AND THE COW BURNED

AND THE COW BURNED

Animals and Philosophy in the Cinema of Andrei Tarkovsky

RAYMOND SCOTT DE LUCA

INDIANA UNIVERSITY PRESS

This book is a publication of

Indiana University Press
Herman B Wells Library
1320 East 10th Street
Bloomington, Indiana 47405 USA

iupress.org

© 2026 by Raymond Scott De Luca

All rights reserved
No part of this book may be reproduced or utilized in any form or by any means, electronic or mechanical, including photocopying and recording, or by any information storage and retrieval system, without permission in writing from the publisher.

For customers in the European Union with safety or GPSR concerns, please contact Mare Nostrum Group B.V., Mauritskade 21D, 1091 GC Amsterdam, The Netherlands. Email: gpsr@mare-nostrum.co.uk

First Printing 2026

Cataloging information is available from the Library of Congress.
ISBN 978-0-253-07467-6 (hdbk.)
ISBN 978-0-253-07468-3 (pbk.)
ISBN 978-0-253-07469-0 (web PDF)
ISBN 978-0-253-07470-6 (ebook)

*For Joseph,
and for all the animals we may have yet*

CONTENTS

Acknowledgments ix

Note to Readers xiii

Introduction: Tarkovsky and the Animals   1
1. Horses   32
2. Dogs   77
3. Birds   123
4. Cows   167
5. Horses of Another Color   217

Conclusion: The Wary Gaze   259

Filmography   265

Bibliography   271

Index   297

ACKNOWLEDGMENTS

THIS BOOK BEGAN IN A way that I could not have possibly foreseen: on a snowy day in 2014 at my parents' home in Red Bank, New Jersey, where I watched *Stalker* for the first time. In truth, not a day has gone by since then where I have not thought of that film. As absorbing as it is alienating, as ponderous and indulgent as it is gorgeous and searching, *Stalker* haunts (indeed, stalks) my imagination. The task of this book is to understand how Tarkovsky creates such heightened, wondrous viewing experiences while also remaining clear-eyed to Tarkovsky's flaws, his excessiveness, and his cruelty. What, in other words, do we miss about Tarkovsky when we let enchantment saturate our thinking? I often joke that I hate to love Tarkovsky but also love to hate him, and I hope this book conveys that ambivalence. Like all books, this one would not have been possible without the unstinting support of numerous colleagues, institutions, mentors, friends, and family members.

The first word of gratitude must go to Marina Rojavin of Bryn Mawr College and Middlebury College's Kathryn Wasserman Davis School of Russian. In the summer of 2016, Marina led a graduate seminar on Tarkovsky at Middlebury, and it was there that I encountered the fullness of his work. I am thankful for Marina's guidance, erudition, and open-mindedness—and to all my peers in that class, some of whom are no longer with us—for fostering one of the most intellectually invigorating experiences of my life.

My puzzlement and misgivings about Tarkovsky propelled me into a PhD program at Harvard University, where I planned from the outset to write (at least part of) my dissertation on him. I would especially like to thank my dissertation committee—Justin Weir, Stephanie Sandler, and Daria Khitrova—whose seminars and feedback not only laid the groundwork for this study but also provided me a model for the sort of teacher and scholar whom I aspire to be. My time at Harvard was also enriched by my coursework and conversations with Julie Buckler, William Mills Todd III, Micheal Flier, Nariman Skakov, Aleksandra Kremer, Giuliana Bruno, Tom Conley, and all my colleagues at the Mahindra Humanities Center, which generously supported my dissertation.

After graduate school, my work on Tarkovsky brought me to the University of Kentucky, and it was there that I decided to spin my dissertation chapter on Tarkovsky into a full-blown monograph. I am grateful to Molly Blasing, Karen Petrone, Jeanmarie Rouhier-Willoughby, Jeff Peters, and Leon Sachs for their intellectual camaraderie, mentorship, and always splendid company. I'd also like to thank Karen Tice, Dwight Billings, Srimati Basu, Mónica Díaz, Ed Lee, Ken Slepyan, Kristin Seymour, Simona Fojtova, Martin Chan, Liang Luo, Peter Kalliney, Pearl James, Jeorg and Lola Sauer, Carol Mason, Miyabi Goto, Marro Inoue, Leni Ribeio Leite, Doug Slaymaker, and Nisrine Slitine El Mghari. Each of them made my transition from a graduate student into a faculty member seamless and exciting. In Lexington, I also had the opportunity to lead a retrospective film series on Tarkovsky at the storied Kentucky Theatre—the pearl of Lexington—thanks to its enterprising directors, Lisa Meek and Hayward Wilkirson.

In 2024, I moved to Emory University in Atlanta, Georgia, where this book entered its final stages. I am grateful to Elena Glazov-Corrigan, Mikhail Epstein, Vera and Oleg Proskurin, Juliette Stapanian Apkarian, Matthew Payne, Julia Bullock, Maria Franca Sibau, Cheryl Crowley, Christina Crawford, Sarah Mellors Rodriguez, and Ceila Campbell. Their enthusiasm about my work not only led to a wonderful new job but also offered me a needed burst of energy as this project made its way down the home stretch.

This book, and my broader habits of mind, have greatly profited from the conversations—formal and informal, real and imagined, in person and in print—that I have carried on with a range of scholars whose thinking, in one way or another, has informed my own: Michael Kunichika, Jason Merrill, Robert Bird, Emma Widdis, Masha Shpolberg, Lilya Kaganovsky, Birgit Beumers, Amy Nelson, Lida Oukaderova, Jane Costlow, Nancy Condee, Akira Mizuta Lippit, Erica Fudge, Laura McMahon, Michael Lawrence, Jonathan Burt, Elaine Scarry, Laurie Anderson, Eric Hobsbawm, Matthew Calarco, and Anat Pick. No list of acknowledgments would be complete, moreover, without recognizing my sensational undergraduate professors at Haverford and Bryn Mawr College—Tim Harte, Liza Allen, Lisa Jane Graham, and Linda Gerstein—who taught me how to think, write, and ask the good questions. Now, as a professor myself, I am indebted to my terrific students; I have had the pleasure of exposing them to Tarkovsky and learning from all their confusion and wonderment with fresh eyes.

At Indiana University Press, I am grateful to Bethany Mowry—this book's earliest champion—Sophia Hebert, Alyssa Lucas, Sabrina Black, Jennifer Wilder, Anna Garnai, Katie Huggins, and David Miller. Their care and attentiveness have made the difference every step of the way. I would also like to thank the press's anonymous readers, whose incisive and generous commentary immeasurably improved the shape of this book's arguments. Additional thanks are owed to Layla Aleksander-Garrett, Alesia Batsman, Irina Brown, Michael Shulman, and Gueorgui Pinkhassov, who permitted the use of several images and quotations within this book that have enriched its contents. This book's trusty indexer, Alexander Trotter, also deserves a debt of gratitude.

Finally, this book is a product of the love and support of my entire family, particularly my parents—Raymond and Debra De Luca—whose encouragement has meant everything. (They are anxiously, and adorably, awaiting their signed copy.) I would be remiss not to thank my closest friends and fellow cinephiles who have listened to me bang on about Tarkovsky for over a decade now: Caroline Oddo, Ryan Carr, Christopher Selden, and Colleen and Emily Kinslow. Above all, this book simply would not exist were it not for the curiosity, devotion, and patience of Joseph Rager—this book's finest editor—whose loving fingerprints are on every page, as they are my world.

NOTE TO READERS

THERE ARE SEVERAL IMAGES AND descriptions in this book that deal with graphic instances of animal cruelty. Most of this material comes from the director's cut of Andrei Tarkovsky's second feature film, *Andrei Rublev* (1966), which resurfaced only after the filmmaker's death in 1986. I have made the decision to include these images and descriptions not for their shock value (as Tarkovsky had intended them) but because they texturize the claims advanced in this study concerning Tarkovsky's cruelty, his excessiveness, and his pathological commitment to gritty cinematic realism. These images and descriptions magnify what I understand as the central paradox to Tarkovsky's visual ecologies: How does a filmmaker who gives us some of the most exquisite images of animal life ever committed to celluloid also produce some of the most gruesome scenes of animal death? This material is essential to the clear-eyed reevaluation of Tarkovsky—his biography, cinema, and legacy—that this book undertakes.

AND THE COW BURNED

INTRODUCTION

Tarkovsky and the Animals

"I used to like Andrei Tarkovsky's movies. But when I found out that, once during a shoot, he burned a cow alive . . . Tarkovsky, for me, ceased to exist."

—Kira Muratova, "Kogda ia uznala," interview
with *Bul'var Gordona*, 2006

AT THE END OF EVERY showing I have ever attended of a film by the legendary Russian director Andrei Tarkovsky—whether in a classroom, an arts theater, or a living room; in Saint Petersburg or Moscow; in Paris, Rome, Stockholm, Atlanta, or Cambridge; in Middlebury, Vermont, or Lexington, Kentucky—someone has asked a question about the animals abounding across Tarkovsky's cinema. Where did those dogs come from? What types of birds did we hear in the background, and how were they so loud? Why were there horses everywhere? And did he *really* burn a cow alive?

This book continues these conversations, for there has never been enough time to discuss all that could be said about Tarkovsky's animals. It aims to shed light on the above queries but also on a much larger set of questions: Why are we so fascinated by Tarkovsky's animals? What convinces us that, if we could just understand Tarkovsky's animal images, we could unlock the secrets of this most beguiling of filmmakers? The urgency behind these bigger inquiries, lurking beneath our local curiosities about Tarkovsky's animals, suggests that their answers extend beyond Tarkovsky and into the fraught domain of human-animal relations. Tarkovsky's cinema presents multitudinous ways of thinking about animals, not only because it is replete with animals but also because it actively reflects on animals as they exist alongside us, caught in a dragnet of violence, compassion, and mystery in all their varieties: as pets, metaphors, marvels, and meat. Tarkovsky's filmography is an exercise in animal philosophy, spanning from Plato to Haraway, that invites us to consider what animals mean and how these different meanings beget paradoxical interspecies encounters and exchanges.

Since the early 2000s, there has been a surge of interest in the question of "the animal" across the arts, humanities, and sciences. This "animal turn" has been attributed to the growing disillusionment around classical notions of Western humanism; spirited debates among contemporary ethicists and philosophers; the rise of cybernetic technologies that have catalyzed the field of posthumanism; and remarkable new findings in animal behavior.[1] This burgeoning field of inquiry, known as animal studies, is dedicated to historicizing and rethinking our relations with animals, central to every aspect of human existence.[2] This transdisciplinary field "challenges the very core" of human knowledge by "reminding us" that our human-centered pursuit of knowledge does not "straightforwardly reveal truths, but offers partial, messy, and impure methodologies, practices and theories for understanding life."[3] Animal studies bears the potential to fundamentally reorient our sense of the world and, thus, ourselves in it. Only recently, however, has animal studies begun to exert its influence on film studies and, to a lesser degree, Slavic studies.[4] A goal of *And the Cow Burned* is to demonstrate how animal studies can enrich our understandings of Soviet culture and cinema, in addition to exploring what Tarkovsky—and the Soviets—might contribute to animal studies in return.

In spite of the striking ways in which Tarkovsky portrays animals, the lack of scholarly attention paid to these animals—inversely proportional to the interest they pique among viewers—is perhaps not coincidental. Jonathan Burt, a leading scholar of animals in film, has accused critics of "a willful blindness" when it comes to animals in cinema because of the difficult questions their use poses about the violence, cruelty, and coercion central to their history on screen.[5] Almost never, Randy Malamud reiterates, have animals benefited from the making of a movie: "To restate the obvious, people make these films, and people make money from making these films. . . . Where, in this nexus, does the animal come in? Do the animals profit in any way from this interaction, from the human gaze? Can they? Should they? Even if no animals were harmed in the making of these movies, is that the best we can hope for? Were any animals *helped* in the making of these movies?"[6] Animals are usually worse off for their encounters with cinema, which often leave them traumatized, injured, or dead. Indeed, Tarkovsky's hauntingly beautiful images of animals are accompanied by antithetically grisly scenes of animal death that undercut his cinema's refined artistry. It is as if our admiration of Tarkovsky's work has dissuaded us from confronting its darker side, exemplified by his cruel treatment of animals—in particular the cow he set on fire in *Andrei Rublev* (1966), to whom this book's title pays tribute. *And the Cow Burned* insists that we not avert our gaze from Tarkovsky's cruelty but rather treat it as central to our understanding of his cinema, which serves as a case study of the perennial problem concerning the relationship between ethics and aesthetics. Tarkovsky's films, then, raise another question: Why do recordings of animals so often backslide into violence?

The few scholars who have turned their attention to Tarkovsky's animals have limited their analyses to animals' symbolic or metaphorical implications to elucidate Tarkovsky's narrative concerns.[7] This line of analysis, while certainly valuable, ignores the actual animals conscripted into Tarkovsky's cinema and saddled with demands to perform and, in some cases, die on screen. Tarkovsky's animals are not merely placeholders for abstract ideas but flesh-and-blood beings whose lives were altered by their encounters with Tarkovsky. Still, we cannot sideline the rich figurative meanings that subtend Tarkovsky's animal images. Any analysis of Tarkovsky's animals must "incorporate symbolic approaches with social and material history" because human-animal relations are neither fully metaphorical nor fully corporeal.[8] The term "material-semiotic" has been used to describe how animals' "bodies and meanings coshape one another," how "trope and flesh are always cohabitating, always co-constituting."[9] *And the Cow Burned* evaluates how Tarkovsky both represents animals in terms of their figurative significance and *re*-presents animals before a camera, staying tuned to animals' place in the world as beings with lives of their own that can go better or worse.

And the Cow Burned joins a growing movement of scholars pursuing theoretical, clear-eyed readings of Tarkovsky's films rather than the reverential, hagiographic, or quasi-mystical approaches that have dominated previous studies. As one critic notes, most scholarship on Tarkovsky—no fewer than (at the time of writing) thirty-one monographs, several edited volumes, and an ocean of journal articles—have betrayed "fascination with the Russian master" at the expense of a more "level-headed approach" that could balance "cinephilic enthusiasm with academic expertise."[10] (Two particularly notable exceptions to this critical tendency are Nariman Skakov's *The Cinema of Tarkovsky: Labyrinths of Space and Time* and Nathan Dunne's edited volume *Tarkovsky*, both of which deftly engage cultural and aesthetic theory.)[11] *And the Cow Burned* illuminates Tarkovsky's work from the perspective of animal studies by engaging classical and contemporary debates concerning ethical philosophy, psychoanalysis, critical theory, and animality.[12] It reveals how Tarkovsky's animal images not only dilate his cinema's salient aesthetic and thematic preoccupations but also demystify his mysteriousness, which has been used, especially by Russian critics, to deify Tarkovsky and reify his illegibility for Western audiences. *And the Cow Burned* focuses on the animals of Tarkovsky's cinema to solve the puzzles posed by his visual enigmas and integrate his work into the broader trajectory of global film history, Western philosophy, and twentieth-century culture and thought. Thus, another of this project's primary goals is to unriddle the exclusivist peculiarity and mystique that is Tarkovsky's "Russianness."

The remainder of this introductory chapter outlines Tarkovsky's attitudes toward animals and the historical context and philosophical traditions on which they draw. Tarkovsky's motley ideas about animals created conditions that accommodate both his affection for and aversion to animals and, in turn, his ostensibly incompatible depictions of animal life and animal death. From there, *And the Cow Burned* presents a series of case studies organized around the different types of animals encountered across Tarkovsky's filmography: horses, dogs, birds, and cows. *And the Cow Burned* makes the case that a full understanding of Tarkovsky's cinematic and philosophical project is simply not possible without deep consideration of the animals therein.

POSTWAR HUMANISM

"What an extraordinary country," wrote a seething Tarkovsky in 1972 after learning that the Soviet Union's censors were obstructing the release of yet another of his films, *Solaris*.[13] "Don't they want an international artistic triumph, don't they want us to have good new films and books? They are frightened by real art. Quite understandably. Art can only be bad for them because it is humane, whereas their purpose is to crush everything that is alive, every shoot of humanity, any aspiration to freedom, any manifestation of art on the dreary horizon."[14] This statement perfectly captures not only Tarkovsky's personality—his self-importance, contemptuousness, flair for metaphor, defiance, and sense of victimhood—but also his worldview: his belief that the redeeming, humane power of art, indicative of humanity's inalienable freedom, could ameliorate his bleak historical circumstances. Throughout his career, Tarkovsky thought a lot about what he as a filmmaker owed humankind, and he devoted his work to exploring profound questions about the human condition. Indeed, the words "humanity," "humankind," and "human" appear with astonishing frequency in Tarkovsky's diaries, interviews, and artistic manifesto, *Sculpting in Time* (*Zapechatlennoe vremia*, 1985), published shortly before his death in December 1986.[15]

Where does Tarkovsky's fixation with humanity come from? Why did a filmmaker, pestered by censors but never truly threatened like some of his peers, understand his work in such lofty, grandiose terms?[16]

Born in 1932, Tarkovsky came of age during a highly turbulent era. His childhood coincided with Joseph Stalin's breakneck campaign to modernize Russia, which culminated in an outbreak of mass political terror. Tarkovsky's father, a poet who began his career as a translator—later commissioned by Stalin himself—abandoned his family and enlisted in the Red Army during World War II, a conflict that utterly shattered Soviet society.[17] Tarkovsky's memories of Stalin's crimes and punishments, the shock of paternal abandonment, and the traumas of wartime evacuation and famine shaped both his autobiographical cinema and his outlook on modern life. Beleaguered by historical forces beyond his control, Tarkovsky maintained that the dignity of human life had to be recovered in the postwar era by individuals banding together in spite of their miserable predicaments. "In a world where there is a real threat of war," Tarkovsky wrote, "where social ills exist on a staggering scale; where human suffering cries out to heaven—the way must be found for one person to reach another. Such is the sacred duty of humanity towards its future, and the personal duty of each individual."[18] The scars of history, Tarkovsky upheld, could only be redressed by recuperating values of decency, beauty, art, unity, and love on a person-to-person basis. Elucidating his worldview, Tarkovsky adopted the time-honored language of what he viewed as the noblest of intellectual traditions: humanism.

With conceptual origins in ancient Greece among the Sophists, humanism emphasizes human beings' capacity for self-betterment. Although the Greeks lacked a term for humanism, the theme of "the human" occupied much of Greek thought: "Wonders are many," Sophocles wrote, "and none is more wonderful than man."[19] As the historian Perez Zagorin notes, Greek humanism was a cultural program "for an elite of free men of aristocratic background and independent means who had the leisure for the pursuit of excellence. It was predicated on the idea of an inherent superiority of the Greeks over the barbarian."[20] Humanism sought to cultivate a specific kind of human thriving against other forms of self-organization, betraying a universalist notion of what constitutes "the human" to reinforce the perceived exemplariness of Greek life.[21]

Humanism as a philosophy coalesced in the Italian Renaissance, as elite culture's "highest aim" became the development of "a Christian gentlemen—classically educated, morally sound, accomplished in the arts of speaking and writing, competent to advise and serve in the governments of kings, princes, and cities, and possessed of the manners to make a credible appearance at royal and princely courts."[22] The ideas promulgated in the Renaissance solidified an enduring vision of what it means to be human in modern life. Humanism grew ever more independent from the church as Enlightenment-era thinkers exalted reason and science over faith and superstition, enthroning "humanity and its progress as the supreme meaning of history."[23]

These ideals of self-mastery and progress became the reigning ideology of the European bourgeoisie in the nineteenth century, and during the first decades of the twentieth century, Soviet communists pushed the Enlightenment's humanist legacy to a radical extreme.[24] Bolshevik revolutionaries were driven by bottomless faith in the human ability to transform into a maximally efficient subject: the New Soviet Man (*Novyi sovetskii chelovek*). "Man," Leon Trotsky wrote, "will be able to harmonize his own nature. He will take control of all unconscious processes: breathing, blood circulation, digestion. He will bring himself up to a new level, becoming a higher, social-biological type; a superman."[25] In their will to power, the Bolsheviks not only drew on an undercurrent of utopian thinking that had long percolated in Russian intellectual life but also turbocharged Enlightenment ideas by propounding humanity's ability to hasten its destiny toward a postcapitalist future of self-determination.[26]

The calamities of the twentieth century, particularly the catastrophe of World War II, smashed these views of human perfectibility. Belief in human potential and the unbroken path of progress no longer seemed tenable in the wake of industrial warfare, genocide, nuclear bombs, and the destruction of the European continent. The most important discussions about humanism in the decades after World War II reveal that, indeed, a philosophy of *anti*humanism had taken hold among leading intellectuals. The German philosopher Martin Heidegger, for example, penned his "Letter on Humanism" (*Über den Humanismus*) in 1946, perhaps as an attempt to rehabilitate his own reputation after having spoken favorably of Nazism (and stayed disquietingly silent about the extermination camps).[27] Heidegger argued that humanism empowers individuals to impose their will on the world without understanding the true essence of "Being" (*Dasein*) beyond human subjectivity. Humanism, Heidegger concluded, should be abandoned for the philosophical obliviousness it instills, which can lead to incalculable suffering and bedlam. Likewise, the French thinker Vincent Descombes wrote that humanism, "a term of ridicule," should "be entered among the collection of discarded 'isms,'" and the Romanian French playwright Eugène Ionesco described humanism as a set of ideas that had "gone to pieces."[28] Some years later, Michel Foucault hammered the nail in humanism's coffin by proclaiming "the death of man" in *The Order of Things* (*Les Mots et les Choses*, 1966).[29] Foucault contended that, far from a transcendent concept, "man" is a recent invention—a product of the eighteenth century—developed to reinforce dominant ways of thinking in service of extant political elites and ideologies. After Europe's near suicide in World War II, philosophers wondered how any notion of human progress or virtue could be seriously entertained.

Yet Heidegger's "Letter on Humanism"—a key document of midcentury antihumanism—was a response to the French thinker Jean-Paul Sartre's cautious gambit to recoup a vision and praxis of humanism for the postwar world, a world traumatized by death camps and in need of (secular) salvation. A crucial thinker for the school of thought known as existentialism, Sartre objected to accusations that he believed life to be ugly and pointless. Rather, Sartre argued that existentialism is a *type* of humanism. Precisely because human beings are randomly thrown into existence, it is incumbent on us to build a morally decent world through our own actions and choices without recourse to divine authority. "Man," Sartre wrote, "is nothing else but what he purposes, he exists only in so far as he realises himself, he is therefore nothing else but the sum of his actions, nothing else but what life is ... condemned to be free."[30] Existentialism redoubles the spirit of humanism by appealing to humanity's better angels to foster goodness for its own sake, simply because we can; it is a godless morality for the politically and spiritually shaken.

Sartre's backdoor defense of humanism vis-à-vis existentialism reveals that, amid the avalanche of antihumanist thought in the postwar era, the embers of humanism still flickered. Discussing English novelists like E. M. Forster and Virginia Woolf, literary scholar Marina MacKay—citing Woolf's 1940 essay for the *New Republic* in which she decried the "subconscious Hitlerism in the hearts of men"—argues that wartime writers explored how the "forces of sadism and cruelty ... that so insistently prove liberal humanism vulnerable also prove it indispensable."[31] This literary culture, MacKay contends, catalyzed the formation of the British welfare state, which exemplified the humanist ideals of generosity and compassion. Analogously, as cultural historian Kenan Malik notes, just as antihumanist ideas had sedimented among leading postwar European intellectuals, major thinkers of the developing world, such as Che Guevara and Franz Fanon, reenergized the ideas and language of classical humanism.

> Despite the critique of Western humanism as a camouflage for the dehumanization of non-Western peoples, humanism remained a central component of the ideology of Third World liberation struggles of the postwar era, virtually all of which drew on the emancipatory logic of universalism. Indeed, Western radicals were often shocked by the extent to which anticolonial struggles adopted what the radicals conceived of as tainted ideas. The concepts of universalism and social progress, the French anthropologist Claude Lévi-Strauss

observed, found "unexpected support from peoples who desire nothing more than to share in the benefits of industrialisation; peoples who prefer to look upon themselves as temporarily backward than permanently different."[32]

Many anticolonial thinkers argued that humanist ideals of self-determination and universal justice could be cleansed of their checkered legacies and uncoupled from the predatory practices of imperialism. These radicals were *revisionist* humanists—anti-antihumanists—whose residual support for humanism conveyed its resilience in the postwar period.

The soft glow of postwar humanism radiated most brightly from Soviet Russia, of all places. Under Stalin, the Soviet Union had become a kind of moral black hole on Europe's outer rim, a place where a philosophy of terror and human disposability—a politics of antihumanism if there ever was one—had evacuated human life of all value whatsoever. Yet stalin's death in 1953 triggered a period of liberalization in Soviet politics and culture known as the Thaw (*ottepel'*). Artists and intellectuals began emphasizing the need to foster a more humane world in contrast with the dark Stalinist past.[33] The political event that jump-started the Thaw was Nikita Khruschev's "secret speech" delivered at the Twentieth Congress of the Communist Party in 1956. Khruschev denounced Stalin's legacy in explicitly moral terms for excessive cruelty and megalomania that debased the "spiritual good of humanity."[34] Whereas early Soviet culture had pursued the optimal rationalization of the human subject—the New Soviet Man—the Thaw focused on nurturing society's moral imagination to recoup a sense of *humanity*: a culture of care, integrity, stewardship, creativity, and individuality that echoed age-old principles of classical humanism.

Beginning his career in the moral wreckage of World War II and Stalinism, Tarkovsky aspired to revive humanist ideals of truth, beauty, and goodness. Almost every aspect of Tarkovsky's biography epitomizes the humanistic undertow of post-Stalinist life: his longing for creative freedom; his love of the classical arts; his elevated sense of style; his lyrical movies; his high-mindedness; and his desire to comport himself decently. "Human existence," Tarkovsky wrote, "demands constant moral effort to do good in order to realize our lives, and at the same time bring our own positive contribution to the universal human process."[35] The tragedy of the twentieth century, relentlessly eroding the worth of human life, renewed Tarkovsky's commitment to humanity, just as it had Sartre's. "The true artist," Tarkovsky believed, "strives to immortalise man within the world."[36] It is not by chance that after seeing *Ivan's Childhood*, Tarkovsky's debut film about a child soldier's warped humanity, Sartre himself wrote: "We have often known Evil . . . where Evil comes from, when it pierces the Good with its countless pinpricks, it reveals the tragic truth of man and of historical progress.... Of course, there is no need to draw from that any kind of pessimism. No more than facile optimism. But only the will to fight without ever losing sight of the price to be paid."[37] Sartre praised Tarkovsky for advancing a clear-eyed vision of humanism that did not take progress for granted, deny humanity's capacity for evil, or surrender the humanist ideals of justice, decency, and peace. Through his poetic films, Tarkovsky, like Sartre, hoped against hope that people might recover their shared humanity in the war-torn world and "fight together" in pursuit of a brighter future.[38]

A GATHERING OF ANIMALS

As his career unfolded, however, Tarkovsky's longing for a revival—a renaissance—in humanistic values bled into a dark, deep-seated pessimism, which cast a long shadow over his writings and films. There was, according to Tarkovsky, "a monstrous and self-evident spiritual crisis affecting" humankind as a result of the deleterious forces unleashed by the modern world, which included everything from consumer capitalism to hidebound communist bureaucracy, the rise of postwar counterculture (particularly the feminist movement), and, above all, technological progress, especially the threat of nuclear war.[39] "It is obvious to everyone," Tarkovsky wrote, "that man's material aggrandisement has not been synchronous with spiritual progress. The point has been reached where we seem to have a fatal incapacity for mastering our material achievements in order to use them for our own good. We have created a civilisation which threatens to annihilate mankind."[40] Far from celebrating the rebirth of humanism in the postwar era, Tarkovsky lamented humanism's limited appeal. It appeared to Tarkovsky, in the wake of World War II, that society had been broken beyond repair, too psychologically damaged or coarsened to be morally rejuvenated; indeed, he "diagnosed" the modern world "as being spiritually impotent."[41] We "know so little about the soul, we're like lost dogs. We feel comfortable when we're speaking about politics, art, sports, love of women," but "as soon as we touch upon spirituality, we lose our way, we're no longer cultured, we lack any preparation in that domain."[42] What did Tarkovsky mean by "spirituality," and why did the term so often attend his brooding, threnodic reflections on the difficulty, even impossibility, of resuscitating humanist values in the postwar period?

Tarkovsky understood spirituality as one's capacity to think deeply, that is, "a person's interest in what has been called the meaning of life."[43] While Tarkovsky indisputably evinced certain religious influences throughout his career—from pietism to mystical Russian Orthodoxy to Buddhism—he was secular in a classically humanist sense. Religion, for Tarkovsky, was simply a vehicle to activate one's spirituality, an inducement to ask the ultimate questions about life, what cultural critics have called "the accursed questions" stirring the great works of nineteenth-century Russian literature: "What do we live for? Where are we going? What is the meaning of our presence on this planet over the course of . . . the eighty years or so that we live on Earth?"[44] A work of art, for Tarkovsky, functions like religion because it serves as a catalyst for mental activity and, therefore, moral awakening. "In the case of someone who is spiritually receptive, it is therefore possible to talk of an analogy between the impact made by a work of art and that of a purely religious experience. Art acts above all on the soul, shaping its spiritual structure."[45] To be spiritual—to contemplate life's headiest questions—is to reaffirm our humanness, even if no answers are gleaned in the end: "If he's interested in these questions, if he simply asks himself these questions, he's already saved spiritually. It's not the answer that's important. I know that from the moment man begins asking questions he will be unable to live as he has before."[46] The very act of introspection, per Tarkovsky, ennobles humanity. Those who "do not ask themselves these questions," by contrast, "are individuals without spirituality."[47] And, lacking spirituality, these people are hardly *people* at all: "they exist on the level of animals."[48]

If, as Tarkovsky maintained, humanity's essence lies in its spiritual activity—its willingness to ponder life's greatest mysteries—then "the point of an animal's life is life itself, the continuation of the species."[49] Animals live purely biological, material existences with no trace of an inner world. They are all body, no mind. "An animal carries out its slavish activities because it can feel the point of its life instinctively," Tarkovsky wrote. "Therefore its sphere is restricted. Man, on the other hand, claims to aspire to the absolute."[50] Tarkovsky believed that because humans can contemplate their own existence, people are intrinsically superior to animals. Those who do not think deeply are "like men who don't know how to clean their teeth," primitive hominids whose mode of being is no different from an ape's.[51] Humanness, for Tarkovsky, can be nurtured or neglected; we are not automatically human at birth so much as we *become* human through sustained self-reflection, which lifts us out of the instinct-driven world of animality.

In Tarkovsky's estimation, however, modern man ("the human," for Tarkovsky, is always and only coded as male) has lost all interest in self-examination. This has obstructed the mind's development and stalled humanity's evolutionary trajectory. "A civilization without spirituality," Tarkovsky said, "without belief in the immortality of the soul, is no more than a gathering of animals. It no longer is a civilization; it's already the end, the decline."[52] The spiritual crisis Tarkovsky believed to be befalling society was an ontological one, a crisis of *devolution*, with modern people failing to nurture their intellect and slipping from humanness back toward the animal. Recalling the image of a horse carriage plunging into an abyss at the end of Nikolai Gogol's classic literary work *Dead Souls* (*Mertvyie dushi*, 1842), Tarkovsky wrote that "the spiritual half of man has been separated further and further from the animal, the material, and now in an infinite expanse of darkness we can just make out, like the lights of a departing train, the other half of our being as it rushes away, irrevocably and forever."[53]

The fault line Tarkovsky drew between thinking human beings and mindless, purely reflexive animals is plainly indebted to a schema plotted by the seventeenth-century French philosopher René Descartes. In his treatise *Discourse on Method* (1637), a seminal text of Enlightenment thought, Descartes explains how all beings, including humans, adhere to the hyperrational laws of nature. For Descartes, there is no metaphysical property to differentiate any being from a lifeless machine. However, buried in the cavities of the human brain is an ingenious piece of corporeal engineering that, Descartes claims, encompasses the human soul: the pineal gland (so named because it resembles a pine cone). The pineal gland, per Descartes, is a valve system regulating blood, visual processing, emotional intelligence, and sensory information in a highly complex fashion that turns human beings into self-aware subjects and lifts us out of the machinelike existence governing forms of nonhuman life.[54] The soul, for Descartes, is a unique physiological component of humanity, which makes human beings—even "the most dull-witted of men"—not merely more cognitively sophisticated than other animals; the soul is what ontologically trademarks and, therefore, elevates humanity as a category of species.[55]

Descartes codified ideas about human exceptionalism that had been percolating since the ancient Greeks, generating the basis for what later became known as "anthropocentrism" or "speciesism," a conviction that humanity is of singular importance on Earth.[56] If the first principle of Cartesian philosophy states, "I think, therefore I am," then only beings with access to this "I" have the faculties for autonomy, reducing animals, emptied of a mind, to automatons: insensate brutes beholden to their physical constitution. "If there were such machines," Descartes writes, that had "the organs and outward shape of a monkey or some other irrational animal, we would have no means of knowing that they were not of exactly the same nature as these animals."[57] To prove his hypothesis, Descartes and his acolytes would reportedly nail dogs to display boards and mutilate them alive in early examples of modern-day vivisection.[58] Descartes dismissed the dogs' spasms and cries as sensory-motor reactions to external pressure no different from "a whining gear that needs oil."[59] Cartesianism thus "gives humans an alibi for their lack of concern for, or even cruelty towards, animals."[60] Descartes even avoided the word "animal," which crept into popular vernacular in the 1600s, given its etymological link to the Latin term "anima," which bears a relation to the idea of a soul; he preferred the term "beast" (*bête*) to reiterate the mutually exclusive nature of the human-animal divide.[61]

Though Tarkovsky's work has seldom been analyzed from a Cartesian perspective—and Tarkovsky never directly referenced Descartes in writings or interviews—his thoughts on the human's ensouled essence echo Descartes's postulations.[62] Describing what animal he would like to be, Tarkovsky said, "It's difficult wanting to be an animal" because "it would be necessary to want to descend spiritually lower, the soul would need to be paralyzed."[63] Animals, Tarkovsky suggested, are inherently inferior, and they possess a qualitatively different kind of soul—if they have one at all. "I won't deny that I have seen very happy cats," Tarkovsky once stated. "I especially like Kipling's. But in this case how does a person differ from an animal? . . . We are different from animals in that we are conscious of ourselves. . . . We see ourselves at the center of the world . . . but for some reason we have ceased to be amazed by this phenomenon."[64] Tarkovsky parroted Descartes's logic by claiming that the "soul" is an "essentially human thing" that resides in every person like a "crystal."[65] Tarkovsky characterized the soul as a mineral or gem, recalling Descartes's descriptions of the pineal gland—that is, the soul as a solid material rather than some sort of vapor or ether. "Despite the fact . . . that every soul has the capacity to accumulate what is eternal and good, as a mass people can do nothing but destroy. . . . Human history looks all too like some monstrous experiment . . . a kind of vivisection."[66] For Tarkovsky, we think, therefore we are—and, therefore, are *not* animals.

In addition to Descartes, the immense significance Tarkovsky attributed to the soul invokes the well-trodden discourse about the life-giving quality of the soul in Russian culture—the vaunted "great Russian soul" (*velikaia russkaia dusha*)—that has long been a cliché of nationalistic propaganda.[67] Perhaps unsurprisingly, Tarkovsky deeply admired the nineteenth-century novelist Fyodor Dostoevsky, no stranger to Russian chauvinism, whose fiction has become synonymous with the examination of Russia's soul. The onset of Tarkovsky's career in the 1950s coincided with a major reconsideration (and recirculation) of Dostoevsky's prose in Soviet society. Thaw-era literary critics reoriented the social, class-based analyses that had dominated under Lenin and Stalin in favor of exploring Dostoevsky's more humanistic themes of life, death, dignity, and suffering, which gained fresh cultural currency in the wake of Stalin's death.[68] As one literary historian notes, "the post-Stalin 'thaw' marks the beginning of a gradual revival of *Dostoevskovedenie* in the Soviet Union. The one hundred and fiftieth anniversary of the writer's birth, celebrated in November 1971, gave a new impetus to the study of Dostoevsky and prompted a number of articles, research studies, and monographs devoted to Dostoevsky's personality, creative writings, and *Weltanschauung*."[69] Channeling this Dostoevskian renaissance, Tarkovsky hoped to adapt Dostoevsky's novels on screen—*Crime and Punishment* (*Prestuplenie i nakazanie*, 1866), *The Idiot* (1868–69), and *Demons* (*Besy*, 1871–72).[70] He wrote: "For the moment I must read. Everything Dostoevsky wrote. Everything's that been written about him... Dostoevsky could become the whole point of what I want to do in cinema."[71] In Tarkovsky's view, Dostoevsky probed life's deepest questions, initiating the sort of spiritual activity necessary for people to reclaim their humanity and amount to something more than a mindless "gathering of animals." Yet for Tarkovsky, modern society's pathogenic influences had fogged the human mind and left the soul—that precious "organ of belief"— "atrophied," jettisoning far too many across the Cartesian divide, away from Dostoevskian spirituality and toward soulless animals.[72]

THE SOVIET ROUSSEAU

Despite his Cartesian antipathy toward animals, Tarkovsky inundated the screen with their images. And while Tarkovsky did often treat these animals cruelly, he also portrayed them tenderly, beautifully, and mysteriously, thereby belying Cartesianism's (and his own) callous and mechanistic understanding of animal life. Tarkovsky's hostile views on animals may strike those unfamiliar with his interviews or writings as surprising, as these views cannot easily be inferred from most of his animal images. Tarkovsky drew on intellectual traditions beyond Cartesianism to formulate his ideas about animal life, counterbalancing his feelings of aversion with affection, wonder, and nostalgia.

Bemoaning modern society, Tarkovsky allied himself with an enduring countercurrent of Western thought exemplified by the eighteenth-century philosopher Jean-Jacques Rousseau. Earlier Enlightenment thinkers, such as John Locke and Thomas Hobbes, saw the development of society as necessary for humans to thrive. Only a well-ordered society, they argued, can subordinate nature, the chaos and rapacity of which pose serious obstacles to human flourishing. Centuries later, these ideas inspired Soviet communists, who, as Oxana

Timofeeva argues, understood nature "in a Hegelian-Marxist spirit, in terms of unfreedom, suffering, and exploitation . . . a model of a society that should be transformed."[73] The Bolsheviks believed that insofar as dominion persists in nature—a world of a Hobbesian dog-eat-dog ethic—the equality of beings more generally can never be achieved. All iterations of the class struggle are simply symbolic reworkings of the violence inhered in nature's original fight for survival. The October Revolution, in short, promised to lift human beings *out* of nature and into a perfect(ed) society.[74]

However, unlike Locke and Hobbes (and, later, the Bolsheviks), Rousseau argued that it is *society* that corrupts humanity—in nature, people are happy and good. Rousseau contended that humans are essentially self-sufficient, compassionate, and altruistic, but when we began organizing ourselves into communities, a shift in our development occurred. We drifted into competition with one another for goods, sexual partners, wealth, and recognition. Rousseau calls this new human trait *amour propre*: self-love, a concern about one's comparative success in a social setting, which propelled humanity along its wayward trajectory and into the dissolute society in which we find ourselves today.[75]

In remarkably similar language, Tarkovsky articulated a Rousseauian view of history: "Man has, since the Enlightenment, dealt with things he should have ignored. He began to turn toward material things. . . . It began when man decided to defend himself against nature and other men. Our society developed on this faulty basis. People don't relate to each other in love, in friendship . . . but from the impulse to take advantage. . . . I believe Man would have survived in any case, because he is human, not animal. We know examples where Man lived in harmony with nature and achieved astonishing things."[76] Society, per Tarkovsky, warps humanity, whereas in nature, we exist in an unadulterated state more conducive to our healthy development. "A city man knows nothing about life," Tarkovsky said. "He doesn't feel how time passes. The child finds assurance of its future in nature, in nature he educates his will."[77] Tarkovsky's use of terms like "children," "will," and "education" in delineating what "society" and "nature" mean only deepens his philosophical indebtedness to Rousseau, who upheld pedagogy as a means to dissimilate people, especially the young, from the reigning social order.

Furthermore, Rousseau maintained that the "original man" bore qualities similar to those of animals: self-reliance, diligence, and a requisite concern for those nearest of kin. Unlike Descartes, Rousseau saw humans and animals not as opposites but more "in terms of one another." He offered a more "balanced view of their relationship . . . according to a model of fundamental continuity," which, to be sure, faintly echoed Charles Darwin's nineteenth-century theories of human evolution.[78] Unlike Darwin, however, Rousseau understood the difference between humanity and animality as related less to biology than to the creative capacity "to raise oneself up," that is, *"perfectibility"*: the human ability to lift ourselves figuratively (and literally) off the ground and take charge of our fate in ways that animals, unduly constrained by their respective environments, cannot.[79] Humans exceed the "narrowest possible adjustments of the body and senses" to do great things, whereas animals lack "the faculty of self-improvement—a faculty which . . . progressively develops all our other faculties, and which in man is inherent in the species."[80] In Rousseau's cosmology, animals possess intelligence but not ingenuity.

Tarkovsky similarly understood human beings as superior to animals, yet he conceded our lineage within nature: "We are the result of its evolution. . . . Nature always gives us a sense of truth," and his films, to restate, are awash in images of plants, animals, and the elements.[81] By not abandoning nature altogether, Tarkovsky, like Rousseau, subscribed to a softer version of Descartes's theory of human exceptionalism. Untainted by society, animals bear elemental wisdom about life in its purest state. "A person has no need of society," Tarkovsky wrote. "A person must live in isolation, close to nature, to animals and plants, and be in contact with them."[82] For Tarkovsky, the path out of society's crisis of devolution, ironically, runs *through* animals. People can, Tarkovsky hoped, affirm the fullness of their humanity without losing what is redeemable about animality. Tarkovsky's ambivalent understanding of animals ought to be understood as *anti-anthropocentric anthropocentrism*—that is, it expressed a highly critical view of humankind while arguing that we can only recover a morally enlightened sense of humanness by learning from otherwise degenerate animals. Tarkovsky's Janus-faced attitude toward animals thus accounts for his seemingly incompatible depictions of animals, which vacillate between affection and violence. Our task, per Tarkovsky, is to (re)learn how to live with animals—not as equals but as helpers, neighbors, and reminders that are, in the end, always subject to human dominion. But if such a reorientation to animals is possible, how can it be achieved? "We have to start living differently," Tarkovsky wrote, before adding, somewhat sheepishly, "but how?"[83]

A CINEMATIC RETURN TO NATURE

To reanimate our relations with animals and nature, Tarkovsky somewhat counterintuitively turned to cinema: the very art form he viewed as emblematic of society's degraded condition. Commercial films, Tarkovsky wrote, "corrupt the public to an unforgiveable degree, denying them the experience of true art."[84] Yet Tarkovsky believed that films could be used and made differently. "Our starting-point," he argued, "should be the essential principles of cinema," which have nothing to do with entertainment or consumerism but everything to do with time.[85] According to Tarkovsky, people go to the movies "for time lost or spent or not yet had" because cinema "widens, enhances, and concentrates a person's experience" by "mak[ing] it longer, significantly longer."[86] A movie crafted by the right hands, per Tarkovsky, can foster durational bouts of introspection, prompting the sort of deep thinking Tarkovsky longed for and exercising a salutary effect on the psyche—therefore assuaging society's yawning spiritual crisis.

The purpose of his art, Tarkovsky said, "is to prepare the human soul for the perception of good," which can be achieved in part by reenchanting our experience of the natural world.[87] "Nature," Tarkovsky wrote, "exists in cinema in the naturalistic fidelity with which it is recorded; the greater the fidelity, the more we trust nature as we see it in the frame . . . in its authentically natural likeness. . . . Rain, fire, water, snow, dew, the driving ground wind—all are part of the material setting in which we dwell; I would even say the truth of our lives. . . . In commercial cinema nature often does not exist at all; all one has is the most advantageous lighting and exteriors for the purpose of quick shooting."[88] Tarkovsky's portrayals of nature—which clearly pay homage to those of his cinematic muse, the Ukrainian director Oleksandr Dovzhenko, and particularly his 1930 masterwork, *Earth (Zemlia)*—were to immerse viewers in the organic experiences from which we are alienated in modern society.[89] By evoking nature's textures and rhythms on screen—its "very smell" and "moisture"—Tarkovsky hoped his images would enable us to reconnect with the elemental truths he regarded as necessary for spiritual revival.[90] Discussing his conviction that the metaphysical can be accessed through sustained encounters with the natural world, Tarkovsky (likening himself to Dovzhenko) said, "I feel very close to pantheism," and called for the "spiritualization of nature" vis-à-vis cinematic images.[91] Nature offered Tarkovsky a kind of "comfort zone" to which he wanted, like Rousseau, to "return" both himself and others.[92] Hence, at the end of *Mirror*, Tarkovsky's camera pulls back into the woods in a Rousseauian return to nature, leaving viewers "in darkness and silence," safely "engulfed by weeds" and moss.[93] This concluding sequence rhymes with the image of Tarkovsky's protagonist in *Stalker* lying in the grass with bugs on his face and hands. For the French philosopher Gilles Deleuze, Tarkovsky's ecological (and rain-soaked) films seem to be asking incessantly, "What is Russia, what is Russia?"[94] The answer is "frozen" somewhere "in [his] sodden, washed and heavily translucent images, with their sometimes bluish, sometimes brown surfaces, while the green environment seems, in the rain, to be unable to go beyond the condition of a liquid crystal which keeps its secret . . . constantly bring[ing] us back to the question: what burning bush, what fire, what soul, what sponge will staunch this earth?"[95]

Tarkovsky's lush visual ecologies were in part a response to the environment's worsening conditions in the latter half of the twentieth century, particularly in the Soviet Union, which had endured untold ecological destruction as a result of World War II and decades of extractive state policies.[96] This ecological degradation became an acute concern among Soviet intellectuals in the 1960s–1980s, and late Soviet films often express environmental themes, as in Larisa Shepit'ko's *Heat* (*Znoi*, 1964), Andrei Konchalovsky's *Siberiade* (*Siberiada*, 1978), and Elem Klimov's *Farewell* (*Proshchanie*, 1983). Tarkovsky distinguished himself in Soviet cinema's "green turn" for the messianic significance he ascribed to his recordings of nature.

To activate what he understood as nature's latent spiritual potential, Tarkovsky above all relied on his signature aesthetic technique: the long take, the significance of which will be paid special attention throughout this book. At its most basic, a long take is a single durational shot that lasts longer than a shot in a typical editing pace. As one scholar writes, long takes foster "a cinema of slowness" that dwells "on the interstices between events or on moments within events during which nothing much happens" and allows "a different temporality, meaning, and value to come into being, thereby questioning the notion of an 'event' . . . and unsettling the very foundation of what constitutes a film's narrative."[97] Throughout his cinema, Tarkovsky uses long takes to unhurriedly study the terrestrial realm in its organic state of unfolding, inviting us to encounter the world's textures, sounds, pulsations, and temporalities in ways that otherwise escape our attention. This sustained viewing experience, per Tarkovsky, can catalyze profound spiritual experiences of (self-)reflection and (self-)discovery.

Tarkovsky's lovingly elongated depictions of the natural world not only inspired other filmmakers—such as Béla Tarr, Claire Denis, Terrence Malick, and Apichatpong Weerasethakul—to return to nature in highly innovative, durational ways but also influenced a more recent genre of avant-garde filmmaking called the "slow animal documentary."[98] A short list of these works includes Claude Nuridsany and Marie Pérennou's *Microcosmos* (1996), Jacques Perrin's *Winged Migration* (2001), Lucien Castaing-Taylor's *Sweetgrass* (2009), Nicholas Philibert's *Nénette* (2010), Emmanuel Gras's *Bovines* (2011), Denis Côté's *Bestiaire* (2012), Viktor Kossakovsky's *Gunda* (2020), and Andrea Arnold's

Tarkovsky's camera retreats into the woods, enacting a Rousseauian "return to nature." Still from *Mirror*, 1975.

Stalker lies in the grass with bugs on his hand; nature as a kind of "comfort zone." Still from *Stalker*, 1979.

Cow (2021). These documentaries, learning from Tarkovsky's aesthetic of languorous detachment, arose as a polemical response to popular wildlife films, such as Luc Jacquet's *March of the Penguins* (*La Marche de l'empereur*, 2005) and the British Broadcasting Corporation's *Planet Earth* (2006–), which tend to blend action-packed narratives with informational material about animals, a potent combination known as "edutainment."[99] By contrast, slow animal documentaries cultivate "a mode of sustained engagement with the time of animals in which supposedly 'nothing happens,' asking us to see these lives anew" beyond their entertainment or educational value.[100] This durational attentiveness, indebted to Tarkovsky's torpid visuality, endeavors to capture an animal's experience of reality without backsliding into anthropomorphism, which often redoubles human ways of being in the world.[101] These drawn-out documentaries also focus on less cinematically captivating animals, like pigs and cows, as opposed to the more charismatic species—megafauna—that prevail in mainstream wildlife productions, such as whales, big cats, and polar bears. The slow animal documentary proposes a new kind of realism, a "*zoomorphic* realism" in which "the editorial power of the human artist to purposively direct the scene or try to determine its effects is suspended" in favor of observing the mundane habitation of animals involved in their surroundings.[102] In this light, Tarkovsky's sustained attentiveness to the natural world vis-à-vis the long take helped forge a pathway out of cinema's dominant anthropocentric viewing position.

Crucially, though, unlike slow animal documentaries, Tarkovsky's films do *not* extend to animals a spirit of beneficent disinterest. More often than not, animals provoke Tarkovsky's more interventionist tendencies. Through meticulous editing, staging, and, too often, violence, Tarkovsky manipulated animals for his own creative purposes. It appears that he accorded greater respect to the sovereign existence of trees, plants, and the elements than he did animals, whose agency seemed to trigger Tarkovsky, as if he could not tolerate independent life forms indifferent to his directorial will.[103] It stands to reason, then, that Tarkovsky did not fully regard animals as part of nature; rather, he understood them as extensions of human needs and wants, hence his preponderant use of *domesticated* animals: livestock (horses, cows) and pets (dogs). The paradox at the heart of Tarkovsky's cinema is, thus, between his impulse to let nature be and his tendency to coercively extract mimetic images from animals and relentlessly tinker with those images. Tarkovsky's inability to refrain from (ab)using animals—and their imagistic likenesses—betrays a deeper human compulsion, "simultaneously sympathetic and pathological," to assimilate animals into every aspect of human life in our quest to better understand ourselves.[104] If anything, slow animal documentaries, even if their slowness is identifiably Tarkovksian, are *correctives* to Tarkovsky's relentless interference in animal lives.

When the contemporary philosopher Frederick Jameson powerfully argued that "the deepest contradiction in Tarkovsky" is his failure to concede that his "valorization of nature" is achieved by "the highest technology of the photographic apparatus," Jameson, it seems, did not have Tarkovsky's treatment of animals in mind.[105] Jameson critiqued Tarkovsky for articulating a naive and reductive theory of cinematic realism that essentializes images of nature as somehow more authentic than mainstream cinema's depictions without appreciating his own aesthetic interpositions. Jameson did not, however, acknowledge the extent of Tarkovsky's knowing and unremitting editing of his images of animals, which serve as little more than a sieve for his technologized subjectivity. Jameson's claim that Tarkovsky's lack of self-reflexivity "threatens to transform Tarkovskian nature-mysticism into the sheerest ideology" is correct, but not in the way he anticipated.[106] It is precisely Tarkovsky's deliberate manipulation of animals—their bodies, their images, and their deaths—that exposes the "second hidden presence" of the beliefs, ideas, and cultural prejudices structuring Tarkovsky's visual ecologies, which seem to flourish amid human absence as if "drawing [their] blood from the extinction of the human."[107] While Tarkovsky did indeed cultivate the resources necessary for the ethical and nonanthropocentric viewing experiences fostered by slow animal documentaries (long takes, dead time, stillness, etc.), he consistently chose *not* to apply those aesthetics to his portrayals of animal life. Tarkovsky's cinematic, Rousseauian "return to nature"—his zoomorphic realism—exists in suspended tension with his incursive handling of animals, which often backslides into reprehensible cruelty.

To understand why Tarkovsky refused to extend the same observational impassivity to animals as he did to many of his other cinematic subjects is the task of this book. By negative example, Tarkovsky's relentless exploitation of animal lives invites us to entertain the possibility of *dis*entangling ourselves from animals, of resisting the urge to further ensnare animals in our parochial dramas. To put too fine a point on it, the lofty terms Tarkovsky used to describe his cinema—"spirituality," "return," "time," "humanity," "soul," "nature"—meant nothing to the animals encountered therein, indifferent to Tarkovsky's creative project but not, obviously, unaffected by it. What is at stake for *them* in Tarkovsky's starry-eyed goal to save humanity's soul through cinematic images? How and why are animals' lives altered, aestheticized, and, at times, extinguished for the sake of one man's spiritually searching art? What do these animals disclose about Tarkovsky that his writings, movies, and ideas cannot on their own?

THE PRESENT STUDY

The preceding introduction has outlined Tarkovsky's idiosyncratic ideas about animals as well as the philosophical traditions from which they extend. The subsequent chapters focus on the different animals encountered across his cinema and their respective portrayals: horses, dogs, birds, cows, and *dead* horses. This study marshals a range of interpretive frameworks to analyze these animals, particularly critical theory, film history, and psychoanalysis. Though any scholar, it is worth noting at the outset, should exercise due caution when psychoanalyzing an artist's work, Tarkovsky frequently places animals in his characters' dreams and associates them with childhood, mourning, and mother figures, soliciting Freudian interpretation.[108] Where possible, this study tries to distinguish between Tarkovsky's subjectivity and the subjectivity of his films themselves. It pursues intensely focused readings of Tarkovsky's animal images to shed light on the desires, chronic tendencies, and pathologies saturating Tarkovsky's cinematic universe—the unconscious of Tarkovsky's work—rather than exclusively fixating on Tarkovsky's peculiar psychology, though the two remain, of course, inextricably linked. This study traces the latticework of Tarkovsky's recurrent, convoluted images, as elusive as they are allusive, to pursue its claims. *And the Cow Burned* teases out surprising connections between Tarkovsky's animal images—and the visual ecologies in which they dwell—to reveal how animals were always at the center of Tarkovsky's creative imagination and practice.

Recentering animals in our understanding of Tarkovsky's life and work, this book also integrates Tarkovsky's animals into the broader history of animals on screen, offering readers a useful, if not exhaustive, primer to the phenomenon of animals in cinema. Recent scholars have begun uncovering the synergistic relationship between cinematic technology and animal life, linking each in urban modernity to the "postindustrial spectacles" of zoos, fairgrounds, and photography.[109] "The animal inevitably questions the origins of cinema," writes the French film critic Hervé Aubron, "because the animal was its first model. But also because cinema was fused with animals in its earliest stages."[110] Media scholar Akira Mizuta Lippit evocatively refers to this cinematographic-zoological correlation as "cinemality."[111] *And the Cow Burned* throws into focus Tarkovsky's cinemality: the ways in which film technology and animal life collide across Tarkovsky's oeuvre with wondrous, baffling, and terrifying consequences that embroil the Soviet filmmaker in major ethical and aesthetic debates about the presence of animals on screen.

A productive tension animating this study, then, is its attempt to (re)view Tarkovsky's cinema from the perspective of animal studies in ways that can accommodate, without entirely succumbing to, the critical tradition that has dominated previous studies on Tarkovsky—what scholars refer to as "auteur theory." Arising in the 1940s in response to the wave of creative filmmaking after World War II, auteur theory holds that a director oversees every element of a motion picture; far from acting as a guiding or distant managerial presence, filmmakers are authors in complete artistic control of their productions.[112] The ways in which Tarkovsky imposes himself on our experience of his films—achieved vis-à-vis incessant motifs, a fatalistic worldview, and self-referentiality—replicate how he impressed himself on his subordinates throughout his career: on actors, writers, cameramen, and, above all, comparatively defenseless animals. Tarkovsky's thirst for auteurist control is, indeed, what generated his stunning depictions of animals, which occasionally lapse into spectacles of violence that lay bare his obsessiveness.

A strictly auteurist view of film, however, mistakenly conceives of cinema as an individualist enterprise rather than a joint undertaking shaped by screenwriters, technicians, actors, and others, including—certainly in Tarkovsky's case—animals themselves.[113] While animals were often coerced in their interactions with Tarkovsky, they were never fully divested of possibilities for self-directed activity. If a being's agency is understood "not as some innate or static thing which an organism always possesses, but rather in a relational sense which sees agency emerging as an effect generated and performed in configurations of different materials," then power never entirely precludes animals' autonomy, however drastically eroded.[114] Elaborating on this idea, Deleuze insists that there is more to power than the saturated field of domination (*pouvoir*); he highlights "power as potential" (*puissance*) as a corrective to the negative model of power as circumspection.[115] Rather than belonging to individuals as a fixed quantity, power is a system of relations flowing through individuals in complex, unequal, and unpredictable ways. "There is a chance," philosopher Cary Wolfe writes about animals, "for life to burst through power's systematic operations in ways difficult to anticipate" that stymie the will of the mighty.[116] Notwithstanding the lopsidedly vulnerable status of Tarkovsky's animals, their capacity to act otherwise—to "burst through" and (re)direct Tarkovsky's designs—discloses their *puissance*. And the Cow Burned studies Tarkovsky's animals because, despite the cruelty and death, they call attention to *life*, both facilitating and frustrating Tarkovsky's work. This study uses

Tarkovsky's animals not only to better fathom his biography and fixations but also to understand animals and our relations to them more fully, on and off screen. Tarkovsky's animals help us inch beyond the depressingly circular analyses that have governed prior studies, in which all interpretive roads lead back to Tarkovsky, the great auteur.

To begin this study, chapter 1 explores the centrality of horses to Tarkovsky's cinema, a protagonism that parallels horses' catalytic significance for the origins of cinematic technology in the mid-nineteenth century. Tarkovsky uses horses to reflect on and, ultimately, eulogize film history. The haunting beauty of Tarkovsky's horses betrays their elegiac qualities, conveying Tarkovsky's mourning for what he saw as cinema's squandered potential to rekindle viewers' spiritual sensibilities. Besides using horses to lament cinema's lost promise, Tarkovsky also relies on them to grieve bygone values that once purportedly structured Russian men but then eluded them during what scholars have described as the postwar "crisis of masculinity."[117] Horses, for Tarkovsky, symbolize an aspirational yet thwarted masculine ideal, which explains why he juxtaposes feckless (and often impotent) male heroes against images of vibrant horses. Finally, Tarkovsky's pessimism about modern society is reified by the disappearance of horses *themselves* across his cinema. In step with John Berger's 1977 essay "Why Look at Animals?," which suggests that society's modernization has rendered animals obsolete in the industrial era, Tarkovsky uses ghostly images of horses to draw our attention to their increasing absence in contemporary life.[118] Modern society, for Tarkovsky, has warped horses into compensatory facsimiles of themselves in the forms of dreams, art, photographs, automobiles, memories, and spectral cinematic images.

The dogs traipsing about Tarkovsky's films are the focus of chapter 2. Depicted beside cerebral characters, these dogs exemplify the canine's legacy in the Western canon as the "philosopher's pet."[119] Thinkers have long claimed that dogs do with their sense of smell what philosophers do with their mind: track down knowledge. Dogs, in this light, accompany Tarkovsky's errant characters on their quests to unlock life's secrets across disparate spatiotemporal planes. Tarkovsky's film dogs are also associated with the tenets of philosophical Cynicism, whose adherents were, in fact, derided as "dogs" for their offbeat, countercultural behavior.[120] The Cynics even cast themselves as guard dogs because, like Tarkovsky, they sought to protect humanity from the excesses of modern society. Despite Tarkovsky's affection for dogs—he himself was a proud dog owner aligned with the trends of postwar Soviet pet keeping—Tarkovsky's canine representations preclude genuine companionship. As Donna Haraway argues, instances of interspecies companionship yield opportunities for humanity to rethink our deep-seated prejudices toward our pets.[121] Yet Tarkovsky emphasizes dogs' submission and fealty above all else, neutering possibilities for a more dynamic human-canine exchange.

The subject of chapter 3 is the rich menagerie of birds encountered across Tarkovsky's work. The culturally stifled atmosphere of late Soviet life inspired Tarkovsky's portrayals of birds, aviation technologies, and levitating characters as means to escape a bleak reality. These visions of flight, moreover, draw inspiration from Leonardo da Vinci's anatomical bird drawings, suggesting Tarkovsky's desire to revivify his gray Soviet milieu with Renaissance-style ingenuity. Tarkovsky's identification with Leonardo, whom he revered as *the* consummate artist (another great auteur), also links him to a desire for mastery over a craft. Thus, despite symbolizing freedom, Tarkovsky's birds are subjected to his heavy-handed directorial techniques, as Tarkovsky was extremely particular about where birds should be seen and heard (or not) across his work. This fixation with control also unites Tarkovsky's avian representations with the proto-cinematic studies of Étienne-Jules Marey, who atomized birds' flight patterns in a self-proclaimed display of technical mastery over the natural world. Additionally, Tarkovsky's use of birds, especially cuckoo birds—harbingers of death in Russian folklore—bears morbid implications. This connection between birds and mortality, channeling the demonic flocks of Alfred Hitchcock's *The Birds* (1963), taps into the burgeoning ecological concerns of the postwar era to relay ominous messages about the apocalypse, as if anticipating the Chernobyl disaster that coincided with the end of Tarkovsky's career.

Chapter 4 concerns Tarkovsky's decision to burn a cow alive in *Andrei Rublev*, a source of long-standing controversy, the contours of which this book brings to light in full detail. Though Tarkovsky intended for the attack to make plain the violent reality of medieval Russia, it reveals Tarkovsky's utter disregard for animal life. Given age-old associations between cows and the maternal, the immolated cow also exposes Tarkovsky's retrograde attitudes toward women. Tarkovsky blamed postwar feminism for ruining society, a view that squarely locates him in the reactionary riptide of late Soviet culture, typified by Aleksandr Solzhenitsyn's fire-and-brimstone denunciations of Western decadence. Relying on Jacques Derrida's theory of "carnophallgeocentrism"—which argues that the violence humanity directs toward animals mimics violence against women—I argue that the burning cow cannot be disentangled from Tarkovsky's degrading treatment of female actors and characters.[122] Yet cows signified something different toward the end of Tarkovsky's life as he succumbed to bronchial cancer, perhaps contracted amid the latent chemical haze on the set of *Stalker*.[123] Looking to Eastern spiritualism and Friedrich

Nietzsche's theory of "eternal return," both of which link cows to the cyclical nature of existence, Tarkovsky uses cows to allay fears about his own impermanence.[124]

The final chapter, "Horses of Another Color," returns to Tarkovsky's horses. The elegiac images of horses beginning *Andrei Rublev* are replaced by grisly scenes of equine death, which evoke the same apocalyptic implications as the massacred mare in Dostoevsky's *Crime in Punishment*. The ghastly visuals in *Andrei Rublev* reveal how Tarkovsky's mourning for horses lapses into what Sigmund Freud described as "melancholia," a psychological condition that targets violence against objects of loss.[125] The apparent disposability of horses in *Andrei Rublev* also invokes Heidegger's theory of animals' metaphysical "poverty": since animals have no conception of death, their lives are meaningless and, therefore, expendable.[126] A Freudian-Heideggerian reading of Tarkovsky's callous treatment of horses in this final chapter circles back to Descartes's theory of animal soullessness beginning this book. In cinematic terms, Tarkovsky's animal cruelty also establishes his relationship with Sergei Eisenstein—the leading light of Soviet cinema—whose films, which feature graphic scenes of animal slaughter, Tarkovsky detested. In killing a horse, Tarkovsky attempts to outshine Eisenstein and symbolically destroy his legacy, a textbook case of what Harold Bloom calls "the anxiety of influence."[127]

Finally, Tarkovsky's slaughtered horse in *Andrei Rublev* is emblematic of his position in a dark subculture of postwar avant-garde cinema known as "the arthouse," which is replete with animal violence. The history of animal cruelty on screen, as will be shown, relates to entrenched cultural taboos placed on the sight of animal slaughter in modern industrial society. Animals afforded art directors like Tarkovsky—Jean-Luc Godard, Ingmar Bergman, Rainer Werner Fassbinder, and others—a means to viscerally probe the existential matters of life and death on screen in ways that fainthearted and bourgeois Hollywood cinema could not. These directors' willingness to record nonsimulated scenes of dead animals became an authenticator of their aesthetic and philosophical seriousness. However, whatever transgressive potential these filmmakers thought they were activating by butchering animals on camera merely redoubled the conventions of mainstream society they strove to resist. What could be more conventional, after all, than needlessly destroying animals for human ends? Tarkovsky's grisly episodes of horse death are nothing more than demonstrations of raw power bereft of any redemptive significance. Tarkovsky's animal cruelty thus exposes the senseless violence human beings target against animals for violence's own sake, simply because they can. Tarkovsky's cinema forces us to grapple with the mutually *inclusive* relationship—the troubling tautology—between violence and vulnerability in humanity's dealings with animals, "a strange twinning" that is "reluctantly pondered by theorists and activists because it too painful, seemingly hopeless, or inordinately dark."[128] Where else would violence turn, Tarkovsky asks, if not toward the vulnerable?

Ironically, in his quest to revive humanist values in postwar life, Tarkovsky betrayed humanism's ethical limits, which—as his cruel treatment of animals makes searingly apparent—are fortified by gratuitous violence in service of human domination. To look for useful meaning in Tarkovsky's animal cruelty is to undertake a futile search for significance where there is none.

NOTES

1. For the animal turn, see Weil, *Thinking Animals*.

2. For several major animal studies texts, see Baker, *Postmodern Animal*; Rothfels, *Representing Animals*; Wolfe, *Animal Rites*; Fudge, *Animal*; Calarco, *Zoographies*; Gruen, *Critical Terms for Animal Studies*; Young, *Immense World*.

3. Ryan, *Animal Theory*, 14.

4. For animals and film studies, see Bousé, *Wildlife Films*; Lippit, *Electric Animal*; Burt, *Animals in Film*; Pick, *Creaturely Poetics*; Lawrence and McMahon, *Animal Life & the Moving Image*; McMahon, *Animal Worlds*. For animals and Slavic studies, see Costlow and Nelson, *Other Animals*; Mondry, *Political Animals*; Timofeeva, *History of Animals*, 151–81.

5. Burt, *Animals in Film*, 17.

6. Malamud, *Introduction*, 78.

7. See, e.g., Turovskaya, *Tarkovsky*; Johnson and Petrie, *Films of Andrei Tarkovsky*, 213–15; Robinson, *Sacred Cinema of Andrei Tarkovsky*, 169–70.

8. Pearson and Weismantel, "Does 'The Animal' Exist?," 17.

9. Haraway, *When Species Meet*, 2, 383.

10. Toymentsev, "Introduction: Refocus on Tarkovsky," 3. In addition to the studies already cited, see Le Fanu, *Cinema of Andrei Tarkovsky*; Green, *Andrei Tarkovsky*; Synessios, *Mirror*; Evlampiev, *Khudozhestvennaya filosofia Andreia Tarkovskogo*; Boldyrev, *Stalker*; Bird, *Andrei Rublev*; Jónsson and Óttarsson, *Through the Mirror*; Bird, *Andrei Tarkovsky*; Salynskii, *Kinogermenevtika Tarkovskogo*; Redwood, *Andrei Tarkovsky's Poetics of Cinema*; Perepelkin, *Slovo v mire Andreia Tarkovskogo*; Martin, *Andrei Tarkovsky*; Alexander-Garrett, *Andrei Tarkovsky*; Dyer, *Zona*; Bould, *Solaris*; McSweeney, *Beyond the Frame*; Pontara, *Andrei Tarkovsky's Sounding Cinema*; Boyadzhieva, *Andrei Tarkovsky*; Efrid, *Andrei Tarkovsky*; Hunter-Blair, *Poetry and Film*; Fomina, *Costumes for the Films of Andrei Tarkovsky*; Kozin, *Andrei Tarkovsky's Mythopoetics*; Robinson, *Andrei Tarkovsky*; Petrushenko, *Nostalgia for the Absolute*; Artamonov, *Posle Tarkovskogo*.

11. See Dunne, *Tarkovsky*; Skakov, *Cinema of Tarkovsky*.
12. For this book's conceptual origins, see De Luca, "Tarkovsky's Cine-Safari," 511–36.
13. Tarkovsky, *Time within Time*, 60.
14. Tarkovsky, *Time within Time*, 60–61.
15. By my count, versions of these words appear at least sixty-one times in Tarkovsky's diaries, eighty-eight times *Sculpting in Time*, and seventy-six times in his collected interviews.
16. Unlike other persecuted Soviet filmmakers of his era, such as Kira Muratova and Sergei Parajanov, Tarkovsky had all his films approved for domestic and foreign (albeit limited) release. While "Tarkovsky was at times inconvenient for the system, he was its greatest international star throughout the 1960s and '70s, an invaluable advertisement for Soviet art and the source of scarce hard-currency earnings. In short, Tarkovsky and the system found it within their mutual interests to achieve an accommodation, however tense and uncomfortable." Bird, *Andrei Tarkovsky*, 27–28.
17. For his father's career, see Kutik and Gibbons, "Poet Who Survived Stalin's Poems."
18. Tarkovsky, *Sculpting in Time*, 205–206.
19. Quoted in Zagorin, "On Humanism," 87.
20. Zagorin, "On Humanism," 87.
21. For more on the emergence of humanism, see Celenza, "Humanism and the Classical Tradition."
22. Zagorin, "On Humanism," 88.
23. Zagorin, "On Humanism," 89.
24. For the humanist ideology of the nineteenth-century bourgeoisie, see Hobsbawm, *Age of Capital*, 305–19.
25. Trotsky, *Literatura i revoliutsiia*, 197.
26. See Masing-Delic, *Abolishing Death*.
27. Heidegger, "Letter on Humanism." For Heidegger's fraught relationship to Nazism, see Rothman, "Is Heidegger Contaminated by Nazism?"
28. Quoted in Zagorin, "On Humanism," 90; Ionesco, *Antidotes*, 18.
29. Foucault, *Order of Things*, 373.
30. Sartre, "Existentialism Is a Humanism."
31. MacKay, "World War II, the Welfare State, and Postwar 'Humanism,'" 160; "Virginia Woolf Reflecting on Peace During an Air Raid."
32. Malik, "Humanism, Antihumanism, and the Radical Tradition"; Lévi-Strauss, "Disappearance of Man."
33. See Kozlov and Gilburt, *Thaw*; Rutten, *Sincerity After Communism*.
34. See "Khrushchev's Secret Speech."
35. Tarkovsky, *Time within Time*, 169.

36. Tarkovsky, *Sculpting in Time*, 168.

37. Sartre, "Letter on the Critique of *Ivan's Childhood*," 45. Sartre was, in fact, defending Tarkovsky against Marxist film critics, mostly in Italy, who lambasted *Ivan's Childhood* for its lack of political content. Sartre emphasized the film's pacificist humanism, which, he argued, was a formidable political statement.

38. Sartre, "Letter on the Critique of *Ivan's Childhood*," 45.

39. Tarkovsky, *Sculpting in Time*, 236.

40. Tarkovsky, *Sculpting in Time*, 234.

41. Tarkovsky, *Sculpting in Time*, 42.

42. Tarkovsky, *Interviews*, 87.

43. Tarkovsky, *Interviews*, 145.

44. Tarkovsky, *Interviews*, 145.

45. Tarkovsky, *Sculpting in Time*, 41.

46. Tarkovsky, *Interviews*, 174.

47. Tarkovsky, *Interviews*, 145.

48. Tarkovsky, *Interviews*, 145.

49. Tarkovsky, *Time within Time*, 15.

50. Tarkovsky, *Time within Time*, 12–13.

51. Tarkovsky, *Interviews*, 87.

52. We hear Tarkovsky utter these words in a 2019 documentary titled *Andrei Tarkovsky: A Cinema Prayer*, made by his youngest son, Andrei.

53. Tarkovsky, *Time within Time*, 18.

54. For Descartes's understanding of the pineal gland, see Senior, "Souls of Men and Beasts."

55. Descartes, *Discourse on Method*, 46.

56. For anthropocentrism, see Ryan, *Animal Theory*, 5–12.

57. Descartes, *Discourse on Method*, 46.

58. Francione, *Introduction to Animal Rights*, 2.

59. Quoted in Francione, *Introduction to Animal Rights*, 2.

60. Ryan, *Animal Theory*, 9.

61. For the terms "animal" and "beast," see Midgley, "Beasts, Brutes, and Monsters," 35–46.

62. For a rare Cartesian analysis of Tarkovsky's cinema, see Tumanov, "Philosophy of Mind and Body in Andrei Tarkovsky's *Solaris*."

63. Tarkovsky, *Interviews*, 87.

64. Tarkovsky, *Interviews*, 145. Tarkovsky here is likely referencing the English writer Rudyard Kipling's story "The Cat That Walked by Himself," which, in 1968, was adapted into a Soviet cartoon (*Koshka, kotoaria ruliala sama po sebe*) by Aleksandra Snezho-Boltskaya. For Kipling in Soviet culture, see Hodgson, "Poetry of Rudyard Kipling in Soviet Russia." The title of Tarkovsky's fifth feature film, *Stalker*—based on the Soviet sci-fi novel *Roadside Picnic* (*Piknik na*

obochine, 1972) by Boris and Arkady Strugatsky—refers to a man whose profession (i.e., stalking) entails illegally shuttling people into a biohazardous wasteland. The designation "stalker" was at least in part inspired by Kipling's mischievous schoolboy character Stalky in his collection of stories *Stalky & Co.* (1899). For the Strugatskys' indebtedness to Kipling, see Strugatsky and Strugatsky, *Roadside Picnic*, 197.

65. Tarkovsky, *Sculpting in Time*, 199.
66. Tarkovsky, *Time Within Time*, 18–19.
67. See Pesmen, *Russia and Soul*.
68. For Dostoevsky's Thaw-era revival, see Shneidman, "Soviet Theory of Literature and the Struggle around Dostoevsky." As Vladimir Golstein also notes, like many nineteenth-century Russian writers, Tarkovsky "challenge[d] the material pressures that threaten humanity, insisting on the duty of an artist to suffer, sacrifice, and save the world. . . . One finds in Tarkovsky a full dose of what is commonly known as 'Tolstoevsky.'" See Golstein, "Energy of Anxiety," 177.
69. Shneidman, "Soviet Theory of Literature and the Struggle Around Dostoevsky," 526.
70. For Tarkovsky's proposed Dostoevsky adaptations, see Apostolov, "Khronika velikoi nevstrechi." Additionally, in both *Mirror* and *The Sacrifice*, Tarkovsky's characters repeatedly quote Dostoevsky.
71. Tarkovsky, *Time Within Time*, 2.
72. Tarkovsky, *Interviews*, 68.
73. Timofeeva, *History of Animals*, 166.
74. For Bolshevik visions of nature, see Josephson et al., *An Environmental History of Russia*, 60–65.
75. See McLendon, *Psychology of Inequality*.
76. Tarkovsky, *Interviews*, 115–16. Though Tarkovsky rarely referenced Rousseau in his writings, he has a child in *Mirror* read a passage from Rousseau's "Discourse on the Arts and Sciences." Tarkovsky also habitually cited Henry David Thoreau in his diaries, whose project of returning to nature clearly drew on Rousseau's. See Tarkovsky, *Time Within Time*, 322–23. See, also, Lane, "Thoreau and Rousseau."
77. Tarkovsky, *Interviews*, 45.
78. Guichet, "Animality and Anthropology in Jean-Jacques Rousseau," 156.
79. Guichet, "Animality and Anthropology in Jean-Jacques Rousseau," 151.
80. Guichet, "Animality and Anthropology in Jean-Jacques Rousseau," 151; Rousseau, *Discourse on Inequality*, 88.
81. Tarkovsky, *Interviews*, 48.
82. Tarkovsky, *Time Within Time*, 157–58.
83. Tarkovsky, *Time Within Time*, 158.
84. Tarkovsky, *Sculpting in Time*, 167–68.

85. Tarkovsky, *Sculpting in Time*, 63.
86. Tarkovsky, *Sculpting in Time*, 63.
87. Tarkovsky, *Interviews*, 68.
88. Tarkovsky, *Sculpting in Time*, 212.
89. "Dovzhenko," Tarkovsky said, "made his films as if they were vegetable gardens, as if they were gardens. He would water them himself, he would make everything grow with his own hands.... His love of the land of the people made his characters grow, as it were, from the earth itself. They were organic, complete. I would very much like to resemble him in this respect." Tarkovsky, *Interviews*, 21.
90. Tarkovsky, *Sculpting in Time*, 213.
91. Tarkovsky, "'I'm Interested in the Problem of Inner Freedom.'"
92. Totaro, "Nature as 'Comfort Zone' in the Films of Andrei Tarkovsky." See, also, Jones, "Stalking the Sublime."
93. Costlow, *Heart-Pine Russia*, 214.
94. Deleuze, *Cinema 2*, 75.
95. Deleuze, *Cinema 2*, 75.
96. For late Soviet environmental policies, see Josephson et al., *Environmental History of Russia*, 184–251.
97. Lim, *Tsai Ming-liang*, 30–31.
98. McMahon, *Animal Worlds*, 3–8.
99. Chris, *Watching Wildlife*, xii.
100. McMahon, *Animal Worlds*, 6.
101. Slow animal documentaries, in other words, set anthropomorphism against anthropocentrism; they creatively, sensitively, and consciously uncouple personification from the imaginative act of re-creating an animal's point of view on screen. Perhaps, political ecologist Jane Bennett wonders, "a touch of anthropomorphism" is useful to "uncover a whole world of resonances and resemblances—sounds and sights that echo and bounce far more than would be possible were the universe to have a hierarchical structure." Bennett, *Vibrant Matter*, 99.
102. Pick, "Animal Life in the Cinematic *Umwelt*" (italics mine), 219; Shukin and O'Brien, "Being Struck," 193.
103. For Tarkovsky and nonanimal forms of life, see Loughlin, "Tarkovsky's Trees." As one of Tarkovsky's characters in *Mirror* says after falling on the ground: "Now that I'm down here, there are all kinds of things. Roots, branches. Have you ever thought, has it ever occurred to you, that plants feel and are aware and maybe even understand?"
104. Shukin, *Animal Capital*, 108.
105. Jameson, *Geopolitical Aesthetic*, 100.
106. Jameson, *Geopolitical Aesthetic*, 100.
107. Jameson, *Geopolitical Aesthetic*, 99–100.

108. For psychoanalytic takes on Tarkovsky, see Pourtova, "Andrei Tarkovsky"; Roitman, "Dreaming Birth for an Unborn Child."
109. Lippit, "Death of an Animal," 12.
110. Quoted in Lippit, "Death of an Animal," 12.
111. Lippit, "Death of an Animal," 12.
112. For auteurism, see Cook, *Cinema Book*, 390–404.
113. For a thorough critique of auteurism, see Sellier, *Le culte de l'auteur*.
114. Philo and Wilbert, *Animal Spaces, Beastly Places*, 17.
115. "Gilles Deleuze," *Stanford Encyclopedia of Philosophy*.
116. Wolfe, *Before the Law*, 32–33.
117. See Zdravomyslova and Temkina, "Krizis maskulinnosti v pozdnesovetskom diskurse."
118. Berger, *About Looking*, 3–28.
119. Fudge, *Pets*, 76–79.
120. Calarco, *Boundaries of Human Nature*, 29–32.
121. See Haraway, *Companion Species Manifesto*.
122. For "carnophallogocentrism," see Derrida, "Violence Against Animals."
123. For the aesthetics of pollution in *Stalker*, see Madson, "Zones."
124. See Nietzsche, *Thus Spoke Zarathustra*, xxii.
125. Freud, "Mourning and Melancholia," 243–58.
126. Heidegger, "Letter on Humanism," 268.
127. Bloom, *Anxiety of Influence*.
128. Pick, "Vulnerability," 411.

ONE

HORSES

HORSES APPEAR IN ALMOST ALL of Tarkovsky's seven feature films, and his depictions of horses have been lauded as some of the most striking images not only in his work but in all of world cinema. Of the many types of animals teeming across Tarkovsky's movies, horses epitomize his art. Like many artists since the dawn of civilization, Tarkovsky viewed horses as noble and majestic beings; they singularly enthralled his imagination.[1] "This may be my internal subjective vision, but the fact is, when I see a horse," Tarkovsky once said, "it seems to me that I have life itself before me. Because it is at the same time very beautiful, very familiar, and very significant in Russian life."[2] Horses, in Tarkovsky's view, embody all that is good in the world: beauty, vitality, intimacy, and home—precisely the sort of lofty, spiritual values Tarkovsky found sorely absent from modern life. Through horses, Tarkovsky hoped to reinvigorate in his viewers the qualities he believed were needed to stave off spiritual disaster.

Yet Tarkovsky's cinema also includes one of the most gruesome instances of violence ever committed against a horse on celluloid. Halfway through *Andrei Rublev*, Tarkovsky's medieval epic about the life of the fifteenth-century iconographer, a horse falls down a flight of stairs. It breaks its back on impact with the ground before being stabbed to death with a spear.[3] There exist conflicting reports about whether, during the shoot, the horse was pushed down the stairs, stabbed, or shot in the neck (by Tarkovsky himself, it has been alleged) to induce its fall.[4] In any case, Tarkovsky presents an extreme act of cruelty at odds with his affection for horses, which indicts him, perhaps irredeemably, for forcing generations of viewers to confront this scene, somehow making us accomplices to the animal's slaughter. The horses that, for Tarkovsky, exemplify everything good in the world are the same animals against which he unleashes frightening brutality. Why? How can Tarkovsky accommodate both exquisite images of horses and antithetically grisly scenes of their death? Horses, I argue, demarcate the two opposite poles of Tarkovsky's visual ecology, a spectrum along which all of Tarkovsky's animal images can be plotted. This study, therefore, is bookended by chapters on horses: chapter 1 deals with Tarkovsky's beautiful horses and chapter 5 with their brutalized counterparts.

This chapter begins by considering the central importance of horses in Tarkovsky's filmography, which, I argue, parallels their catalytic role in the development of the cinematic medium itself, beginning with Eadweard Muybridge's equine motion studies in the late nineteenth century.[5] Throughout his movies, Tarkovsky recovers horses' fulcrum link with motion picture technology to reflect on cinema's essence and evolution, which, in Tarkovsky's eyes, had reached a breaking point by the mid-1960s. The pressures of Hollywood and an uncultured mainstream had, per Tarkovsky, evacuated cinema of its true artistic potential. In response, Tarkovsky turned to images of horses to elegize the squandered promise of film as an art form capable of reviving viewers' spiritual sensibilities. Yet while Tarkovsky's gorgeous images of horses have been praised by critics, there has been little engagement concerning what purpose their haunting beauty serves. This chapter suggests that Tarkovsky uses beautiful images of horses to impress on his spectators a sense of their comparative inferiority—that is, humanity's ungainliness and ineptitude as a species. Humans, especially Tarkovsky's feckless male protagonists, pale in comparison to the visual splendor of horses. Channeling the postwar crisis of Soviet masculinity, Tarkovsky's horses present an idealized yet increasingly remote configuration of virility.[6]

This chapter, then, explores Tarkovsky's pessimistic vision of modern society: the death of cinema, the crisis of masculinity, and the waning possibility for spiritual renewal. The concatenation of these forces, seen as a consequence of social and technological changes wrought in the latter decades of the twentieth century—particularly against the destructive backdrop of World War II— occasioned the disappearance of horses in everyday human life. Across his films, Tarkovsky depicts how, in contemporary society, horses have been relegated out of humanity's habitat and into the realms of dreams, memories, art, and technology. These equine reproductions, proposes the critic John Berger, are compensatory facsimiles that proliferate in urban modernity in response to the destruction of the natural world, reiterating the ongoing fact of animals' relentless marginalization.[7] Tarkovsky's attempt to reconnect with horses vis-à-vis film merely redoubles his feelings of loss. His equine-rich cinema is an index of horses' vanishing in modern industrial life; it exists in inverse relation to horses' off-screen disappearance, an absence Tarkovsky mourns by relentlessly producing ghostly images of horses.

In the end, however, Tarkovsky's elegiac depictions of horses betray the limits of mourning as a conceptual framework through which to understand animals in modern life. An overemphasis on mourning fails to account for the material and ethical consequences of how Tarkovsky uses—and abuses—horses on screen, the topic of chapter 5. *And the Cow Burned* contends that any consideration of Tarkovsky's animals must begin and end by evaluating his portrayals of horses, which are equal parts enchanting, mournful, and macabre.

FILM HISTORY

The baffling prologue of *Andrei Rublev*, which follows a medieval balloonist plummeting to his death, ends with an exquisite image of a horse lying on the ground. The horse begins pitching back and forth in the dirt in what equine behavioralists call a "horse roll," typically a way of communicating strength, comfort, and pleasure.[8] This scene, captured by a static camera, lasts for half a minute; it occurs in total silence as the horse completes two full rotations before rising and trotting out of the visual field.[9]

The image of a careening horse at the start of *Andrei Rublev* is structured by Tarkovsky's signature aesthetic technique: the long take. A long take denotes a continuous shot of a longer duration than is typical in the editing pace of mainstream cinema, in which shots last for only a few seconds.[10] Long takes generate alternative experiences of time that invite contemplation and concentrate spectatorial focus on details that might otherwise escape attention, especially in the fast-paced market economy of Hollywood.[11] With extreme examples like Andy Warhol's *Empire* (1965) and Chantal Akerman's *Jeanne Dielman, 23 quai du Commerce, 1080 Bruxelles* (1975), the long take defined the cinema of Tarkovsky's postwar avant-garde milieu. By holding the camera's focus on a rolling horse in *Andrei Rublev*, Tarkovsky dilates our perception of the animal's grace, beauty, and power as it stretches its neck, flails its forelimbs, sashays its tail, and spools its sinewy body in the dirt.

As critics note, Tarkovsky's durational images are perhaps the clearest example of what French philosopher Gilles Deleuze—himself inspired by Tarkovsky's languid visuals—calls the "time-image."[12] In the second volume of his sweeping history of cinema, Deleuze describes a representational mode of film devoid of any ostensible action that, instead of plot, offers viewers experiences of "pure time."[13] The time-image, unyoked from the narrative logic of cause and effect, emerged in the films of Italian neorealism as a response to the

A horse pitches back and forth in the dirt, one of Tarkovsky's most exquisite images. Still from *Andrei Rublev*, 1966.

disorientation of perception precipitated by World War II. Movies like Vittorio De Sica's *Bicycle Thieves* (1948) and Robert Rossellini's *Germany, Year Zero* (1948) pioneered a directionless aesthetic in which the camera drifts through the ruins of postwar life.[14] These films absorb viewers in a "direct presentation of time" that presents reality's subtlest pulsations and rhythms.[15]

The time-images of postwar Italian cinema influenced a generation of Soviet filmmakers during their formative years at Moscow's All-Union Institute of Cinematography (VGIK) in the 1950s—especially Tarkovsky, for whom the long take acquired metaphysical import for its capacity to "sculpt time," as detailed in his artistic manifesto.[16] Through the time-image of a rolling horse at the start of *Andrei Rublev*, Tarkovsky solicits viewers' unstructured thoughts and emotions as inspired by a horse that has nothing to do with the film's plot.

This digressive image generates an open-ended experience of temporal drift, exemplified by the horse's unhurried rocking that replicates the back and forth of a metronome and lulls us into a dreamlike stupor. The horse—and time itself—becomes the subject of *Andrei Rublev*'s hypnotic prologue.

In the slow films of postwar cinema, Deleuze also discovers a "new race of characters" unable to accomplish anything of note as they wander around shambolic, war-torn worlds.[17] These characters, lost in the folds of time, can only bear witness to the wreckage of history. "This is a cinema of the seer," Deleuze writes, "and no longer of the agent."[18] It is telling, then, that Tarkovsky describes the horses in *Andrei Rublev* as the film's onlookers, condemned to "witness" all "the horror of violence" that human beings inflict on each other, the natural world, and horses themselves across the film's several vignettes.[19] Indeed, wherever there is suffering in *Andrei Rublev*, there are horses: after the balloonist's death in the prologue; amid a man's persecution in "The Jester"; during the arrest of the pagans in "The Holiday"; through the sack of Vladimir in "The Raid"; and while a bell caster, having sentenced a man to corporal punishment, comes clean in "The Bell." Horses are the film's internal audience, stoically observing human beings' dysregulated pursuit of progress as they wade through the medieval era.

In one of the most brutal episodes of *Andrei Rublev*, Tarkovsky depicts a band of traveling stonemasons having their eyes gouged out by men on horseback. Tarkovsky re-creates on screen the mayhem of Paolo di Dono's Renaissance painting *The Hunt* (1465–70), suggesting how humans, like preyed-on animals, are liable to fall victim to random acts of violence. Several horses stand by, mutely watching the havoc. They fulfill the role of Deleuze's "new race of characters," fated to watch society's hopelessness in the aftermath of world war. The horse's status as bystander in *Andrei Rublev* is reiterated in the scene's final image, which depicts a stonemason stumbling around the woods with bloodied and emptied eye sockets. Tarkovsky confers horses the gift of vision in *Andrei Rublev* and, therefore, the burden of eye-witness testimony: a burden Tarkovsky recapitulates with alater image of a courier who is blindfolded, fed molten metal, tethered to a horse, and dragged to death.[20] Tarkovsky implies that human beings have lost their moral perspicuity, while horses must bear witness to the world's excessive brutality. When a Mongol invader at one point asks a Russian whether he feels guilty about the destruction of an Orthodox church, the camera pans to the stoic face of a horse motionlessly dwelling in space, impassively observing the maelstrom as if casting judgment. To what film scholar Elena Gorfinkel describes as art cinema's catalog of "dilated temporality" and

Tarkovsky's horses bear witness to human suffering. Still from *Andrei Rublev*, 1966.

"corporeal lexicon of exhaustion"—from Robert Bresson's "dedramatized 'models'" to Tsai Ming-Liang's "itinerant sleepy drifters" to "Agnes Varda's vagabonding Mona and Pedro Costa's Vanda"—we must add Tarkovsky's horses.[21]

Deleuze, however, predicates his theory of the time-image in response to a crisis in what he calls the "movement-image," which shaped cinema up until World War II.[22] The movement-image, culminating in Alfred Hitchcock's detective films, stands for narrative cinema in which characters are depicted as functional units capable of navigating space and fulfilling tasks: "The cinema of action depicts sensory-motor situations: there are characters, in a certain situation, who act . . . according to how they perceive the situation. Actions are linked to perceptions and perceptions develop actions."[23] Time in the movement-image yields to forward-moving, often suspenseful plotlines that usually resolve in the hero's favor—the way classical Hollywood cinema traditionally presents the passage of time.

The movement-image, according to Deleuze, has origins in cinema's prehistory in the late nineteenth century with Eadweard Muybridge's equine motion studies. Commissioned in 1872 by American industrialist Leland Stanford to determine whether all of a horse's hooves leave the ground during gallop,

Muybridge, an eccentric English photographer, began conducting research on Stanford's ranch in Palo Alto, California. After six years of experiments, Muybridge captured a series of twelve photographs of a horse named Sallie Gardner running at forty miles per hour around a track. Muybridge procured these images, titled *The Horse in Motion*, through a battery of cameras equipped with stereoscopic lenses with what was then considered lightning-fast shutter speeds of 1/1000th of a second.[24] Besides proving that horses are momentarily aloft during gallop, *The Horse in Motion* demonstrates how photographs can spatialize the flow of time into a sequence of observable, discrete instants— what the French physiologist Étienne-Jules Marey calls the first example of "chronophotography."[25]

Deleuze describes how Muybridge's "equidistant snapshots"—a sly pun on the equally spaced intervals between the photographs and the use of an equine—disintegrated a horse's canter into a series of "any-instant-whatevers": a succession of snapshots that detach a being's motion trajectory from a fixed chronology.[26] Somewhat paradoxically, Muybridge made moving images by reassembling a real enactment of motion into a semblance of itself, thereby entering the original movement trajectory into a new time horizon. The movement-image, Deleuze explains, entails both the de- and re-temporalization of motion, which creates the preconditions for cinematic storytelling vis-à-vis editing and montage.

Yet Deleuze only glancingly appreciates that the novelty of cinema hinged on a horse: "Until the mysteries of animal locomotion had been rigorously analyzed down to their smallest physical variations ... cinema could not even properly be thought of as such; for cinema is what follows diligently from ... the stilled data of an exhaustive analysis of the animal."[27] Muybridge's work thus inaugurated a biological-technological synthesis in which the destinies of "cinema (the moving image)" and horse—"the moving organism"—were made coconstitutive.[28] After *The Horse in Motion*, Muybridge perfected a device he called the "zoopraxiscope," a crude forerunner to the cinematograph introduced by Louis and Auguste Lumière in 1895, that could quickly cycle through photographs to create an illusion of continuous motion.[29] Horses' linchpin role in the development of cinema signifies their status in human culture as, above all, figures of movement. Impressed by Muybridge's studies, the American businessman Henry Ford embraced the metaphor of "horsepower" (discussed later) to promote the first mass-assembled, high-speed automobile, the Model T, the development of which culminated in the Ford Mustang later in the century.[30]

Therefore, despite their qualities as Deleuzian time-images, Tarkovsky's horses are also, inevitably, movement-images that invoke the fulcrum link between equine locomotion and cinematic technology. While often depicted in long takes, Tarkovsky's horses are also seen in bouts of kinetic activity as they navigate and inhabit his settings. We are reminded of the horses that burst into the visual field in *Ivan's Childhood*, scavenging for apples on a sun-drenched beach in a vertiginous dream sequence; the horse that elliptically loops around the grounds of a lush country estate in the beginning of *Solaris*; the grazing white horse blanketed in fog in *Nostalghia*; and the myriad horses abounding throughout *Andrei Rublev*. Tarkovsky's horses are indicative of time as much as motion.

The intersection between cinema, movement, and horses in Tarkovsky's oeuvre is no more apparent than in the image of the rolling horse at the start of *Andrei Rublev*. As it flails its hooves, tousles its mane, and rocks back and forth before rising and charging out of the frame, this horse exemplifies the kinetic activity that propelled cinematic technology. It is as if the incantatory rhythm produced by Tarkovsky's rocking horse summons the ghost of Muybridge, who likewise proffered intimate insight into the subtleties of equine locomotion. The image preceding the horse in *Andrei Rublev*, moreover, is a freeze-frame shot (the only one in Tarkovsky's cinema) of the grassy topsoil onto which the wayward balloonist crashes, which introduces photography into the diegesis.

This static shot, whose "motionlessness is manifestly non-cinematic," exposes cinema's material base as invented by Muybridge.[31] Tarkovsky also refers to the most iconic horse in all of Soviet cinema, the tradition with which he is most familiar: the galloping white horse brought to a standstill in Dziga Vertov's avant-garde masterwork *Man with a Movie Camera* (*Chelovek c kinoapparatom*, 1929). As film theorist Laura Mulvey astutely writes,

> [Vertov's] sequence begins as the cameraman films a carriage drawn by a white horse as it canters down a Moscow street, ferrying passengers from the railway station to their home. At a moment when the horse fills the frame, the film frame freezes into a still "photograph." The build-up to this moment, the spectator realizes retrospectively, had been geared around movement.... It asserts the moment at which that one frame was recorded, even as it is duplicated to create a freeze effect.... The photograph's freezing of reality... marks a transition from the animate to the inanimate, from life to death. The cinema reverses the process, by means of an illusion that animates the inanimate frames of its origin.[32]

In *Man with a Movie Camera*, Vertov acknowledges the life-giving powers of cinema—a perceptual illusion achieved by spinning a series of photographs into motion—vis-à-vis an allusion to the very first film image, Muybridge's galloping horse. In *Andrei Rublev*, Tarkovsky similarly juxtaposes a moment of stillness—a freeze-frame shot of the balloonist's death—with a lively image of a horse in motion, returning to cinema's founding documents in both Western culture (Muybridge) and Soviet culture (Vertov). The image of a horse at the start of *Andrei Rublev* is a deeply intertextual one that recovers cinema's origins, its equine genetic code: the *horse-ness* of film.

Additionally, muybridge's photographic (re)assemblage of a horse's gait appeared slower than a horse's actual movement. To study the intricacies of horse motion, Muybridge needed to decelerate "a sweaty, snorting, quivering mass of horseflesh" into a durational version of itself—"a dynamo performing an endlessly repetitive sequence of actions"—that defamiliarizes popular perceptions of a horse's seamless agility.[33] *The Horse in Motion* makes it appear as if Muybridge's mechanical means of gathering data have been transposed onto the subject of his study. In later decades, cinematographers sought to enhance film's relation to reality by overcoming the distortive effects of slow and staccato motion encountered in *The Horse in Motion*. Through the use of new recording techniques, standardized aspect ratios, and, most notably, sound, cinema achieved far greater degrees of kinetic realism in the ensuing decades.

Though it is now commonplace, slow motion (slo-mo) did not take hold as an aesthetic technique in narrative cinema until the 1950s. It was catapulted into fashion among artistically minded filmmakers of the postwar era by Akira Kurosawa's *Seven Samurai* (1954), a magisterial film set in medieval Japan and teeming with horses that greatly influenced *Andrei Rublev*, Tarkovsky's own feudal epic.[34] A slow-motion image is made by recording something at a higher-than-normal aspect ratio—which, per convention, hovers around twenty-four frames per second—and then playing the resultant footage back at normal speed. Throughout *Seven Samurai*, Kurosawa uses slow motion to heighten dramatic moments and create oneiric atmospheres, just as Tarkovsky does across his work, particularly with images of horses in *Andrei Rublev*.

Besides elongating our encounter with the metronomic horse in *Andrei Rublev*'s prologue through a long take, Tarkovsky also deploys the then-novel technique of slow motion to distend our view of it. As in Muybridge's *The Horse in Motion*, Tarkovsky denaturalizes the horse's movement through technological deceleration. Tarkovsky's use of slow motion thus breaks the spell of mimesis, impressing on us that we are, unmistakably, watching a movie. In *Andrei Rublev*, Tarkovsky revives the patently artificial but beguiling visual qualities of Muybridge's (and Vertov's) horse to reiterate how the first cinematic image was, in fact, captured in slo-mo. Tarkovsky recovers not only the horse-ness of film but also the *filmic-ness* of film by abandoning any pretense of visual realism for a de- and re-temporalization of equine locomotion.

Tarkovsky's slow-motion image of a galloping horse alludes to both Muybridge's and Vertov's depictions of equine locomotion. Still from *Andrei Rublev*, 1966.

Dziga Vertov's metacinematic image of a galloping horse, which evokes Eadweard Muybridge's equine motion studies. Still from *Man with a Movie Camera*, 1929.

This convoluted yet potent matrix of a long take, freeze-frame shot, slow motion, and horse at the beginning of *Andrei Rublev* suggests that Tarkovsky accords horses significance throughout his cinema to acknowledge their foundational role in the emergence of film as a medium of vision. In less than half a minute, Tarkovsky's slow-motion portrayal of a horse draws on the protracted images of plotless time in postwar cinema while also returning to the medium's earliest days in the 1870s, when viewers were stupefied by Muybridge's mechanical reproduction of equine movement. The horse in the prologue of *Andrei Rublev* is, in a way, a retelling of all of film history as plotted by Deleuze up until the onset of Tarkovsky's career. It is both a time-image—digressive, elongated, languorous—and a movement-image: gyrating, atemporal, decelerated. Tarkovsky recovers horses' legacy in film history to meditate on the medium's essence and evolution, which, in his eyes, had reached an end point by the mid-1960s. The image of a horse in (slow) motion in *Andrei Rublev* is Tarkovsky's tribute, his monument, to cinema on the cusp of its undoing.

THE END OF CINEMA

Among his litany of complaints about the modern world, Tarkovsky felt that, by the 1960s, cinema had wasted its potential as a meaningful art form. Tarkovsky worried that cinema, as a result of Hollywood's dominance and the emergence of mass consumer culture in the wake of World War II, had lost its way. Audiences went to the movies above all to be entertained by ready-made genre films, which were, in Tarkovsky's view, "cold as a tomb" in terms of creative value:[35] "Any talk of genre in cinema refers as a rule to commercial films—situational comedy, Western, psychological drama, melodrama, musical, detective, horror or suspense movie. And what have any of these to do with art? They are for the mass consumer."[36] Films, for Tarkovsky, had become yet another consumer product. The "most meaningless, unreal commercial film can have just the same kind of magical effect on the uncritical and uneducated cinemagoer as that derived by his discerning counterpart from a real film. The tragic and crucial difference is that if art can stimulate emotions and ideas, mass-appeal cinema, because of its easy, irresistible effect, extinguishes all traces of thought and feeling irrevocably. People cease to feel any need for the beautiful or the spiritual and consume films like bottles of Coca-Cola."[37] In Tarkovsky's view, there were only "a few people of genius in the cinema" (among whom he included himself): Bresson, Kurosawa, Bergman, Fellini, Antonioni, Buñuel, Ozu, and Mizoguchi.[38]

According to Tarkovsky, while cinema reached a breaking point in the postwar era, the seeds of its crisis had been sown during the medium's inception in the nineteenth century. "From the moment it was born," Tarkovsky wrote, "cinema has been developing not according to its vocation but according to purely commercial ideas."[39] Filmgoers have always preferred commercial schlock to more poetic cinema, which incentivizes filmmakers to cater to an unrefined mainstream. "The dilemma of the filmmaker," Tarkovsky said, "boils down to the fact that he's deeply dependent on money. Cinema is the only art that has its origins in the bazaar."[40]

It is unsurprising, then, that Tarkovsky negatively depicts money throughout his films. In *Solaris, Stalker, Nostalghia,* and *The Sacrifice,* images of coins, often atop religious icons like Jan van Eyck's *The Ghent Altarpiece* (1432), suggest that money has warped humanity's moral compass. (That the coins in *Solaris* are emblazoned with Lenin's visage epitomizes Tarkovsky's critique that, despite its collectivist aims, Soviet communism also fell prey to capitalism's petty materialism and individualism.) Reminding us of the New Testament's account of Christ expelling merchants outside the temple in Jerusalem, Tarkovsky asserts that money has tainted the secular church of cinema: "The cinema is a whore. First, she charges a nickel, now she charges five dollars. When she learns to give it away, she will be free."[41] Tarkovsky's lewd and gendered personification of cinema, resonating with the biblical theme of adultery, recycles the fears of the medium's first critics in the early twentieth century, who likened filmgoing to prostitution: "The cheap luxury, the emotional repetitiveness, the sense of entering a perverse and criminal world, of being totally immersed in the life of the city, and finally the egalitarianism of the street—these are the qualities that turned the cinema and the brothel into another pair of 'heterotopic siblings.'"[42] The promise of cinema, for Tarkovsky, was thus damned from the outset, which perhaps explains why coins in his movies are usually seen submerged in water, as if in a baptismal font, suggesting that the medium was cursed at birth by commercialism.

The mercantile essence of cinema begins, indeed, with Muybridge's *The Horse in Motion*. Commissioned to maximize Stanford's racetrack winnings, Muybridge's work was inspired by human society's long-standing exploitation of horses: "By controlled breeding, which goes back 4,000 years, humans have been able to produce horses that are more suited to pulling or speed, more agile or athletic, taller or shorter, and to at least aim at certain colours or markings" for social, economic, and cultural ends.[43] Muybridge's photographic experiments contributed to the modern view of horses as a "biotechnology" to be altered and improved for human use.[44] The "technological methods utilized to produce" Muybridge's images were "continuous with the means deployed to produce the subject of the images."[45] *The Horse in Motion* enabled the further (mis)use of horses in industry and sport and opened a new frontier where horses could be monetized as spectacle: cinema.

The nexus of horses, cinema, and capital is on display in what historians recognize as the first film: Louis Lumière's *Workers Leaving the Factory* (*La Sortie de l'Usine Lumière à Lyon*, 1895), which depicts a throng of laborers exiting a factory's gates. It is only on leaving a place of work that human beings present themselves before a camera, suggesting that cinema, allied with leisure, begins as the workday ends. However, there is one instance of labor's unmistakable presence in *Workers Leaving the Factory*: the horse pulling a carriage out of the factory gates. Saddled, strapped, and guided by a driver, this horse is the only character actually at work in Lumière's film about work.[46] The horse is covered in bits, blinders, and harnesses that reiterate its status as material for human use. (Another version of Lumière's film shows the driver cracking his whip over the horse's back, making plain the logic of exploitation underwriting the workplace.) It is not the "end of a day's work" for Lumière's horse "but its continuation."[47] *Workers Leaving the Factory* is, in part, about the role of equine labor in the rise of cinema as a commercial enterprise. The horse is exiting Lumière's own film factory in Lyon, France; it is in the *literal* business of film production and circulation, stressing the medium's inaugural ties to the market.

The sweep of commercial cinema since *Workers Leaving the Factory* attests to the medium's reliance on horses. Save perhaps dogs, horses have appeared on screen more than any other type of animal, in films like Victor Sjöström's *The Phantom Carriage* (1922), Clarence Brown's *National Velvet* (1944), Carroll Ballard's *The Black Stallion* (1979), Gary Ross's *Seabiscuit* (2003), and Robert Redford's *The Horse Whisperer* (1998). Across his films, Tarkovsky acknowledges horses' inextricability to motion picture technology. In *Andrei Rublev*, for instance, images of horses in quadrilateral compositions repeatedly replicate on screen an image of a screen. At one point, Rublev (Anatoly Solonitsyn) watches his fellow iconographer Kirill (Ivan Lapikov) after Kirill leaves their makeshift dwelling in a barn to report a peasant to local authorities. This scene of snitching, to be sure, alludes to the culture of tattling informants (*donoschiki*) that blighted Soviet life under Stalin, yet we watch Rublev spy on Kirill through a slat resembling a movie screen. Rublev becomes the film's internal audience, and through this screen within a screen, he gazes at a horse. By way of this metacinematic *mise-en-scène*, Tarkovsky re-creates a sight that has shaped cinematic culture since its inception, including our experience of his own films: a viewer distantly admiring a horse's likeness on a flat pictorial surface. Later in *Andrei Rublev*, the camera holds focus on several horses grazing in a field across the threshold of a barn's gates. This image, besides foreshadowing *Andrei Rublev*'s

Tarkovsky frames horses in quadrilateral compositions that replicate on screen the image of a screen. Still from *Andrei Rublev*, 1966.

spectacular finale, frames horses within its frame. It functions as a *mise en abyme* for horses' centrality to the cinematic medium.

The violent, vast, and equine-rich world of *Andrei Rublev* also recalls two cinema marquee genres that hinge on horses: war epics like Steven Spielberg's *War Horse* (2011) and Westerns such as Fred Zinnemann's *High Noon* (1952), John Ford's *The Searchers* (1956), and Sergio Leone's *Once upon a Time in the West* (1968), which inspired the rise of "the Eastern" (*ostern*) in late Soviet cinema.[48] Shot in central Asia or the Caucuses, films like Vladimir Motyl's *White Sun of the Desert* (*Beloe solntse pustyni*, 1970) and Nikita Mikhalkov's *At Home among Strangers* (*Svoi sredi chuzhikh, chuzhoi sredi svoikh*, 1974) draw on motifs of deserts, outlaws, and horses, providing escapist entertainment for the stagnated atmosphere of late Soviet culture. Yet Tarkovsky, as noted, loathed genre films like Westerns. On his 1983 trip to the United States, Tarkovsky said that "upon seeing Utah for the first time," he realized "Americans were vulgar because they filmed westerns in a place that should only serve as backdrop to films about God."[49] To activate what he perceived as film's metaphysical potential, Tarkovsky rejected mainstream cinema's cheap thrills by reappropriating its aesthetics, including horses, to evoke wonder about life's mystery and beauty. Tarkovsky himself often wore a cowboy hat on the set of his films, suggesting that he did, despite his critique, recycle the aesthetics of Westerns for his own purposes.[50] *Andrei Rublev* is, in a way, an anti-Western Western: a *spiritualized* Western.

In the background of many scenes in *Andrei Rublev*, horses meander across the visual field from frame left to frame right, heading to some unknown location. Their trajectory replicates the path of Tarkovsky's wandering monks who—foreshadowing the itinerant threesome in *Stalker*—shuttle across the frame on a left-right axis. This "universal migration to some off-screen destination ... communicate[s] a clear directionality," and "most episodes ... begin or end on rivers which link them into a single journey across a unified space, even if we sometimes do not know where we are."[51] Tarkovsky's rightward-moving horses and monks, which re-create the movement in Rublev's icon *The Last Judgment: Procession of the Righteous Women to Heaven* (*Strashnii sud: Shestvie prevednyykh v rai*, 1408), direct our attention to that which transcends the visible. These horses invite us, like Rublev, to take a leap of faith, to envision an invisible realm that requires conviction, humility, and imagination—that is, belief—to access. Tarkovsky focuses on horses throughout *Andrei Rublev* to rekindle the lofty, spiritual values he found sorely missing in modern life.

As Anne Eakin Moss writes, citing the French philosopher Pierre Hadot's writings about the life-affirming necessity of "everyday spiritual activity," Tarkovsky's "films can be seen as vivid narrative illustrations of spiritual exercises" because they demand from his characters and viewers "extreme forms of mental concentration, focused on goals that depart from the everyday" in pursuit of a "transcendent aim."[52] The horses in *Andrei Rublev* embark on a path, a pilgrimage, toward the unknown, somewhere beyond the soul-crushing tedium of ordinary life. Tarkovsky's spiritual exercises do not transmit specific "doctrinal content"; rather, Tarkovsky encourages viewers to "traverse a certain itinerary," perceptually and emotionally, to enrich their inner worlds.[53] It is as if *Andrei Rublev*'s ambling horses could help us answer the questions raised by Tarkovsky's beguiling and inscrutable films, the meaning of which, it appears, extends beyond the bounds of the diegesis. On-screen space, for Tarkovsky, is aestheticized to reinvigorate viewers' off-screen spirituality, to expand their psychic horizons in the real world.

Through special effects like spatial discontinuity, asynchronous sound, and slow motion, Tarkovsky posits a link between cinematic spectacle and the miraculous in *Andrei Rublev*. That is, his images depart from direct presentations of reality to "reproduce mimetically the experience of the miraculous" for secular, modern viewers in ways that draw attention to the director's powers to transform reality and confound the viewing experience.[54] Though skeptical of cinematic trickery for its own sake, Tarkovsky nonetheless technically distorts his images of horses—especially the slow-motion horse careening in dirt at the beginning of *Andrei Rublev*—to generate an experience of wonder akin to the awe evoked by miracles. As S. Brent Plate writes, usefully analyzing how filmmakers "borrow millennia-old aesthetic tactics" from religion, "Cameras and rituals *frame* the world, *selecting* particular elements of time and space to be displayed. These framed selections are then projected onto a broad field"—an altar or a screen—"in a way that invites its viewers/adherents to become participants, to share in the experience of this re-created world."[55] Cinema, for Tarkovsky, is a kind of miracle machine.

Despite the awestriking qualities of the slow-motion horse in *Andrei Rublev*'s prologue, Tarkovsky described it as a creature "who looks sad."[56] It is sad, he claimed, because it is lamenting the violence and stupidity humanity will enact—against itself, art, churches, nature, etcetera—throughout *Andrei Rublev*. This portrayal of a horse eulogizes humanity's spiritual demise and, by turn, its inability to appreciate true cinematic art. Present-day spectators, Tarkovsky concluded, do *not* wish to follow his horses to locations unknown in pursuit of unseen truths. Tarkovsky detected no meaningful signs of spiritual renewal in modern life despite his best cinematic efforts. "But strange developments are occurring in cinema," Tarkovsky said, "I would even say catastrophic developments. For viewers have gotten what they wanted, and, in general, they have stopped going to the cinema. . . . The situation is very, very disheartening. In short, the crisis has arisen out of our lack of spirituality."[57] It is not by chance that the only time we see Rublev handle an icon in the film, he is polishing one that was burned in a Mongol raid: an analogy for how the public neglects art, which is preserved only by a few loyal disciples. Modernity, for Tarkovsky, is medieval: "Is progress leading us in the right direction? If one compares the number of victims caused by the Inquisition to those victims of concentration camps, one would say that the Inquisition was a Golden Age. The greatest absurdity of our times is thinking that, united together, people of a spiritually inferior character are able to bring happiness to the rest of humanity."[58] Humanity is beyond redemption, cinematic or otherwise. Tarkovsky's sense of doom is darkly illustrated by the slaughter of horses throughout *Andrei Rublev*. The destruction of the very animals that catalyzed cinematic technology, to which we return in chapter 5, conveys what Tarkovsky viewed as the "death" of genuine cinematic art, what he called "real film." For Tarkovsky, there could be no cinema, no secular salvation, without horses.

BEAUTY

Despite the "sad" qualities of Tarkovsky's horses, they are unmistakably beautiful. They have inspired countless tributes in the form of poems, performances, and videos; Tarkovsky's horses, indeed, have become a shorthand for the idea of beauty itself.[59] Yet what exactly makes these horses so beautiful? In critics' breathless rush to admire Tarkovsky's horses, the specific aesthetic qualities constituting their striking appearances have been overlooked.

On its own, as Elaine Scarry teaches us, "beauty" is a freighted concept with a definition that is difficult to locate. While "we know with relative ease what a beautiful horse or beautiful man or possibly even a beautiful pot is ... it is much more difficult to say what 'Beauty' unattached to any object is."[60] Notwithstanding beauty's elusiveness, when we encounter something beautiful, we instinctively recognize its presence: "Beauty quickens. It adrenalizes. It makes the heart beat faster. It makes life more vivid, animated, living, worth living.... The beauty of the thing at once fills the perceiver with a sense of conviction about that beauty, a wordless certainty—the this! here!"[61] The facility with which we recognize beauty led the German philosopher Immanuel Kant to hazard a connection between beauty and morality, because beauty "prepares us to love something ... apart from any interest ... to esteem something highly even in opposition to our (sensuous) interest."[62] Beauty, Kant argues, reroutes our self-interest in favor of the beautiful thing before us, fostering bonds between the beholder and the beheld. Building on Kant's ideas, Scarry argues that beauty "is an occasion for 'un-selfing'" because it facilitates a more capacious regard for that which lies outside us, whether that be another individual, a horse, or the world itself.[63] Our

> daily unmindfulness of the aliveness of others is temporarily interrupted in [beauty's] presence ... alerting us to the requirements placed on us by the aliveness of all persons, and the same may take place in the presence of a beautiful bird, mammal, fish, plant.... Beauty seems to place requirements on us for attending to the aliveness or (in the case of objects) quasi-aliveness of our world, and for entering into its protection. Beauty, then, is a compact, or contract between the beautiful being (a person or thing) and the perceiver. As the beautiful being confers on the perceiver the gift of life, so the perceiver confers on the beautiful being the gift of life. Each "welcomes" the other.[64]

Tarkovsky echoed these Kantian notions about the ennobling virtue of beauty: "And is it possible to help such people to experience inspiration and beauty and the noble impulses that art touches off in the soul? ... My function is to make whoever sees my films aware of his need to love and to give love, and aware that beauty is summoning them."[65] Beauty, for Tarkovsky, expands our moral concern beyond the self, entering us into a "reciprocal pact" with the beautiful thing before us.[66]

The conclusion of *Andrei Rublev*, an eight-minute sequence backdropped by hymnal music that cycles through Rublev's religious art, enacts Scarry's and Kant's ideas about beauty. Tarkovsky's close-ups of Rublev's paintings, heightened through an altogether unexpected—that is, miraculous—shift to color footage, contrast with the black-and-white film stock used to shoot *Andrei Rublev*. Presented in their full colorful glory, the saturated colors of Rublev's artwork, acclaimed for its blues, yellows, and pinks, offer Tarkovsky's viewers an experience of aesthetic pleasure after having dwelled in the bleak medieval world for over three hours. Composed of a series of tracking shots, this sequence reenacts a medieval worshipper's roving gaze, the camera scanning the surface of the icons. Tarkovsky fosters a shared perceptual experience between fifteenth-century churchgoers and twentieth-century filmgoers: beauty facilitates connectedness with objects and others beyond the self across time and space. Tarkovsky's loving presentation of Rublev's icons, which survived the throes of history (including the tumult of the Soviet period), evokes gratitude and wonderment, making us aware of our "need to love and to give love."[67] Rublev's paintings, in other words, circuit our self-interest in the continuation of our own lives on behalf of the beautiful artwork before us.

This dazzling spectacle culminates in an equally colorful image of horses grazing in a thunderstorm, which, like Rublev's frescos, juxtaposes *Andrei Rublev*'s grayscale composition. In cinematic terms, Tarkovsky's shift to Technicolor horses reminds us of the fantastical Horse of a Different Color in Victor Fleming's *Wizard of Oz* (1939), a film that ushered in a new era of color cinema. Dorothy (Judy Garland) encounters the white (then mauve, then red, then yellow) horse upon entering the Emerald City. Just as Muybridge used horses to innovate cinematic motion, Fleming used them to experiment with the new possibilities of color film stock. With *Andrei Rublev*'s finale, Tarkovsky reveals how, throughout film history, directors have turned to horses at junctures in the medium's technical evolution to generate profound experiences of wonder and aesthetic pleasure, designed to send viewers over the rainbow.

Tarkovsky introduces the final image through a lap dissolve during a close-up of Rublev's icon *Christ the Redeemer* (*Khristos Vsederzhitel'*, 1410), which fades into the horses as rainfall and rolls of thunder overtake the visual frame. The use of this cinematographic technique posits an analogy between the beauty of Rublev's icons and Tarkovsky's horses. Made possible by rewinding the negative in a camera's film chamber and rerecording over it, a dissolve shot involves the distortion of one image as it gives way to another.[68] The technique simulates proximity between two images on screen beyond that of traditional montage alterations. In *Andrei Rublev*, a fusion of icons and horses briefly overtakes the frame, blurring the coordinates between nature and culture—further evidence of Tarkovsky's religious reverence for horses.

A dazzling color image of horses that rhymes horses with
Andrei Rublev's icons, along with the Technicolor horses from
The Wizard of Oz. Still from *Andrei Rublev*, 1966.

For thirty seconds, Tarkovsky holds our gaze on these horses blanketed by rain. Just as with Rublev's frescos (some of which feature horses), Tarkovsky has us observe these animals in all their resplendence through a long take, echoing the durational image of the rolling horse at the beginning of *Andrei Rublev*. Unlike that decelerated image, however, Tarkovsky does not cinematographically tinker with these horses. They are immune to the overtures of his aesthetic imagination, suggesting that their beauty is self-evident. Beauty, Scarry writes, "permits us to be adjacent while also permitting us to experience extreme pleasure, thereby creating the sense that it is our own adjacency that is pleasure-bearing. This seems a gift in its own right, and a gift as a prelude to or precondition of enjoying fair relations with others."[69] The epilogue of *Andrei Rublev* lets horses alone; it salutes the sovereignty of beings outside the human. Tarkovsky "cede[s] ground to the" horses grazing before us, which evoke an "opiated adjacency," a deep pleasure, despite offering no material benefit.[70] This nonutilitarian form of value and exchange is precisely what Kant identified as evidence of beauty's moral essence: "purposiveness without a purpose."[71] The stunning horses at the end of *Andrei Rublev* inspire a more capacious regard for the natural world. "It is not that we cease to stand at the center of the world," Scarry concludes, "for we never stood there. It is that we cease to stand at the center of our own world."[72]

Another aspect of beauty identified by Scarry is that beautiful things evoke an "impulse toward begetting": a desire to duplicate beauty by whatever aesthetic means available.⁷³ "Beauty brings copies of itself into being. It makes us draw it, take photographs of it, or describe it to other people."⁷⁴ That beauty catalyzes its own replication explains why we find many re-creations of Tarkovsky's striking images across world cinema, as in the films of Claire Denis, Carlos Reygadas, Lars von Trier, Bi Gan, and Terrence Malick. Beauty's (self-)replicability accounts not only for why many of Tarkovsky's images reenact canonical paintings, such as Alexander Ivanov's *The Appearance of Christ to the People* (1837–57) in *Andrei Rublev*, but also for why Tarkovsky's visuals repeat *themselves* across his cinema: burning houses, windswept fields, heavy rainfall, lacy fabrics, and majestic horses. As Stephanie Sandler writes, "Repetition is perhaps the strongest technical feature of Tarkovsky's films.... Repetition has great psychological force, allowing a filmmaker or poet to hold onto words or images, to keep them from disappearing."⁷⁵ Tarkovsky's beautiful aesthetic both begets beauty and is begotten by the beautiful. Indeed, the exquisite slow-motion image of a horse in the prologue of *Andrei Rublev* reprises the slow-motion image of horses drifting out of frame in the opening scene of *Zvenigora* (1929), a film by the Ukrainian director Oleksandr Dovzhenko, whom Tarkovsky adored.⁷⁶ What is beautiful, Scarry writes, "prompts the mind to chronologically move back in the search for precedents and parallels, and to move forward into new acts of creation, to move conceptually over, to bring into relation, and does all this with a kind of urgency as if one's life depended on it."⁷⁷

Tarkovsky's use of slow motion in his depiction of the rolling horse in *Andrei Rublev* further corroborates beauty's iterability. The simplest manifestation "of the requirement beauty places on us to replicate ... is the everyday fact of staring ... the desire to duplicate not by translating the glimpsed image into a drawing or a poem or a photograph, but simply by continuing to see."⁷⁸ Not only does the use of slow motion create an illusion of decelerated time, lengthening the period in which the animal is available for our gaze, but it also literally requires double the celluloid and twice the number of frames than in standard aspect ratio. "No matter how long beautiful things endure, they cannot out-endure our longing for them," but "efforts may be made"—such as Tarkovsky's use of slow motion—"to prolong our access" to beauty.⁷⁹ Thus, the beauty of Tarkovsky's horses is found both in their capacity to enrich viewers' moral imagination and in their iterative essence. Yet it behooves us to ask, What makes horses *themselves* so beautiful? Why are horses considered by so many to be beauty incarnate?

In his essay "The Academic Horse," French philosopher Georges Bataille outlines what he calls "Hellenic genius": the ancient Greek philosophical notion that all the world's beings and things adhere to a set of perfect cosmic laws.⁸⁰ Bataille argues that the Greeks looked to the mathematical, "academic" precision of horses, which contrasts with the obvious ineptitudes and failings of human beings, as evidence of the universe's metaphysical harmony.

> [A horse] is one of the most accomplished expressions of the *idea* ... as Platonic philosophy or the architecture of the Acropolis. All representations of this animal during the classical age can be seen to extol ... a profound kinship with Hellenic genius. Everything happened ... as if the forms of the body as well as social forms or forms of thought tended toward the sort of ideal perfection from which all value proceeded, as if the progressive organization of the horse sought gradually to satisfy the immutable harmony and hierarchy that Greek philosophy tended characteristically to ascribe to ideas.⁸¹

The pleasure afforded by the sight of a horse is not merely a matter of geometric symmetry but an ideal of metaphysical wholeness to be admired by comparatively graceless human beings. For the ancients, horses embodied the best of nature and offered a possibility to commune with it. It is not by chance, then, that horses became "symbols of status" for ancient elites, whose nomenclature of class and rank presupposed horse ownership: *hippeis* in Athens and *equites* in Rome.⁸² In *Andrei Rublev*, Tarkovsky depicts the medieval world's privileged and ornately dressed upper classes astride horses: Russian princes, Mongol equestrians, and Italian dignitaries invited to the unveiling of a spectacular bell, which is itself emblazoned by a horse's likeness.⁸³

To echo Scarry's theory of beauty's links to (re)iteration and begetting, when we look at a horse, we are, perhaps, looking at the most idealized yet unobtainable version of *ourselves*. We associate horses with beauty because they embody a flawlessness in form and function that human beings, with all their defects and ungainliness, can never hope to attain.

> When we look at a horse, we see a body capable of motion and coordination much like our own. ... This silent echo of our own being also exists in another plane of knowledge beyond the capacity of sight. The great power of those bodies, those full muscular forms that so far excel our own ... share their command of the world with us. We can know their mobility almost as they know it, tactile and kinesthetically, when we ride and run with them. ... This endows the image of the horse with a special quality that makes us see it differently from other animals, and this we find reflected in artistic representations of the horse. Even without humanized and sentimentalized distortions, the animal itself embodies something as deeply longed for and admired as the most formally accomplished representation of the human body.⁸⁴

We see in horses not ourselves but the faintest ideal version of ourselves. The sight of a horse recapitulates our inadequacies as a species, the inescapable failings of the human mind and body.

Thus, horses—and Tarkovsky's exquisite images of them—are so beautiful because we see ourselves as a *mis*begotten copy of them: a pale imitation or silent echo of the metaphysical harmony translated into the perfectly proportioned equine body. It is not a coincidence that, at the end of *Andrei Rublev*'s prologue, the camera alternates between images of a gracefully careening horse and the splayed-out human corpse of the balloonist lying in the wreckage of his deflated flying contraption, which hisses and swells like a failing organ. The human, Tarkovsky suggests, is a pathetic copy of the horse's elegant, effortless power. The horse's motion trajectory even inverts the balloonist's: "take off—flight—crash—wallow—leaving."[85] This reversal insinuates what Tarkovsky considered to be the superiority of earthbound horses over humanity's skyward delusions—a literal flight of fancy, to which we return in chapter 3.

EQUINE MASCULINITY

The point of comparison for Tarkovsky's beautiful horses, however, is not humanity writ large but rather the *men* encountered across his cinema. In step with the great authors of nineteenth-century Russian literature, who likewise idealized horses, Tarkovsky portrays horses as model configurations of masculinity. According to Mikhail Epstein, "In the Russian poetic system of animal images, the horse occupies, without a doubt, the most important place."[86] Whether in Aleksandr Pushkin's "The Bronze Horseman" (*Mednyi vsadnik*, 1833), Nikolai Gogol's *Taras Bulba* (*Taras Bul'ba*, 1835), Lermontov's *A Hero of Our Time* (*Geroi nashero vremeni*, 1840), or Leo Tolstoy's *Anna Karenina* (1878) and "Kholstomer" (1886), horses are often "a marker of the status gained by a male hero moving 'outward' to a public position and the successful domination of his (feminized) nature, toward a culture beyond domesticity, women, and the body.... The horse is often a representation of limitlessness, of wandering motifs in the tradition of violence and masculinity."[87] The most common words for "horse" in Russian are *loshad'* and *kon'*, and each word behaves differently. The former is grammatically feminine, comes from the Turkic word *alasha*, and refers to the general category of horses as a species, while the latter, grammatically masculine—likely from the Mongolian term for "herd leader"—connotes steeds, stallions, and warhorses.[88] Russian cultural projections of horses frequently draw on the essentially masculine traits entailed by the word *kon'*: power, daring, freedom. Thus, as the canonical Russian writers before him,

Tarkovsky uses horses to juxtapose his era's prevailing norms of masculinity. If Tarkovsky's horses are synonymous with his films, then this status must be extended to his brooding male heroes, who look to horses to better apprehend themselves.

After World War II, both sides of the Iron Curtain underwent what has been described as a "crisis of masculinity," which persisted through the Cold War.[89] This crisis was precipitated by numerous factors, all of which threatened men's traditional position as the apex of society: economic automatization, adherence to norms of domesticity, a gnawing lack of purpose after fascism's defeat, and the burgeoning presence of women in the workforce. In Soviet culture, male feelings of social dislocation led to a revival of the trope of the "superfluous man" (lishnii chelovek), which powerfully shaped nineteenth-century Russian literature.[90] Tarkovsky, whose regressive ideas about women are explored in chapter 4, believed that Russian men, besieged and supplanted, had lost their morale in the postwar era. "For me there is nothing more unpleasant than a woman with a big career. Not because I fear for my male rights, but because I see it as something unnatural. There is a woman taking a route that she should have ignored. Only a misleading, competitive feeling for the man has caused her to do it. . . . We never speak of the fact that a woman is a woman and a man is a man. . . . To be a man is as hard as it is to be a woman. The misery is based on something else. Man's spiritual level is very low."[91] Throughout his films, Tarkovsky turns to horses to reanimate men's dignity and virility in the face of male disaffection.

Tarkovsky's arthouse riff on the science fiction genre, *Solaris*, illuminates his disenchantment with contemporaneous gender politics. The movie opens with the astronaut protagonist, Kris Kelvin (Donatas Banionis), moodily walking around his father's estate the morning before his disastrous expedition into outer space. *Solaris*'s first shot depicts a babbling creek in the currents of which we see undulating reeds. Kelvin admires the mist-laden setting, seemingly committing to memory Earth's sights, sounds, and smells. These nature motifs signal a departure from the dominant aesthetics of the science fiction genre, as canonized in 1960s and '70s films like Stanley Kubrick's *2001: A Space Odyssey* (1968), Spielberg's *Close Encounters of the Third Kind* (1977), and George Lucas's *Star Wars: A New Hope* (1977).[92] The lush visuals in the beginning of *Solaris* call on telluric tropes found in Russian Village Prose (*derevenskaia proza*), one of the most popular literary genres of the late Soviet era. Like Tarkovsky, Village Prose writers expressed skepticism about the modern world's fast-paced changes by romanticizing pastoral life.[93] From its outset, *Solaris*—an extraterrestrial film—locates humanity's destiny in its *terrestrial* origins. Tarkovsky beckons Kelvin back to Earth. "We don't need other worlds; we need a mirror," says one of the film's jaded astronauts, alluding to Tarkovsky's follow-up film, *Mirror*.

Another leitmotif of Village Prose on which *Solaris* leans is horses. Works like Konstantin Paustovskii's "Grey Gelding" (*Sivyi merin*, 1963) and Vasilii Belov's *Business as Usual* (*Privychnoe delo*, 1966) rhapsodize horses to conjure an idyllic past as an escape from the woes of modern industrial life, in which men (and horses themselves) have become extraneous.[94] As Kelvin morosely traipses about his father's estate in *Solaris*, we see a horse trot across the visual field. Its breezy canter contrasts with Kelvin's pensive amblings. The horse embodies the manly traits evacuated from late Soviet masculinity: brawniness, resolve, action. It is, indeed, a movement-image in contrast to the durational time-images of Kelvin ruminating, prevaricating, and sleeping seen throughout the film. Kelvin is out of step with the celebrity cult of Soviet cosmonauts typified by Yuri Gagarin. Following his death in 1968 (a few years before *Solaris*'s release), Gagarin came to embody a triumphant, sci-fi vision of virility in popular culture.[95] Conversely, Kelvin epitomizes the existential crisis of Soviet masculinity, as do all of Tarkovsky's male protagonists: the title character of *Stalker* is an unheeded prophet; Andrei Gorchakov (Oleg Iankovskii) in *Nostalghia* is a hapless, suicidal émigré; Aleksandr (Erland Josephson) in *The Sacrifice* is a washed-up stage actor; and the iconic iconographer in *Andrei Rublev* briefly abandons his craft. Tarkovsky's heroes all struggle to make something of themselves, and they are frequently juxtaposed against vigorous, agile, and beautiful horses.

Besides Village Prose, Tarkovsky's portrayals of horses also align with those enshrined in the lyrics of the Soviet bard Vladimir Vysotsky. In songs like "Ambler's Race" (*Beg inokhodtsa*, 1970) and "Fastidious Horses" (*Koni priveredlivye*, 1972), Vysotsky "conveys an intimacy between man and horse that is both mental and physical, creating a powerful unit of understanding and kinetic communication."[96] Through images of galloping and rogue horses, Vysotsky conferred on his lyric persona an uncompromising freedom unafforded by the repressive atmosphere of late Soviet life.[97] Even Vysotsky's grave site, located in Moscow's Vagankovskoye Cemetery, consists of a sculpture of him tethered by rope to both a guitar and a wild horse, evidence of the tension between aspirational, equine freedom and external cultural constraints.

Literary scholars have also situated Vysotsky in a "rarely identified" movement of "Neo-Romanticism" in postwar Soviet culture that bequeathed artists stylistic and imaginative resources to assert their "individual freedom" against the state's "depersonalizing political and cultural forces."[98] The horse, an

A horse cuts across the visual field, its agility contrasted against
Kelvin's morose amblings. Still from *Solaris*, 1972.

exemplar of nineteenth-century Romantic art, embodies the values Vysotsky
vied to recoup.[99] Perfectly intoned by his gravelly (hoarse) voice, Vysotsky's
lyrics personify horses as renegades bucking the codes of ordinary life. Likewise, Tarkovsky uses horses in *Andrei Rublev* and *Solaris* to reinvigorate the two
male protagonists, an astronaut and an artist, whose identities are restricted by
society as they grapple with crises of self-worth. Despite Tarkovsky's distaste
for literary Romanticism—a "sickness," he called it, that expresses hostility
toward the simple pleasures of "daily habit"—Tarkovsky's "free and unembarrassed use of such terms of 'genius,' 'transcendence,' 'spiritual vision,' 'beauty,'
etc." seems to place him as "an inheritor of a Romantic tradition," regarded
by Western intellectuals in the 1960s and 1970s "as being outmoded and discredited."[100] Rublev and Kelvin are, indeed, paragons of the Romantic hero:
rogue voyagers on quests to redeem their errant worlds. They can be likened
to the paradigmatic Romantic (anti)hero in Caspar David Freidrich's painting
Wanderer above the Sea of Fog (1818), who defiantly turns his back on the portraitist.[101] Tarkovsky, a filmmaker with larger-than-life (Romantic) ambitions
to spiritually reinvigorate humankind and save the world, uses horses—such
as the one that enters a desecrated church after Rublev forswears painting—to
reconnect his protagonists with life's beauty, mystery, and grace. Through insistent appeals to the Romantic trope of the horse as the epitome of freedom,
both Vysotsky and Tarkovsky extra-diegetically assert their own masculine
identity in late Soviet culture.[102]

Yet Tarkovsky's horses also betray the unattainability of the idealized masculine qualities they anthropomorphize. The free-wheeling horse of *Solaris*'s opening scene, for example, strikes us as a kind of mirage because its appearance is, albeit subtly, highly spatially disjunctive. The sequence in which the horse appears begins with Kelvin gazing at his father's home across a pond and then traipsing out of the frame. The next shot, with a rightward angle, presents an alcove at the pond's edge where Kelvin pauses with his back turned toward the camera (not unlike Freidrich's wanderer). The camera, positioned on slightly higher ground, looks down at Kelvin, as if assuming what Tarkovsky believed to be postwar society's condescending attitude toward men. The next shot, tilted to the left, shows the horse entering the frame and running in a circle. The camera, now stationed on slightly lower ground, *looks up* at the horse, figuratively elevating it as a kind of cultural and physical ideal. These shots' alternating angles, axes, and elevations suggest that the horse is seen from Kelvin's vantage point. The cinematography implies that the horse appears behind Kelvin and inspires him to turn around and look at it. Kelvin's rotational perspective can also be inferred by the horse's 360-degree loop around the visual field; its orbital canter mimics Kelvin's revolving gaze.

The following shot, however, does *not* show Kelvin looking at the horse: it is, unexpectedly, a tracking shot of Kelvin meandering along the pond. This shot alteration abandons conventional shot-reverse-shot montage, flouting cinema's "180-degree rule," which states that camerawork should establish a coherent left-right axis between things on screen to ease viewers' perceptual experience of a film setting.[103] Before even launching into space, then, *Solaris* disorients viewers by violating the normative rules—the physics—of continuity editing.[104] The discontinuous spatial relations between Kelvin and the horse suggest that it materialized elsewhere in the woods, much farther from Kelvin than we initially presumed. Thus, if Tarkovsky understood horses as symbols of masculinity, this horse's disparate spatial relation to Kelvin insinuates that his manhood is just out of reach—present but unlocatable within the frame. The horse in *Solaris* represents not only masculinity but also masculinity's remoteness. The horse even has a bridle attached around its head, denoting its domestication. A far cry from Vysotsky's rambunctious stallions, the masculine traits of Tarkovsky's horses have been inhibited.

Later in *Solaris*, the same horse is heard neighing from within a garage repurposed into a stable. The horse's cries frighten a young boy (Vitalik Dvorzhetsky), who rushes to a woman (Tamara Ogorodnikova) for protection. We see the horse standing in its stall, obscured in darkness. In no way does it resemble the sinewy animal Kelvin encountered earlier. This enchained horse, casting its shadow onto a wall, is but a trace of its former self. The boy even fails to ascertain it: "What's standing over there?" The horse has been defamiliarized to the point of unrecognizability. Through the horse's neighs, Tarkovsky foreshadows the strange, terrifying noises aboard Kelvin's spaceship, resonantly captured by the film's clangorous electronic soundtrack. Additionally, the horse's looming presence—"It's in the garage, staring at me," the boy frets—portends Kelvin's sense of dread that he is being watched in outer space, an unease enacted by the film's surreptitious camerawork. Bridled and secluded, the horse in *Solaris* is no longer an embodiment of masculinity. It now resembles the alien monsters that dominate sci-fi films, such as Don Siegel's *Invasion of the Body Snatchers* (1956), Ridley Scott's *Alien* (1979), and John Carpenter's *The Thing* (1982). Tarkovsky implies that domestication warps horses into monstrosities to be kept out of view. The horse in *Solaris* becomes a simulacrum of itself, not unlike the alien-replicants generated aboard the Solaris space station, known by Tarkovsky's characters as "guests" (*gosti*).

The child's terror at the sight of the horse also recalls Sigmund Freud's well-known study of "Little Hans," a boy who has nightmares about being bitten by a horse.[105] Freud concluded that the horse manifests Little Hans's fear of being punished—symbolically castrated—by his father for his incestuous desire toward his mother.[106] The horse, per Freud, symbolizes punitive paternal authority. Later feminist critics, de-emphasizing Freud's patriarchal inclinations, reinterpreted this case study by arguing that the horse, in fact, symbolizes the castrating power of Hans's *mother*, who holds the keys to the boy's sexual maturity.[107] The horse of Hans's dream relays not the threat of paternal authority but a menacing maternal influence capable of obstructing the boy's libidinal development. In *Solaris*, it is a dour woman—portrayed in an unsympathetic light as an incessant nag—who consoles the boy. "It's gentle," she says of the horse, suggesting that, in her eyes, horses acquire value once they have been sequestered, enchained, and neutered. In psychoanalytic terms, this woman represents a maternal power that inhibits the flourishing of male sexuality. In all likelihood, the horse in *Solaris* is castrated: a gelding—in Russian, a *merin* (still grammatically masculine)—that signifies what has become, in Tarkovsky's view, the dejected condition of Russian men in postwar society. It is no wonder that Kelvin is himself impotent in *Solaris*. He cannot consummate his romance with the alien-ghost of his ex-wife, Hari (Natalia Bonderchuk), because he is haunted by memories of his mother (whom he at one point even dreams of in Hari's clothes).[108] Kelvin, like a gelding, has a severely diminished libido as a result of female power; he is a faint echo of a man, just as the bridled horse has become a shadow of the rowdy stallion, the *kon'*, it once was.

Thus, Tarkovsky's would-be-renegade protagonists are portrayed as victims. To be sure, the Soviet crisis of masculinity fueled "a victimization discourse" that impugned modernization in all its forms for men's dislocation, a politics of sexist grievance that continues to resonate in present-day Russia.[109] It is not the fault of Tarkovsky's heroes that they are castrated. Rather, Tarkovsky blames outside forces—feminism, technological advancement, cultural decadence, Westernization—for conspiring against Russian men, which explains why so many characters in *Solaris* bear non-Russian names: Sartorious, Hari, Burton, Snaut, and, in a nod to the British mathematician, Kelvin. The foreign experience of modern life, for Tarkovsky, is emasculating.[110] Industrial modernity is itself culpable for the confused, timid, and (self-)destructive behavior of Tarkovsky's male heroes, who are all variously estranged from the elemental values embodied by horses. If Tarkovsky relies on beautiful horses to mourn the death of cinema, he also uses horses to lament the thwarting of an idealized—unmistakably Romantic—vision of masculinity.

THE END OF HORSES

Tarkovsky no better presents what he considered to be modern life's alien qualities than in the "city of the future" scene in *Solaris*.[111] When a retired astronaut by the name of Henri Burton (Vladislav Dvorzhetsky) leaves Kelvin's family residence, he travels by car through a sprawling metropolis at night. This nocturnal setting contrasts with the woods where *Solaris* began. We see concrete tunnels, traffic jams, skyscrapers, and overpasses, all illuminated by neon-lit billboards, headlight beams, and red brake lights. Guided by elastic camerawork, this long (four-and-a-half-minute) and winding sequence is soundtracked by the din of car engines and dissonant synth music. It simulates a space launch, perceptually jettisoning Tarkovsky's spectators into the alien world of space-age modernity.[112]

Ironically, this episode—by far the most futuristic in *Solaris*—takes place on Earth. Tarkovsky suggests that the future is *now*, already upon us. Tarkovsky filmed the scene along the Akasaka-Mitsuke highway in Tokyo, a city that, in the latter half of the twentieth century, became synonymous with innovation and cutting-edge devices, such as the JVC stereo system that plays bamboo flute music in *The Sacrifice*: a sonic fusion of ancient and modern. Indeed, the Akasaka-Mitsuke highway was expressly designed as a symbol of technological progress to project a modern image of Japan in anticipation of the 1964 Tokyo Olympics.[113] Japanese political elites sought to announce to the world that Japan's postwar period of poverty, ruination, and American occupation had decisively ended. Yet Tarkovsky believed that humanity faced no graver threat than that "posed by the relentless march of technology," which had obliterated the natural

The Akasaka-Mitsuke highway at night in Tokyo, presented by Tarkovsky as a futuristic vision of hell devoid of organic life. Still from *Solaris*, 1972.

world.[114] The foreign, ultramodern city of Tokyo represents, for Tarkovsky, a metallic hell devoid of organic life, natural light, and nonmechanical sound.

The highway scene also insinuates that, in the future, there will be no horses. The increasingly automotive culture of postwar society, which witnessed a surge in car ownership in more developed parts of the West in the latter half of the twentieth century, embraced "the physical displacement of animal traction by new locomotive powers."[115] As noted earlier, the American industrialist Henry Ford likened the mass-produced car—the Model T—to horses through the analogy of "horsepower." The term, coined by Scottish inventor James Watt in the late eighteenth century in reference to the steam engine, relayed Ford's hope that automobiles would usher in a new, more efficient method of transportation. Since ancient times, horses had served as humanity's primary mode of transport; cars began physically replacing them as our principal locomotive means in the early twentieth century and, in doing so, relegated horses out of human life. The automobile, retaining "traces of an incorporated animality" through the mimetics of effortless speed and seamless mobility, became an equine substitute.[116] "Once considered a metonymy of nature, animals came to be seen as emblems of the new, industrialized environment."[117]

The highway scene in *Solaris* thus envisions what Ford hailed as a glorious "horseless age," a catchphrase that served as the title of one of the twentieth century's first car magazines, promoting Ford's automobiles for early motor enthusiasts.[118] Cars became the new horses, as if the latter had merged with the very technologies replacing them, efficiently yet insensately shuttling human beings through urban space. The rows of cars stuck in traffic along the Akasaka-Mitsuke highway even bear a resemblance to columns of transport animals in the forward-moving march to predetermined destinations, such as the workhorse in Lumière's *Workers Leaving the Factory*. It is not by chance, then, that the horse encountered on Kelvin's family estate in *Solaris* is also seen locked up in a garage next to a car, an image documenting horses' increasing irrelevance in modern life. (That Burton travels in a self-driving car as he recumbently makes video calls encapsulates humanity's desire for autonomous machines.) Reflecting the Cartesian thesis about the machinelike essence of animals, *Solaris*'s animals-as-robots motif is one that structures a subset of dystopic science fiction cinema—the animatronic owls in Scott's *Blade Runner* (1983), for example—that has earned the designation "techno-horror."[119]

An underappreciated fact about Tarkovsky's cinema, then, is its antagonism toward the automobile—its amaxophobia—captured through repeated images of abandoned, rusty, and immolated vehicles. In *Ivan's Childhood*, cars are war torn and dilapidated, and in *Stalker*, run-down cars (along with several tanks) are in various states of disrepair, as if the Zone's overgrown topography has made ruins out of modernity's Fordist triumphs. Throughout his films, Tarkovsky figuratively punishes cars for having displaced horses in contemporary life. In *The Sacrifice*, images of cars betray the victory of atavism over the rationalizing forces of modern industrial life: a broken-down car is seen at the entrance of a witch's den, another appears in Aleksandr's hallucinations of a postapocalyptic city, and yet another catches on fire because of Aleksandr's irrational decision to burn his home (which leads to him being shuttled away in an ambulance). In the beginning of *The Sacrifice*, Tarkovsky superimposes bits of Aleksandr's brooding soliloquy—"Humanity is on the wrong road, a dangerous road"—over an image of a car. Tarkovsky's negative associations with cars therefore explain why his protagonists reject automobiles as a mode of transportation; they opt instead to walk through their respective worlds, intimating a desire to (re)connect with the earth. The trio in *Stalker*, for example, must abandon their vehicles—an armored car and a railway trolley—before entering the Zone on foot. Only Gorchakov in *Nostalghia* is regularly encountered in a car—in Italy, no less, the epicenter of postwar industrial prosperity, the land of Fiats and Ferraris. Gorchakov's status as an automobile passenger (a woman, in fact, chauffeurs him around) crystallizes his alienated and emasculated psychology. While Tarkovsky's protagonists rarely drive cars, they are not seen astride horses, either. Though Tarkovsky's heroes refuse automobiles,

A horse locked in a garage aside an automobile, documenting the irrelevance of horses in modern life as they are replaced by industrial modes of transportation. Still from *Solaris*, 1972.

they also fail to reconnect with horses, as these animals have become increasingly absent in human society.

The dissolution of horses in Tarkovsky's cinema aligns with the argument pioneered by English philosopher John Berger in his essay "Why Look at Animals?," the publication of which coincided in 1977 with the height of Tarkovsky's career.[120] Berger argues that society's modernization has broken the primordial link between humans and animals through the relentless encroachment of industry into the natural world, an intrusion Tarkovsky acknowledges through the recurrent motif of telephone poles in remote woodland areas, symbols of humanity's technical expanse.[121] "The 19th century," Berger writes, "saw the beginning of a process, today being completed by 20th corporate capitalism, by which every tradition which previously mediated between man and nature was broken. Before this rupture, animals constituted the first circle of what surrounded man."[122] For Berger, the origins of human identity derived from close interactions between humans and animals, which made humanity aware of itself as a distinct category of being: a species capable of language separate from but adjacent to wildlife. Animals' disappearance, therefore, has evacuated the conceptual conditions for a dialectical notion of humanness. The dislocation of animals in modern society "lessens the fullness of *our* world.... It is now the human world that suffers from the exclusion of animals, whereas before, it was precisely the removal of animals that allowed human beings to establish their autonomy."[123]

To cope with the loss of animals, Berger maintains that people fill their lives with facsimiles of animals rather than letting them pass into an authentic state of nonexistence: "Zoos, realistic animal toys and the widespread commercial diffusion of animal imagery, all began as animals started to be withdrawn from daily life.... Such innovations were compensatory."[124] As animals vanish in real space, they proliferate as warped copies of themselves in virtual space. These replicas, belonging "to the same remorseless movement as was disappearing the animals," are faint reminders of the once-formative relations that structured human-animal encounters, now reduced to simulations. Animals, in other words, "no longer remain in the realm of ontology," a "catastrophic break in the genealogy of animal being."[125] Any contact between humans and these animal-esque copycats recapitulates our alienation from animals. Berger's theory of animal vanishing can account for the remote and lachrymose qualities of Tarkovsky's horses. It is as if the cars on the Akasaka-Mitsuke freeway in *Solaris* are alien-like restorations of horses that remind us of both our former closeness with real horses and the impossibility of recovering those bonds; the car engine is nothing more than an "equine crypt."[126] Modernity, Akira Mizuta Lippit writes, spawns "a new breed of animals" that "surrounds the human populace"—a genus of vanishing animals whose existence is paradoxically constituted by disappearance. The animal becomes, as stated by Jacques Derrida, "a memory of the present."[127]

The end of the highway scene in *Solaris* exemplifies the spectral essence of modern animals. It concludes with an abrupt return to Kelvin's family home: Tokyo's roar is overtaken by the quiet of the woods, and Kelvin is again walking the grounds to bask in nature's richness before launching into outer space. The horse, last seen in the garage, again trots across the visual field. While Kelvin failed to notice the horse earlier, he now longingly gazes at it, taking a mental snapshot he will bring into space (along with photos of his ex-wife and home movies). This horse is the last thing we see Kelvin see on Earth; the next shot is an image of a starry sky, indicating the onset of his voyage. Kelvin's last memory of Earth, then, is of a horse, implying that horses have become vestiges, ghosts of humanity's earthbound past. This parting exchange between the horse and Kelvin is filmed with a blue filter that creates an oneiric atmosphere. Appearing in another metacinematic quadrilateral frame, the blue-tinted horse, recalling the Technicolor horses in *Andrei Rublev* and *The Wizard of Oz*, resembles a dream figment more than an actual animal. Even before liftoff, horses *already* occupy the realm of fantasy, memory, and history.

Recounting a dream of his that echoed these sequences in *Solaris*, Tarkovsky wrote: "I was in Moscow... which was full of cars and people.... Suddenly, in the midst of the noise and rush of the city, I saw a cow, a most beautiful cow, the colour of dark chocolate, with a head like Isis and horns like a lyre, and deep,

The last thing Kelvin sees before outer space is a horse, filmed with a blue-tinted filter, which suggests that horses occupy the realm of fantasy, memory, and history. Still from *Solaris*, 1972.

human eyes. She came up to me, I stroked her, and she crossed the street and went off down the pavement. I still remember the smell she left on the palm of my hand: the penetrating, tender, homely smell of life and happiness."[128] While the importance of cows in Tarkovsky's cinema is explored in chapter 4, Tarkovsky's dream is significant here because it substantiates Berger's argument that animals have been evacuated from urban modernity and reappear only in altered states of reality or consciousness. "Modernity can be defined by the disappearance of wildlife from humanity's habitat and by the reappearance of the same in humanity's reflections on itself: in philosophy, psychoanalysis, and technological media, such as the telephone, film, and radio."[129] The dream cow offered Tarkovsky an experience of tactile immediacy and emotional contact unafforded by the soulless, concrete, car-ridden city typified by Tokyo in *Solaris*.[130]

Aboard the spaceship, Kelvin enters the office of the late Dr. Gibarian (Sos Sargsyan) and discovers the room in complete disarray, presumably the result of a search or abduction—Tarkovsky's not-so-subtle allusion to KGB apartment raids. Gibarian's office is littered with mnemonic objects that evoke Earth, including pictures of horses hanging on the walls. Gibarian turned to graphic reproductions of horses to reanimate his lost connection with Earth before committing suicide, intimating how, in the future, horses become otherworldly, ancient aliens. Gibarian suffered from an acute case of intergalactic homesickness, and he longed, futilely, to be "buried with the worms"—a desire in sharp

Kelvin gazes at a picture of a horse; Tarkovsky
gives us images of images of horses, corroborating horses'
ongoing absence in human life. Still from *Solaris*, 1972.

contrast with the sight of his plastic-wrapped corpse aboard the spacecraft. In *Solaris*, Tarkovsky presents images of *images* of horses: horses removed from their actual selves, as the stuff of dreams, memories, art, and automotive reincarnation. The horse, for Tarkovsky, is a phantom crackling within his and his characters' imaginations; horses are what Slavoj Žižek ingeniously describes as "the thing from inner space" in *Solaris*.[131]

Similarly, in *Ivan's Childhood*, horses only appear in a dream of the child protagonist, Ivan (Nikolai Burlyayev), which unfolds in a lush forest that juxtaposes the industrial hell of his wartime reality. This dream depicts Ivan and a girl shuttled through the woods in a lorry full of apples during a rainstorm. The cart exits onto a beach, apples spill out of it, and horses burst into the frame and nibble the fruit in an homage to Dovzhenko's *Earth*, which also unites images of horses, apples, and rain. The dream in *Ivan's Childhood* is backdropped by lilting string music, which turns the beach into an Arcadian paradise where horses (still) roam.

That horses inhabit fantasylands accessed through dream states in Tarkovsky's cinema bears a relation to Freud's curious hypothesis that because "geese dream of maize," all dreams are biological attempts at wish fulfillment.[132] "If, as Freud believes, the origins of dream wishes are revealed in regression, then [his] recourse to animality here suggests a point of contact between the deepest recesses of memory and the animal world."[133] The horses of *Ivan's Childhood* and *Solaris* creep out of humanity's deep-seated desire for

Ivan dreams of horses on a beach in an image starkly at odds with his war-torn (and horseless) reality. Still from *Ivan's Childhood*, 1962.

a premodern world before its technological exhaustion, for a civilizational infancy predating the spiritual fall, hence Tarkovsky's foreboding, Edenic leitmotif of bitten apples. As Berger writes, "What man has to do in order to transcend the animal... within himself, and what his unique spirituality leads to, is often anguish. And so, by comparison... the animal seems to him to enjoy a kind of innocence. The animal has been emptied of experience and secrets, and this new invented 'innocence,' begins to provoke in man a kind of nostalgia. For the first time animals are placed in a *receding* past."[134] This nostalgia for lost innocence subtends all of Tarkovsky's horse images. It is thrown into sharp relief in a deleted scene from *The Sacrifice* that shows Aleksandr dreaming of his own funeral, in which his son leads a white stallion across the frame. This image—found on the cover of this book—aligns horses with childhood, dreams, and pessimism about humanity's industrial future, which has torn people and animals asunder: Aleksandr's nightmare is triggered by the outbreak of nuclear war.[135] The white horse, a Christian symbol of the apocalypse, heralds the passing of one world into a different world—one in which horses, Tarkovsky insinuates, will be absent. The looming threat of ecological barrenness in *The Sacrifice* is also captured by the dead tree Aleksandr plants in the film's opening scene. The unnervingly empty, savanna-like grasslands in *The Sacrifice* are haunted by the ghosts of horses. Everything about Tarkovsky's gossamer equine images is tinged with nostalgia and longing for an unblighted natural world, which Berger wistfully recalls in "Why Look at Animals?"

Paradoxically, then, Tarkovsky implies that cinema—the technology of industrial modernity par excellence—is not itself a product of society's modernization. The "technological contrivances" and "symbols of human error" that Tarkovsky (and Berger) vilify for destroying nature are precisely what enable his creative project, the art of mechanical reproduction.[136] It is as if Tarkovsky tries to leverage twentieth-century imaging technology for premodern ends, endeavoring "to chase the genie of spirituality back into the bottle of modernity by using the most modern of the arts."[137] Tarkovsky is, in many ways, an "anti-avant-garde avant-gardist" whose experimental films yearn to revive a mode of premodern simplicity, faith, and wonder: a world *before* the industrial triumph of cinema.[138] Yet, as cultural theorist Svetlana Boym demonstrates, the word "nostalgia"—proceeding from the Greek *nostos*, meaning "return home," and *algia*, "longing"—arose in the seventeenth century, which makes it a distinctly "modern condition."[139] Tarkovsky's desire, vis-à-vis film, to escape society, "live close to nature," and "again be in contact with animals," is a result of the very modernity that hastened humanity's split from animals in the first place.[140] Tarkovsky betrays a patently *modern* form of whimsy.

Caught in this light, Tarkovsky's horse-drenched cinema can be understood as a response to horses' vanishing in real space. Tarkovsky's films reiterate Berger's thesis that as "animals were disappearing from the immediate world, they were reappearing in the mediated world of technological reproduction.... Animals found a proper habitat in the recording devices of technological media."[141] This insight bears the potential to recast not only Tarkovsky's filmography but also all of film history, as it suggests that cinema begins as animals end. Cinema emerged as a response to the off-screen disappearance of animals, and it turned the likeness of those bygone animals into mimetic yet lost objects to be mourned—not unlike ghosts. "The alliance between animals and cinema brings together two poles of traditional opposition, animals and technology," resulting in a radically new species of "electric animals."[142] Describing Muybridge's *The Horse in Motion*, which Tarkovsky invokes in the beginning of *Andrei Rublev*, Lippit writes, "By capturing and recording [the horse's] every

A dead tree being planted symbolizes the barrenness of Tarkovsky's apocalyptic final film, as if its savanna-like grasslands are haunted by the ghosts of horses. Still from *The Sacrifice*, 1986.

gesture, pose, muscular disturbance, and anatomical shifts with such urgency, Muybridge seemed to be racing against the imminent disappearance of animals from the new urban environment."[143] The proliferation of horses in Tarkovsky's films—and, in truth, all of cinema—exists in inverse proportion to their physical disappearance in reality. These images, pace Berger, are compensatory: they entice us with the possibility of reconnecting with horses, but the impossibility of such contact only intensifies our longing, begetting more images that induce deeper craving for contact. Cinema, Lippit concludes, functions as a medium in not only a technological sense but also a clairvoyant one. It channels the ghosts of modernity's vanishing animals as they undergo a shift "from body to an image; from a living voice to a technical echo."[144]

This feedback loop, Lippit continues, reenacts Freud's theory of mourning, discussed in greater detail in chapter 5, which upholds that children, distinguishing between self and other, recognize a residue of themselves in the other entities to which they cling, forever grieving the loss of their preformed egos; animals become humanity's "narcissistic object" retaining a trace of the bygone self.[145] To mourn the loss of animals is to mourn "a self that became dehumanized in the very process of humanity's becoming human."[146] Cinema, then, is nothing but a "massive mourning apparatus, summoned to incorporate a disappearing animal presence."[147] Tarkovsky's equine-rich filmography, therefore, is not a monument to horses but a horse *mausoleum*, "preserv[ing] the radically absent other in a state that can be defined neither as life nor death."[148] Tarkovsky's sad horses, per this line of reasoning, are nothing more than phantasmal facsimiles—equine corpses brought back to life on screen by modernity's electric illusionism—that redouble his and his protagonists' acute feelings of loss. We gaze at Tarkovsky's characters mournfully gazing at spectral reproductions of horses, themselves reproduced by Tarkovsky's mournful equine imagination. The mourning, then, occurs on a diegetic and extradiegetic level—a *double mourning*—that reifies our ever-widening distance from real horses.

However, to consign Tarkovsky's horses to only the themes of mourning, absence, and simulacra is to "reinforce at a conceptual level the effacement of the animal that is perceived to have taken place in reality even whilst criticizing that process."[149] The theory of animal vanishing developed by Berger and Lippit (and corroborated by Tarkovsky's cinema), "which appears to be so much on the side of animals," stages yet another flight from animals. It reenacts the themes of its own analysis—emptiness, disappearance, mourning—because it seems interested less in the treatment of animals as they continue to exist in, and be threatened by, modern industrial life and more in shifts in the psychology of man's self-confirmation as a being in the world.[150] Ironically, *actual* animal lives vanish in the theory of animal disappearance. If Berger were to respond to the titular question of his essay—"Why Look at Animals?"—rather than answering "'because we need to re-evaluate human-animal relations by paying attention to the contexts in which we look at animals,' or 'because we need a considered and attentive looking to appreciate the animal world more,' Berger would probably answer 'too late.'"[151] The nature of modernity has rendered any meaningful human-animal exchange impossible because "animals and humans are now too alienated for the look to register anything of consequence beyond exemplifying their degree of alienation."[152] The theory of animal absence is, thus, an analytical dead end. It ensnares animals in an infinitely regressive cycle of disappearance, nostalgic mourning, and compensatory reappearance that recapitulates the crisis in human ontology and elides attention to the condition, treatment, and behavior of animals as they still exist in our lives.

For their part, Tarkovsky's elegiac images of horses betray greater concern for what horses' vanishing means for humanity—for *Tarkovsky*—than for horses themselves. Tarkovsky's equine imagery, which, on its face, appears to be so much on the side of horses, reduces horses into little more than indices of human alienation, undercutting whatever concern he harbored for actual horses. Tarkovsky reacts to horses' disappearance by fetishizing them, humanity's "narcissistic object," and then dwelling in—thereby intensifying—the feelings of loss occasioned by their ongoing absence. The mournful undertow to Tarkovsky's horses befogs the conditions, often coercive, determining *how* horses appear within his settings.

This chapter ends on the mournful riptide at work on Tarkovsky's horse images. We return to horses in chapter 5 to account for the ways in which Tarkovsky exploits horses not as abstract ideas or symbols about beauty, masculinity, or modernity but as *bodies*: flesh-and-blood beings whose lives were dramatically altered and sometimes extinguished by their encounters with Tarkovsky. He reneges on the "contract"—the "reciprocal pact"—described by Scarry as forged between the object of beauty and its beholder. Rather than safeguarding the beautiful thing from all bad fortune can destroy, Tarkovsky subjects horses to his most heavy-handed interventions. By concentrating on *how* Tarkovsky's horses are made available to our gaze, we can construe a fuller sense of human-horse relations in modern life than the latently anthropocentric theory of animal vanishing can.

NOTES

1. For horses in culture, see Johns, *Horses*. There also exist many photographs of Tarkovsky aside horses; see, e.g., "Andrei Tarkovsky Photos."
2. Tarkovsky, *Interviews*, 25.
3. There are two versions of *Andrei Rublev*: the 175-minute edition and the 205-minute director's cut. The redacted version depicts the horse's fall but not its stabbing. For *Rublev*'s fraught editing process, discussed in chapter 3, see Johnson and Petrie, *Films of Andrei Tarkovsky*, 79–85.
4. For accounts of the horse's death, see Kuniaev, *Moi pechal'nye pobedy*, 562; Aksenova, "Zhertvoprinosheniia."
5. For horses in cinema, see Mitchum, *Hollywood Hoofbeats*.
6. On the postwar Soviet crisis of masculinity—and horses therein—see Rosenholm, "Of Men and Horses," 190–92.
7. Berger, *About Looking*, 3–28.
8. For horse rolls, see Donoho, "Why Do Horses Roll?"
9. In the edited version of *Andrei Rublev*, this scene is abbreviated: we see the horse careening on the ground, but we do not see it rise.
10. The average shot length in Hollywood cinema has decreased from ten seconds in the mid-1960s to about four seconds in the 1990s. See Bordwell, *Way Hollywood Tells It*, 121–24. By contrast, the average shot length in Tarkovsky's work increases from twenty seconds in *Ivan's Childhood* to about a minute, if not well

over, in his later cinema. See Schillaci, "Evolution of Form in Andrei Tarkovsky's Films."

11. For the history of the long take, see de Luca and Barradas Jorge, *Slow Cinema*.

12. Deleuze, *Cinema 2*, 42–43; see also Efrid, "Deleuze on Tarkovsky."

13. Deleuze, "On *The Time-Image*," 59.

14. Tarkovsky's image of a crumbling Italian church at the end of *Nostalghia* has been compared directly to the "desolate finale" of a ruinous urban landscape in *Germany, Year Zero*. Bird, *Andrei Tarkovsky*, 66–67.

15. Deleuze, *Cinema 2*, 36.

16. See Tarkovsky, *Sculpting in Time*.

17. Deleuze, *Cinema 2*, xi.

18. Deleuze, *Cinema 2*, 2.

19. Tarkovsky, *Interviews*, 25.

20. To underscore the grotesque nature of the man's death, Tarkovsky has him played by Yuri Nikulin, a beloved Soviet actor known for his lighthearted, comedic roles.

21. Gorfinkel, "Weariness, Waiting," 311.

22. Deleuze, *Cinema 1*. See also Toymentsev, "Crisis of the Soviet Action-Image."

23. Deleuze, "On *The Movement Image*," 51.

24. O'Rourke, "Birth of Film."

25. See Scharf, "Marey and Chronophotography."

26. Deleuze, *Cinema 1*, 5–6.

27. Murphet, "Pitiable or Political Animals?," 102.

28. Murphet, "Pitiable or Political Animals?," 102.

29. For the zoopraxiscope, see Lawrence, "Muybridgean Motion/Materialist Film," 75.

30. For Ford, horses, and automation, see Shukin, *Animal Capital*, 119.

31. Skakov, *Cinema of Tarkovsky*, 43.

32. Mulvey, *Death 24x a Second*, 13–15.

33. Ott, "Iron Horses," 414.

34. In 1972, Tarkovsky composed a list of his ten favorite films, which included *Seven Samurai*. See Wakamiya, "Zvyagintsev and Tarkovsky," 253.

35. Tarkovsky, *Sculpting in Time*, 150.

36. Tarkovsky, *Sculpting in Time*, 150.

37. Tarkovsky, *Sculpting in Time*, 179.

38. Tarkovsky, *Interviews*, 135.

39. Tarkovsky, *Time Within Time*, 396.

40. Tarkovsky, *Interviews*, 66.

41. Quoted in Ebert, "Solaris."

42. Tsivian, *Early Cinema in Russia and Its Cultural Reception*, 29.
43. Walker, *Horse*, 64.
44. Greene, *Horses at Work*, 4.
45. Lawrence, "Muybridgean Motion/Materialist Film," 75.
46. For the matter of human (and animal) labor in Lumière's film, see McMahon, *Animal Worlds*, 103–105.
47. McMahon, *Animal Worlds*, 104.
48. For Soviet "Easterns," see Bohlinger, "'East Is a Delicate Matter.'"
49. Quoted in Ma, *Severance*, 266. There is also footage of Tarkovsky's American trip in Kidlat Tahimik's *Why Is Yellow the Middle of the Rainbow?* (1994), in which he is seen petting a horse. See "Andrei Tarkovsky's American Visit in 1983."
50. See "Andrei Tarkovsky Photos."
51. Bird, *Andrei Rublev*, 38.
52. Moss, "Cinema as Spiritual Exercise," 210–11.
53. Moss, "Cinema as Spiritual Exercise," 210.
54. Moss, "Cinema as Spiritual Exercise," 221.
55. Plate, *Religion and Film*, xiii, 3.
56. Tarkovsky, *Interviews*, 25.
57. Tarkovsky, *Interviews*, 139–40.
58. Tarkovsky, *Interviews*, 85.
59. See, for instance, Tafdrup, *Tarkovsky's Horses*; Fürholzer, "Living Oblivion"; Sider, "Tarkovsky's Horse"; "Tarkovsky's Horse 2008."
60. Scarry, *On Beauty*, 9.
61. Scarry, *On Beauty*, 24–25, 28–29.
62. Kant, *Critique of Judgement*, 98.
63. Scarry, *On Beauty*, 113.
64. Scarry, *On Beauty*, 90.
65. Tarkovsky, *Sculpting in Time*, 179, 200.
66. Scarry, *On Beauty*, 90.
67. In 1918, shortly after the Bolshevik Revolution, several of Rublev's icons were recovered from an old barn in the Russian town Zvenigora, where they had been stored under firewood. Skakov, *Cinema of Tarkovsky*, 225.
68. The first dissolve shots occurred in Georges Méliès's *Cinderella* (1899), a film about wondrous transformations emblematic of Méliès's magician background; Méliès acquired Harry Houdini's Paris theater in 1888.
69. Scarry, *On Beauty*, 114.
70. Scarry, *On Beauty*, 112, 114.
71. Kant, *Critique of Judgement*, 57.
72. Scarry, *On Beauty*, 112.
73. Scarry, *On Beauty*, 9.
74. Scarry, *On Beauty*, 3.

75. Sandler, "Absent Father, the Stillness of Film," 128.
76. In Tarkovsky's words, "I would like to say that, if one should absolutely need to compare me to someone, it should be Dovzhenko. He was the first director for whom... atmosphere was particularly important." Tarkovsky, *Interviews*, 21.
77. Scarry, *On Beauty*, 30.
78. Scarry, *On Beauty*, 5.
79. Scarry, *On Beauty*, 50.
80. Bataille, *Undercover Surrealism*, 238.
81. Bataille, *Undercover Surrealism*, 238.
82. Kalof, "Introduction: Ancient Animals," 4.
83. The scene of skeptical Italians admiring a work of art created by a young Russian inevitably refers us to Tarkovsky's own success at the 1962 Venice Film Festival, where winning the grand prize—the Golden Lion—for *Ivan's Childhood* catapulted his career.
84. Bullock, "Watching Eyes, Seeing Dreams, Knowing Lives," 99.
85. Skakov, *Cinema of Tarkovsky*, 44.
86. Epstein, *Priroda, mir, tanik vselennoi*, 92.
87. Rosenholm, "Of Men and Horses," 181.
88. "Proiskhozhdenie slova loshad.'"
89. For the postwar crisis of masculinity, see Dumančić, *Men out of Focus*; Zdravomyslova and Temkina, "Krizis maskulinnosti v pozdnesovetskom diskurse."
90. For this trope's revival, see Dumančić, *Men out of Focus*, 254–65. Themes of male impotency are explored in late Soviet films like Marlen Khutsiev's *I Am Twenty* (*Mne dvadstat' let*, 1965)—in which a boyish Tarkovsky cameos—and Andrei Smirnov's *Belorussian Station* (*Belorusski vokzal*, 1971).
91. Tarkovsky, *Interviews*, 111–13.
92. Tarkovsky famously called Kubrick's film "phony" (*lipa*). See Russell, "Stanley Kubrick Film That Andrei Tarkovsky Hated." Additionally, according to his son, Tarkovsky knew "every little detail" of *Star Wars*, which he eschewed throughout his forays into sci-fi cinema. For example, Tarkovsky begins *Stalker* by repurposing the upward-tracking yellow font that Lucas uses to introduce *Star Wars*. The strange quality of Tarkovsky's yellow text—a kind of sci-fi Cyrillic full of ellipses and question marks—emphasizes *Stalker*'s thematic inscrutability, as opposed to the clear-cut narrative of *Star Wars*. Furthermore, in contrast to Lucas's orchestral score, Tarkovsky pairs the yellow text with electronically distorted bamboo flute music (scored by Eduard Artemiev on a synthesizer), a mix of the archaic and futuristic that redoubles *Stalker*'s mysteriousness. For Tarkovsky on *Star Wars*, see Dax, "'This Is Not a Coincidence.'"
93. For Village Prose, see Lewis, "Peasant Nostalgia in Contemporary Russian Literature."

94. Rosenholm, "Of Men and Horses," 185–88.

95. Jenks, "Conquering Space," 129–49.

96. Rosenholm, "Of Men and Horses," 189.

97. Vysotsky's love of horses is also archived on film. Playing a jaded White Army officer during the Russian Civil War in Evgenii Karelov's *Two Comrades Were Serving* (*Sluzhili dva tovarishcha*, 1968), Vysotsky follows his stallion into the Black Sea to their mutual demise, symbolically betraying hopelessness about the communist future.

98. Kahn et al., *History of Russian Literature*, 599–605.

99. For horses in Romantic art, see Pickeral, *Horse*, 210–31.

100. Johnson and Petrie, *Films of Andrei Tarkovsky*, 31–32. For Tarkovsky on Romanticism, see *Interviews*, 176, 184. Tarkovsky also explored what he perceived as the dangers of Romanticism in an abandoned screenplay entitled *Hoffmanniana* about the life of the Romantic author E. T. A. Hoffman, which he completed after filming *Mirror* in 1975.

101. Bird also compares the church at the end of *Nostalghia* to Friedrich's "hyper-romantic" painting *Ruin at Eldena* (1824). See Bird, *Andrei Tarkovsky*, 66–67.

102. Vysotsky's and Tarkovsky's fascination with masculinity is also revealed by the popularity of Ernest Hemmingway among late Soviet readers. As a film student, Tarkovsky even adapted one of Hemmingway's short stories, "The Killers" (1927). For this film, see De Luca, "Tarkovsky Screens Hemingway."

103. For the 180-degree rule, see Elsaesser and Hagener, *Film Theory*, 103.

104. This scene's perceptual disorientation is also relayed by the presence of a balloon suspended in midair, discussed more in chapter 3, and the uncanny reflection of Kelvin's surroundings in the pond water, which creates an image of the image within itself.

105. For this Freudian parallel, see, also, Bould, *Solaris*, 42.

106. Freud, "Analysis of a Phobia in a Five-Year-Old Boy."

107. For a reinterpretation of Freud's case study, see Creed, *Monstrous-Feminine*, 88–104.

108. We also see Kelvin staring at headshots of his deceased mother, which, psychoanalytically glossed, "resemble the phallic threat to masculinity posed by the Medusa's severed head." Bould, *Solaris*, 43.

109. Zdravomyslova and Temkina, "Krizis maskulinnosti v pozdnesovetskom diskurse," 449.

110. When Kelvin enters his bedroom on the spacecraft, Tarkovsky, channeling Jacques Tati's farcical film about the pitfalls of modernist architecture, *PlayTime* (1967), presents an antiseptic picture of the minimalist trends in midcentury Soviet homemaking as homogenizing and feminizing. Tarkovsky juxtaposes Kelvin's bedroom against the spacecraft's library, which, with its wooden walls,

antiques, dark colors, and stained glass, resembles a medieval library. For modernist design in postwar cinema, see Oukaderova, *Cinema of the Soviet Thaw*, 150–79.

111. Bird, *Andrei Tarkovsky*, 159.
112. The scene clearly draws inspiration from the kaleidoscopic Stargate sequence at the end of Kubrick's *2001*.
113. Tomizawa, "Transformation of Akasaka Mitsuke in 1964."
114. Tarkovsky, *Sculpting in Time*, 222.
115. Shukin, *Animal Capital*, 119.
116. Lippit, *Electric Animal*, 187.
117. Lippit, *Electric Animal*, 187.
118. See "'Horseless Age,'" Henry Ford.
119. For *Solaris* and *Blade Runner*, see Robinson, *Sacred Cinema of Andrei Tarkovsky*, 394–97.
120. Berger, *About Looking*, 3–28.
121. Additionally, the motif of ringing phones in *Nostalghia*, *The Sacrifice*, and *Stalker*—even in the remotest corners of the Zone, where someone dials the wrong number for a clinic (which Stalker assumes is the Zone playing tricks)—suggests what Tarkovsky viewed as the scope of technology's inexorable expanse.
122. Berger, *About Looking*, 3.
123. Lippit, *Electric Animal*, 17.
124. Berger, *About Looking*, 26.
125. Berger, *About Looking*, 26; Lippit, *Electric Animal*, 53.
126. Lippit, *Electric Animal*, 248.
127. Lippit, *Electric Animal*, 3; Derrida, *Memoires for Paul De Man*, 60.
128. Tarkovsky, *Time Within Time*, 291.
129. Lippit, *Electric Animal*, 2–3.
130. The protagonist of *Blade Runner* also dreams of horses (unicorns, it appears) in response to a dystopic future city bereft of animals (Los Angeles in *Blade Runner*, Tokyo in *Solaris*).
131. Žižek, "Andrei Tarkovsky, or the Thing from Inner Space."
132. Quoted in Lippit, *Electric Animal*, 163.
133. Lippit, *Electric Animal*, 164.
134. Berger, *About Looking*, 12.
135. Though deleted from the final cut of *The Sacrifice*, this image can be found in Alexander-Garrett, *Andrei Tarkovsky*, 188.
136. Tarkovsky, *Interviews*, 173.
137. Bird, *Andrei Tarkovsky*, 12.
138. Schlegel, "Der antiavantgardistiche Avantgardist."
139. Boym, *Future of Nostalgia*, xiii.
140. Tarkovsky, *Time Within Time*, 157–58.

141. Lippit, *Electric Animal*, 25.
142. Lippit, *Electric Animal*, 25.
143. Lippit, *Electric Animal*, 185.
144. Lippit, *Electric Animal*, 21.
145. Lippit, *Electric Animal*, 17.
146. Lippit, *Electric Animal*, 18.
147. Lippit, *Electric Animal*, 188.
148. Lippit, *Electric Animal*, 189.
149. Burt, *Animals in Film*, 29.
150. Burt, *Animals in Film*, 29.
151. Burt, "John Berger's 'Why Look at Animals?,'" 206–207.
152. Burt, "John Berger's 'Why Look at Animals?,'" 207.

TWO

DOGS

IN ONE OF THE MOST memorable and unexpectedly comical human-animal encounters in the history of Western philosophy, French thinker Jacques Derrida, naked as a jaybird, found himself caught by the gaze of his house cat after stepping out of the shower one morning.[1] Under the scrutiny of his cat, the disrobed Derrida was overcome by unease and embarrassment. Yet this shame quickly gave way to curiosity about the nature of human-animal relations. Why should a human, Derrida wondered, feel ashamed—embarrassed of being embarrassed—before a cat with no sense of nakedness or, by extension, humanness? What exactly was Derrida's inquisitive little cat seeing at that moment?

> It is generally thought, although none of the philosophers I am about to examine actually mentions it, that the property unique to animals, what in the last instance distinguishes them from man, is their being naked without knowing it. Not being naked therefore, not having knowledge of their nudity, in short, without consciousness of good and evil . . . The animal, therefore, is not naked because it is naked. It doesn't feel its own nudity. . . . Man would be the only one to have invented a garment to cover his sex. He would be a man only to the extent that he was able to be naked. . . . Before the cat that looks at me naked, would I be ashamed *like* a beast that no longer has the sense of its nudity? Or, on the contrary, *like* a man who retains the sense of his nudity? Who am I, therefore? Who is it that I am (following)? Whom should this be asked of if not of the other? And perhaps the cat itself?[2]

This encounter of an animal's literal and metaphorical view of a philosopher with no clothes launched Derrida's landmark meditation *The Animal That Therefore I Am*, in which he explores the relegation of animal life in the Western philosophical canon, the ethics of slaughter, and the fundamental instability of human identity. The cat's gaze on the naked philosopher—encountered, after all, in the bathroom, "a place of the body," far away from the study, a realm of the mind—inspired Derrida to challenge the arrogance of human knowledge.[3] The very title of Derrida's essay takes aim at the Cartesian dictum "I think therefore I am," which has long underpinned ideas about humanity's sense of authority over supposedly inferior animals.[4]

Interestingly, Andrei Tarkovsky also once found himself thinking about an animal's gaze. Reflecting in an interview on his decision to remain abroad for good after leaving Russia in 1983, Tarkovsky recalled the moment he bid farewell to his pet dog, a German shepherd named Dakus, the subject (or star) of this chapter, whose name has been mistranslated into English as Dark.[4] "When I had to leave Russia," Tarkovsky recalled, "[Dakus] sat motionless, he no longer even looked at me."[5] Unlike the nude Derrida, Tarkovsky (presumably clothed) actively solicited visual contact with his pet. Tarkovsky *wanted* to be seen by his dog, as if the animal could acknowledge and affirm his tormented psychology on the cusp of exile. If Derrida inadvertently exposed his sex to a cat, Tarkovsky hoped to lay his soul bare before his dog, for it might enable the two to commiserate. Tarkovsky's, then, was a very different kind of cross-species encounter than Derrida's, one with far more to do with anthropomorphism, companionship, and emotional identification than ontological uncertainty, shame, awkwardness, and self-effacement.

It would not be surprising if, during his exchange with Dakus, Tarkovsky had been attired in one of his characteristically chic and impeccably coordinated outfits. Inspired during his student years by the 1950s *stilyagi* youth movement—"the dandified Russian equivalent of the Beat Generation"—that reacted against the staid trends in Soviet life by embracing Western fashion, Tarkovsky always dressed smartly to assert his refined sense of self.[6] Clothed, perhaps rather stylishly, under an animal's gaze, Tarkovsky, unlike Derrida, was figuratively insulated by humanness, shielded from having his subjectivity thrown into question. If Derrida's cat dislodged the coherence of human identity, then Tarkovsky's German shepherd reified it. The divergence of Tarkovsky's and Derrida's animal encounters, as pet philosopher Erica Fudge teaches us, exposes the epistemic differences between cats and dogs, which persist in oft-repeated clichés about these animals (and the "cat people" and "dog people" who love them): the feline disrupts our human-centric worldview, whereas the canine reaffirms and abides by it.[7]

Tarkovsky's attempt to commune with his dog on the eve of exile thus presents an ideal point of entry into Tarkovsky's canine representation. The chapter begins by situating Tarkovsky's affection for dogs in the rise of Soviet pet keeping in the

1950s, which coincided with the beginning of Tarkovsky's career.[8] Dogs, it was claimed, could help Soviet citizens recover a sense of humanity in the wake of their country's traumatic, Stalinist past. The chapter then turns to the philosophical implications of Tarkovsky's film dogs, drawing on the canine's legacy in the Western canon as "the philosopher's pet."[9] Dogs' keen sense of smell, which allows them to track down quarry, inspired classical philosophers to liken themselves to dogs in their own pursuit of deep, metaphysical truths. If, for Derrida, a cat incited infinite, open-ended questions about the nature of being, dogs, for Tarkovsky, helped track down answers to life's mysteries, leading us to Plato, the ancient Skeptics, the Cynics, and posthumanist theory.

In the end, however, the knowledge pursued by Tarkovsky's dogs does *not* interrupt the hierarchical relations between humans and animals upended by Derrida's cat. While Tarkovsky adored dogs, especially his own, his depictions of dogs ultimately succumb to his stubborn belief in human supremacy. Tarkovsky admired dogs for their willingness to yield to (his own) authority in a way people and circumstances would not. Tarkovsky's elusive canine images reiterate human ascendency over dogs by emphasizing loyalty and submission as dogs' most treasured traits.

THE NEW SOVIET PET

There is nothing novel about encountering dogs on screen. They have appeared in film since the medium's earliest days in such works as Lewin Fitzhamon's *Rescued by Rover* (1905) and Chester M. Franklin's *Where the North Begins* (1923) and dominated later blockbusters like Fred M. Wilcox's *Lassie Come Home* (1943), Robert Stevenson's *Old Yeller* (1957), Duwayne Dunham's *Homeward Bound: The Incredible Journey* (1993), and David Frankel's *Marley and Me* (2008). The presence of dogs in narrative cinema "has not only contributed to their steadily growing popularity over the last century, but also created powerful assumptions about what dogs 'are' and, concomitantly, what sort of relationships we 'should' have with them."[10] Indeed, dogs on screen frequently steal the limelight from their human costars, dramatically driving up box office returns and becoming celebrities in their own right: Strongheart, Rin Tin Tin, Uggie, Benji, (Air) Buddy, and Beethoven (a Saint Bernard who shares the name of the German composer whose music is, as we will see, bound up in Tarkovsky's canine representation).

Very often, filmmakers deploy dogs as "moral exemplars" that instruct human beings in "the values of simplicity, goodness, and happiness."[11] Dogs in this light are found training people on screen, not the reverse. The media theorist Anne

Friedberg calls this representational practice "petishism," a mode of human-canine identification that invites us to see dogs' traits as extensions of our idealized selves.[12] Upstanding characteristics, displaced onto dogs, refract back onto us: "Part of our desire to project animals can be traced to that centripetal identification that sees animals as 'better,' the other that affirms our own (lost) innocence."[13]

Psychological identification with dogs as a means to uplift humanity's self-image became a particularly pronounced feature of Soviet cultural life after Stalin's death in 1953. During the Thaw, as discussed in the introduction, Soviet artists began emphasizing matters of sincerity, truth, and compassion in an attempt to recoup life's dignity after long years of terror and war.[14] The desire to cultivate society's moral imagination helps account for the rise of pet ownership, which Soviet communists had historically regarded as ideological anathema, in post-Stalinist culture.

The early Bolsheviks dismissed pets as "parasitic" vestiges of bourgeois decadence, inimical to the revolutionary values of collectivity, cleanliness, labor, and order.[15] Such a view of pets is on display in the early Soviet director Abram Room's *Bed and Sofa* (*Tret'ia meshchanskaia*, 1926) through the recurrent motif of a house cat yawning, napping, and licking itself. The Soviets associated pets with exploitative imperial-era Russian landowners, who, it was claimed, treated their dogs better than their serfs.[16] A long-standing legend in Russian folk culture held that landowners made their female servants breastfeed puppies; this myth became formalized within Soviet school curriculum to illuminate the dehumanizing injustices of czardom.[17] In 1911, on the fiftieth anniversary of the liberation of the serfs, painter Nikolai Kasatkin made a controversial portrait of a peasant breastfeeding a dog: *Serf Actress in Disgrace, Breast-Feeding Her Master's Puppy* (*Krepostnaia aktrisa v opale, kormiashchaia grud'iu barskogo shchenka*). It went into broader circulation after the iconoclastic Soviets had it printed on postcards.[18]

Interestingly, the early Bolsheviks' disparaging views about pets anticipated critiques proffered by more contemporary Western critics, who argue that pet ownership—symptomatic of industrial alienation under modern-day capitalism—is "a universal but personal withdrawal into the private small family unit, decorated or furnished with mementos from the outside world."[19] Pets, it is said, have neutered the revolutionary politics of the street and commodified nature. Committed to humanity's ideological and physiological transformation, the Bolsheviks viewed animals, especially dogs, as scientific test subjects that could facilitate the development of a New Soviet Man (*Novyi sovetskii chelovek*). This positivist understanding of animal life is exemplified by Ivan Pavlov's canine experiments, which the Soviet filmmaker Vsevolod Pudovkin captured on film in his chilling documentary *Mechanics of the Brain* (*Mekhanika golovnogo mozga*, 1926).[20]

After Stalin's death, however, Soviet authorities began encouraging pet keeping, specifically dog ownership (Nikita Khrushchev, for instance, had pet dogs throughout his term in office—two Chihuahuas gifted by Fidel Castro and later a beloved German shepherd). Officials argued that pets could, in fact, cultivate the kind-heartedness, stewardship, and emotional honesty needed to revive—*humanize*—communism in postwar life: "Official Soviet culture may have lauded the efforts of the collective and encouraged individual commitment to the abstract causes of the state, but ... Soviet urban denizens, like their Western and prerevolutionary counterparts, treasured their dogs for their personal loyalty and devotion. Investing animals with qualities highly valued but rarely encountered in people ... Dogs offered their owners companionship, a literally 'selfless' ideal of friendship and a connection with the outside world. They also facilitated the moral development of people, especially children."[21] From the late 1950s on, pet-care manuals, novels, and films popularized dog ownership in Soviet society, as did improved economic conditions that enabled citizens to migrate out of communal apartments and into single-family residences more conducive to household animals.[22]

For his part, Tarkovsky attributed the privacy of the domestic sphere as having been essential for bringing animals into his life. "It's the first time I've ever owned my own home," he said of his cabin in Myasnoye (a town two hundred miles outside Moscow). "This is how I came to have a relationship with animals."[23] In one of the many lists of chores Tarkovsky inventoried in his diary—mimicking Henry David Thoreau's meticulous ledger keeping in *Walden* (1854), a book Tarkovsky cherished—he wrote the action item: "Acquire a dog (Alsatian)" in an entry dated January 2, 1975.[24] Tarkovsky followed this note with a directive to "put a fence around the house," an act of domestic self-enclosure (undertaken in part to raise his new German shepherd) that manifested the qualms of early Bolsheviks who understood pet ownership as an excessively insular, bourgeois preoccupation.[25]

> Imagining himself as a martyr persecuted by Goskino censors, [Tarkovsky] was hoping to find shelter in the village outside the city, which was also viewed as an attempt to reproduce the tranquil environment of his childhood. To put this drama in Tarkovsky's own terms, we could say that in order to escape from *travlya* or persecution in the city, he wanted to hide in *trava* [grass] near the country house, which required him to spend much of his energy and money, or *trata*. These three words, derived from the same root *tra-* ... denote the principal trajectories of the semantic associations in Tarkovsky's life as well as the psychanalytic logic of his anxieties and fantasies, all of which are centered around his primal fantasy of the home.[26]

Tarkovsky with his pet German shepherd Dakus; a dog lover and aspiring homemaker, Tarkovsky typified Soviet society's postwar embourgeoisement. © Gueorgui Pinkhassov/Magnum Photos.

A dog lover and aspiring homemaker, Tarkovsky typified Soviet society's postwar embourgeoisement. Caught in a certain light, then, Tarkovsky's poetic motif of cottages relays little more than a quaint middle-class desire for the peace and quiet of an ordinary life with a dog.

The capacity of dogs to help recoup one's humanity in midcentury Soviet society also bore implications for cinema. Theorizing the place of animals in popular culture, Jonathan Burt argues that "humane behavior is not simply a matter of deeds but is also a matter of being *seen* to behave humanely.... The mark of a more civilized society—a common trope of animal welfare literature generally—is the way in which a society *displays* its humanity. The appearance and treatment of the animal body becomes a barometer for the moral health of a nation."[27] To project post-Stalinist goodness and virtue, Thaw-era filmmakers frequently thematized the close bonds between people and their pet dogs, as in Marianna Roshal and Vladimir Shredel's *White Poodle* (*Belyi pudel'*, 1955); Leonid Gaidai's *Dog Barbos and the Unusual Cross* (*Pes Barbos i neobychnyi kross*, 1961); Semen Tumanov's *Here, Mukhtar!* (*Ko mne, Mukhtar!*, 1964); Nikolai Koshelev's *Salty Dog* (*Solenyi pes*, 1973); and Naum Birman's *Three Men in a Boat (To Say Nothing of the Dog)* (*Troe v lodke* [*ne schitaia sobaki*], 1979). All these films revel in their protagonists' close, morally nutritious relationships with their pet dogs. Even in Yuri Norstein's existential cartoon *Hedgehog in the Fog* (*Ezhik v tumane*, 1975), it is a cocker spaniel that mysteriously emerges out of the fog and reunites the disoriented hedgehog protagonist with his misplaced parcel. Thaw-era filmmakers wanted to be seen displaying their humanity vis-à-vis good treatment of dogs, to be caught in the act of animal care.[28] "The dog becomes the repository of those model human properties that we have cynically ceased to find among humans. . . . How we treat animals becomes a litmus test of our 'humanness.'"[29] If the 1960s was a decade marked by the idea of "socialism with a human face"—a slogan referring to a more humane form of politics after Stalin's death—the culture of the Thaw could also be called "socialism with a dog's face."[30] Post-Stalinist society was to be rescued not by the New Soviet Man but by the New Soviet Pet.

Channeling the Thaw's pet-keeping ideals, dogs accompany many of Tarkovsky's world-weary protagonists in pursuit of moral clarity: Kris Kelvin (Donatas Banionis) in *Solaris*, Stalker (Aleksandr Kaidanovsky) in *Stalker*, and both Andrei Gorchakov (Oleg Iankovskii) and Domenico (Erland Josephson) in *Nostalghia*. Just like the dogs from the films of Italian neorealism, such as Vittorio De Sica's *Umberto D.* (1955), Tarkovsky's dogs help (re)awaken what he perceived as the best of humanity's traits—loyalty, authenticity, integrity—in his characters. "Dog owners' relationships with their pets replicated the affective bonds of familial and other personal relationships. At the same time, the canine-human friendship could be embraced as more genuine and less flawed by human weakness than the human-animal variant. This was possible at least in part because dogs' mutable, plastic nature facilitated their owners' efforts to invest them with idealized versions of desirable 'human' qualities."[31] Tarkovsky's canine-rich filmography documents the visibility and idealization of dogs in midcentury Soviet life more broadly.

Across his work, Tarkovsky also associated dogs with children, as did many other Soviet directors in films like Ilia Gurin's *Give Me Your Paw, Friend!* (*Dai lapu, drug!*, 1967); Roman Balian's *Kashtanka* (1975); Stanislav Rostotsky's *White Bim, Black Ear* (*Belyi Bim, Chernoe ukho*, 1976); and Konstantin Bromberg's *Adventures of an Android* (*Prikliucheniia Elektronika*, 1980). A scene in *Solaris*, for instance, shows two children playing with a dog outside while the adults remain indoors, morosely discussing space travel. Kelvin later watches an old home movie in which we see his mother cradling a puppy as one would a child. In *Nostalghia*, children are seen beside a German shepherd in lyrical black-and-white daydreams, and in *Mirror*, a puppy clumsily explores the set of Tarkovsky's replicated childhood home, as if an infant. Dogs' vivacity and innocence parallel the vitality of children, who similarly played a role in Thaw cinema's mission of moral rehabilitation.[32] "The desire to have a pet was often characterized as a universal urge of childhood, the youthful manifestation of the 'natural love of animals.'... Pet-keeping advocates urged parents to indulge their child's longing for a pet, asserting that pets played an important role in the upbringing (*vospitanie*) of the young generation."[33] Dogs, like children, could rejuvenate the qualities needed to redeem Soviet society's monstrous history. It should come as no surprise, then, that Tarkovsky expressed deep paternalistic affection for his pet German shepherd. He wispily sketched Dakus and often photographed the dog near his son Andriusha, the two of whom, per Tarkovsky's diary notes, shared a birthday (August 7).[34] Echoing the petishistic, bourgeois culture of Thaw-era society, Tarkovsky described Dakus as a "member of my family."[35]

It is not a coincidence, then, that dogs resembling Dakus appear in *Stalker* and *Nostalghia*, the productions of which occurred during Tarkovsky's final days in Russia and earliest days of exile in Italy. These German shepherds entangle with Tarkovsky's feelings of loss, alienation, and desire for companionship abroad, memorializing Tarkovsky's wistfulness for his own lost German shepherd and, by extension, homeland.[36] Asked why he kept a picture of Dakus in his Paris apartment—after (somewhat disingenuously) insisting that "Man ought to be able to live without anything"—Tarkovsky said, "It's a Russian dog, a member of my family who has remained in Russia."[37] The German shepherds in *Stalker* and *Nostalghia* convey Tarkovsky's psychic dislocation abroad, his feelings of being homesick and sick of his adoptive home(s) in France, Italy, and Sweden as he bounced around Europe like a stray dog. "Nostalgia," Tarkovsky said, "is a complete, total feeling... powerlessness in the face of the world, this pain of being unable to transmit one's spirituality to other people."[38] For Tarkovsky, there could be no home without Dakus: "Larochka! Tyapus! Dakus! How I miss you all!"[39] To mourn his lost home and those inhabiting it, Tarkovsky re-creates everything in *Nostalghia*: the Russian countryside, his cabin, his children, his wife, and—vis-à-vis images of a German shepherd—Dakus. These uncanny reanimations, besides redoubling Tarkovsky's embrace of Romantic literary tropes like doppelgängers, mimic the loss-induced psychological spiral experienced by the detective protagonist Scottie (Jimmy Stewart), who futilely tries to re-create the objects of his affection, in Alfred Hitchcock's *Vertigo* (1958), a film Tarkovsky admired.[40] As evidenced by Tarkovsky's wistful canine portrayals, the pet dogs of postwar Soviet cinema reflect middle-class mores of sentimentality, individuality, and domesticity, all but confirming the early Bolsheviks' anxieties about the incipient bourgeois values attendant to

A dog cradled by Kelvin's mother as if she is holding a child.
Still from *Solaris*, 1972.

pet keeping. Dogs became avatars of the spiritual and cultural aspirations of those who benefited most from the Thaw's socioeconomic liberalization: the post-Stalinist middle class.[41]

Yet unlike the dogs portrayed by mainstream Thaw-era filmmakers, Tarkovsky's canine representations also complicate and resist the conventions of domesticity. At one point in *Nostalghia*, for example, Tarkovsky alternates between shots of a German shepherd bounding through the Russian countryside and images of a small white cocker spaniel tethered to a leash. The latter dog is being led through a hotel lobby by an Italian woman dressed in white, reminding us of the bourgeois heroine in Anton Chekhov's short story "Lady with a Little Dog" (*Dama s sobachkoi*, 1899), which the Soviet director Iosif Kheifits made into a film in 1960. Like the cocker spaniel in *Nostalghia*, Chekhov's white dog (also encountered at a foreign resort) "resembles a lapdog in a middleclass boudoir," and Chekhov refers to it with the German word *Shpits* (Spitz), a breed associated with the pampered upper classes.[42] As Amy Nelson notes, Soviet dog owners (despite living in cramped apartments) often preferred "massive dogs" like German shepherds, Saint Bernards, and Great Danes for their symbolic indomitability, a status marker of larger-than-life vivacity in the face of social constraints.[43] In *Nostalghia*, Tarkovsky's German shepherd signifies the freedom and disinhibition associated with the unruly, overgrown Russian countryside, while the cocker spaniel, portrayed as an obsequious lapdog, represents confinement and materialism. The German shepherd is associated not only with Tarkovsky's homeland but also the sights and sounds of nature—it runs through a puddle chasing a stick—whereas the cocker spaniel is correlated with the geometrical space of a dimly lit hotel, which Tarkovsky auralizes through the screech of an iron door. Though Tarkovsky embraced the trend of Soviet pet keeping, he was skeptical of its endemic parochial and bourgeois values, from which he distanced himself by having his film dogs stray into heady philosophical territory.

STALKING

The most curious character in all of *Stalker* is not the film's title character, who is illegally commissioned to lead people through a biohazardous wasteland, the Zone, to fulfill their innermost desires, but a black German shepherd. The dog first appears halfway into the film, when Tarkovsky's trio of characters—Writer (Anatolii Solonitsyn), Professor (Nikolai Grinko), and Stalker—lie down to take a nap.[44] Professor and Writer are heard squabbling, and Writer calls Stalker "Chingachook," the name of a noble-savage character in the American novel series *Leatherstocking Tales* (1827–41) by James Fenimore Cooper. Like Chingachook, Stalker claims to possess secret, elemental knowledge about the world. Preaching a pseudo-Taoist philosophy of nonviolence and interconnectedness, Stalker, whose bald head lends him the look of a Buddhist monk, exudes meditativeness—a zoned-out state of mind—indicative, in Tarkovsky's understanding, of Eastern spiritualism, discussed more in chapter 4.[45] These Zen-like qualities are also typified by the electronically distorted bamboo flutes of the film's soundtrack, designed by Eduard Artemiev. Stalker is a figure of the mind, an unheeded prophet on the hunt for spiritual transcendence in the modern world.

As Stalker listens to his quarrelsome companions, a black German shepherd cautiously approaches. The color film stock used to record this scene suddenly shifts to sepia-toned footage, and dissonant flute music fills the background, signaling a poetic moment of heightened presence. The camera embarks on a lateral glide over an embankment; this tracking shot ends with a close-up of Stalker lying face down on a small island. The sepia-toned image of Stalker switches back to color, and we see Stalker in a different position, lying face up in the grass. The shot then reverts *again* to the sepia image of Stalker. This elusive scene's "alternating monochrome and colour photography launches the dislocation of space and time."[46]

A black German shepherd cautiously approaches Stalker and lies beside him in a moment of diegetic instability. Stills from *Stalker*, 1979.

The abrupt switching of colors in *Stalker*, as in *Andrei Rublev*'s finale of horses grazing in the rain, again calls forth *The Wizard of Oz* (1939), which experimented with the possibilities afforded by color film stock. When Dorothy (Judy Garland) enters Oz, the black-and-white film that began in windswept Kansas bursts into dazzling Technicolor. Similarly, when Tarkovsky's characters escape their gray Soviet setting and enter the Zone, *Stalker* switches from sepia to color. Humanity's drab realities are juxtaposed by the wondrous lands of Oz and Zone, Oz(one). Tarkovsky's allusion to *The Wizard of Oz* suggests *Stalker*'s metacinematic reflection on cinema's capacity to transport unsuspecting audiences—Dorothy, Writer, Professor—to loftier planes of existence, awash in color.[47] Stalker's black dog materializes precisely at, or perhaps even triggers, moments of diegetic instability, which Tarkovsky visualizes through irregular colorization.[48] First in color and then in sepia, the dog runs to Stalker and lays at his feet. If *Andrei Rublev*'s finale—like *The Wizard of Oz*—thrills us with a Horse of a Different Color, *Stalker* gives us a Dog of a Different Color. The German shepherd's alternating hues suggest that, like Stalker (to whom the dog clearly seems attached), the canine exists on multiple diegetic planes and carries deep philosophical meaning, as if representing a "concentrated idea of dog."[49]

Since antiquity, dogs have been associated with formidable thinkers—not unlike Stalker—committed to the discovery of "absolute truth," namely Plato and Aristotle.[50] Dogs have been linked to an intellectual tradition that presupposes that answers to the accursed questions of existence are ultimately discoverable, an idea that Sextus Empiricus, a second-century Greek philosopher, referred to as "dogmatic": "Those who are called Dogmatists in the proper sense of the word think that they have discovered truth—for example, the schools of Aristotle and Epicurus, and the Stoics, and some others."[51] In classical philosophy, dogs became synonymous with the Dogmatists. As the fourth-century philosopher Basil of Caesarea wrote:

> Pursuing his quarry and finding that the tracks part in different directions, the dog examines the tracks, and with little trouble he works out his syllogistic reasoning. The prey, he reasons, has escaped hither or tither, or in quite a different direction, and, since it is neither here nor there, only one direction remains. Thus, by eliminating the erroneous alternatives, the dog discloses the truth. So do also those grave men of thought, who, seated in front of geometrical figures, draw lines in the sand and, confronted with three propositions, have to discard two in order to discover the truth of the one that remains.[52]

The dog's skills are likened to the philosopher's, as they each "sniff towards the truth."[53] Great thinkers do with their mind what dogs do with their keen sense of smell. A dog's instinct, Plato writes, "'shows discrimination and a truly philosophic nature'" because "'a creature that distinguishes between the familiar and the unfamiliar on the grounds of knowledge or ignorance must surely be gifted with a real love of knowledge.'"[54] The "nose knows something" of philosophy, and the dogs in *The Republic* create a "cognitive map" that leads to Plato's "central teachings" about justice, tyranny, and law-abidingness.[55] The dog in pursuit of quarry proves "that the quarry exists (how else would a scent be left?) and thus can be (although isn't always) caught, so for the thinker, truth exists and is attainable (although is not always found)."[56] The dog's propensity to track thus determines the epistemological basis of its existence. "Looking for its master in a wood," the ancient Greek philosopher Chrysippus once recounted, a dog—not unlike the German shepherd in *Stalker*—"comes to a triple fork" in the path, where it "sniffs down two of the branches and finds no scent of his master. He then without sniffing darts down the third branch, thus proving his reasoning powers."[57] The dog's legacy as a truth seeker—a retriever of certainty—is precisely what Tarkovsky invokes in *Stalker*.

Known as "Stalker," a term referencing those who stealthily pursue or poach an object of desire in an obsessive, often illicit manner—from the Old English *-stealcian*, as in *bestealcian*, "to steal along, walk warily"—Stalker compulsively (and unlawfully) shuttles himself and others in and out of the Zone in search of answers to life's mysteries.[58] He sniffs them out alongside his trusty German shepherd. Not unlike a guide dog, Stalker leads lost souls through the Zone toward profundity. It is not by chance, then, that Stalker's decrepit home (where the black German shepherd of the Zone is later found) is lined wall to wall with books, tomes of religion and philosophy, which have presumably aided Stalker in his quest to unlock the universe's secrets.[59]

Yet Stalker's fellow travelers, Professor and Writer, do not share his thirst for knowledge. They doubt Stalker's hunt for truth and the progress he has made. "The world is so boring," Writer says, "There's no telepathy, no ghosts, no flying saucers." Writer expresses, in no uncertain terms, disbelief in Stalker's quest.[60] He enters the Zone (with a few bottles of booze) as a kind of day trip, a leisure activity. From one angle, Writer appears to echo the certitude of a Dogmatist. He is convinced of the universe's brassbound laws and references Pythagoras, a key influence on Plato: "There's no Bermuda Triangle, only A, B, C." Writer does not believe that there is knowledge beyond humanity's cognitive grasp; he is convinced of reality's unchangeability. In the context of *Stalker*, then, Writer is less of a Dogmatist and more of a nonbeliever who mocks Stalker's resolute pursuits. Such suspicion aligns Writer with a parallel (and polemical) group of thinkers in relation to the ancient Dogmatists: the Skeptics, who distrusted the possibility of knowledge's attainment and avoided grand explanatory theories.[61] In *Stalker*, Writer doubts humanity's ability to learn more than it already knows, mistrusting Stalker's conviction that the world is *more* enigmatic than it appears. Tellingly, the Skeptics are associated not with dogs but with a different kind of animal—the dog's natural antagonist, the cat.

Correlated with French philosophers such as Michel de Montaigne and, as noted, Derrida, cats in the Western philosophical canon, unlike dogs, symbolize wariness, if not outright disdain, for human enlightenment because of their nocturnal nature; cats are far less likely than dogs to acquiesce to human lifestyles and behaviors.[62] "When I play with my cat," Montaigne famously asked, "who knows if I am not a pastime to her more than she is to me? . . . We entertain each other with reciprocal monkey tricks."[63] This question anticipates (four hundred years later) Derrida's existential uncertainty as he stared at his cat in the bathroom, wondering who (or what) he was. Montaigne's analogous query advances a speculative if not mocking attitude toward the human intellect. His question about what he does (or does not) know about his cat follows remarks about "human vanity," which leads us to distinguish our mental abilities "from the horde of other creatures."[64] What right, Montaigne wonders, do we have to appoint ourselves as the world's truth seekers? "The most vulnerable and frail of all creatures is man, and at the same time the most arrogant. . . . How does he know, by the force of his intelligence, the secret internal stirrings of animals? By what comparison between them and us does he infer the stupidity he attributes to them?"[65] How would we even know the truth if we found it? "Presumption is our natural and original malady."[66] Truth, for Montaigne, is always vague, provisional; certainty is a fool's errand. A cat is "the anti-pet *par excellence*" because, rather than bringing clarity and being trainable like a dog, cats are "much more independent—less homely—animals" that, rather than help "construct a domestic space," could "well be understood as a challenge to it."[67]

Though Stalker does exhibit certain feline characteristics—roguishness, furtiveness, slinkiness—he does not evince any of the irony, contempt, or equivocality endemic to cat-loving (i.e., ailurophiliac) philosophers, hence his canine, not feline, companion. Stalker is *dogmatically* convinced that humanity needs to be dissuaded out of sneering suspiciousness. People succumb to Skepticism, according to Stalker, whenever they lose faith in the truth. It is not incidental, then, that cats rarely appear in Tarkovsky's films. One of the few cats materializes in *Andrei Rublev* after a Mongol raid has massacred hundreds of people and desecrated a church, events that shake the protagonist's faith in humanity. A black cat—an age-old symbol of satanic power—appears at the onset of Rublev's existential crisis as he forswears painting, abandoning his pursuit of metaphysical truth.⁶⁸ Tarkovsky's cinema is *ailurophobic*, allergic to the epistemic traits anthropomorphized by cats; it prefers instead dogs' certainty, earnestness, obedience, and fidelity. A contemporaneous song, "There Is No More Horrible Beast than the Cat" (*Strashnee koshki zveria net*, 1968), by popular Russian musician Evgenii Kliachkin perfectly captures Tarkovsky's aversion to the feline. In Kliachkin's tune, cats epitomize the unseemly traits, such as complacency and opportunism, that were needed to thrive in late Soviet society, as portrayed in the characters Writer and Professor. "In the symbolic dog-cat dichotomy, those in opposition" to official Soviet culture, such as Stalker, are scrappy and earnest "underdogs" and, therefore, "expressly anti-cat."⁶⁹ Moreover, cats are coded as feminine, which explains why the cat in *Andrei Rublev* appears as the holy fool girl—the *durochka* (played by Tarkovsky's first wife, Irma Rausch)—is seen braiding the hair of a dead woman; cats had little appeal to Tarkovsky's gendered animal imagination.⁷⁰ Like a (male) dog, Stalker hounds the truth, and this pursuit, alongside his German shepherd, philosophically ennobles him. It is not by chance that *Stalker*'s dominant cinematographic technique is the tracking shot, a canine-like camera movement that follows its subjects as they move through space. The tracking shot took hold in moody, slow-paced films of the postwar period, like Orson Welles's *Touch of Evil* (1958), Mikhail Kalatozov's *I Am Cuba* (*Soy Cuba*, 1964), and Stanley Kubrick's *Barry Lyndon* (1975). The camerawork of *Stalker*, as if assuming the perspective of Stalker's pursuant black dog, surreptitiously follows—stalks—Tarkovsky's protagonists on their ambling spiritual journey.

For Tarkovsky's viewers, too, *Stalker* hints at the promise, the quarry, of deep meaning through disorienting colorization, mesmerizing cinematography, and cryptic dialogue. For example, soon after the German shepherd lies beside Stalker, a reading from the book of Revelation begins, and the camera scans a pool of water, in the depths of which we see a series of semantically rich objects: clocks, coins, syringes, and religious icons. This episode bears interpretively dizzying, "infinite possibilities" that stoke our curiosity about *Stalker*'s ultimate significance.⁷¹ Despite Tarkovsky's rejection of the use of symbols on screen—"I am an enemy of symbolism," he once stated. "An artistic image cannot be decoded"—Tarkovsky's mysterious films, especially *Stalker*, stoke our curiosity, seducing our desire to sniff toward answers by asking what things mean.⁷² One wonders whether his disavowals of symbolism were, in fact, intended to further incentivize decryptions of his imagery. Constantly told that *Stalker* lacks any symbols—"It's just a black dog," Tarkovsky cautioned a critic who asked what the German shepherd in *Stalker* "meant"—we begin to see nothing *but* symbols.⁷³ We find ourselves, like Tarkovsky's lost characters

Tarkovsky at his desk aside Dakus, an image that situates Tarkovsky in the iconographic tradition of great male philosophers at work in the company of dogs. © Gueorgui Pinkhassov/Magnum Photos.

(and their dog), wandering through the Zone in search of answers. Through allegorically potent motifs, Tarkovsky's images cannot help but inflame our intrigue, as if promising a rewarding payoff (or treat) at the end of their scent trail.[74] *Stalker*, in a way, makes us doglike by inducing our urge to track down hidden truths and allusions.[75] If Stalker's dog symbolizes anything, it is the interpretive process itself: a promise that, somewhere in the depths of *Stalker*, truth can be found (however many viewings may it take). The long takes and tracking shots in *Stalker* generate time and space for us to ponder Tarkovsky's enigmas, enticing us to hunt for meaning as philosophers do with their dogs.

Through dogs, Tarkovsky stylized himself as a philosopher-filmmaker in pursuit of wisdom. It is not by chance that Tarkovsky was often photographed with his dog at his feet, situating him in an iconographic tradition of great male philosophers dutifully at work in the company of dogs, as in Albrecht Dürer's engraving *Saint Jerome in His Study* (1514) and Jean-Léon Gérôme's painting *Diogenes* (1860), an ancient Greek philosopher discussed more later. Dogs, for Tarkovsky, inspire what he regarded as the noblest tradition of philosophical inquiry: the search for truth.

METAPHYSICAL ENVOYS

Muddied and humbled, Tarkovsky's protagonists return from the Zone to the tavern where *Stalker* began, and Stalker's wife (Alisa Freindlich) enters to see her husband feeding the black German shepherd we last saw in the Zone.[76] "Where did that dog come from?" she asks. Stalker says that it "tagged along" and that he "couldn't leave it behind." Wary of the added responsibilities of caring for a dog—on top of her renegade husband and "mutant child"—Stalker's wife offers it to Professor or Writer: "Anyone want a dog?" Writer scoffs and says he already has "five at home," a comment that locates him, like Tarkovsky, in the pet-keeping culture of postwar Soviet society. Like many world-weary Soviet citizens of the 1960s and '70s, Writer betrays his desire for companionship amid the banalities and injustices of everyday life; dogs have a salutary effect even on Tarkovsky's most jaded (indeed, skeptical) character. Shuttling back and forth between disparate metaphysical realms, Stalker's little black dog is an emissary or envoy from the Zone, inverting the nineteenth-century literary trope of Chekhov's little white dog.

This German shepherd also upends the breed's historical function in Soviet culture. As war with Nazi Germany loomed under Stalin in the 1930s, the threat of foreign invasion fueled an official campaign to fortify USSR borders.[77] In response, a cult following formed around border patrolmen and their trusty German shepherds.[78] As a breed, German shepherds originated in nineteenth-century Germany under Max Emil Friedrich von Stephanitz, an ex-calvary captain who selectively bred dogs for tactical military work. The success of Von Stephanitz's genetic experiments led German shepherds to become the favored breed among policemen and prison guards around the globe.[79] In the Soviet context, German shepherds, officially rebranded in 1964 as "East European shepherds" to gainsay the breed's cultural origins, were valorized as defenders of the nation.[80] In films like Vladimir Shneiderov's *Dzhul'bars* (1935), Vasilii Zhuravlev's *The Border Is Locked* (*Granitsa na zamke*, 1937), and—coinciding with the Soviet Union's invasion of Afghanistan in 1979—Yuliy Fait's *Border Dog Alyi* (*Pogranichnyi pes Alyi*, 1980), German shepherds signified not the porosity of borders but their ironclad integrity.[81] The German shepherds of 1930s Stalinist cinema upheld political order in the Soviet East—just as Hollywood's most famous German shepherd, Rin Tin Tin, had in the American West during the 1920s.

By contrast, Tarkovsky's German shepherd in *Stalker* shakes off the breed's Stalinist legacy by destabilizing and transgressing fixed borders, both real and imaginary. Stalker's dog (re)introduces mystery and ambiguity into the static settings of Soviet cinema. Indeed, the Zone has been compared to an abandoned Stalinist prison camp, and Stalker, with his shaved head and emaciated physique, bears the look of a gulag inmate, a "zek."[82] Rather than a site of internment patrolled by menacing German shepherds—the type encountered, for instance, in Sergei Dovlatov's contemporaneous novel *The Zone: A Prison Camp Guard's Story* (*Zona: zapiski nadziratelia*, 1982)—Tarkovsky's Zone has mutable topography, the volatility of which is anthropomorphized by the black dog's diaphanous (de)materializations across the film.[83]

Breaking from depictions of German shepherds under Stalin, Stalker's enigmatic dog also has non-Soviet cinematic antecedents. As explored in chapter 1, Louis Lumière's *Workers Leaving the Factory* (1895), considered the first film, depicts a series of laborers exiting an industrial workplace. The film consists of a single shot in which a pair of factory gates, along with a smaller door to the right, swings open as workers begin streaming toward the camera. As the factory empties, a stray dog emerges amid the workers, and it exits and (re)enters the visual field at will. The dog traipses out of the frame alongside a few people before reemerging and trying to catch the attention of several workers. The dog then appears in the corner of the shot, whereafter it cuts across the camera's field of vision, as if announcing its presence. The dog's lateral movement contrasts with the workers' longitudinal trajectory. Finally, the dog strolls back into the frame and, yawning, stares at the workers before coming to a standstill. The dog's comings and goings counterpose the crowd's unidirectional motion, which replicates the flow of the assembly-line factory from which these workers are escaping. The free-wheeling dog thus undercuts the film's choreographed spectacle; it is the only character *not* working for the film image. It is a figure of leisure and spontaneity inimical to Lumière's production line.

This stray dog, then, makes *Workers Leaving the Factory* an early study about cinematic space. As Akira Mizuta Lippit writes, "The very architecture of [*Workers Leaving the Factory*], the series of flat surfaces that moves from screen to wall to interior background, suggests that this cinema is an exploration of depth. An imaginary, impossible depth extends into the screen . . . revealing a virtual interiority and distance, far away."[84] The Lumière dog's haphazard journeys into an abyssal, unknown dimension—a zone—beyond the frame discloses the film image's tenuous relation to reality: its susceptibility for distension and rupture as it straddles on- and off-screen space. Like Toto, the Carin terrier in *The Wizard of Oz* who travels with Dorothy to and from Kansas and the Emerald City, Lumière's dog establishes a precedent for Tarkovsky's spatially sinuous German shepherds.

In the final scenes of *Stalker*, Stalker's wife, now accompanied by her new pet dog, exits the tavern with her husband and daughter as they walk home. The German shepherd scampers around the trio, surveying the area for risk and danger, not unlike its owner in the Zone. This image re-creates the earlier sight of three characters sauntering through space escorted by a black dog; Stalker's family has been gifted a guardian from the Zone. This dog darts in and out of the camera's line of sight. It not only crosses boundaries internal to the film's diegesis between the Zone and Stalker's shanty neighborhood but also transgresses borders separating Tarkovsky's film from its extra-diegetic reality as it zigzags in and out of the frame. Seemingly born of the Zone, the black German shepherd embodies its spatial instability. Throughout Tarkovsky's cinema, dogs prove difficult to fix within a single space-time continuum.

In *Solaris*, for example, the protagonist's pet boxer is initially encountered in the opening scenes, on his father's wooded estate.[85] Yet the boxer inexplicably materializes on the spacecraft when Kelvin, surrounded by mirrors, undergoes a fever dream that disrupts all distinctions between past and present, adulthood and adolescence, Earth and outer space. Kelvin's dog frustrates a spatiotemporally contiguous understanding of *Solaris*. The boxer again appears in the film's stupefying finale when Kelvin disembarks on the planet Solaris and makes contact with an uncanny extraterrestrial replica of his childhood home. The dog is, indeed, the first thing that greets Kelvin in this "new-old" world. When Kelvin collapses at the knees of his alien father, Tarkovsky re-creates Rembrandt's painting *The Return of the Prodigal Son* (1661–69) on screen, yet this painterly *mise-en-scène* is marred by the presence of the boxer, staring doggedly at the camera. The dog is what Žižek describes as "a monstrous Thing" that reminds us of the universe's "infinite void" glaring back at us.[86] Tarkovsky's evocation of Rembrandt signals the dissonance between Kelvin's future space-age exploration and the archaic past of Renaissance art—not unlike *Solaris*'s soundtrack of electronically distorted music by Johann Sebastian Bach, another unnerving mix of classical culture and dystopic future.[87] The boxer, like Kelvin, is lost in time and space. Stuck abroad in the 1980s, Tarkovsky himself might as well have been marooned on a distant planet, fantasizing about his pet dog while conceding the impossibility of their reunion. The boxer in *Solaris* intimates Kelvin's and, by turn, Tarkovsky's unattainable longing for homecoming—that is, the hopelessness of spatiotemporal synchronicity.

A boxer eerily stares at the camera during a father-son reunion, intimating Tarkovsky's unattainable longing for homecoming. Still from *Solaris*, 1972.

In a similar timbre, the German shepherd in *Nostalghia* is initially associated with Gorchakov's memories of Russia. Yet it also appears in the present in Italy, where it enigmatically materializes in Gorchakov's hotel room and knocks over a glass bottle as he drifts in and out of sleep, patting the dog's head. The animal exists on the cusp of Gorchakov's consciousness. After Gorchakov wakes up, the camera cuts to the same German shepherd walking alongside Domenico, the Italian madman who convinces Gorchakov to commit suicide to achieve peace—as if the dog is leading Gorchakov to Domenico, foreshadowing his imminent self-sacrifice. It is fitting, then, that the German shepherd is also lying beside Gorchakov in *Nostalghia*'s final shot, perhaps Tarkovsky's most iconic: an impossibly utopian image of a Russian cottage nestled inside the ruins of an Italian church, the San Galgano Abbey in Tuscany. *Nostalghia*'s German shepherd populates each of the film's spatiotemporal planes—Gorchakov's prelapsarian past (Russia), his eschatological present (Italy), and his quixotic future (Russo-Rome). The dog acts as the connective tissue between characters, cultures, languages, geographies, and temporalities, enacting Gorchakov's wish expressed at the beginning of the film to "abolish the world's frontiers."

Dogs appear precisely at moments of (meta)physical dislocation in Tarkovsky's cinema when "time is out of joint," as Shakespeare memorably writes

Gorchakov, Tarkovsky's autobiographical alter ego, lies in the ruins of an
Italian abbey beside a German shepherd, who acts as connective tissue between
characters, cultures, geographies, and temporalities. Still from *Nostalghia*, 1983.

in *Hamlet*—a play Tarkovsky staged in Leningrad in 1977.[88] In *Andrei Rublev*, a dog is found among those trudging alongside Christ during Tarkovsky's recreation of the Crucifixion, which he relocates to a wintry Russian landscape far from Golgotha. Likewise, in *Mirror*, a dog inexplicably traipses out of an attic (and the cinematic frame) after a door swings open in a flashback of the child protagonist's mother peeling potatoes. These dogs are phantasmal creatures floating between otherwise mutually exclusive planes of existence. They are, in a way, arthouse manifestations of Laika, Belka, and Strelka: the three most famous Soviet space dogs who (along with more than seventy others) were rocketed off Earth between 1951 and 1961.[89] Like these interstellar canines, Tarkovsky's dogs are threshold beings, neither fully here nor there.

The disorienting effect dogs have on the diegetic coherence of Tarkovsky's cinema has led some scholars to compare them to mythical watchdogs of the netherworld, patrolling the boundary separating life from the afterlife.[90] That the Zone in *Stalker* is littered with skeletons guarded by a German shepherd suggests that the dog, like Cerberus or Anubis, fulfills a mythological purpose. Indeed, in several of Tarkovsky's polaroid photographs of his dog, we see Dakus alone in a field, eerily gazing into the foggy distance as if looking across the

River Styx toward another world.⁹¹ It is not by chance that in *Stalker*, the black German shepherd's second appearance occurs immediately after Tarkovsky's characters cross a polluted stream in a treacherous area of the Zone known as the "meatgrinder," moving toward their final reckoning. Stalker's canine has also been compared to the Black Shuck of English folklore, the ghost dog said to terrorize the British Isles, and to the dogs in Rembrandt's etchings for his painting *Supper at Emmaus* (1648), which depicts the resurrected Christ blessing bread as he did at the Last Supper.⁹² Dogs, for Tarkovsky, traverse the borders between this world and the underworld, the living and the dead: Tarkovsky's dogs belong to Hades as much as they do to Plato and Aristotle.

Freely roaming other worlds, Tarkovsky's dogs are often heard off camera. Upon entering the Zone, Writer and Professor are startled by the howl of a dog signaling they have trespassed into a new world with fateful consequences. The howling canine in *Stalker* joins the chorus of barking in *Andrei Rublev*, *Solaris*, *Mirror*, *Nostalghia*, and *The Sacrifice*, emanating from some faraway place to which we do not have access. These distant, often faint sounds plunge Tarkovsky's viewers into a struggle "to believe in the diegesis," which replicates the experience of Tarkovsky's heroes on their own faith-seeking quests.⁹³ Tarkovsky "uses sound to embody this internal process by drawing a parallel between 'two leaps of faith': that of accepting that a sound proves the existence of an unseen object and that of believing in the existence of an invisible spiritual world. Because we posit a source for every offscreen diegetic sound, we believe in the existence of this source even when we cannot produce a visible mental image of it. We believe, although we cannot explain or prove. This paradox is one of the bases of religious faith."⁹⁴ Tarkovsky's distantly barking dogs signal a collision between the physical world and a numinous realm—a mysterious, inaccessible place somewhere within the on-screen world, a zone—suggesting that there is more to reality than can be captured by the movie camera.

The elusiveness of Tarkovsky's dogs deepens his cinema's philosophical indebtedness to Plato, who claimed that there were two planes of existence in perpetual interaction: the physical realm and the spiritual realm. The world exists in its truest form beyond the perceivable, and we catch glimpses of it from our position in the physical world. In *The Republic*, Plato explicates his bifurcated theory of reality through the allegory of the cave, in which prisoners enchained in a cavern spend their lives watching shadows on a wall projected by the light of a fire. When a prisoner escapes, he perceives the world outside and realizes that there is a greater reality than was afforded to him by the cave. This allegory distills the relation Plato ascertained between reality's material and metaphysical dimensions.⁹⁵ The barking dogs heard across Tarkovsky's films seem to hail from the spiritual realm of Platonian philosophy. Haunting—that is, dogging—Tarkovsky's visual ecologies, dogs prove that there is something beyond the coordinates of humanity's bleak reality, which Tarkovsky visualizes in *Stalker* through images of industrial decay and belching smokestacks (his reprise, in a Soviet key, of the English poet William Blake's "dark Satanic mills" of early nineteenth-century British industrialization).[96] Tarkovsky's dogs invite us to take a leap of faith, to believe that there is more to life than meets the eye. "Our life is a metaphor," Tarkovsky said. "Everything that surrounds us is a metaphor"—nothing but the flickering shadows of Plato's realm of forms.[97] In his films, Tarkovsky reimagines the vaunted "kino-eye" of early Soviet cinema, said to pierce through the trappings of reality to disclose society's Marxist core, with the *canine-eye*: an altogether different nonhuman gaze capable of penetrating through our reality's dilapidated facades in search of higher truths.[98]

Through dogs, Tarkovsky challenges what postwar film theorists like André Bazin champion as the "reality effect" of cinema, which purportedly maintains a direct, mimetic relation to the world it archives on celluloid. "Only the impassive lens, stripping its object of all those ways of seeing it . . . that spiritual dust and grime with which my eyes have covered it, is able to present it in all its virginal purity."[99] Yet Tarkovsky refused to "strip" the world of "spiritual dust"; he did not elide the phantasmagoric appearances of what he understood as a higher, truer realm of being. Tarkovsky's characters, as Nariman Skakov argues, "enter an intermediary domain of abstract illusion and concrete reality, and face situations where the boundaries between nominally real and nominally illusory events are unstable, or at times even completely effaced. Their temporally anomalous and spatially abnormal journeys do not lead them to greater clarity, but into uncertainty wrapped in a sense of cosmic homelessness."[100] Dogs surface in Tarkovsky's universe when the phenomenal and the metaphysical interweave, disclosing the presence of underworlds and elsewheres, afterlives and infinities, in excess of human vision—somewhere over the rainbow.

TARKOVSKY THE CYNIC

For Tarkovsky, however, the barking dogs in *Solaris, Mirror, Stalker, Nostalghia,* and *The Sacrifice* were calling out to nowhere, their cries falling on the deaf ears of people uninterested in higher truths. Humanity, Tarkovsky believed, had lost its way: the "confused state of the soul, its decline and inadequacy, are becoming an ever more chronic syndrome in modern man, who could be diagnosed as being spiritually impotent."[101] In his later cinema, Tarkovsky began using his protagonists as mouthpieces to air his ever-growing pessimism about modern life. "They call themselves the intelligentsia," Stalker bewails. "Writers! Scientists! They don't believe in anything. Their capacity for faith has atrophied." Somewhat uncharacteristically given his classicist tastes, Tarkovsky even praised James Cameron's *The Terminator* (1984) for its desolate vision of humanity's future: "The brutality and low acting skills are unfortunate, but as a vision of the future and the relation between man and his destiny, the film is pushing the frontier of cinema as an art."[102] It is not coincidental, then, that Tarkovsky's increasingly grim view of humanity's fate paralleled the heightened visibility of dogs in his films. As Tarkovsky said, by way of a canine analogy, "We know so little about the soul, we're like lost dogs."[103] The twinning of Tarkovsky's criticism about modern life and dogs is no better on display than in the bewitching end of *Stalker*.

Throughout *Stalker*, characters whisper about the "mutant child" with whom Stalker was "cursed" because of the Zone's latent radioactivity; apparently, it warped the genes his daughter inherited. The film's finale reveals that Stalker's daughter (Natasha Abramova), who cannot walk or talk, is telekinetic, as she begins moving glassware across a table with her mind. Stalker's German shepherd, resting beneath the girl's feet, senses the gravitational disturbance and begins whimpering. The presence of dogs in Tarkovsky's cinema becomes palpable whenever reality glitches, not unlike the déjà vu effect in the Wachowskis' *The Matrix* (1999). Stalker's daughter knocks a glass onto the floor, and this noise duplicates the sound of the bottle felled by the German shepherd in Gorchakov's hotel room in *Nostalghia*, allying Stalker's dog—and his extrasensory daughter—with Gorchakov and Domenico's mysterious canine companion.

After the girl's telekinetic stunt, the sound of a roaring train fills the frame, as it did during the film's opening; Stalker's family (perhaps squatters) resides dangerously close to train tracks. Curiously, the clamor of the train is accompanied by Beethoven's "Ode to Joy" from his Ninth Symphony (1824), the "paradigmatic example of triumphant and celebratory music" in Western culture, as musicologists note.[104] As the train's din and Beethoven's music fade, the camera slowly approaches—stalks—Stalker's daughter, whose dispassionate expression, the last thing we see before the film cuts to black, juxtaposes the ceremonial spirit of "Ode to Joy." What to make of this baffling conclusion: a mishmash of telekinesis, trains, dogs, and Beethoven?

When asked about his use of classical music in *Stalker*—which, besides "Ode to Joy," also includes snippets of Claude Joseph Rouget's "La Marseillaise" (1792), Richard Wagner's *Tannhäuser* (1845), and Maurice Ravel's *Boléro* (1928)—Tarkovsky said he wanted the music to "express the theme of humanity's social destiny," that is, to be expressly political and indicative of civilizational "progress."[105] Known as the "Marseillaise of Mankind," Beethoven's "Ode to Joy" is an encomium to Western society, a full-throttled celebration of its "scientific progresses, our grand political and ideological projects, the perceived teleology of human history, in short, the meanings of our jointly constructed 'lifeworld.'"[106] The ode, at the time of its composition, indeed captured the triumphal spirit of the self-proclaimed "masters of history": the ascendant bourgeoisie of Western Europe that exalted the ideals of rationality, liberty, and enterprise in post-Napoleonic society.[107] It is all too fitting, then, that Tarkovsky couples "Ode to Joy" with the noise of a train, the quintessential sound of bourgeois industrialism. "It is impossible not to share the mood of excitement, of self-confidence, of pride, which seized those who lived through this heroic age of the engineers. . . . Such men thought in continents and oceans. For them the world was a single unit, bound together with rails of iron and steam engines, because the horizons of business were like their dreams world-wide. For such men human destiny, history, and profit were one and the same thing."[108] Through Beethoven and railway locomotion, *Stalker* seems to broadcast the gloriousness of Western culture. "Ode to Joy" did, in fact, acquire fresh currency during Tarkovsky's career when, in 1972, the Council of Europe, a forerunner to the European Union, named it "The Anthem to Europe," a modern-day celebration of harmony, peace, and progress.

For Tarkovsky, however, Beethoven's music epitomizes Europe's arrogance because the West "is forever shouting: 'This is me! Look at me! Listen to me suffering loving! How unhappy I am! How happy! I! Mine! Me!'"[109] For a generation of Russians, "Ode to Joy" rang of Nazism, for it had been lionized by Hitler's propagandists as proof of German exceptionalism.[110] Given Tarkovsky's negative views of Beethoven, the train that accompanies "Ode to Joy" at the end of *Stalker* draws not on the railway's heroic symbolism but on its more ominous legacy in nineteenth-century Russian literature. Trains, as enshrined in Tolstoy's *Anna Karenina* (1878) and Dostoevsky's *The Idiot* (1868–69), signify the victory of "godless European enlightenment"; trains are symbols of doom because they move, "like 'atheistic' logic, along iron rails without any higher reason for being."[111] The railway, moreover, displaced more organic forms of horse-drawn transportation, underscoring for Tarkovsky the terrifying and alien essence of trains that ripped humanity away from the natural world. As detailed in chapter 1, Tarkovsky was not only amaxophobic—ill disposed to cars—but also *siderodromophobic*, distrustful of trains. Tarkovsky uses Beethoven and railway locomotion in *Stalker* to demonize the West, hence the camera's tight focus on Stalker's mutant daughter as the uproar fades. This otherworldly girl will outlast the supposed mightiness of Western culture and civilization—her name, tellingly, is Monkey (*martyshka*).

The Russian term *martyshka* is a diminutive for "marmoset," a term adults use to refer to children. Yet the common use of this nickname was not Tarkovsky's only motivation to call Stalker's daughter Monkey. *Stalker* is based on the 1972 novel *Roadside Picnic* by Boris and Arkady Strugatsky, in which things bear curious sobriquets: "Red," "mosquito mange," "witches' jelly," etcetera.[112] (The term "zone," *zona*, was itself a Soviet epithet for "prison camp.") As *Roadside Picnic* unfolds, the daughter of the stalker-protagonist behaves more and more erratically, losing her voice and growing furry paws ("overgrown with coarse brown hair"), a confirmation of the genetic deformities conferred to her by the Zone.[113] Monkey, in other words, evolutionarily regresses; she comes to resemble more of a simian than a girl, anthropomorphizing the traits of her (pet) name.

The moniker "Monkey," furthermore, calls forth Charles Darwin's *On the Origins of Species* (1859), which challenges humanity's assumed apartness from the animal kingdom by positing that we are, in fact, decedents of certain species of primates. Published at the height of Europe's nineteenth-century self-confidence—symphonically consecrated by Beethoven's "Ode to Joy"—Darwin's "dramatic or rather traumatic" discovery "abolished the special status of man as hitherto conceived. The violence with which evolution was resisted was ideological. How could man, created in God's image, be no more than a modified monkey?"[114] Indeed, Darwin's theory of natural selection, per Sigmund Freud, landed the second of three great blows against "the universal narcissism of men" that unmoored humanity's exceptionalist self-image.[115] The Copernican Revolution scored the first by proving that Earth, humanity's habitat, is not the center of the universe; the third, by Freud himself, revealed how humans are not the masters of their own minds. For his part, Darwin proved that human beings are nothing more than animals. In *Stalker*, Tarkovsky preserves the bestial qualities of the Strugatskys' simian character, which conjure the specter of Darwinism and underscore the extent of the Zone's disturbing physiography.

Yet Stalker's daughter is not merely a "modified monkey"; she is, as mentioned above, a telepath (perhaps a fourth challenge to "the universal narcissism of men"). Monkey is a combination of the atavistic and the extraterrestrial—an alien-animal—who predates *and* postdates Western civilization as glorified by Beethoven and trains.[116] Monkey subverts human self-aggrandizement by confronting us with a life form that both antecedes human rationality (e.g., Darwinian primates) and exceeds it (e.g., telekinesis). To accentuate Monkey's unfathomability, the camera magnifies her expressionless face, recycling the

Stalker's daughter—Monkey—blankly stares at the camera with a dog beneath her feet. Her Darwinian nickname implies that she antecedes human rationality, while her telekinesis suggests she exceeds it. Still from *Stalker*, 1979.

close-up of a goat's jarring and inscrutable stare from the start of *Ivan's Childhood*. The close-up, used throughout film history to make characters' interior states of mind more legible, is repurposed here to emphasize Monkey's unknowable (animal) essence, the alterity separating her from human norms. Her autumnal gold-brown headscarf even echoes the "subtle shades of gold and red" illuminating the Zone's wish-room, putting her in metonymic sympathy with the chimerical realm.[117] The bestial yet paranormal Monkey turns *Stalker* into a post- and *pre*-apocalyptic film.

Stalker's Darwinian critique of modern society situates Tarkovsky's cinema in yet another ancient philosophical tradition: Cynicism. Inspired by Socrates—who warned against the accumulation of wealth in the building of an ideal society—the Cynics and their leader, Diogenes of Sinope, shunned all cultural amenities. (A bust of Socrates, it should be noted, appears several times in *Solaris*.) Rejecting most forms of dress, food, and shelter, the Cynics pursued an abstemious lifestyle close to nature. A meaningful life, for the Cynics, can emerge only after human beings cast off that which distracts from introspection and self-reliance. "The central idea animating Cynic philosophy," Matthew Calarco writes, spotlighting the human-turned-bear (and then bear-food) protagonist of Werner Herzog's remarkable documentary *Grizzly Man* (2005), "was that a happy life, the life most worth living, was a life lived according to nature.... The Cynics set this ideal in opposition to the way of life adopted by most people in city-states, a way of life governed by customs, conventions, and social norms.... This latter form of existence represented a perilous deviation from the path leading to genuine happiness; hence, they argued, dominant cultural practices should be held at bay and actively resisted."[118] The Cynical ideal rejects desire as informed by society in favor of "nature," which the Cynics viewed as a realm of harmony and modesty better able to teach humanity about living mindfully and minimally. Diogenes wore a tattered cloak, ate readily available food, and slept in a barrel. For the Cynics, it is vanity and social artifice—not lack of wealth—that immiserate humankind.

Tarkovsky articulated an analogous worldview: "Modern mass culture, aimed at the 'consumer,' the civilization of prosthetics, is crippling people's souls, setting up barriers between man and the crucial questions of his existence, his consciousness of himself as a spiritual being."[119] Unlike the character Writer, Tarkovsky is not a Skeptic but a *Cynic*, and he aligns his protagonists, namely Stalker and Domenico, with the Cynics' embrace of asceticism and iconoclasm.[120] Both Stalker and Domenico live a stripped-down existence on the outskirts of their cities in ramshackle domiciles, sustaining themselves on a diet of bread and fruit and dressing austerely. "I am drawn to the man," Tarkovsky wrote, "who is ready to serve a higher cause, unwilling—or even unable to—to subscribe to the generally accepted tenets of a worldly 'morality': the man who recognizes that the meaning of existence lies above all in the fight against the evil within ourselves, so that in the course of a lifetime he may take at least one step toward spiritual perfection."[121] In *Nostalghia*, Domenico reiterates Tarkovsky's haze of discontent: "Society must be made whole again, instead of so disjointed. Look at nature, and you'll see that life is simple. We must go back to where we were, to the point where we took the wrong turn!"

In step with the Cynics, neither Domenico nor Stalker withdraws from society in their struggle against it. Rather, they pursue a transformation of the social order from within, albeit on society's edges. The Cynics "didn't cloister themselves in seclusion outside the city but instead... insisted on conversing, arguing, debating with—even berating—human beings who were not caring for their own souls."[122] Stalker illegally leads skeptical "tourists" through a shape-shifting wasteland to a room that fulfills people's deepest longings, while Domenico stages an elaborate public demonstration to espouse his starry-eyed ambitions: "If you want the world to go forward, we must hold hands! We must mix the so-called healthy with the so-called sick!" The Cynics "do not simply recommend returning to or trying to recover our nature, for this nature is all too amenable to the temptations offered by culture. . . . Rather, the Cynics believe it is necessary for those who are tempted by and have become habituated to the ease of cultural life to undergo a joint process of de-habituation (losing old habits and dispositions learned from the dominant culture) and re-habituation (gaining new, better habits and dispositions that can resist the temptation of culture)."[123] The Cynics are not misanthropes but, in fact, idealists committed to the Socratic vision who have not yet given up on humanity. In an appeal for social "de-habituation" and "re-habituation," Domenico in *Nostalghia* says, "We must go back to the foundations of life without dirtying the water." Domenico's public demonstration culminates with him lighting himself on fire in an act of protest that recalls the self-immolations of dissidents remonstrating against political injustice during the Cold War: the South Vietnamese monk Thích Quảng Đức, the Czech university student Jan Palach, and the Romanian painter Liviu Cornel Babeş.[124] Tarkovsky backdrops Domenico's self-immolation with "Ode to Joy," conjoining Domenico to Monkey's "Cynical" critique of modern civilization in *Stalker* when she moves glassware with her mind (a variation of Montaigne's "monkey tricks") while a dog whimpers at her feet. As Domenico burns, Beethoven's music stops after the tape recorder on which it is playing malfunctions (another of Tarkovsky's not-so-subtle potshots against modern society's unreliable gadgets). The frame is filled by Domenico's screams, suggesting what, for Tarkovsky, Beethoven's hubris bequeaths humankind.[125] "The greatness of modern man lies in protest," Tarkovsky wrote. "Thank God for people who burn themselves alive in front of an impassive, wordless crowd, or who walk out into squares with placards and slogans condemning themselves to reprisals, and all those who say 'No' to the go-getters and the godless."[126]

It is telling that Domenico, like Stalker, appears alongside a German shepherd. Domenico and the dog are seen strolling together, and the dog (when in Italy) lives in Domenico's cave-like dwelling, where rain pours in: Tarkovsky's dogs thrive in liminal spaces. Domenico even says to the dog at one point, "I know what you're thinking," as if he, like Monkey, is capable of telepathic communication with animals—a modern-day Saint Francis of Assisi, whose spiritually rich but materially poor life put the Cynics' spartan ideals into practice. When Domenico lights himself on fire, the German shepherd is the only character to respond appropriately. It alertly rises when Domenico strikes his match, and it recoils and howls after Domenico bursts into flames. Meanwhile, a street performer mocks Domenico, a woman fixes her makeup, and others look on impassively. The dog is stirred by the sight of anguish in a way that the Italian bystanders are not.[127] The onlookers—"the godless "go-getters"

Domenico's German shepherd howls at the sight
of him burning alive, reacting in a way the Italian bystanders do not.
Stills from *Nostalghia*, 1983.

Tarkovsky scorned"—exhibit the narcissistic traits of modern life against which the Cynics revolted.

Domenico's close relations with a scruffy dog typify the tenets of Cynicism because the Cynics were themselves known as "dogs." Hence, the Greek word for "dog," *kyon*, is a source for the English word "cynic."[128] The shamelessness of the Cynics in defying social conventions—Diogenes defecated and masturbated in public—motivated their comparison to mangy canines. Yet the Cynics embraced this moniker because they believed that "human flourishing lies not within removing ourselves from animality... but in newly aligning ourselves with it."[129] As Domenico thunders in *Nostalghia*, "We must listen to the voices that seem useless. The buzzing of insects must return." Domenico urges us to reopen ourselves to nature, much like Stalker does by immersing himself in the grass, water, and mud of the Zone. "Our most profound happiness, [the Cynics] insist, is to be found not by separating ourselves from animals, but in learning to live like them."[130] In *Nostalghia*, the unkempt Domenico models himself on a dog's simple life, exemplifying Tarkovsky's exhortation "to start living differently... closer to nature and animals and plants."[131]

Another reason why the Cynics embraced association with dogs was because dogs have historically performed a guardian role in human life. The Cynics, like dogs, "lived on the margins of human cities but remained visible within them. They believed that their way of life and worldview led to genuine human flourishing, and they hoped to share that worldview and way of life with fellow human beings."[132] The Cynics, through extreme methods, stylized themselves as protectors of humanity, seeking to warn human beings against their own callowness. "The eyes of all mankind," Domenico says, "are looking at the pit into which we are plunging." Like the Cynics, Domenico claims to have humanity's best interest at heart, just as dogs—especially Domenico's chosen breed of a German shepherd, the consummate guard dog—are known for their loyalty. A possible source for the word "dog" in Russian, *pes*, derives from the Latin *specio*, meaning "to look," which gave rise to the Russian *smotret'* ("to watch") and *storozh* ("watchman").[133] The Cynics appealed to dogs' alertness to safeguard humanity's very humanness. If nothing else, the onslaught of watchdogs made famous by Hollywood cinema, such as Lassie, substantiates the Cynics' belief that we turn to dogs to warn, protect, and uplift us. Analogously—by circuitously bringing together Beethoven, telekinesis, iconoclasts, trains, dogs, and Darwinism—Tarkovsky echoed the Cynics' canine-inspired philosophy by proclaiming that his films "served" a "higher and communal idea" that strove to shield humanity from the excesses and vanities of modern life.[134] Fulfilling the role of the German shepherd, Stalker, Domenico, and Tarkovsky himself—these human watchdogs—endeavor to protect us from ourselves.

COMPANIONSHIP

The closeness between human beings and dogs in Tarkovsky's cinema unavoidably refers us to the theory of "companion species" pioneered by the posthumanist thinker Donna Haraway.[135] Though Haraway develops her thesis on companionship in her later writings, she first broaches these ideas in an earlier essay, "A Manifesto for Cyborgs: Science, Technology, and Socialist Feminism in the 1980s." Haraway demonstrates how distinctions between people, animals, and machines have been breached in modern life, as evidenced by devices and practices like transplant surgery, prosthetics, microchips, chemical consumption, and artificial intelligence. Humans, Haraway argues, are inescapably coconstituted subjects, interwoven into the world's (in)organic textures. "This messy, complex notion of human subjectivity makes it necessary to discard the traditional conception of the human individual as a distinct and cleanly separated organism and replace it with an image of the individual as cyborg—that is, a hybrid creature that has been assembled in and through various and more-than-human beings and influences."[136] In her later work, Haraway—a scientist by training with a PhD in developmental biology from Yale University—extrapolates her cyborg theory of organismal relationality to upend human-animal binaries through the concept and practice of companionship.

For Haraway, companionship as an ontological category is *the* fundamental building block of every being's existence. Life forms are not atomistic individuals awaiting interaction but products—Haraway uses terms like "hybrids," "mosaics," and "chimeras"—of their relations with others; all life is networked.[137] Deploying the term "companion," Haraway does not mean "pet," a word originating in the seventeenth century to refer to "hand-reared lambs" and spoiled children.[138] Haraway rejects the servile, bourgeois connotations of the term "pet" as scorned by capitalism's critics (including the early Bolsheviks), and her work embraces the more egalitarian word "companion" to rehabilitate the significance of domesticated animals in human society: "Changes in terminology can signal important mutations in the character of relationships—commercially, epistemologically, emotionally, and politically.... 'New' names mark changes in power, symbolically and materially remaking kin and kind."[139] Nomenclature, for Haraway, assumes ethical and ontological importance, and she riffs on the etymology of the word "companion," which derives from the Latin *cum*, meaning "with," and *pain*, "bread."[140] We break bread with our human companions just as we share food—often underneath the table—with our pets (as Stalker, Domenico, and Gorchakov do with their dogs in *Stalker* and *Nostalghia*). Humanity's task, per Haraway, is to reconceive itself as a companion species alongside other beings in ways that do not privilege humanness as an idealized category. "To be a genuine companion, a true comrade, is to care about" our entanglements with others "and to learn how to better inhabit them."[141]

Given their proximity to human beings, dogs are uniquely positioned to prompt reconsideration of humans' grandiose self-conception. As the Cynics make apparent, dogs have long straddled the boundary between nature and culture—they have been domesticated for at least fourteen thousand years (by far the longest of any species) and are part of our families, households, and public spaces.¹⁴² Despite dogs' integration into human society, however, certain canine traits refuse domestication, reminding us that there is a world outside human culture. The mythological trope of dogs transgressing metaphysical planes, as in Tarkovsky's cinema, takes its cue from dogs' literal traversal of outdoor and indoor spaces, the street and the home, nature and culture. Dogs are a threshold species, neither human nor fully animal; they throw into relief humanity's emotional, physical, and cultural entanglements with animals. "If I have a dog," Haraway writes, "my dog has a human."¹⁴³ Spotlighting her Australian shepherd Cayenne Pepper, Haraway explores how she and Cayenne exist in a never-ending "dance of relating," an "ontological choreography" that upends traditional human-animal hierarchies.¹⁴⁴ This pair of "reproductively silenced females"—"canid, hominid; pet, professor; bitch, woman; animal, human"—are "significantly other to each other" and each betray "a nasty developmental infection called love."¹⁴⁵ The term "nasty," which Haraway uses affectionately, stems from the unavoidably embodied—slobbery, hairy, muddy, smelly—relations between dogs and (their) humans. "I bet if you checked our DNA, you'd find some potent transfections between us. Her saliva must have the viral vectors. Surely, her darter-tongue kisses have been irresistible."¹⁴⁶ Together and for each other, "companion species build meaningful worlds, lives, and societies."¹⁴⁷

As discussed throughout this chapter, Tarkovsky recognized what it meant to experience a "nasty developmental infection called love" with a dog of his own—his German shepherd Dakus. The peculiar name Dakus, occasionally mistranslated as Dark, itself insinuates an idea of companionship.¹⁴⁸ It stems from the Russian verb *dakat'*, loosely meaning "to get along with" or "to be agreeable."¹⁴⁹ The name of Tarkovsky's dog thus implies an idea of camaraderie, a notion of cross-species amicability and communicability. Indeed, many photos exist of Tarkovsky and Dakus walking, relaxing, cuddling, sunbathing, playing, and hiking together, suggesting that the two were somewhat inseparable, not unlike Haraway and Cayenne.¹⁵⁰

In his diaries, Tarkovsky mentioned Dakus with increasing frequency as he started traveling to Italy in the late 1970s.¹⁵¹ "Last night I had a dream: it was spring; rain and puddles; I was taking Dakus for a walk. Some boozer fell into a puddle, terrified, and started fending Dakus off with his feet. Dakus of course had no intention of biting anybody."¹⁵² Tarkovsky's dream betokens his desire to be reunited with Dakus, who, Tarkovsky wrote, evinces all the virtuous traits—placidity, protectiveness, vigor—that ordinary people ("some boozer") do not. It is not by chance that in *Nostalghia*, the German shepherd first visits Gorchakov, a Russian émigré in Italy who shares Tarkovsky's first name, as he slips into a dream about his Russian homeland (where the dog also appears). The German shepherd personifies Tarkovsky's longing for companionship abroad. Later in *Nostalghia*, Domenico searches his dwelling for his German shepherd, whose name, we learn, is Zoe: the ancient Greek term for "life," which gave rise to the Latin *zoon*, meaning "animal."[153] "Zoe! Where are you?" Domenico cries. "Zoe, answer me! Zoe, you know I'm scared of being alone." The dog is a kind of emotional support animal for Domenico, just as the nameless black German shepherd—a creature of the Zo(n)e—is for Stalker; like Domenico, he feeds it bread, relating to the etymological origin of the term "com*pan*ion." Yet Stalker's and Domenico's close relations with their dogs throw into focus the emotional and psychological *pain* that Tarkovsky felt while separated from Dakus. Tarkovsky voiced his concern that he may never see Dakus again after the dog fell "ill for four days and nearly died" in August 1979.[154] All these manifestations of care relay the fondness Tarkovsky felt for Dakus, a precondition for Harawayian companionship.

Unlike Haraway, however, Tarkovsky did *not* open himself to a more contingent, "messy" relationship with Dakus that could dislodge his prejudices about human primacy. Besides its implications of agreeableness, the word *dakat'* also bears a pejorative connotation. It is etymologically linked to the Russian word "yes" (*da*) and refers to pushovers and sycophants: those who are incapable of saying anything but "yes" and who cannot think for themselves. Though Dakus's name broaches an idea of human-animal camaraderie, it nevertheless echoes a Cartesian understanding of animals as passive creatures without minds of their own in service of free-thinking humans. Dakus was like a "yes man" who did not subvert or challenge Tarkovsky's elevated humanness. Rather, Dakus, whom Tarkovsky had a habit of simply calling "Dak" (as if the dog's name was "yeah"), reified Tarkovsky's sense of self.[155] "Our dog is very human," Tarkovsky said. "He understands words, he truly feels human emotions."[156] Tarkovsky personified Dakus less as a "significant other" and more as an inferior, an extension of his own psychology—a "little human" or pet—kept for his personal edification, precisely the sort of anthropomorphic attitude toward domesticated animals Haraway adamantly rejects.

Whenever Tarkovsky described dogs that were not his own, he employed a far more dismissive vocabulary: "slavish," "tired," "lost."[157] Dog as an abstract category of species caused Tarkovsky's affection for the species to wane. The German shepherds in *Stalker* and *Nostalghia* are depicted reverentially and poetically because they resemble Dakus, whose memory, for Tarkovsky, triggered deeply personal associations. These German shepherds, in other words, are extensions of Tarkovsky, stripped of their independent, obstreperous "dogness." We should not be surprised, then, that several dogs (who did *not* resemble Dakus) were harmed in the making of Tarkovsky's most violent film, *Andrei Rublev*. When one of the film's medieval iconographers, Kirill (Ivan Lapikov), learns that he has not been invited to Moscow to paint the Cathedral of the Annunciation, he abandons his monastery in protest. Kirill's dog chases after him, looking for companionship, but Kirill bludgeons it to death. Though Kirill expresses concern for his dog earlier in the film—he twice asks his apprentice whether the dog has been fed—Tarkovsky has Kirill slay the dog to convey the savagery lurking in all human beings, even an otherwise pious monk. By killing the dog, Kirill (who earlier claimed that he would "serve" his mentor "like a dog" until the day he died) surrenders a critical piece of his humanity necessary for making art. We hear the dog's cries as Kirill beats it, and we then see a close-up of the dog's body splayed out in the blood-stained snow, flailing its limbs before its last breath escapes it.[158]

This extreme close-up of a small, furry creature dying before a camera replicates a shot from *Rules of the Game* (*La règle du jeu*, 1939) by Jean Renoir, whom Tarkovsky venerated.[159] Halfway through Renoir's film, the refined, bourgeois, and (like Tarkovsky) stylishly dressed characters embark on an afternoon hunt. This infamous scene turns Renoir's picture into a snuff film in which scores of pheasants and rabbits are dispatched with ruthless efficiency. At one point, Renoir magnifies an image of a wounded rabbit convulsing on the ground before it expires, an image Tarkovsky re-creates in *Andrei Rublev* vis-à-vis Kirill's bludgeoned dog. Both Renoir and Tarkovsky enlisted real animal death for narrative ends: Renoir had a rabbit destroyed to convey the latent cruelty of the European bourgeoisie—the hunt a metaphor for the rise of fascism among the French upper class in the 1930s—while Tarkovsky had a dog killed in *Andrei Rublev* to stress the consequences of turning one's back on faith. Yet the dead dog in *Andrei Rublev* carries far greater affective charge than the rabbit in *Rules of the Game* because dogs are considered in Western society, particularly in the pet-crazed culture of the Soviet 1960s, to be outside the category of the edible and, therefore, killable. Whereas rabbit hunting is—as implied by the title of Renoir's film—"fair game," dogs are "animals to be petted, not potted."[160] The slaying of a dog in *Andrei Rublev* viscerally impresses the film's themes of callousness and cruelty on Tarkovsky's viewers, many of whom, like Tarkovsky, were dog owners themselves.

Later in *Andrei Rublev*, a band of Mongols arrives at another monastery and instigates a fight among a pack of dogs. The camera dwells on the snarling

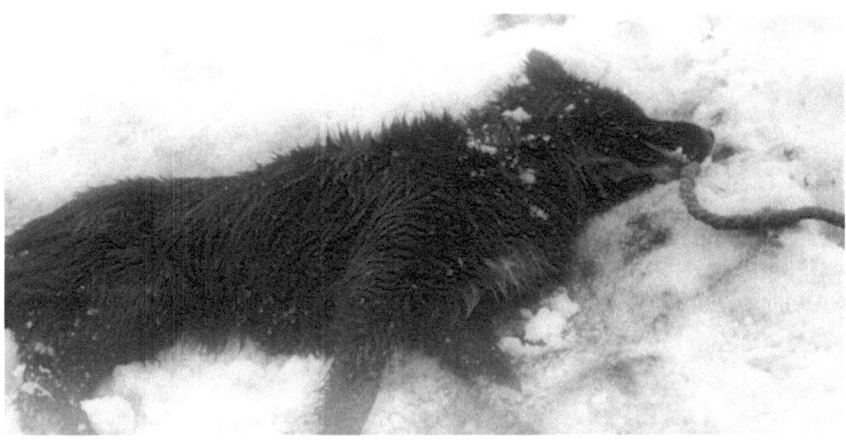

A dog clubbed to death by a rogue monk, a brutal image that conveys the limits of Tarkovsky's affection for dogs. Still from *Andrei Rublev*, 1966.

canines as they viciously swarm each other. This dogfight reenacts an identical scene from Konstantin Iudin's *Frontier Post in the Mountains* (*Zastava v gorakh*, 1953), a Stalin-era war film about the imperviousness of Soviet borderlands. Early in Iudin's film, we see some Tajik tribesmen, just like the Mongols in *Andrei Rublev*, "take pleasure" in a dogfight in contrast to "more humane" Russians, who look on with horror and treat *their* canine companions with compassion.[161] Tarkovsky reenacts Iudin's dogfight in *Andrei Rublev* to convey what he perceived as Russia's cultural superiority over ostensibly savage Easterners. Rublev, tellingly, turns his back on the dogfight. Even if Tarkovsky condemns the mistreatment of dogs by the Mongols, he nevertheless indulges in images of cruelty that betray his perception of animals as usable (and, ultimately, disposable) resources to project his worldview. In one fell swoop, Tarkovsky conjoins prejudicial ethnic commentary with animal abuse, revealing the ease by which notions of human supremacy—whether cultural or species—can reinforce one another, a topic explored in chapter 4.

Throughout his cinema, then, Tarkovsky relies on dogs as symbolic devices capable of incarnating his attitudes toward humankind. Tarkovsky could be accused of fetishizing dogs, treating them, in the words of the French philosophers Gilles Deleuze and Félix Gauttari, as "Oedipal animals": animals—often pets—that "invite us to regress" and "draw us into narcissistic contemplation."[162] Human analyses of culture frequently hinge on ascribing animals certain human features that turn them into "objects of symbolic capture," negating the promise of reciprocal companionship posited by

Haraway.¹⁶³ If for Haraway, dogs are "not a projection, nor the realization of an intention, nor a telos of anything," then by contrast, dogs for Tarkovsky exist *for* his filmography; he leaves dogs no choice but to assent (*dakat'*) to his symbolic, ideological, and aesthetic designs.¹⁶⁴ Unlike Haraway, Tarkovsky does not "narrate this co-constitutive history" of human-canine "co-evolution in natureculture."¹⁶⁵

In *Nostalghia*, Domenico points to a gaggle of decadent Italians (including the owner of the cocker spaniel with which this chapter began) and asks his German shepherd: "Have you heard their talk, what they're interested in? You've got to be different!" In Domenico's formulation, the humans are dehumanized and debased, while Domenico's dog is commanded to acquiesce to his standards of behavior. Ironically, Domenico implies that modern-day people have become animalistic, whereas human beings' true yet forgotten essence flickers in his pet dog. "Individuals without spirituality," Tarkovsky said, "exist on the level of animals."¹⁶⁶ In turn, as implied by Domenico, Tarkovsky correlated what he understood as dogs' best traits—persistence, authenticity, nonconformity—with human potential, while he associated dogs' worst traits with dogs themselves: aggressiveness, ignorance, impulsivity. It is not by chance that in *Andrei Rublev*, Kirill is slandered as "a dog" before beating his own dog to death. Kirill indulges a predatory economy of aggression—a dog-eat-dog world—indicative of the wilderness.

The one frontier that Tarkovsky's dogs do not cross, then, is the frontier separating humanity from animality. Dogs, for Tarkovsky, accompany and edify humans without dislodging dominant conceptions of anthropocentrism. Dogs remind us not to stray from the core humanist values Tarkovsky believed were lost in modern life. Somewhat counterintuitively, Tarkovsky uses dogs to warn us from becoming too doglike. Despite being a dog lover, Tarkovsky is largely unconcerned with what is at stake for *dogs* in their encounters with humanity. Rather, he is preoccupied with only one-half of human-dog relations: What effect do dogs have on us? Humans can learn from dogs, but we should never curb our ideals on their behalf.

By any stretch of the imagination, then, Tarkovsky is not a posthumanist. Posthumanists like Haraway couple their critiques of human society with a rejection of "essentialist and hierarchical divisions between culture and nature" to foster "non-anthropocentric worldviews" that embrace humanity's "ontological entanglements."¹⁶⁷ By contrast, Tarkovsky is an obstinate humanist—a neohumanist—dedicated to reinvigorating an enlightened human subject in opposition to purportedly soulless animals. Tarkovsky's cinema refuses an ontologically disruptive, Harawayian experience of human-canine camaraderie.

Though Tarkovsky harbored deep affection for dogs, humanity's position over dogs remains intact throughout his cinema. © Gueorgui Pinkhassov/Magnum Photos.

For all of Tarkovsky's film dogs' links to classical philosophy, these dogs are only *like* philosophers. Dogs are dogs, not Dogmatists; "humans think, whereas dogs scent (we are mind, they are body)."[168] Tarkovsky relates to dogs as symbols, ideas, and templates but never *with* dogs as partners or companions with lives mutually, albeit asymmetrically, at stake in human-canine encounters. In Tarkovsky's filmography, our position over dogs remains intact—the hierarchy endures—as corroborated by the numerous photographs of Tarkovsky towering over Dakus. The dog is (still) not at the philosopher's side but dutifully at his feet.

NOTES

1. See Derrida, *Animal That Therefore I Am*.
2. Derrida, *Animal That Therefore I Am*, 4–5.
3. Fudge, *Pets*, 84.
4. Tarkovsky, *Interviews*, 87.
5. Tarkovsky, *Interviews*, 87.
6. Martin, "Stilyaga from Siberia," 140.
7. Fudge, *Pets*, 74, 79.
8. For Soviet pet keeping, see Nelson, "Bringing the Beast Back In."
9. See, e.g., Gaita, *Philosopher's Dog*.
10. McLean, "Introduction: Wonder Dogs," 9.
11. Burt, *Animals in Film*, 22.
12. Friedberg, "Der vierbeinige Andere und die Projektion im Kino," 4.
13. Marks, *Touch*, 25.
14. For Thaw culture, see Rutten, *Sincerity After Communism*, 74–77.
15. Nelson, "Bringing the Beast Back In," 45.
16. For the dog-serf-master hierarchy, see Mondry, *Political Animals*, 39–46. Mondry notes that it was Aleksandr Pushkin who first thematized this relationship in his story "Dubrovskii" (1841), published only posthumously because it so negatively portrayed landowners.
17. Mondry, *Political Animals*, 34–35.
18. Mondry, *Political Animals*, 34–35.
19. Berger, *About Looking*, 14.
20. Mikhail Bulgakov notably satirized these positivist attitudes toward animals in his contemporaneous novella *Heart of a Dog* (*Sobach'e serdtse*, 1925).
21. Nelson, "Hearth for a Dog," 126.
22. Nelson, "Bringing the Beast Back In," 54.
23. Tarkovsky, *Interviews*, 48.
24. Tarkovsky, *Time Within Time*, 114. Tarkovsky called *Walden* "a wonderful book" and regularly quoted Thoreau in his diaries. See Tarkovsky, *Sculpting in Time*, 46.
25. Tarkovsky, *Time Within Time*, 114.
26. Gornykh, "*Trava-Travlya-Trata*," 43.
27. Burt, *Animals in Film*, 36.
28. Dogs' salutary effect on humans is also a perennial theme of post-Stalinist literature, as in Georgii Vladimov's *Faithful Ruslan: The Story of a Border Dog* (*Vernyi Ruslan: Istoriia karayl'noi sobaki*, 1975) and Varlam Shalamov's "Tamara the Bitch" ("Suka Tamara," 1959).
29. Garber, *Dog Love*, 15.
30. Mondry, *Political Animals*, 8.

31. Nelson, "Bringing the Beast Back In," 50.
32. For the motif of children in Thaw-era cinema, see Prokhorov, "Adolescent and the Child in the Cinema of the Thaw."
33. Nelson, "Bringing the Beast Back In," 51.
34. For these photographs, see Chiaramonte and Tarkovsky, *Instant Light*, 27, 33, 37; Tarkovsky, *Time Within Time*, 182, 190, 327.
35. Tarkovsky, *Interviews*, 86.
36. Tarkovsky had a habit of calling his family while abroad to speak with Dakus, who, he reported, had in one instance "learnt some new songs" for him to "sing" over the telephone. See Tarkovsky, *Time Within Time*, 364.
37. Tarkovsky, *Interviews*, 86.
38. Tarkovsky, *Interviews*, 169–70.
39. Tarkovsky, *Time Within Time*, 300. "Larochka" and "Tyapus" are, respectively, nicknames for Tarkovsky's second wife (Larisa) and his youngest son (Andrei). "Tyapus" is, tellingly, also a common name used for dogs in Russian, reiterating the connection Tarkovsky posited between dogs and (his own) children.
40. For Hitchcock's influence on Tarkovsky, see Robinson, *Sacred Cinema of Andrei Tarkovsky*, 146–47, 192.
41. For the applicability of the term "middle class" to postwar Soviet culture, see Chernyshova, *Soviet Consumer Culture in the Brezhnev Era*, 103–13. It is telling that many Soviet film dogs had names, as if full-fledged members of the middle-class household: Mukhtar the German shepherd; Bim the English setter; and Ressi the Airedale in *Adventures of an Android*.
42. Mondry, *Political Animals*, 184.
43. Nelson, "Hearth for a Dog," 134–35.
44. *Stalker* was in part inspired by the 1957 nuclear explosion in Chelyabinsk, making it a "prophetic vision of the forthcoming Chernobyl tragedy." See Skakov, *Cinema of Tarkovsky*, 149. It is also rumored that Tarkovsky—along with his wife Larisa and Solonitsyn—died because of a cancer contracted while filming *Stalker*, which took place near several defunct power plants in Soviet Estonia. It is as if the air of the film—*Stalker*'s nuclear mystique—imprinted itself into Tarkovsky's skin like an image imprinted onto celluloid.
45. For the Buddhist undercurrent in late Soviet culture, which enabled secular art "to reach out to the divine on its own terms," see Kahn et al., *History of Russian Literature*, 589. The Buddhist turn in late Soviet culture is no better exemplified than by Dmitrii Prigov's chanting—"Buddhist manner"—performances of Pushkin's *Evgeny Onegin* (1833). Kahn et al., *History of Russian Literature*, 590.
46. Skakov, *Cinema of Tarkovsky*, 147.
47. The connection between *Stalker* and *The Wizard of Oz* is made more explicit by Stalker's remark after entering the Zone that "the flowers for some

reason don't smell." When Dorothy arrives at Oz, the camera pays special attention to the myriad flowers ensconcing her, obviously made from cellophane. These fake, candy-coated flowers underscore the artificial and self-reflexive nature of Oz as a specifically cinematic site; film is an audiovisual medium, not an olfactory one, so the flowers in Oz and the Zone, by definition, cannot emit smell. For the metacinematic elements of *Stalker*, see Foster, "Where Flowers Bloom but Have No Scent." Additionally, the attributes represented by the trio of Oz characters—Lion, Scarecrow, and Tin Man—respectively map onto Tarkovsky's: Stalker (courage), Professor (brain), Writer (heart). For *Stalker* and *The Wizard of Oz*, see Barceló, "En la Zona de Oz."

48. *Stalker*'s belabored production history also accounts for the clashing colors. See Johnson and Petrie, *Films of Andrei Tarkovsky*, 137–38.

49. Dyer, *Zona*, 81.

50. Fudge, *Pets*, 76–77.

51. Sexton, *Outlines of Skepticism*, 3.

52. Quoted in Fudge, *Pets*, 76.

53. Fudge, *Pets*, 77.

54. Plato, *Republic*, 372.

55. Long, "Who Let the Dogs Out?," 132. For Tarkovsky on Plato, see *Sculpting in Time*, 108.

56. Fudge, *Pets*, 77

57. Cited in Boas, "Theriophily," 384.

58. *Oxford English Dictionary*, "stalker." As Tarkovsky writes, "'Stalker,' is from the word 'to stalk'—to creep." *Time Within Time*, 148.

59. Besides pet keeping, Stalker also reflects the postwar Soviet trend of book collecting. See Lovell, "Publishing and the Book Trade in the Post-Stalin Era." Throughout Tarkovsky's cinema, we frequently encounter images of burned books and textual documents (dissertations, photographs, and, in *Nostalghia*, a collection of his father's poetry). The motif of charred books is so prominent that Robert Bird describes Tarkovsky as a "bibliomachist," suggesting that for Tarkovsky, the written word possessed secret, potentially subversive knowledge against which political authorities sought to guard themselves through book burning. See Bird, *Andrei Tarkovsky*, 22. Tarkovsky's biblioclasm locates him in an age-old discourse about the enduring power of literature in Russian culture and cinematically enacts the famous line from Mikhail Bulgakov's *The Master and Margarita*—"manuscripts don't burn" (*rukopisi ne goryat*)—a novel released at the height of Tarkovsky's career that, discussed in chapter 3, he hoped to adapt on screen. See Tarkovsky, *Time Within Time*, 163.

60. Writer's mistrustful monologue about the Zone echoes Han Solo's misgivings about "the force" in *Star Wars: A New Hope* (1977), a film, cited in chapter 1, that Tarkovsky immensely enjoyed. "I've never seen anything to make me

believe there's one all-powerful force controlling everything," Solo says. "It's all alotta simple tricks and nonsense." In *Stalker*, Tarkovsky recycles Lucas's binary between skeptical outsiders (Han Solo, Writer) and mystical believers (Obi-Wan Kenobi, Luke Skywalker, Stalker) who preach the faith in Yoda-like riddles.

    61. Fudge, *Pets*, 78–87.
    62. Fudge, *Pets*, 81.
    63. Montaigne, "Apology for Raymond Sebond," 401.
    64. Montaigne, "Apology for Raymond Sebond," 401.
    65. Montaigne, "Apology for Raymond Sebond," 401.
    66. Montaigne, "Apology for Raymond Sebond," 401.
    67. Fudge, *Pets*, 79; Kete, *Beast in the Boudoir*, 56.
    68. The black cat here also recalls the most famous black cat of Russian literature, Behemoth in Bulgakov's *The Master and Margarita*, one of the devil's henchmen who terrorizes Moscow just as the Mongols wreak havoc on an Orthodox church in *Andrei Rublev*.
    69. Mondry, *Political Animals*, 299–300.
    70. Fudge, *Pets*, 78.
    71. Skakov, *Cinema of Tarkovsky*, 148.
    72. Tarkovsky, *Interviews*, 122.
    73. Quoted in Johnson and Petrie, *Films of Andrei Tarkovsky*, 38.
    74. Tarkovsky's dense imagery also situates him in the "Aesopian language" of late Soviet culture, which afforded writers and artists a "system of hints and allusions" to smuggle nonconformist ideas past censors, much like Stalker sneaks "tourists" into the Zone under the nose of state authorities. See Kahn et al., *History of Russian Literature*, 551.
    75. Skakov concludes that, in *Stalker*, Tarkovsky "speak[s] without saying anything concrete," deliberately leaving "gaps in the viewer's perception" that "pass on 'hope'" to viewers, hungry for answers. This line of reasoning resonates with my argument that Tarkovsky incites us, like dogs, to sniff out answers. Skakov, *Cinema of Tarkovsky*, 153.
    76. The character's elliptical journey that ends with everything changed while paradoxically the same cannot help but (again) remind us of Dorothy returning from Oz to Kansas in *The Wizard of Oz*. As Salman Rushdie writes, "So Oz finally *becomes* home. The imagined world becomes the actual world, as it does for us all, because the truth is that, once we leave our childhood places and start to make up our lives, armed only with what we know and who we are, we come to understand that the real secret of the ruby slippers is not that 'there's no place like home,' but, rather, that there is no longer any such plays *as* home—except, of course, for the homes we make, or the homes that are made for us, in Oz. Which is anywhere—and everywhere—except the place from which we began." See Rushdie, "Out of Kansas."

77. See Widdis, "Border."
78. Mondry, *Political Animals*, 252–56.
79. See Flaim, "German Shepherd Dog History."
80. Levshakova, "Angely-khraniteli," 43.
81. The famous Ukrainian border dog trainer Nikita Karatsupa was featured on Soviet currency in the 1930s. Mondry, *Political Animals*, 253.
82. Žižek, "Andrei Tarkovsky, or the Thing from Inner Space," 170.
83. In Dovlatov's novel, "The prison guard dogs' lack of loyalty towards anybody reflects" Dovlatov's attitude "towards the patriotic discourse that created a cult of the police dog.... Given a chance, these dogs would tear apart their handlers." Mondry, *Political Animals*, 244.
84. Lippit, *Atomic Light*, 56.
85. The boxer, it should be noted, was a beloved breed among Soviet pet owners, popularized in part by Leonid Gaida's sensational blockbusters *Operation Y and Shurik's Other Adventures* (*Operatsiia "Y" i drugie prikliucheniia*, 1965) and *The Diamond Arm* (*Brilliantovaia ruka*, 1969). See "5 Porod sobak, kotorye byli zhutko populiarny v SSSR."
86. Žižek, "Andrei Tarkovsky, or the Thing from Inner Space," 155–56.
87. Bach, in Tarkovsky's estimation, was free of the "vanity which is typical of the West," and his music is, accordingly, linked with deep spirituality and religiosity. See Tarkovsky, "Andrei Tarkovsky on *The Sacrifice*." Tarkovsky subscribed to the myth that took hold in the postwar years of Bach as a humble, spiritual craftsman closer to God than his Enlightenment contemporaries. "The view of Bach which prevails today," wrote Theodor Adorno, "in him, it is said, there is once again the revelation—in the middle of the Century of Enlightenment—of the time-honored bounds of tradition, of the spirit of medieval polyphony, of the theologically vaulted cosmos." Adorno, *Prisms*, 135. Tarkovsky's understanding of Bach's music as a spiritual balm against the soullessness of technical modernity was distinctly modern.
88. See Surkova, "'Gamlet' Andreia Tarkovskogo."
89. Nelson, "Cold War Celebrity and the Courageous Canine Scout," 137. In another major Soviet film, *Nine Days of One Year* (*Deviat' dnei odnogo goda*, 1962) by Mikhail Romm—Tarkovsky's film school advisor—we see a close-up of a laboratory dog staring at the camera through a cage. This morose image, a kind of anti-Laika, rebukes the Soviet space program for neglecting animal compassion.
90. See Green, *Andrei Tarkovsky*, 103. For mythological watchdogs, see McHugh, *Dog*, 40–42.
91. Chiaramonte and Tarkovsky, *Instant Light*, 15, 23.
92. Bird, *Andrei Tarkovsky*, 165.
93. Truppin, "And Then There Was Sound," 235.
94. Truppin, "And Then There Was Sound," 236.

95. Some scholars have analogized filmgoers to Plato's prisoners and the experience of watching a film to Plato's cavern walls. See, e.g., Anderson, *Shadow Philosophy*.

96. These images of industrial decay also recall Michelangelo Antonioni's *Red Desert* (*Il deserto rosso*, 1964), written by Italian screenwriter Tonino Guerra, who collaborated with Tarkovsky on *Nostalghia*.

97. Tarkovsky, *Interviews*, 85.

98. See Vertov, *Kino-Eye*.

99. Bazin, *What Is Cinema?*, 15.

100. Skakov, *Cinema of Tarkovsky*, 221.

101. Tarkovsky, *Sculpting in Time*, 42.

102. Quoted in Russell, "One James Cameron Action Film That Andrey Tarkovsky Loved."

103. Tarkovsky, *Interviews*, 87. Fascinatingly, in an exploration of the culture of socioeconomic dislocation in the United States of the 2010s, American journalist George Packer spoke with a displaced IT worker who, having taken part in the Occupy Wall Street protests of 2011, cited Tarkovsky's "strange" film about "three guys traipsing through the woods" as his favorite movie. It is as if *Stalker*'s lost characters capture the experience of being adrift in the postindustrial American economy, which, as Packer notes, fueled the political rise of Donald J. Trump. See Packer, *Unwinding*, 364–65.

104. Pontara, "Beethoven Overcome," 304.

105. Tarkovsky, *Interviews*, 52.

106. Pontara, "Beethoven Overcome," 307, 309.

107. For the European bourgeoisie's triumphalist ideology, see Hobsbawm, *Age of Capital*, 230–50.

108. Hobsbawm, *Age of Capital*, 55, 57.

109. Tarkovsky, *Sculpting in Time*, 240.

110. See Kämpf, "Beethoven's Music Gone Astray." For Tarkovsky, "Ode to Joy" may have also negatively evoked memories of Stalinism: "In the mid-1930s, articles in journals exhorted composers to turn to the symphony . . . as the form most appropriate for the heroism of the age; Beethoven's famous revolutionary work with its choral finale hymning universal brotherhood was held up as the ideal. . . . The high point of influence came in 1936 when it was performed (along with Georgian folksongs and extracts from Georgian operas, all in honor of Stalin) at the Bolshoi Theater as part of the celebrations marking the signing of the Soviet Constitution." Bullock, "Musical Imagination of Andrei Platonov," 55.

111. Bethea, *Shape of the Apocalypse in Modern Russian Fiction*, 58.

112. See Strugatsky and Strugatsky, *Roadside Picnic*.

113. Strugatsky and Strugatsky, *Roadside Picnic*, 185.

114. Hobsbawm, *Age of Capital*, 259.

115. Freud, "Difficulty in the Path of Psycho-analysis," 139–44.
116. Whereas the Soviets launched dogs into space, the Americans sent monkeys, most notably a chimp named Ham in 1961, which adds a further sci-fi inflection to Monkey in *Stalker*.
117. Johnson and Petrie, *Films of Andrei Tarkovsky*, 153.
118. Calarco, *Boundaries of Human Nature*, 30.
119. Tarkovsky, *Sculpting in Time*, 42. Tarkovsky's critique of modern society is also implied by the fate of Stalker's mentor, Porcupine (*Dikobraz*), who, like Monkey, bears an animal nickname. We learn that Porcupine once entered the Zone's wish-room, hoping that it would grant his late brother a renewed lease on life. When Porcupine left the Zone, however, he learned that his brother had not been restored, and, instead, he had won tremendous wealth. This suggests that Porcupine's most deeply held desire—which the Zone intuited better than he—was not love for his family but self-enrichment. In response to this unbearable truth, Porcupine hangs himself, much like Judas. The parable of Porcupine, Tarkovsky implies, shows how deep seated humanity's materialistic desires have become in modern society, turning human beings, as alluded by Porcupine's name, into "warped" or "wild" (*dikii*) images (*obraz*) of their true selves.
120. Stalker and Domenico have also been aptly compared to medieval holy fools. See Efrid, "Holy Fool in Late Tarkovsky."
121. Tarkovsky, *Sculpting in Time*, 209.
122. Calarco, *Boundaries of Human Nature*, 39.
123. Calarco, *Boundaries of Human Nature*, 34.
124. Swedish filmmaker Ingmar Bergman incorporated footage of Đức's self-immolation into *Persona* (1966), a film Tarkovsky saw "a great many times." Tarkovsky, *Sculpting in Time*, 166.
125. Earlier in *Nostalghia*, the noise of a buzzsaw supplants Beethoven's music, again signaling Tarkovsky's deep-seated antipathy toward Beethoven's triumphalism.
126. Tarkovsky, *Time Within Time*, 21.
127. Domenico's dog also recalls the German shepherd in Robert Bresson's *L'Argent* (1983), which howls at a money-hungry axe murderer, a character clearly indebted to Raskolnikov in Dostoevsky's *Crime and Punishment* (*Prestuplenie i nakazanie*, 1866). *L'Argent* was itself based on Leo Tolstoy's novella *The Forged Coupon* (*Fal'shivyi kupon*, 1911). For Tarkovsky's admiration of Bresson, see *Sculpting in Time*, 94–95.
128. Calarco, *Boundaries of Human Nature*, 32.
129. Calarco, *Boundaries of Human Nature*, 40.
130. Calarco, *Boundaries of Human Nature*, 38.
131. Tarkovsky, *Time Within Time*, 157–58.
132. Calarco, *Boundaries of Human Nature*, 39.

133. "Proiskhozhdenie slova pes," *Etimologicheskie onlain-slovari russkogo iazyka*.
134. Tarkovsky, *Sculpting in Time*, 38.
135. See Haraway, *Companion Species Manifesto*.
136. Calarco, *Animal Studies*, 48.
137. Haraway, "Manifesto for Cyborgs," 177.
138. Fudge, *Pets*, 88.
139. Haraway, *When Species Meet*, 135.
140. Haraway, *When Species Meet*, 17.
141. Calarco, *Boundaries of Human Nature*, 133.
142. McHugh, *Dog*, 16.
143. Haraway, *Companion Species Manifesto*, 54.
144. Haraway, *When Species Meet*, 25, 67.
145. Haraway, *When Species Meet*, 15.
146. Haraway, *Companion Species Manifesto*, 1.
147. Calarco, *Boundaries of Human Nature*, 133.
148. Tarkovsky, *Interviews*, 87.
149. See "Leksicheskoe znachenie clova dakat'."
150. For photographs of Tarkovsky and Dakus, see Gueorgui Pinkhassov's collection of photos (some of which are found in this chapter) at *Magnum Photos*. Tarkovsky invited Pinkhassov, a fellow alum of Moscow's Institute of Cinematography (VGIK), to document the making of *Stalker*.
151. See, e.g., Tarkovsky, *Time Within Time*, 190.
152. Tarkovsky, *Time Within Time*, 356.
153. *Oxford English Dictionary*, "zoon (n.)."
154. Tarkovsky, *Time Within Time*, 220.
155. Tarkovsky, *Time Within Time*, 188, 211.
156. Tarkovsky, *Interviews*, 87.
157. Tarkovsky, *Interviews*, 83; Tarkovsky, *Time Within Time*, 15, 225.
158. Tarkovsky excised this image from the final cut of *Andrei Rublev* at the behest of Soviet censors.
159. Tarkovsky, *Sculpting in Time*, 90.
160. Fudge, *Animal*, 35.
161. Mondry, *Political Animals*, 261.
162. Deleuze and Gauttari, *Thousand Plateaus*, 240.
163. Ryan, *Animal Theory*, 31.
164. Haraway, *Companion Species Manifesto*, 11.
165. Haraway, *Companion Species Manifesto*, 12.
166. Tarkovsky, *Interviews*, 145.
167. Ryan, *Animal Theory*, 69.
168. Fudge, *Pets*, 77.

THREE

BIRDS

IN A DIARY ENTRY DATED a month after he learned that the censorious studio officials at Mosfil'm had accepted *Solaris*—a movie about an intergalactic voyage—without requesting any major alterations, Andrei Tarkovsky expressed his incredulity and recounted a dream about zero gravity flight.

> I was looking up at the sky; and high, high above me it seemed to be slowly boiling, like light had materialized, like the fibres of sunlit fabric.... And those tiny fibres, light-bearing, living threads, seemed to be moving and floating and becoming like birds, hovering so high up that they could never be reached. So high that if the birds were to lose feathers the feathers wouldn't fall, they wouldn't come down to earth, they would fly upwards, be carried off and vanish from our world.... "They're storks," I suddenly heard someone say.[1]

Tarkovsky characterized birds, specifically storks, as alien-like beings removed from humanity's earthbound habitat. Etymologically, the word "human" comes from the Latin *humanus*, which is related to the term "soil" (*humus*). By contrast, the origins of the word "bird" bear a relation to the Germanic *fleug*, a term denoting an instance of flight, which gave rise to the English "fowl" and German *Vogel* for "flying creature," the exact meaning of the Russian term *ptitsa*.[2] Fundamentally, human beings are creatures of the ground, and birds are creatures of the air: inhabitants of entirely separate worlds.

Despite their divergent evolutionary trajectories, however, humans and birds have much in common. Both rely on high-acuity vision to navigate their surroundings, unlike animals more reliant on olfactory capabilities; both are highly mobile yet construct semipermanent domiciles (nests, houses); both are bipedal and endothermic; both are migratory, comprising somewhat of a global community; and both are relatively monogamous, with the nuclear family constituting their societies' basic unit. "Many birds even lock beaks in what looks like a human kiss. Like human beings, birds don't quite seem to be animals; in fact, we often speak of 'birds and animals' as though these were separate categories."[3] Yet for all our similarities, birds, because they dwell above us, seem distant from humanity's everyday activity—even if they are the only wild animals many people of the late twentieth and early twenty-first centuries encounter on a daily basis.

The French anthropologist Claude Lévi-Strauss noted these fundamental (in)congruencies between avian and anthropological ways of life: "[Birds] form a community which is independent of our own but, precisely because of this independence, appears to us like another society, homologous to that which we live."[4] Birds, in other words, exist in a parallel civilization that is identifiably human, on the one hand, and deeply unfamiliar, on the other. What person has not dreamed of flight, the ultimate metaphor for escaping the human condition? "Consequently everything objective conspires to make us think of the bird as a metaphorical human society: is it not after all literally parallel to it on another level?"[5] Birds, then, play an opposite role in human life than dogs do. Dogs—far from constituting a parallel civilization—have been fully integrated into humans' daily lives (literally at our feet), whereas birds are kept as pets much less frequently, freely roam the wild, and (certainly unlike dogs and cats) are still hunted, taxidermized, and eaten.

Thus, Tarkovsky's depictions of birds are the reverse of his representations of dogs. Birds are rarely encountered in his films as singular beings capable of commanding the camera's attention. They are never named, and they do not accompany his characters—except, of course, the rooster kept as a pet by the raving madman in *Ivan's Childhood*, whose home and family were destroyed by the Nazis. That this man finds companionship not with a dog but with a bird (kept on a leash, no less) signals, for Tarkovsky, the depths of his insanity. Unlike dogs, birds occupy the background rather than the foreground of Tarkovsky's settings, yet they are nevertheless omnipresent in his films. We find birds even where we would least expect them, as in *Solaris*, where birds are heard aboard a spacecraft at the edge of the known cosmos.

While birds saturate the soundscape of Tarkovsky's cinematic universe, we rarely see them. As in life, birds surround us, but their precise locations remain unknown or unnoticed; they are everywhere and nowhere, heard but only sporadically seen, their lives unfolding above our heads in treetops and the sky. This ubiquity makes birds the least striking animals of Tarkovsky's films but also perhaps the most significant. Unlike horses, dogs, and cows—the animals captivating Tarkovsky's imagination—most of Tarkovsky's birds are not domesticated. They exist independently within his settings; they are the animals he most closely associates with freedom.

Additionally, in contrast to Tarkovsky's other on-screen animals, very few of the birds we encounter throughout his films are of the same species. Across Tarkovsky's movies, we find categorically distinct types of birds: roosters, cuckoo birds, seagulls, swans, parakeets, swallows, doves, and sparrows, a veritable aviary. Occasionally, Tarkovsky aestheticizes and thematizes specific species of birds based on the cultural connotations they have accrued over the centuries. Cuckoo birds, for example, always represent death for Tarkovsky because of their foreboding connotations in Russian folklore.[6] At other times, though, Tarkovsky simply treats birds as birds—that is, as indistinct flocks, chirps, and airborne creatures representing catch-all ideas about beauty, freedom, flight, and spiritual passage. Tarkovsky's birds are heterogeneous and homogeneous, vague and particular. The ambivalent and ambiguous status birds occupy in human life as our world's (in)congruent analogs inscribes itself into Tarkovsky's avian portrayals.

This chapter begins by exploring how birds inspire much of Tarkovsky's beguiling cinematic aesthetic, which often replicates the elastic and weightless qualities of a flying bird. Through depictions of flight, Tarkovsky uncovers how the history of human aviation paralleled the history of cinema, revealing that film technology is itself symptomatic of humanity's desire to take to the skies and become birdlike. Tarkovsky's interest in flight also links his work to a Renaissance polymath similarly captivated by aeronautics: Leonardo da Vinci. Like Leonardo, Tarkovsky understood birds as symbols of creative freedom, and his innovative movies sought to reenergize his bleak Soviet milieu with Renaissance-style ingenuity. Tarkovsky's longing for escapist flight culminated with a surprise declaration of self-imposed exile in 1984.

For Tarkovsky, da Vinci was *the* consummate master of the arts, suggesting that Tarkovsky's admiration betrayed a desire to exert similar command over his creative practice. Though Tarkovsky's birds symbolize freedom, they also, ironically, expose his obsessive drive toward control, as Tarkovsky sought to painstakingly regulate birds' sounds, movement, and visual presence. Tarkovsky's manipulation of birds evokes the experiments of avian chronophotography conducted by nineteenth-century scientist Étienne-Jules Marey, whose work not only proclaimed technical mastery over nature but also prefigured cinematic technology.

The next section considers how Tarkovsky's portrayals of birds tangle with his depictions of women. Birds, for Tarkovsky, are often coded as feminine, hence the storks—a universal symbol of motherhood—in his dream recounted above. Tarkovsky sought to subject his female actors to the same control he exercised over his birds, as evidenced by his attempt to cajole the heroine of *Mirror* to kill a rooster on camera. The cruel implications of Tarkovsky's desire to spectate as a woman beheads a bird set the tone for this book's latter two chapters, which explore the image of the burnt cow in *Andrei Rublev* as well as that film's grisly episodes of horse death.

This chapter ends by turning to the long-standing cultural connections between birds and human demise that Tarkovsky activated throughout his work.[7] The deathly connotations of Tarkovsky's birds foretell the ecological calamity of Chernobyl, which coincided with the release of his final film, *The Sacrifice*. Drawing on Alfred Hitchcock's demonic fowls in *The Birds* (1963), Tarkovsky presciently uses birds to imagine the consequences of nuclear fallout.[8] Yet while Tarkovsky portrays birds as portents of doom, he also links them to experiences of spiritual renewal. Tarkovsky's bird images channel humanity's deep-seated ambivalence toward mortality, reflected in what Swiss psychologist Carl Jung described as a universal archetype of culture that maintains we defer our anxiety of death through the promise of rebirth.[9]

BIRD'S-EYE VIEW

Andrei Rublev begins with an image of an unidentified flying object, a bulbous contraption resembling a mushroom, hovering in the air. The stone facade of a twelfth-century Russian Orthodox church—the Church of the Intercession on the Nerl—backdrops this levitating material. The camera tracks downward to reveal several peasants tethering the contrivance to the ground through an elaborate system of ropes. Steam hisses from the contraption and blankets the peasants struggling to keep it earthbound. It dawns on us that this apparatus is a hot-air balloon, and these peasants are, in fact, medieval aeronauts preparing for takeoff. In this opening shot, Tarkovsky brings together religion and technology, spiritual piety and industrial ingenuity. Arrayed in cables and pulleys, the hallowed grounds of the church resemble a laboratory, a secular church of science from which humanity attempts to decipher the mysteries of creation.

We then see a man, Efim, coming to assist the balloonists as he is chased by a throng of angry peasants. The public, Tarkovsky implies, does not welcome this crude foray into aviation technology or the prospect of medieval engineers—men playing God—defying the laws of physics and disrupting the celestial order. From one angle, Tarkovsky depicts the mob of peasants as cultural reactionaries stuck in the Dark Ages, attempting to foil scientific progress. Their hostile and suspicious reaction to human creativity mirrors what Tarkovsky characterized as the negative response *Andrei Rublev* elicited from Soviet officials: "If the Committee insists on cuts, I'll tell them to go to hell.... What are they all fussing about?... Today some official, a journalist, said... 'Apparently Tarkovsky has been given permission to take a condemned prisoner... so that he'll die on screen'!!!?"[10] The peasant mob in *Andrei Rublev* represents the credulous and conspiratorial powers that be, then and now. To play Efim, Tarkovsky even cast Nikolai Glazkov, the poet who coined the term "samizdat," the "pre-Gutenberg" system of underground publishing through which Soviet writers and creatives manually circulated work to avoid censorship.[11] The jury-rigged hot-air balloon in *Andrei Rublev* typifies the subversive, do-it-yourself approach to cultural production that defined the late Soviet period.

As Efim approaches the launch site, the camera records him in an impressive elliptical tracking shot, as if Tarkovsky's camerawork, like the airborne balloon, defies gravity's limitations. The gray, dismal setting of *Andrei Rublev* becomes a staging ground for both primitive aeronautics and cinematic virtuosity. Atop the church's belfry, Efim mounts the balloon; he is lifted into the air after the balloonists lose the ropes, pummeled by the mob. An aerial shot of the church, which Tarkovsky captured from a helicopter—another synthesis of medieval and modern—depicts Efim's elevated perspective as he drifts through the air.[12] "I'm flying!" he cries out to the astonished earthbound peasants, who have stopped fighting to gawk at the overhead spectacle.

Tarkovsky's image of a medieval peasant atop a balloon re-creates a Russian folk legend that gained popularity in midcentury Soviet society. Supposedly, an eighteenth-century peasant named Kryakutnoy constructed a hot-air balloon in 1731—fifty years before the Montgolfier brothers in France, classically understood as the pioneers of human-carrying flight technology. Keen to mythologize whatever aspects of Russian history marked the Soviet Union as more advanced than its Western adversaries, Soviet officials celebrated the bicentenary of Kryakutnoy's flight in 1956 and emblazoned his feudal aircraft on a series of commemorative stamps with an image that distinctly resembles Efim's dirigible in *Andrei Rublev*.[13] The Soviets instrumentalized the (now debunked) Kryakutnoy myth as proof of their country's technological prowess during the Cold War as they contested their spaceflight superiority. Kryakutnoy's image began surfacing in Soviet culture exactly five years before the Russian astronaut Yuri Gagarin became the first man to enter outer space.

Efim, a medieval pilot, launches into the sky aboard
a hot-air balloon in one of Tarkovsky's most famous depictions
of human flight. Still from *Andrei Rublev*, 1966.

During this time, the Soviets also publicized a folktale from the seventeenth century that recounts how a serf—"a Russian Icarus"—escaped his master's estate by building wings, an act that resulted in his beheading.[14] This story, it was claimed, demonstrated how aviation technology could liberate Russia "from the constraints of the past"—that is, from the clutches of imperial landowners—and jump-start its "rapid transformation into the world's most advanced and powerful nation."[15] Though Tarkovsky (who initially planned for Efim to use wings) depicts the balloon in *Andrei Rublev* as a critique of cultural conformism, he nevertheless indulges the nationalistic mood of midcentury Soviet culture that touted Russia's apocryphal triumphs in aviation technology at the height of the Cold War space race.[16] Indeed, the Apollo 11 moon landing coincided with the 1969 Moscow Film Festival, where *Andrei Rublev* was to premiere before Soviet authorities banned its screening at the last minute.[17] For all its lofty poeticism—traditionally read as a metaphor for "the risks every true artist must take in stepping beyond the boundaries of the known"—*Andrei Rublev*'s opening episode of human flight faintly smacks of Soviet propaganda.[18]

Beyond its indebtedness to peasant lore and politics, Efim's flight also bears a relation to the emergence of cinematic technology, which, as Tarkovsky subtly acknowledges, paralleled breakthroughs in human aviation. After the invention of photography in the 1840s, amateur artists began adhering cameras to kites and balloons (not unlike Efim's) to capture overhead views, the earliest example being Gaspar Felix Tournachon's 1858 photograph of the town Petit-Bicêtre (now Petit-Clamart), a suburb of Paris.[19] These photographs were enhanced by the development of both planes and motion pictures, which, used together, afforded opportunities to capture unprecedented panoramas of cities and land.[20] The very first use of a film camera mounted to a plane occurred in 1909 in an aircraft piloted by none other than Wilbur Wright, the elder half of the American Wright brothers, who had piloted the first successful heavier-than-air flying machine six years earlier in Kitty Hawk, North Carolina.[21]

Commissioned by the French film company Société Générale des Cinématographes Eclipses, the film *Wilbur Wright and His Flying Machine* begins with images of an airplane being prepared for liftoff as a technician affixes a camera to the aircraft's wing. The scene reminds us of the team of peasant engineers in *Andrei Rublev* readying Efim's balloon. After the plane takes off, Wright flies close to the ground, and we see a series of images below: a man on a horse, farmland, and the ruins of ancient Roman aqueducts, scenes of the preindustrial world—literally the relics of antiquity—captured by airplanes and cinema, the signature technologies of industrial modernity. This combination anticipates the contrast between the medieval and the modern typified by Efim's flying machine. The novelty of human flight, in other words, coincides with the invention of motion pictures, accounting in part for the abiding popularity of the "plane film": Tony Scott's *Top Gun* (1986), Martin Scorsese's *The Aviator* (2004), and Jason Reitman's *Up in the Air* (2012).

In this light, Efim is not only a medieval pilot also but a medieval moviegoer, as are the onlookers—Efim's audience—gaping at him from below, as if glued to their seats. Soaring through the air, Efim observes a peripatetic landscape, a *motion picture*, consisting of stampeding animals, coastlines, and medieval hamlets. The lateral tracking shots that Tarkovsky uses to depict the world below, making the ground appear like a conveyor belt, replicate the sight of a strip of celluloid churning through a projector reel. Efim's flight is a metacinematic commentary on the rise of film as a medium of vision. Throughout his flight, we hear Efim's nervous laughter, which re-creates the unnerved reactions of early filmgoers startled by the perceptual unfamiliarity of moving images. A popular urban legend about early filmgoers recounts how spectators jumped out of the way of an image of a barreling train during a screening of the Lumière brothers' *The Arrival of a Train* (*L'Arrivée d'un train en gare de La Ciotat*, 1895).[22] In *Andrei Rublev*, Efim cannot believe his eyes. If Tarkovsky jettisons Efim into the skyward future of modernity, he takes his viewers back to the earliest days of cinema, when an aesthetic of astonishment—a "cinema of attractions"—was in vogue among neophyte cinematographers, especially the Soviet avant-garde, whose influence on Tarkovsky is considered in chapter 5.[23]

The technological continuity between cinema and air travel conveys a longstanding cultural desire to perceive the world free from the earthbound constraints of human vision. Unsurprisingly, then, both Wright's and Tarkovsky's recordings of flight are rendered from the vantage points of pilots. We see the world below as if from the elevated, zero gravity gazes of Wilbur and Efim, who observe untilled fields, animals, and ancient architecture. The first-person perspective of these aerial scenes alters and expands the camera's gaze, making human vision birdlike as we encounter the ordinary world from new speeds, angles, and heights.

Originating in the mid-eighteenth century in the English painter Joshua Kirby's writings about linear perspective, the term "bird's-eye view" connotes a visual representation of something seen from a high-angle vantage point.[24] In cinema, a bird's-eye view refers to a point-of-view (POV) shot that appears rendered from the perspective of a bird looking down at Earth. Usually, POV shots—images that depict the world from the gaze of a character within a scene—are easily located within a diegesis. A POV shot often begins with an image of a character looking, whereafter the camera performs the act of said looking, mimicking a human's rotational, mobile gaze. A memorable early example of this technique occurs in Abel Gance's *Napoléon* (1927), when, during a snowball fight, the camera falls down and, as if defending itself, stands back up and charges forward in a reenactment of a young Napoleon's ocular experience.

By contrast, bird's-eye perspectives need not assume an identifiable location within a film setting. Aerial shots implicitly take on the perspective of birds flying and perching above our heads as they observe the ground below. From great heights, bird's-eye views distance our gaze not only from human eyesight but also, metaphorically, from the smallness of humanity's dramas and activities, reminding us of our own insignificance in the cosmos. As evidenced by Efim's astonishment, the bird's-eye view elicits a wondrous encounter with the world under our feet that excitingly yet unnervingly reanimates our view of humanity's habitat.

Later in *Andrei Rublev*, a young iconographer named Foma (Mikhail Kononov) finds the muddied carcass of a swan in the woods. Its besmirched body inverts the qualities usually associated with swans—elegance, beauty, grace.[25] The blackened swan functions as a metaphor for *Andrei Rublev*'s bleak medieval world, which denigrates all that is beautiful; it reminds us of the foreboding dead gull discovered in Anton Chekhov's *The Seagull* (*Chaika*, 1895). Backdropped by the trills of woodland birds, Foma pokes at the swan with a stick and lifts up its wing. The limpened wing reiterates the swan's unlucky fate of having been struck out of the sky and, as if permanently deplaned, grounded in the medieval world, which cannot compare with the splendor of birds' aerial—and, in the case of swans, aquatic—kingdom.

A swan's carcass serves as a metaphor for Tarkovsky's bleak medieval world, which denigrates all that is beautiful. Still from *Andrei Rublev*, 1966.

In the director's cut of *Andrei Rublev*, the image of the swan's wing catalyzes a lofty sequence in which the camera (again set in a helicopter) soars over Tarkovsky's medieval landscape, re-creating the spectacular overhead vistas of Efim's flight. This time, however, our gaze is accelerated and the cinematography more dizzying, as we assume the vertiginous perspective of the (now dead) swan. Tarkovsky described this scene as the swan's memory, writing in *Andrei Rublev*'s screenplay that the bird once "saw the earth from high above when the flock was in flight, through breaks in the clouds, he saw cloud shadows running over yellow and green fields; dense, dark woods and sparse, light ones, with black, scorched patches from great fires, and little circles, bright as the sky—the lakes for which they longed."[26] Tarkovsky envisioned a bird's gaze onto the world, achieved through the aesthetic elasticity afforded by a movie camera. Compared to static or graphic art forms, film can better imagine a bird's airborne experience, a synergy inferred by the simultaneous emergence of motion pictures and airplanes. During the swan's flight in *Andrei Rublev*, Tarkovsky anthropomorphizes—*avianizes*—the camera as if it is *itself* a migrating swan. We hear the faint patter of flapping wings as the camera undergoes several zero gravity gyrations, and the scene's lilting music reenacts the sound of a songbird—a swan song before the swan's demise. Tarkovsky literalizes how cinematography becomes birdlike vis-à-vis the bird's-eye view.

This swan glides through not only space but also time. We first see water meadows in spring, then snow-covered riverbanks in winter, then sun-drenched fields in summer. The swan's flight blends "spatial continuity" with "(a)temporal displacement," recapitulating Tarkovsky's leaps to "radically other space[s] and times[s]" throughout *Andrei Rublev* by way of flashbacks, hallucinations, and nondiegetic interludes.[27] The swan, for Tarkovsky, transcends both human vision and any fixed space-time continuum. The swan's gaze reorganizes, compresses, quickens, and estranges our perceptual experience of terrestrial reality, not unlike Tarkovsky's experimental films, which beguile our perspective through jump cuts, long takes, slow motion, and tracking shots. Quoting the Russian novelist Mikhail Prishvin, who admired birds across his prose in works like "In the Land of Unafraid Birds" (*V kraiu nepuganykh ptits*, 1907), Tarkovsky posited an analogy between film, aviation technology, and birds: "As I watch films in the cinema, I realize for the first time the great virtue of the theatre, its humanity. It is rather like gazing at an aeroplane and seeing for the first time how delightful is a bird's flight, a bird's feather."[28] Both movie cameras and birds reorient our sense of our world. Tarkovsky's cinematic project to reimagine ordinary reality and our place in it draws inspiration from nature's aviators, the birds sailing over our heads that make humanity's triumphs and tragedies feel so small.

LEONARDO

Tarkovsky's interest in the intersection of birds and cinema—a mechanical art that can simulate experiences of flight—reminds us of a Renaissance polymath who was also enthralled by birds, art, and aviation technology: Leonardo da Vinci. Tarkovsky regularly expressed his admiration for the great Italian artist—"When we recall the work of Leonardo, before us rises a colossal inner human world"—and, channeling the creative spirit of da Vinci's homeland, Tarkovsky shot his penultimate film *Nostalghia* in Italy, along with *Voyage in Time* (*Tempo di Viaggio*, 1983), a documentary about *Nostalghia*'s making.[29] Da Vinci's art regularly appears throughout Tarkovsky's filmography. In *Mirror*, a child leafs through a book of da Vinci prints in a sequence that culminates with a close-up of the portrait *Ginevra de' Benci* (1474–78), whose aloof gaze, per Tarkovsky, "introduces a timeless element" into the diegesis.[30] The painted woman's stringy hair also offered Tarkovsky a template for the look of his Italian heroine in *Nostalghia*, Eugenia (Domiziana Giordano), a beautiful translator who—regularly seen combing, tossing, and blow-drying her free-flowing hair—resembles the blond, windswept goddess in *The Birth of Venus* (1485) by da Vinci's peer Sandro Botticelli. Additionally, *The Sacrifice* begins with a tracking shot of da Vinci's (unfinished) painting *Adoration of the Magi* (1481), which depicts the Virgin Mary and Christ child visited by the three wise men. Tarkovsky pairs this painting with the "Erbarme Dich" from the *St. Matthew*

Passion (1727) by Johann Sebastian Bach, whose creative talents Tarkovsky likened to da Vinci's (and, incidentally, his father's); all great artists, for Tarkovsky, circle back to Leonardo.[31]

Throughout *The Sacrifice*'s opening credits, the camera holds focus on one of the magi kneeling before the newborn, offering the gift of frankincense. As Bach's aria fades, the faint cries of seagulls fill the frame, along with the noise of breaking waves. The camera glides up da Vinci's painting as the sounds of seabirds and lapping water become louder. We see the Christ child, then Joseph, then the angels, then the trunk of the carob tree (the foliage of which canopies Christ's audience), and then a jarring background consisting of ruinous buildings and battling horsemen. Continuing its ascent, the camera pauses at the top of the leafy tree, rendered in da Vinci's signature *sfumato* technique: dexterous blending of colors to create an impression of haze and smoke. The sounds of the gulls and seawater return, and Tarkovsky transitions to the film's opening shot of Aleksandr (Erland Josephson) planting a (dead) tree with his son, Little Man (Tommy Kjellqvist), on the shores of Närsholmen, a nature reserve on the Swedish island of Gotland. The prologue of *The Sacrifice*, a kind of concert overture, establishes a connection between birds, film technology, and Leonardo.

Besides being a superlative draftsman, sculptor, and painter, da Vinci was also an aeronautics pioneer. In 1505, he penned a manuscript devoted to matters of aviation, "Codex on the Flight of Birds," which features over five hundred sketches of flying machines, the qualities of wind, and avian physiology.[32] These scribbles and musings would propel the development of modern aviation technology several centuries later, in the early 1900s. The balloon voyage in *Andrei Rublev*, set in the fifteenth century, concedes that the history of human flight began centuries before the industrial era, albeit in Renaissance Italy and not medieval Russia.

Tarkovsky understood da Vinci—along with Michelangelo and Raphael, two other artists who influenced Tarkovsky's creative practice—as *the* consummate Renaissance artist who hastened the end of the Dark Ages.[33] In Tarkovsky's eyes, Andrei Rublev was da Vinci's Russian equivalent: "Rublev's art represents the pinnacle of the Russian Renaissance."[34] Efim's flying contraption signifies a burst of Renaissance ingenuity akin to Rublev's technically expert and resplendent iconography—each of which bookend Tarkovsky's film—that lit a path out of the medieval era. By dint of association with Rublev, Tarkovsky links his *own* work with da Vinci's genius, which likewise drew inspiration from birds in its union of art, religion, and technology. "It is impossible," Tarkovsky said, "to make a living with non-commercial art.... Famous writers are forced to write screenplays in order to make a commercial picture.... There's no need to speak of any sort of renaissance."[35] It became, therefore, Tarkovsky's mission to spur a renaissance in his own "dark age," the wearying era of the 1970s, by wistfully looking up—as da Vinci had—at airborne birds.

> This conquest of air is always seen as the ultimate expression of Leonardo as aspirant Renaissance man, but these flights of which he dreams are not entirely distinct from those more prosaic flights with which the rest of us are familiar: flights of escape, of evasion, of irresolution—flights semantically referable to fleeing rather than flying.... In his obsession with flight there is a kind of existential restlessness, a desire to float free from his life of tensions and rivalries, from the dictates of warmongers and art-lovers and contract-wavers. He yearns for this great escape, and in failing he feels himself more captive.[36]

Da Vinci's wish for birdlike flight is, ultimately, a longing for escape, the desire to be unfettered.

Though Tarkovsky began his career during the Thaw, a cultural movement that "took off" with the release of Mikhail Kalatozov's avian-themed film *The Cranes Are Flying* (*Letiat zhurvali*, 1957), much of Tarkovsky's output was colored by the "eternal state" of late, or "developed," socialism—that is, the decades that have become known as the "era of Stagnation" (*zastoi*).[37] The period began in the mid-1960s after a cadre of disgruntled bureaucrats, spearheaded by Leonid Brezhnev, ousted Nikita Khrushchev and gradually revived an authoritarian culture in response to the Thaw's chaotic reformism.[38] In exchange for political quiescence, Brezhnev's regime guaranteed a degree of economic stability—achieved through consumer-oriented policies—that proffered Soviet citizens the highest living standards since the October Revolution. Over time, this stability morphed into a kind of sclerotic cultural stasis. Lethargic and cynical feelings saturated everyday life; perfunctory ideological performativity entrenched itself, often through mind-numbingly long public displays of patriotism, such as Communist Party speeches, monument dedications, and military parades, all of which reached a crescendo under Brezhnev.[39]

In response to the stifled cultural atmosphere, Soviet filmmakers turned to escapist fantasies of flight, as in Larisa Shepit'ko's *Wings* (*Kryl'ia*, 1966), Petr Todorovskii's *City Romance* (*Gorodskoi romans*, 1970), and Georgii Daneliia's *Mimino* (1977). Characters in Marlen Khutsiev's *July Rain* (*Iiul'skii dozhd'*, 1966), Il'ia Averbakh's *Fariatev's Fantasy* (*Fantazii Fariat'eva*, 1979), and Roman Balian's *Flights in Dreams and Reality* (*Polety vo sne i naiavu*, 1983) all entertain experiences of disappearance, travel, and alien visitations to cope with feelings of disaffection.[40] This yearning for escapist flight is on display across

Tarkovsky's cinema. Just as he commences *Andrei Rublev*, his second film, with a skyward voyage, Tarkovsky also begins his debut—and, thus, his oeuvre—with a glorious aestheticization of human flight. One of the first shots of *Ivan's Childhood* consists of a fluttering moth, the flight pattern of which is replicated by the child protagonist as he unexpectedly launches into the air, inaugurating Tarkovsky's leitmotif of levitation, which reoccurs in *Andrei Rublev, Solaris, Mirror*, and *The Sacrifice*. Through experiences of weightlessness, Tarkovsky intimates his characters' "desperate attempt to evade the cruelties" and inanities of ordinary life, especially in the dismally gray and hopeless milieu of late Soviet society.[41]

Birds accompany almost all of Tarkovsky's scenes of levitation, whether by sound or appearance, as if their sheer presence triggers characters' escapist fantasies. In *Solaris*, when Kelvin (Donatas Banionis) learns that the spacecraft's orbit has changed, resulting in a brief period of zero gravity, he enters the shuttle's library and finds Hari (Natalia Bondarchuk)—the alien replicant of his ex-wife—admiring a series of paintings (themselves reproductions) by Pieter Bruegel the Elder, namely *The Hunters in the Snow* (1565). The camera, assuming Hari's gaze, lovingly explores the piece, recycling the roving tracking shots that Tarkovsky utilized to tour Rublev's icons at the end of *Andrei Rublev*. Throughout this scene, we hear chirping birds, suggesting that Hari has shed her alien nature for a more humanlike perspective connected to the Earth, as bird noises, for Tarkovsky, are synonymous with the human experience. As Hari stares at the painting, she smokes a cigarette—another unmistakable, somewhat comical indication of her emergent humanity, bad habits and all. Hari's flight of imagination, saturated by birdsong, concludes with a spectacle of levitation in which Hari and Kelvin glide around the room alongside candelabras and books. Instantiating the avian matter of Hari's mind, Tarkovsky makes his protagonists birdlike, allowing them to briefly transcend the difficulties of their doomed life in outer space, a sense of doom Tarkovsky reiterates by punctuating this lofty scene of ascent with a shot of the planet Solaris's menacing topography.

Similarly, in *Mirror*, a small white bird flutters across the screen as Tarkovsky's heroine, Maria (Margarita Terekhova), inexplicably levitates. Maria's flight follows both an image of her estranged husband and an act of animal killing (discussed later) that she performed begrudgingly. The airborne bird signals Maria's successful albeit momentary attempt to rise above the intractability of her sordid predicament and become, like a bird, weightless. At another point in *Mirror*, a bird perches on the head of an orphan after footage of the bombs being dropped by American pilots over Hiroshima at the end of World

War II. The boy clasps the bird, suggesting that, despite the world's chaos, quiet moments of wonder and simplicity endure. The image of the boy holding the bird is set against a wintry backdrop reminiscent of Bruegel's bird-filled *Hunters in the Snow*, the painting that helped humanize Hari in *Solaris*. We also find in *Mirror* newsreel footage of balloon-strapped soldiers (not unlike Efim) servicing a stratospheric balloon used by the Soviets for reconnaissance missions during the Spanish Civil War. These astonishing mid-air visuals, despite their militaristic undercurrent, are backdropped by the baroque composer Giovanni Battista Pergolesi's graceful *Stabat Mater* (1736), another nod to Tarkovsky's Italian influences. These lyrical scenes of flight induce aesthetic, miraculous wonder, inviting Tarkovsky's characters—and, by turn, his rapt audience—to perceive ordinary reality otherwise.

Relatedly, in *Nostalghia*, a white feather falls from the sky during one of the daydreams of the Russian countryside, replete with bird noises, that absorb Andrei Gorchakov's attention. In his fantasy, Gorchakov (Oleg Iankovskii) picks up the feather and discovers an angel traipsing about the grounds of his abandoned home. This daytime reverie occurs while, in reality, a miserable Gorchakov finds himself stuck in a cramped Italian hotel, telling his translator, Eugenia, that Russian literature—specifically the poems of Tarkovsky's father—can never be understood by foreigners. Only Russians, Tarkovsky suggests, can fathom Gorchakov's tortured psychology, indicative of what he describes as "our Russian nostalgia."[42] Tarkovsky wrote,

> I wanted to make a film about Russian nostalgia—about the particular state of mind which assails Russians who are far from their native land. I wanted the film to be about the fatal attachment of Russians to their national roots, their past, their culture, their native places, their families and friends; an attachment which they carry with them all their lives, regardless of where destiny may fling them. Russians are seldom able to adapt easily, to come to terms with a new way of life. The entire history of Russian emigration bears out the Western view that "Russians are bad emigrants"; everyone knows their tragic incapacity to be assimilated, the clumsy ineptitude of their efforts to adopt an alien life-style.[43]

These sentiments echo well-trodden nationalistic tropes asserting that Russians have a special cultural purchase on feelings of wistfulness and homesickness and a unique indisposition for the challenges and changes of modern life. As Svetlana Boym describes, nineteenth-century Russian nationalists, known as the Slavophiles, argued that Russians were singularly ill equipped to the throes of modernity. They turned "spiritual longing (*toska*)" for a simpler, more authentic

Tarkovsky's heroine levitates beside a small bird, suggesting her desire to escape her predicament. Still from *Mirror*, 1975.

A bird perches atop a child's head after images of the nuclear explosion in Hiroshima, conveying Tarkovsky's belief that quiet moments of beauty persist in modern life. Still from *Mirror*, 1975.

past into the essential feature of "the Russian soul and a birthmark of the chosen nation," which sets its sight on the impossible "dream of transcending history and memory."[44] In *Nostalghia*, Gorchakov's—and, by extension, Tarkovsky's—oceanic yearning for a world before the havoc and confusion of modern life is a definitional marker of his Russianness. Gorchakov longs to take to the skies and return to Russia, where—as Tarkovsky mawkishly shows—birds (still) sing and angels walk.[45] The figure of the angel, indeed, "embodies the human dream of becoming one with birds."[46] The angel's feather even leaves a lasting imprint on Gorchakov. He bears a feathery streak of white hair, as do other of Tarkovsky's heroes: Stalker (Aleksandr Kaidnovsky) and, in *Solaris*, Kelvin. These men are marked, grazed—and therefore graced—by birds' feathers, signaling their desire, like Leonardo, to escape reality or, in Gorchakov's words, "to abolish frontiers between states" and achieve spiritual transcendence.

The deep-seated, unbearable longing expressed by Tarkovsky's characters to somehow surmount reality's spatiotemporal constraints is perfectly relayed by close-ups of caged birds in *Solaris*. As two astronauts discuss the folly of Kelvin's impending voyage, we see three parakeets in a birdcage hanging by a windowsill, flanked by pictures of hot-air balloons. We find within the home's cluttered confines a display case filled with taxidermized butterflies (reminiscent of the signature motif of Vladimir Nabokov, a famous literary Russian émigré). These images represent the ways in which Tarkovsky's characters struggle to escape their respective situations. A curious yellow balloon, breaking the rules of gravity, is seen suspended in midair outside Kelvin's family home; it, too, conveys the denial of flight's promise, as do images of birds struggling to break out of window glass in both *Mirror* and *Nostalghia*.

Beyond imaginative flights of fancy in the form of dreams, flashbacks, and hallucinations, Tarkovsky's characters, like these trapped birds, are all stuck in place, spiritually and spatiotemporally taxidermized. Da Vinci reportedly had a habit of setting caged birds free to observe their exodus into the air.[47] Analogously, Tarkovsky's protagonists yearn to be set free by some higher power, but they find no such relief, as their escapist fantasies continually crash back down to Earth—not unlike the felled swan (and, as we will see, Efim) in *Andrei Rublev*. Even though Kelvin rockets out of Earth's atmosphere in *Solaris*, he does so against his will and feels imprisoned aboard the claustrophobic and litter-strewn spacecraft. Like Gorchakov, Kelvin is physically displaced, yet he longs for *meta*physical freedom. Kelvin and Gorchakov's dislocations reflect not only the story of all of Tarkovsky's existentially adrift heroes but also Tarkovsky's own.

In July 1984, Tarkovsky announced at a press conference in Milan that Soviet authorities had denied his request to extend his working stay in Europe,

Gorchakov grazed—and, therefore, graced—by an angel's falling feather, revealing his desire to escape reality and achieve spiritual transcendence. Still from *Nostalghia*, 1983.

where he had spent the lion's share of his time since 1979.[48] It was clear, too, that there was no guarantee of employment upon Tarkovsky's return to the USSR. As a result, Tarkovsky sought asylum in the West, which Italy readily granted, turning Tarkovsky into one of the most famous reluctant Cold War Russian exiles, in the tradition of Joseph Brodsky, Aleksandr Solzhenitsyn, and Andrei Sinyavski. Tarkovsky's cinematic dreams of flight poignantly manifested in his own birdlike escape from the jaws of political persecution, which resulted in his exile in Leonardo's ancient homeland. The avian motifs of levitation, angels, air travel, swan songs, and cages that Tarkovsky recycles throughout his cinema serve as metaphors for his own biography.

MASTERY

Great makers of culture like Leonardo earned from Tarkovsky the appellation of "master," which he considered the highest compliment any artist could be paid: "Artistic creation . . . is related to the more general aim of mastery of the world, it has an infinite number of facets, the vincula that connect man with his vital activity, and even if that path towards knowledge is unending, no step that takes man nearer to a full understanding of the meaning of his existence can be too small to count."[49] Proceeding from the Latin *magis* for "more" to the Italian *maestro*, the French *maître*, and Russian *master*, the term "master" denotes a person with authority, often possession, over something else.[50] Figuratively understood, a master is an artist or performer of consummate skill. "The artist masters ultimate truth," Tarkovsky wrote, "every time he creates something perfect, something whole."[51] Indeed, the words "masterly," "masterful," "mastery," and "masterpiece" pervade Tarkovsky's reflections on art, and these descriptors, in turn, have come to saturate writings about Tarkovsky since his death.

In the Soviet context, however, "mastery" was a highly freighted concept redolent of Stalinism. Besides signifying virtuosity, mastery also connoted brutal state power as Stalinist officials seized control of every aspect of Soviet life, often through terror, during the 1930s.[52] In one of his infamous midnight phone calls, Stalin rang the poet Boris Pasternak to discuss the fate of Osip Mandelstam, another poet. Stalin asked whether Mandelstam was, indeed, a "master" of his craft.[53] This telephone conversation—allegedly recounted by the Russian poet Anna Akhmatova in one of the darker games of telephone ever played—inspired the title of Mikhail Bulgakov's legendary novel *The Master and Margarita* (*Master i Margarita*, 1928–40).[54] The book tells the story of a persecuted writer, a master, under Stalin; it quickly became a masterpiece of Soviet literature and gained circulation in the mid-1960s, at the height of Tarkovsky's career. He hoped to adapt it on screen someday.[55]

Stalinist cinematographers frequently promulgated this ideology of mastery and conquest through the aestheticization of air travel. Made more accessible by Stalinist industry, planes signified a "gift of technology to the nation" that expanded "the potential of the Soviet experience."[56] The bird's-eye view became a mainstay of Stalinist cinema, which valorized pilots as conquistadors capable of mapping—*mastering*—Russia's vastness, its seemingly infinite *prostor*. In Oleksandr Dovzhenko's *Aerograd* (1934), Iulii Raizman's *Pilots* (*Letchiki*, 1935), and Kalatozov's *Valerii Chkalov* (1941)—a film named after the celebrated pilot who flew from Moscow over the North Pole and footage of whom Tarkovsky incorporated into *Mirror* to pacify hostile Soviet censors—aerial perspectives signify a "controlling gaze" aligned with a totalizing, heroic vision of Stalinism's indomitability and limitless surveillance.[57] Indicative of the demigod status attained by pilots in the 1930s, Stalin himself carried the urn of the famous pilot Pavel Fedoseenko during a funeral procession on Red Square in 1934 after Fedoseenko's death in a plane crash that year; Stalin remembered Fedoseenko as one of his "falcons in the stratosphere."[58] Fittingly, then, the bird's-eye view is also known as the god's-eye view, an ascendant vantage point implying that the looker has assumed an omniscient, even condescending gaze onto the terrestrial world and its puny inhabitants.[59]

From one angle, Tarkovsky critiques this Stalinist discourse of mastery with depictions of unsuccessful flight. In the prologue of *Andrei Rublev*, Efim's voyage is backdropped by ominous music and the noise of twisting ropes and hissing air. Shortly after liftoff, Efim crashes down to Earth, depicted in a rare freeze-frame shot underscoring the finality of Efim's fall from grace. This static image of the ground suggests the unforgiving, inevitable reality awaiting Soviet delusions of mastery, subtly acknowledging how even Stalin's most renowned pilots—like Fedoseenko and Chkalov, who himself died in a crash in 1939—failed to conquer the skies and buckled under gravity's limitations, not unlike the American aviator Amelia Earhart had a few years earlier in 1937.[60]

Efim is seen lying dead next to his deflated flying contraption, an image of technological grandeur in ruins. Tarkovsky's medieval epic begins with a depiction of aerial modernity only to punish the pilot.[61] Efim's errant flight anticipates the folly of Kelvin's interstellar voyage in Tarkovsky's follow-up film, *Solaris*, which critiques the Cold War space race. Soviet (and American) officials formulated the race to the cosmos in a discourse of plunder and mastery reminiscent of Stalinism, a rhetoric exemplified by the American flag, a symbol of national conquest, planted on the moon's rocky surface.[62] "We want to extend Earth to the borders of the cosmos," says an astronaut in *Solaris*, "yet we do not know what to do with other worlds."

Thus, across Tarkovsky's cinema, aircraft (like cars and trains) betoken a kind of techno-pessimism. Tarkovsky's characters, as discussed, achieve weightlessness through leaps of imagination and spiritual reckonings, wholly of their own accord and without the assist of a mechanical conduit—except, of course, Tarkovsky's own cinematic mediation. Despite Tarkovsky's critique of industrial mastery, his scenes of flight themselves required savvy technological application accomplished through helicopters, cranes, airborne cameras, and slow motion. The seeming spontaneity of human levitation in Tarkovsky's films—another cinematic miracle—are the result of scrupulous regulation. Tarkovsky's skyward longing for freedom is, ironically, attained through intensive and strict technical control.

Tarkovsky, then, is part of a time-honored tradition of artists, scientists, and photographers who yearned but struggled to accurately portray experiences of

Efim's crash represents Soviet delusions of mastery; unlike the heroic pilots of socialist realism, he fails to take control of the skies. Still from *Andrei Rublev*, 1966.

flight, typified by da Vinci's bird sketches. As explored in chapter 1, the very invention of film technology, originating in Eadweard Muybridge's nineteenth-century equine motion studies, represented a desire to capture the "flying gallop" of a horse—that is, the seemingly miraculous sight of all four of a horse's hooves leaving ground during a sprint.[63] Concurrent with Muybridge's locomotive studies, French scientist Étienne-Jules Marey experimented with sequential photography by detailing physiological processes unavailable to the naked eye, particularly the dynamics of airborne birds.[64] In 1882, Marey invented a "chronophotographic gun" that, capable of capturing twelve images per second, allowed him to atomize birds' flight patterns into a series of observable instances, much like *The Horse in Motion*. These proto-cinematic technologies conveyed fascination with the "representability of the ephemeral" or "the archivability of presence," achieved through invasive and controlling means.[65] Early film practitioners thus used film to study living bodies in ways that conveyed a certain technical mastery over the natural world. "By 1904, the year of his death, the monumental project of physiology's unification and control had become synonymous with Marey's name.... For Marey's followers, cinematography was not a method in itself, but was one among a range of techniques and instruments potentially to be implemented in the apparatus for the dissemination of physiology as the effort to control not only the living body but the scientific study of life as well."[66] Through his photographic study of birds, Marey tried to exert cinematic, godlike control over the natural world, a project that, over a century later, Tarkovsky expressly renewed. As he put it, sounding like one of Marey's followers, "cinema came into being as a means of recording the very *movement* of reality: factual, specific, within time and unique; of reproducing again and again the moment, instant by instant, in its fluid mutability—that instant by which we find ourselves able to gain mastery by imprinting it on film."[67]

In this light, it is no wonder that, filming in a nature reserve on a Swedish island rich with birdlife, Tarkovsky insisted that "no birds be audible" in *The Sacrifice* except exactly where and when he intended—even though he elected to shoot in May, during the highly noisy mating season.[68] With the help of Swedish sound mixer Owe Svensson, Tarkovsky synchronized the seabirds' cries in the studio to make it seem as if they occurred far more sporadically than in reality.[69] The evocative birdcalls in *The Sacrifice* are the result of fastidious curation, which pays homage to Ingmar Bergman's haunting yet regimented soundscapes. Tarkovsky described Bergman as a "master with sound" who "excludes all the incidental circumstances of the sound world that would exist in real life" in the construction of his eerie settings, particularly in *Through a Glass Darkly* (*Såsom i en spegel*, 1961).[70] Tarkovsky had intended to film *The Sacrifice* in the very location Bergman shot *Through a Glass Darkly*, Fårö, but, denied permission by the Swedish government, settled for the neighboring island Gotland, which Bergman also admired. Tarkovsky generated the disquieting atmosphere of *The Sacrifice* by technologically silencing the cacophonous flocks of mating birds.

Similarly, when Tarkovsky's protagonists enter a room full of sand dunes in *Stalker*—this time in tribute to the sandstorms, dust clouds, and quicksand of Hiroshi Teshigahara's *Woman in the Dunes* (*Suna no Onna*, 1964)—a bird soars across the visual field from the left-hand corner of the frame before disappearing midflight. Seconds later, the bird reappears in the frame's right-hand corner, again glides across the setting, and disembarks in the dunes. This beguiling moment, another of Tarkovsky's miracles, was made possible by directing the bird's crisscross flight pattern and then excising and adding several celluloid frames in postproduction to make it seem as if the bird vanished and then rematerialized in midair. This hidden, meticulous coordination similarly structures a scene in *Mirror* in which a bird flies in a straight line from the left-hand corner of the frame and perches atop a boy's head. Accomplished via painstaking precision and trickery, Tarkovsky's avian images direct and lengthen birds' otherwise fleeting and ungovernable presence and flight.

Tarkovsky's invisible directorial control is no better on display than toward the end of *Stalker*, as his protagonists sit on the threshold of the Zone's wish-room.⁷¹ It inexplicably starts raining indoors—another motif repeated in *Solaris*, *Mirror*, and *Nostalghia*—yet the rainwater in *Stalker* falls in a curiously systematized pattern. Water begins trickling down on the right side of the frame, whereafter it extends leftward, resulting in a downpour. After a minute of precipitation, the curtain of rain reverses trajectory, noticeably dissipating rightward. The asynchronous flow of the rainwater makes apparent Tarkovsky's use of a sprinkler rig. The sounds of the synthetically produced water droplets falling into puddles, which resemble "a thousand small explosions of glitter," reverberate in a way that enacts the noise of the chirping birds heard earlier from within the wish-room, as if Writer's and Professor's most deeply held wish was to listen to birds: simulated, indoor rainfall creates simulated, indoor birdsong.⁷²

Throughout this scene, Tarkovsky's characters are encased by the wish-room's entryway. The rectangular framing reenacts the shape of a screen, calling our attention to this moment's cinematic artifice—how film, through clever manipulation of technology and the elements, can reproduce bird noises and sun showers. The magic of cinema is not magical (or miraculous) at all, just a series of coordinated audio-visual tricks that generate beguiling spectacles. In an unwitting act of self-disclosure, Tarkovsky—albeit more subtly than Toto in *The Wizard of Oz*, who pulls back the curtain on the man behind the scenes controlling the show—divulges the directorial intelligence structuring the film experience.⁷³ Tarkovsky's perennial critique of humanity's ambition to master nature is thus belied by the very terms of its mediation. That is, Tarkovsky's striking portrayals of the natural world demand a high degree of sophisticated technical regulation (i.e., mastery).

It seems all the more disingenuous, then, that Tarkovsky often has his protagonists complain about the ways in which industrious human beings mistakenly try to rationalize and control nature. In *The Sacrifice*, Aleksandr bemoans how, as a child, he once reorganized his mother's overgrown garden and cried on seeing the result because the plot had lost all its "naturalness." Yet it is precisely such naturalness that Tarkovsky often extracts from his portrayals of birds and their habitats, even though his grassy (and always windy) outdoor settings—Tarkovsky famously inventoried the exact number of dandelions appearing within certain shots in *Stalker*—conspire to make us believe otherwise.⁷⁴ At one point in *Solaris*, Kelvin is instructed to attach a piece of paper to an air vent so that he can re-create the sound of wind rustling in the leaves to help him sleep aboard his spaceship. Kelvin's generation of fake leaf sounds discloses the artificial nature of the wind Tarkovsky produces across his cinema: the windblown fields in *Mirror*, the dust storm in *Stalker*, and the icy whirlwinds in *The Sacrifice*. These crafted, highly considered aestheticizations of air (not unlike Dorothy's tornado) create the impression of real, wild, and untamed nature, but they are, ultimately, cinematic illusions that remind us of the airtight control Tarkovsky exercised over his visual ecologies.

Tarkovsky's mastery is no better on display than when the Russian town of Vladimir descends into a Mongol raid in *Andrei Rublev*. Tarkovsky presents an aerial view of the mayhem, and gazing onto the pandemonium, we see two white birds—pushed from behind the camera—flap across the frame. To capture these birds' movements, Tarkovsky uses slow motion, as if replicating Marey's ornithological studies, which visualized imperceptible aerial activity and asserted technical control over it. This bird's-eye perspective—full of smoke, ant-like earthlings, and white birds—also reenacts the overhead views of Hitchcock's *The Birds* (1963), a film Tarkovsky admired about a small California town attacked by a flock of crows. Evoking Hitchcock, Tarkovsky assumes the vantage point of God, the all-powerful Wizard, watching the world descend into apocalyptic violence. The technical strategies Hitchcock used, borrowing from Marey, to re-create birds' flight patterns and predation were "intended to encompass a breakdown of nature as a whole"; Hitchcock, like Tarkovsky (and Marey before them), developed a "deceptive naturalism" to proclaim victory over reality.[75]

The interfilmic dialogue Tarkovsky establishes between Marey's chronophotographic aestheticization of birds and Hitchcock divulges something else about the Russian master. An undertow to Hitchcock's thirst for control was his impulse to coerce and cajole women, whom he infamously terrorized and tormented on set, physically and psychologically.[76] Hitchcock, as many critics have noted, leaves the spectator "no choice *but* to identify" with his male protagonists, who exert "an active, controlling gaze over the passive female object."[77] In *The Birds*, Hitchcock's flocks begin staging raids on Bodega Bay upon the disclosure of the heroine's sexual desire for the male hero. In Hitchcock's previous film, *Psycho* (1960)—another movie Tarkovsky revered—the heroine, Marion Crane (Janet Leigh), is poached, trapped, and killed like a baited bird by Norman Bates (Anthony Perkins), a taxidermist who says Marion "eats like a bird." The very name Marion Crane even refers us to both birds and cinema: "Marion" was the name of a vintage camera manufacturer in the early twentieth century. Across his work, Hitchcock brings together women and birds to assert his godlike mastery over both nature and female sexuality; so, too, does Tarkovsky, a topic to which we now turn.

Two white birds fly above a medieval town descending into violence. Still from *Andrei Rublev*, 1966.

CHOKING THE CHICKEN

Perhaps unexpectedly, a palpable eroticism permeates almost all of Tarkovsky's depictions of human flight. In *Solaris*, as Kelvin and Hari soar across the spacecraft's library, the two tenderly gaze at each other, and Hari wraps her arms around Kelvin's shoulders. Kelvin places his hand across her waist, pulls her close, and lays his head on her chest. They spin around the room clasping and embracing each other before descending. Back on the ground, the camera gazes at their motionless bodies, with Kelvin lying face down on top of Hari; she rubs his back and kisses his head. It is clearly a postcoital moment, a denouement of two lovers coming down from the highs of physical excitation. The very next shot is, unpredictably, an image of a bonfire from Kelvin's childhood home movies, which he earlier screened for Hari. The presence of fire, a symbol for sexual passion, intimates Kelvin's entrance into sexual maturity, as if this scene of levitation has (finally) fulfilled his boyhood fantasies.

Likewise, in *Nostalghia*, a flock of small birds flies out of the womb of an effigy of the Virgin Mother during a fertility ritual in a country church. In the background, we see Piero della Francesca's Renaissance painting *Madonna del parto* (1460), which scandalously portrays a pregnant Mary, an all-too-human image that acknowledges the materiality of sex and gestation somewhat at odds with the biblical account of the virgin birth. Birds, for Tarkovsky, are synonymous with women, procreation, and sex, hence the presence of storks in his dream at the outset of this chapter. Birds appear on screen in encounters with female sexuality, which, in Tarkovsky's view, is morally permissible only if directed toward acts of love and creation rather than sensory, animalistic pleasure.[78] Later in *Nostalghia*, Gorchakov dreams of his pregnant ex-wife (Patrizia Terreno) lying on a bed swathed in white sheets against a pitch-black backdrop. The negative space creates the impression that she is suspended in the air, as if on a cloud. Her distended belly, her baby bump, lifts her off the ground heavenward to the (pregnant) Madonna. In *The Sacrifice*, Aleksandr is told that to stave off nuclear war, he must sleep with Maria (Guðrún Gísladóttir), a local immigrant from Iceland rumored to be a witch. When Aleksandr arrives at her residence, Maria (like Kelvin's mother in *Solaris*) washes his hands and comforts him through physical contact. She kisses him, takes off her dress, and the two steal into the air, spinning around the visual field locked in an embrace, just like Kelvin and Hari. This act of airborne intercourse brings an end to nuclear catastrophe, representing, in Tarkovsky's opinion, the triumph of mystery, faith, and love in the modern world. "Maria," Tarkovsky wrote, "is modest, timid, perpetually uncertain of herself.... In the face of imminent catastrophe, [Aleksandr] perceives the love of this simple woman as a gift from God.... Nothing they do complies with the 'normal' criteria of behaviour.... Contemporary man is unable to hope for the unexpected, for anomalous events that don't correspond with 'normal' logic: still less is he prepared to allow even the thought of unprogrammed phenomenon, let alone believe their supernatural significance."[79] Maria and Aleksandr's paranormal midair copulation saves their world from nuclear destruction.

A "timid," birdlike woman, Maria is repeatedly seen astride a bicycle, which in most contexts functions as a symbol for both female independence (associated with women's suffrage) and, relatedly, the fast-paced changes of modern, urban life.[80] In *The Sacrifice*, however, Tarkovsky correlates the bike with the witch, a figure of the premodern era perennially persecuted by her compatriots, as evidenced by the rash of witch trials throughout world history. Wheeling across the frame, Maria (whose headscarf reminds us of *Stalker*'s bewitched Monkey) represents the eccentricity, danger, and seductiveness associated with witches, who, like Maria, can often fly. Maria on her bicycle also evokes the cycling (and dog thieving) Wicked Witch of the West (Margaret Hamilton) in *The Wizard of Oz*. In *The Sacrifice*, the notion of cultural progress typically inferred by the sight of a woman on a bicycle leads *backward* to an archaic past of sorcery and divination. It is not by chance, then, that Aleksandr himself must ride a bike to Maria's home, a modern-day coven, to activate her mystical powers.

Similarly, in *Nostalghia*, Domenico—another antediluvian madman heralding the world's end (performed by Erland Josephson, the same actor who plays

Aleksandr)—rides a stationary bike, pedaling onward to nowhere. Like Maria, Domenico is out of step with the mechanized, fast-paced twentieth-century culture traditionally symbolized by bicycles. This connection between anti-progress and bicycles also explains why in *The Sacrifice*, when Aleksandr's eccentric postman, Otto (Allan Edwall), who knows about Maria's witchcraft, glides into the frame on a bike, Tarkovsky presents the *longest* long take of his filmography: an unbroken nine-minute shot. Following Otto as he loops around the visual field, Tarkovsky's cinematography refutes the bicycle's connotation of progress. The bike, for Tarkovsky, incites experiences of temporal drift, what he called "unprogrammed phenomena." Tarkovsky does away with bicycles' speed and efficiency, which cinema—whose origins coincided with the popularization of bicycles in everyday urban life—often mimics with rapid-fire editing techniques like montage.[81] Through the technical virtuosity of the long take, Tarkovsky contests modern technology's propulsive inexorability, exemplified by montage cutting and bicycles. This refutation of the bicycle's symbolic legacy also accounts for why we see a rusty bike in the Baths of St. Catherine in *Nostalghia* as Gorchakov carries out his (witchlike) act of self-sacrifice in the *second* longest of Tarkovsky's long takes: an eight-and-a-half-minute scene of Gorchakov pacing back and forth, not unlike Domenico cycling in place. The bicyclists of Tarkovsky's cinema—Domenico, Otto, Maria—are the modern world's misfits: black sheep or, in Russian, "white crows" (*belye vorony*).

Maria's "soothsaying," Tarkovsky wrote, is "at variance with the ideas and established rules of the world."[82] To emphasize her apartness from modern, industrialized society, Tarkovsky has Maria come from Iceland, the furthest reaches of Scandinavia and "Europe's last great wilderness."[83] Unlike other disaffected characters in *The Sacrifice*, Maria is close to nature. Her thicketed residence, like Domenico's in *Nostalghia*, lies outside the village center, and sheep, animals steeped in Christian mythology, freely roam there, designating Maria as a redeemer. As Tarkovsky said about his wife Larisa, "When we walk in the forest, birds fly close to her—she is like them. Some country people even call her a sorceress. Now, I know there is no malice in her at all, birds will never approach an evil being."[84] Associating the mother of his second son with birds, Tarkovsky characterizes Larisa, like Maria, as an enigmatic but *good* witch—more Glinda, the Good Witch of the North (i.e., Russia, Iceland), than Wicked Witch of the West—capable of communing with animals. During the aerial sex scene in *The Sacrifice*, Tarkovsky also cycles through a series of hallucinatory images that confirms the onset of Maria's world-saving spells. One of these images bizarrely shows Aleksandr's stepdaughter, Marta (Filippa Franzén), stark naked and chasing away chickens.

Aleksandr's voyeuristic dream of a naked woman with chickens throws into focus how Tarkovsky eroticizes women through birds and flight. Still from *The Sacrifice*, 1986.

This voyeuristic image brings together an eroticized woman, domesticated birds, and a hint of aggression that harkens back to the most iconic fowl of Tarkovsky's work: the rooster decapitated by *Mirror*'s heroine. In one of *Mirror*'s final scenes, Maria (Margarita Terekhova)—note that she bears the same name as *The Sacrifice*'s witch—and her son arrive at a country doctor's estate to pawn jewelry during wartime. Offering to help Maria, the doctor's wife (played by Tarkovsky's second wife, Larisa, whom he likened to a sorceress) asks Maria to kill a rooster for supper. Maria briefly ponders whether her son should perform the slaughter, but she agrees to do it out of a desire to protect him from violence. Maria is handed an axe; the rooster is laid in front of her, and she places her hands on the bird. The camera dwells on the image of the blade and Maria's hands clenching the rooster, a grim inversion of Tarkovsky's usual motif of characters gently clasping small birds. The scene then cuts to a shot of the doctor's wife, who says she feels queasy, whereafter we hear the rooster's cries as Maria severs its head off screen. Traces of the bird's slaughter—flying feathers—burst into the frame, landing on the face of the doctor's wife.

After the bird's death, we see Maria staring directly at the camera. She bears a wickedly triumphant smile that, as if in a horror movie, recalls the "manic stares" of Stanley Kubrick's psychopathic protagonists or, better yet, the diabolical laughter of the Wicked Witch of the West.[85] The next shot is, unexpectedly, a black-and-white close-up of Maria's estranged ex-husband (played by Oleg Iankovskii), who, shirtless, gazes at the camera. In the background, we see white bedding. Maria's ex-husband turns around, and he caresses a woman's hand amid the sheets. The camera embarks on a lateral pan to reveal a naked Maria, wrapped in blankets and floating in the air. A zoom out captures Maria's whole body, motionlessly suspended several feet above her bed in Tarkovsky's most exquisite depiction of human flight. A white bird cuts across the frame, imbuing this scene with all the hallmarks of a Tarkovksian postcoital moment: two lovers, magical levitation, and the presence of a bird. We realize that this disorienting scene is, in fact, a flashback that Maria recalls after decapitating the rooster, a shot alternation that lends this aerial sequence strong psychoanalytic resonance.

In many cultural traditions, roosters are anthropomorphized as men for their virility, brashness, and vigilance.[86] Their crowing, a word that can idiomatically mean "to boast," signals the rising of the sun, figuratively imbuing roosters—along with their strutting gait and elongated necks—a phallic quality correlated with the awakening of male arousal.[87] "This is due in part to the original bright red, blue, and golden brown of its plumage, crest, and wattle. The call of the cockerel is exuberant if not especially musical, and it seems to proclaim, 'Look at me!' These factors combine with its stride to create a

A succession of shots that begins with Maria clenching a rooster before its decapitation, whereafter we see a close-up of her twisted expression and her estranged husband. Stills from *Mirror*, 1975.

lordly demeanour."[88] A rooster's cry, which organized human conceptions of time for millennia, also denotes another kind of male "erection": the resurrection of Christ, who tells his foremost disciple Peter that, like clockwork, he will deny their affiliation in accordance with the cock's crows. Throughout his films, Tarkovsky uses roosters—occasionally heard, as in the New Testament, thrice—to represent ideas of rebirth. In *Mirror*, however, Tarkovsky has the rooster's masculine and metaphysical connotations symbolically killed by a woman, whose avian avatar tends to be the domestic, female hen.[89]

That Maria appears to enjoy killing the rooster in a scene punctuated by a postcoital image of her husband channels what Sigmund Freud described as the "castration complex."[90] Freud hypothesized that throughout their lives, men are driven by an unconscious fear of harm befalling the phallus, which expresses itself more generally as a dread of being degraded and humiliated, especially by a woman. Men, per Freud's logic, are wont to protect their pride—to keep themselves from being made to feel insignificant or like a cuckold—through sexual dominance, physical violence, and arrogant (cocky) behavior. The rooster's cries backdropping Maria's wraithlike yet smug expression signal the sadistic pleasure she apparently derives from figuratively castrating her husband, from momentarily denying him the privileges and power of masculinity through which he wreaked havoc on her by way of infidelity, abandonment, and paternal neglect. Killing the rooster, Maria briefly reclaims the power of the phallus. The scene presents the looking-glass inversion of the vulgar idiom "choking the chicken," which likens the barnyard task of wringing a chicken's neck before slaughter to male masturbation.[91] Maria destroys *the* animal symbol of phallic virility. The alterations between the cockerel, Maria's clenched hands, her taunting gaze, her ex-husband, and her naked, airborne body all suggest Maria symbolically dismembering her feckless lover, exorcising her memories of him vis-à-vis a climactic act of murder.

The cockerel, however, was not actually killed. Terekhova informed Tarkovsky that she could not bring herself to behead the rooster.[92] Tarkovsky flew into a rage, saying that Terekhova's unwillingness would ruin the scene, as it would force him to have the camera pan away at the moment of the bird's slaughter. The "whole point," Tarkovsky claimed, was that Terekhova's character, like the actress herself, had never slaughtered a rooster before, so Terekhova's unease would lend the scene a high degree of authenticity.[93] Tarkovsky instead had to splice a rooster's cries into this scene during production (which prepared him for the sonic editing of bird noises in *The Sacrifice*). Years later, Tarkovsky, still smarting, renounced this episode for its inauthentic staging: "I was playing 'give-away.'... We serve up the emotion we want, squeeze it out by our own—director's—means."[94] It is darkly telling that Tarkovsky, who otherwise indulged highly doctored depictions of birds, sought to record Terekhova killing a rooster in real time, sans cinematic artifice. Indeed, upon learning that Terekhova "felt sick" while gripping the bird, Tarkovsky reportedly yelled, "Very good! Action!"[95] Made aware of Terekhova's distress, Tarkovsky felt that she was better suited to carry out the task. While Terekhova did not kill the rooster—though viewers have little on-screen evidence to think otherwise—this scene should strike us for what Tarkovsky *intended* to capture on camera: a defenseless animal killed by an intimidated actress.

Through this gruesome exchange, Tarkovsky vied to flex—*strut*—his gendered authority over both a defenseless bird and a horrorstruck woman. As media theorist Linda Williams writes, men often "master" the "fear of castration" by entertaining fantasies of phallic violence, sometimes carried out by women, to reassure themselves of their own virility.[96] The whole spectacle of a cockfight, an ancient practice popularized by the Greeks centuries before chickens became part of humanity's diet, consists of men displacing their castration anxieties onto phallic birds that fight each other to the death.[97] Importantly, Williams grounds her argument on feminist thinker Laura Mulvey's influential contributions to film theory, delineated in her 1975 essay "Visual Pleasure and Narrative Cinema." Mulvey argues that "female figures" pose a problem for male viewers because their "lack of a penis" functions as "material evidence" on which "the castration complex" originates.[98] The very sight of a woman incites a man's fear of being made impotent; "thus the woman, as icon, displayed for the gaze and enjoyment of men, the active controllers of the look, always threatens to evoke the anxiety it originally signified."[99] For its part, the "male unconscious" has "two avenues of escape" from this anxiety: the first, "voyeurism," entails "ascertaining guilt, asserting control, and subjecting the guilty person through punishment or forgiveness." The second is "complete disavowal of castration by the substitution of a fetish object... so that it becomes reassuring rather than dangerous."[100] In *Mirror*, Tarkovsky substitutes a rooster ("fetish object") for the phallus, which he intended to have destroyed ("complete disavowal") by a woman as punishment ("voyeurism") for evoking *his* fears of emasculation, thereby enabling him to escape his castration anxiety. The close-up of Terekhova's clenched hands on the rooster, as if gripping a penis, is saturated with Tarkovsky's voyeuristic desire for self-affirmation of gendered authority. This image aligns with what Williams calls mainstream culture's "hardcore spectacles" that "implant a perversion"—an "unprecedented conjunction of pleasure and power"—in debased images of women for the sake of male gratification.[101]

Tellingly, Williams sources Mulvey's ideas of gendered looking all the way back to Muybridge's *Animal Locomotion*, a proto-cinematic study (discussed in chap. 1) that juxtaposes images of animals alongside photographs of objectified naked women whom Muybridge recorded performing domestic tasks while blowing kisses, twirling, and touching themselves.[102] Muybridge's "ostensibly scientific discourse" of biological mechanics, which laid the groundwork for modern motion pictures, "elicits surplus aestheticism in the fetishization of its women subjects."[103] *Animal Locomotion*, in other words, transcodes how female and animal bodies can be elided "under a similar visual structure: the voyeuristic, eroticized, and objectifying gaze"—hence, as Williams notes, patriarchal culture's persistent fantasy of women entertaining sexual relations with animals on screen, such as Jessica Rabbit in Robert Zemeckis's *Who Framed Roger Rabbit?* (1988).[104] Through the (intended) beheading of a rooster in *Mirror*, Tarkovsky vied to exploit both a woman *and* an animal as "socially powerless (though sexually potent)" creatures to produce a disturbingly erotic spectacle that would resonate with those of cinema's founding document.[105]

The scene in *Mirror*, though, ends with Terekhova simply redoubling Tarkovsky's castration complex. That is, Terekhova rebuffed the designs of an officious filmmaker indulging a fantasy of phallic violence to reaffirm his mastery. Indeed, Tarkovsky fumed against Terekhova's defiance in the tormented, self-pitying vocabulary of cuckoldry: "I was playing 'give-away' with the audience," he crossly wrote.[106] Tarkovsky recognized that he had been made a "cuck," a shorthand pejorative for "cuckold" that arose in the eighteenth century to belittle the husbands of unfaithful women.[107] The very word "cuckold" comes from the French for "cuckoo bird" (*coucou*), as female cuckoos lay their eggs in other male cuckoos' nests—mocking them vis-à-vis their infidelity, much like Maria does the memory of her husband in *Mirror*. And just as Maria reclaims the symbolic power of the phallus by beheading a rooster within *Mirror*'s narrative, Terekhova reasserted her agency as an actor by *not* decapitating a rooster outside the film's diegesis. Sparing the bird's life, Terekhova refused Tarkovsky's drive toward phallic sadism to sublimate his gendered anxieties. In the end, Terekhova humiliated Tarkovsky, just as he hoped to humiliate her, which he again tried (and, self-admittedly, failed) to do through the trick editing of *Mirror*, which makes it appear like Terekhova did, in fact, kill the rooster off screen. This sly editing is, in a way, Tarkovsky's cinematic response to cuckoldry. The make-believe simulation of the rooster's slaughter conceals *and* reveals Tarkovsky's castration complex: his angst at acquiescing to a woman who refused to acquiesce. Psychoanalytically glossed, the cut away from the cockerel in Terekhova's hands—in whose grip we also see a phallic axe—onto the face of Tarkovsky's second wife signifies "the cut" that he, like so many men, feared most. This (would-be) beheaded rooster discloses how gender, power, mastery, sex, and birds entangle across Tarkovsky's filmography.

CLOUD CUCKOO LAND

Before the first shot of *Ivan's Childhood*, while the Mosfil'm logo of the Stalin-era sculpture *Worker and Kolkhoz Woman* (*Rabochii i kolokhoznitsa*) lingers on screen, we hear a cuckoo bird. Its call resounds five times before the film cuts to a shot of Ivan (Nikolai Burlyayev), a boy in a bathing suit, looking for the bird. He peers through a spiderweb woven between a conifer tree's branches; unable to find the cuckoo, he retreats into the woods, and the camera tracks up the tree. The next shot consists of a close-up of a goat, followed by an image of Ivan running in the forest. We then see a fluttering moth, triggering Ivan's launch into the air. After reaching a certain altitude, the camera—now assuming Ivan's bird's-eye perspective—descends into the mud amid the twisted roots of the tree over whose canopy Ivan just sailed.

The cuckoo bird's call recommences at the forest's base, and Ivan sees his mother (played by Irma Raush, Tarkovsky's first wife) carrying a bucket of water. Ivan greets her and, not unlike a baby animal, drinks from the metal pail, saying, "Mama, there's a cuckoo bird." The blast of a machine gun suddenly engulfs the frame, and Ivan screams. He jolts up in pockmarked military clothes inside a decrepit windmill, the jagged sails of which replicate the texture of the earlier spiderweb. The camera, capturing Ivan's disorientation, judders through the desolate space as Ivan surveys the war-torn landscape and begins trudging through a bog, inverting his previous appearance: he wore swim trunks while on ground but now swims in military fatigues. We realize that, in the windmill, Ivan was dreaming—Tarkovsky's allusion to the long-standing link between windmills and human imagination as posited by Miguel de Cervantes in *Don Quixote* (1605), a book that Tarkovsky foregrounds (and has characters recite from) in *Solaris*. Channeling Sancho Panza's love of sleep, Ivan dreams his way out of the reality of Soviet Ukraine during World War II to a time before his mother was killed by the Nazis, leaving him an orphan.

The peacefulness of Ivan's woodland dream notwithstanding, omens saturate his subconscious, most palpably transmitted by the cuckoo bird's call. In many folkloric traditions, particularly in Eastern Europe, cuckoo birds betoken death. In Russia, upon hearing a cuckoo bird, it is customary to ask, "Cuckoo bird, cuckoo bird, how much longer do I have left to live?"[108] Cuckoo birds tend to appear during the spring rains; therefore, it is claimed that they carry secret knowledge about the onset of summer, the prime of a forest's life. Such keenness to seasonal change affords cuckoo birds metaphoric insight into how long a person has to live, hence their connection to time, evidenced by the seventeenth-century invention of the cuckoo clock in the Black Forest region of Germany.

The cuckoo bird commencing *Ivan's Childhood* announces not only the death of Ivan's mother but also *his* untimely demise, which occurs at the end of the film in a Nazi prison, where he is hanged. Ivan's childhood is over before it begins. The cuckoo bird's refrain—which also signifies orphanhood, as mother cuckoo birds desert their hatchlings—casts a pall over Tarkovsky's debut and evokes his own experience of childhood abandonment after his father left his family in 1937.[109] The cuckoo bird at the start of *Ivan's Childhood* is just one of many details foretelling Ivan's fate. The matted texture of the spiderweb replicates the look of iron bars, visually imprisoning Ivan as the Nazis later will, and minutes later, Ivan swims through an actual web of barbed wire. The unnervingly magnified close-up of a goat—an animal that, in certain corners of Christianity, bears demonic and pagan implications—foreshadows the hell awaiting child soldiers like Ivan during World War II, and the sparse conifer tree looks more dead than alive, not unlike Ivan, whose youth has been robbed. In concert with a range of nature symbols, Tarkovsky utilizes a cuckoo bird to reveal how his debut film will end: with the death of a child.

The cuckoo's call commencing *Ivan's Childhood* anticipates the bird's importance for Tarkovsky's cinema more generally. In *Andrei Rublev*, a cuckoo bird resounds during the debate about humanity between Theophanes the Greek (Nikolai Sergeyev) and Rublev. "The Last Judgment is coming," Theophanes cries, "and we'll burn like candles." In *Solaris*, a cuckoo bird follows Kelvin as he traipses about his father's estate before his ill-fated voyage. In the opening shot of *Mirror*, a cuckoo bird's call rings out, accompanied by the sounds of a buzzing fly and a ticking clock; together, they allude to Russia's memories of death and decay under Stalin in the 1930s, when much of *Mirror* takes place. And in *Stalker*, a cuckoo bird trails Tarkovsky's protagonists across the Zone, which, littered with corpses, acts as a waystation for lost souls. The peal of a cuckoo bird is also heard during the film's final scene, but now in the form of a clock, an automated timekeeper, as Stalker condemns modern industrial society. This mechanization of the cuckoo bird reiterates John Berger's thesis concerning animals' physical disappearance in modern life and their reanimation as technological facsimiles, detailed in chapter 1. Outside the fantastical Zone, real cuckoo birds have become ever more remote.

For some of Tarkovsky's characters—Stalker, Domenico, Aleksandr—madness is the only reasonable response to the confusion of modern life and the knowledge that we are all doomed; they embrace the cuckoo bird's age-old connotations with insanity. These associations between cuckoo birds and madness originally developed because of the cuckoo bird's self-referential call, as if the bird is constantly talking (nonsense) to itself, not unlike the addled madman in *Ivan's Childhood* who keeps a pet bird.[110] It was the ancient Greek playwright Aristophanes who coined the term "cloud cuckoo land" in *The Birds* (414 BCE), a comedy about an absurd sky kingdom in which fowls supplant the gods. In the nineteenth century, German philosophers like Arthur Schopenhauer and Friedrich Nietzsche repurposed Aristophanes's evocative coinage in their writings about human (ir)rationality.[111] Tarkovsky's protagonists go "cuckoo" as a survival strategy in response to mortality's inescapability and the alienation of modern life, as do characters in *One Flew over the Cuckoo's Nest* (1975) by Miloš Forman, one of Tarkovsky's filmmaking peers who also escaped political persecution in Eastern Europe by fleeing abroad in the 1960s.[112] "We don't know what madmen are," Gorchakov says of Domenico in *Nostalghia*. "They're troublesome, inconvenient, but they're certainly closer to the truth."

It is not by chance that Domenico has an eccentric poster hanging in his home that reads "$1 + 1 = 1$." This wall art crystallizes Domenico's insanity—which climaxes in his self-immolation—by calling for a reintroduction of the irrational into human life, for a departure from the cold, hard logic structuring modern society that has failed to prepare us for death. Domenico's poster evokes the famous antimath passage in Fyodor Dostoevsky's *Notes from Underground* (*Zapiski iz podpol'ia*, 1864). "Two times two is four," the novel's (anti)hero claims, "has a cocky look; it stands across your path, arms akimbo, and spits. I agree that two times two is four is an excellent thing; but if we're going to start praising everything, then two times two is five is sometimes also a most charming little thing."[113] Dostoevsky, the literary heart of the nineteenth-century Slavophile movement, championed an alternative, antimodern worldview that centered Russian mysticism and iconoclasm against Europe's secular rationalism. In *Nostalghia*, Tarkovsky has an Italian madman remind a Russian émigré of *his* country's "troublesome" madness, to which Russia has long turned to antagonize self-assured Westerners. Domenico and Gorchakov sacrifice themselves for a vision of another (Russo-centric) world; Domenico, Gorchakov says, "has faith."

In *The Sacrifice*, Tarkovsky has seagulls perform the funereal role of cuckoo birds. The visual tour of the carob tree in Leonardo's *Adoration of the Magi* commencing *The Sacrifice* is overlaid with seagulls' caws. Though attending to Christ's birth, da Vinci's tree denotes death because, after double-crossing Jesus, Judas, it is said by some theologians, hanged himself from a carob tree.[114] The wise man's gift of frankincense, an antimicrobial resin used to mask the smell of decay during Roman funerals, also alludes to expiry. Leonardo's tree of life is, in fact, a tree of death portending the demise of the Christ child, just as the sparse conifer and cuckoo bird do in *Ivan's Childhood*. The shot after *Adoration of the Magi* shows Aleksandr and his son, who resembles Ivan, planting a barren tree similar to the one in *Ivan's Childhood*. We later see Little Man carrying two tin pails of water, recalling the image of Ivan drinking from a metal bucket at his (dead) mother's feet. Through trees, buckets, and birds—cuckoos and gulls—Tarkovsky dovetails the beginning of his oeuvre with its end, enacting a full life cycle. Indeed, the very last shot of *The Sacrifice* re-creates the first shot of *Ivan's Childhood*: a lateral glide up a gaunt tree.

Acknowledging da Vinci's allusion to the Christ child's demise in *Adoration of the Magi*, Otto says, upon seeing a copy of the painting in Aleksandr's home: "My God, how sinister! I've always been terrified by Leonardo." Otto's words are heard against the shrieks of the gulls, which are superseded by the crackling voice of a television broadcaster announcing that the world has plunged into nuclear war, evoking yet another of Bergman's films, *Shame* (*Skammen*, 1968), about the outbreak of war on a remote Swedish island. The child death first presaged by the cuckoo bird in *Ivan's Childhood*—and then by seagulls during Tarkovsky's tour of *Adoration of the Magi*—culminates in a doomsday proclamation about humanity's fiery extinction in *The Sacrifice*.

The crumbling buildings and battling horsemen in Leonardo's painting, in this light, are omens portending the conflict that Christ's death will occasion, which *The Sacrifice* captures through Aleksandr's hallucinations of a war-torn city full of stampeding people. This postapocalyptic imagery inverts the idea of paradise ironically implied by the phrase "cloud cuckoo land." The seabirds of *The Sacrifice* emanate not from some kingdom in the sky but from a sulfurous underworld. For Tarkovsky, cloud cuckoo land signifies the folly of humanity's progress as measured by the scientific "achievement" of nuclear technology: "Nuclear war? That wouldn't even be a victory for Satan. It would be like a child playing with matches and setting fire to his house. You can't even accuse it of pyromania. Spiritually, man is not ready to survive his bombs. He's not mature enough."[115] Ever threatened by nuclear winter, modern society is, in Tarkovsky's eyes, a kind of cloud cuckoo land deliriously entertaining its own annihilation.

In a dark coincidence, *The Sacrifice* premiered in May 1986, weeks after the Chernobyl explosion, which triggered the worst environmental catastrophe in human history. While Tarkovsky could not have anticipated the disaster, the threat of nuclear war had escalated in the early 1980s as tensions between the Soviet Union and the United States surged, particularly after the Soviets mistakenly downed a Korean passenger plane in 1983. This brinksmanship terrified Tarkovsky, and he used *The Sacrifice* to ponder the world's precarity: "It's that man should aspire toward spiritual greatness, he should leave behind him secrets that a million years from now others will need to decipher, not ruins which only bring to mind traces of catastrophe ... in any event not the nuclear plant at Chernobyl, just the opposite."[116] Nuclear reactors, for Tarkovsky, were monuments to humanity's delusional notions of progress. It was, after all, Swedish authorities, the figures announcing nuclear war in *The Sacrifice*, who first broadcast information about irregular levels of radiation emanating from the Soviet Union in April 1986. Chernobyl, in Tarkovsky's view, became a smoldering shrine to cloud cuckoo land.

The seabirds in *The Sacrifice* portend anthropogenic obliteration in a realization of the twentieth century's worst fears, again channeling Hitchcock's terrifying crows in *The Birds*. Hitchcock's horror movie tapped into ecological concerns raised by the publication of Rachel Carson's *Silent Spring* (1962), a book—banned by the Soviets—that catalyzed the creation of the Environmental Protection Agency (EPA) in the United States through its detailed examination of the effects of synthetic pesticides on the natural world, including bird reproduction.[117] "Where had they gone?" Carson imagines American townsfolk asking after some sort of ecological fallout in the opening pages of *Silent Spring*. "It was spring without voices."[118] Hitchcock's homicidal birds are harbingers of a dying planet increasingly hostile to animal life, just as Tarkovsky's seabirds augur nuclear winter. The sounds of *The Sacrifice*'s cacophonous birds are, indeed, replaced by the roars of nuclear fighter jets in another (sonic) enactment of Berger's (and Carson's) postapocalyptic visions of animal disappearance. Tarkovsky's birds-turned-planes are the logical extreme of da Vinci's dreams of flight, which, recklessly pursued, beget dystopic consequences.

In *The Sacrifice*, however, the worst never occurs thanks to Maria's sorcery: Aleksandr wakes up the next morning after sleeping with Maria and discovers that the world has averted nuclear extermination. The seabirds have returned, and their cries, now replacing the noise of fighter jets, signal not death but exuberant new life. The apocalyptic dread saturating *The Sacrifice* has dissipated, suggesting that, for Tarkovsky, all is not lost. Confronted with nuclear fallout, Tarkovsky hoped that humanity could still somehow be saved: "Hope has a tendency to grow in the face of the most sordid facts of real life. This is simply because horror ... inspires a believer with hope."[119] Tarkovsky's seabirds, then, foreshadow both ruin and renewal, both death and life after death.

This triadic connection between birds, life, and death is commonplace in many cultures, given that birds fly great distances as if embarking on journeys between worlds that offer them information inaccessible to earthbound humans. The psychoanalyst Karl Jung described birds as "soul-images" because their airborne nature represents a kind of "shamanic flight": a metaphor for the human soul's metaphysical transcendence—its ascent (or descent) into the afterlife—upon the body's physical cessation.[120] In his work on the "collective unconscious," Jung posited several unlearned forms of knowledge—"archetypes"—passed down over millennia that represented supposedly universal aspects of anthropological experience, allowing for a shared understanding of human behavior across cultures and languages.[121] One of Jung's archetypes concerns rebirth, the belief that life continues after death, refuting human finitude. This archetype, Jung argued, arose from the need to conciliate our existential anxieties as triggered by the prospect of death's finality; it thus became the bedrock for most world religions so as to prevent us from falling into a void of despair over our impending extinction. The characteristics of birds, particularly migratory birds, that leave our world only to return with the warm season personify such rebirth: "Birds are associated with death not because some are black, eat carrion, or have nocturnal habits, but because they embody the fullness of life."[122] For his part, Tarkovsky portrays birds in this dualistic fashion. They represent wisdom about human demise *and* the enduring and migratory nature of the human soul (a dualism that also informs Tarkovsky's embrace of the Buddhist philosophy of reincarnation, explored in chap. 4).

At the end of *Mirror*, Tarkovsky's autobiographical protagonist—the poet Aleksei (voiced by Innokentii Smoktunovskii)—appears on his deathbed. The camera scans the bedsheets to reveal a wounded sparrow lying beside him. Sparrows, in many cultural traditions, symbolize the wanderlust of the human soul, as they are the most widespread bird in the world. The sparrow's story, then, "seems to be that of the meek inheriting the earth."[123] In *Mirror*, the dying Aleksei reaches out and clasps the sparrow, just as the boy with a bird atop his head did earlier. As Aleksei holds the sparrow, the camera tracks upward, and we hear his final strained breaths. In his last act on Earth, Aleksei releases the sparrow. The image of his outstretched hand and the fluttering bird reenacts Michelangelo's painting *The Creation of Adam* (1512), an image of divine birth. Allegorized by the ethereal sparrow, Aleksei's soul soars to a realm beyond the knowable, echoing the lines of a poem penned by Tarkovsky's father and recited earlier in *Mirror*, "Eurydice" ("Evridika," 1961): "The soul flies out through the cornea / Into the heavenly clearness, / Upon

Tarkovsky's protagonist releases the sparrow held in his hands at the end of his life, suggesting that he has come to terms with mortality. Still from *Mirror*, 1975.

the icy spoke, / Upon the bird-drawn chariot." Through Aleksei's freeing of the bird, Tarkovsky suggests—as he does in *The Sacrifice*—that what we consider to be the worst fate of all, the cosmic nothingness of death, will not befall us; death is not what it seems. "Everything," Aleksei says, holding the sparrow, "will be what will be." Rooted in the Jungian archetype of rebirth, *Mirror*'s soul-image of a flying bird and a man who has come to terms with his mortality, symbolized by his unclenched fist, a literal image of letting go, denies human finitude.

Though we never see Aleksei in *Mirror*—we hear only his voice—we encounter his forearm on his deathbed. It was, astonishingly, *Tarkovsky himself* who stood in for Aleksei's corpse.[124] Tarkovsky playacted his own death in *Mirror* perhaps to reassure himself about the nature of human everlastingness through this deathbed encounter with a sparrow. The scene acquired even more prophetic resonance when, dying from lung cancer in the mid-1980s, Tarkovsky took to sheltering an injured sparrow in his Paris residence, whom he named Tishka or, in English, "the quiet one." Photos of a terminally ill Tarkovsky stroking the bird replicate the images of him, ten years earlier, clasping a sparrow in *Mirror* as Aleksei, his deceased alter ego.

Tarkovsky's craving for immortality is symptomatic of humanity's psychological and emotional incapacity to fathom our own impermanence—that is, humanity's "metaphysical narcissism": our reluctance to believe that the

A terminally ill Tarkovsky took to sheltering an injured bird, whom he named Tishka—the quiet one—in the final months of his life. Photograph © Irina Brown, 1986.

universe will or can go on without us.[125] Human beings, indeed, are never "so self-involved as when they fear death."[126] We assume, perhaps mistakenly, that since animals cannot grasp the abstract concepts of death and (re)birth the way humans can, all animals—including birds—are hopelessly terrestrial. The belief that our souls soar like birds upon death implies that human beings are somehow impervious to the material realities of nonexistence haunting other animals, which, like the felled swan in *Andrei Rublev*, return to the Earth after death—from dust to dust. Humans, as it were, are the "real" birds: heaven sent and skyward bound. Tarkovsky's obsession with death, in art and in life, betrays his unwillingness or inability to let go of his mortal concerns like his alter ego cadaver in *Mirror*. Alexei's unclenched fist (that is, Tarkovsky's) is an image of meekness and humility in the face of death—perfectly embodied by the frail sparrow—that Tarkovsky spent a lifetime trying to achieve. Tarkovsky, in other words, hoped to become *sparrow-like*, attuned to the importance of small and quiet things rather than the cosmic questions of life-and-death seriousness that seemed to seize his every waking thought. Tarkovsky's macabre fascinations make apparent that, of all of Earth's creatures, only human beings spend so much of their lives so preoccupied by the afterlife, as if held hostage by the knowledge of their own mortality. Tarkovsky, like so many of us, hoped that our destiny extends into the sky above us, not into the lunacy of cloud cuckoo land but through heaven's gates and among the angels.

NOTES

1. Tarkovsky, *Time Within Time*, 63.
2. For this etymology, see Sax, *Aviation Illuminations*, 20.
3. Sax, *Aviation Illuminations*, 18.
4. Lévi-Strauss, *Savage Mind*, 204.
5. Lévi-Strauss, *Savage Mind*, 204.
6. Gura, *Simvolika zhivotnykh*, 703–709.
7. See Moreman, "On the Relationship Between Birds and Spirits of the Dead," 481–502.
8. See Soles, "'And No Birds Sing.'"
9. See Jung, "Concerning Rebirth."
10. Tarkovsky, *Time Within Time*, 29.
11. Komaromi, "Material Existence of Soviet Samizdat," 598.
12. Bird, *Andrei Tarkovsky*, 76.
13. See "Robert Bird on *Andrei Rublev*."
14. Banerjee, *We Modern People*, 44.
15. Palmer, *Dictatorship of the Air*, 7.
16. Tarkovsky, *Sculpting in Time*, 79.
17. For the film's (delayed) premier, see Johnson and Petrie, *Films of Andrei Tarkovsky*, 81.
18. Johnson and Petrie, *Films of Andrei Tarkovsky*, 87.
19. See Waxman, "Aerial Photography's Surprising Role in History."
20. For film and airplanes, see Ferguson, "Aviation Cinema."
21. Ferguson, "Aviation Cinema," 310.
22. Gunning, "Aesthetic of Astonishment," 114.
23. Gunning, "Aesthetic of Astonishment," 116.
24. See *Oxford English Dictionary*, "bird's-eye-view (n.)."
25. For the swan's symbolism, see Young, *Swan*, 32–61.
26. Quoted in Skakov, *Cinema of Tarkovsky*, 226.
27. Skakov, *Cinema of Tarkovsky*, 50–51.
28. Tarkovsky, *Time Within Time*, 187.
29. Tarkovsky, *Interviews*, 146.
30. Tarkovsky, *Sculpting in Time*, 108.
31. Tarkovsky, *Sculpting in Time*, 9, 108.
32. See "Codex on the Flight of Birds."
33. Tarkovsky, *Interviews*, 9.

34. Tarkovsky, *Interviews*, 9.
35. Tarkovsky, *Interviews*, 140.
36. Nicholl, *Leonardo da Vinci*, 399.
37. Yurchak, *Everything Was Forever*, 1. Exemplifying Yurchak's idea of the "eternal state" of late socialism, Writer in *Stalker* at one point says, "The future used to be an advancement of the present, its changes loomed somewhere over the horizon. But now the future is part of the present."
38. For post-Thaw politics, see Fainberg and Kalinovsky, *Reconsidering the Brezhnev Era*.
39. For the monotonous culture of stagnation, see Raleigh, *Soviet Baby Boomers*, 220–67.
40. For escapism in stagnation-era cinema, see Harte and Rojavin, *Soviet Films of the 1970s and Early 1980s*.
41. Skakov, *Cinema of Tarkovsky*, 128.
42. Tarkovsky, *Time Within Time*, 295.
43. Tarkovsky, *Sculpting in Time*, 202.
44. Boym, *Future of Nostalgia*, 17.
45. Later in *Nostalghia*, Gorchakov meets a young girl named Angela, another "angel," whose innocence and kindness uplift him.
46. Sax, *Aviation Illuminations*, 8.
47. Sax, *Aviation Illuminations*, 28.
48. Kamm, "Soviet Director Asks Refuge," 20.
49. Tarkovsky, *Sculpting in Time*, 13.
50. See *Oxford English Dictionary*, "master (n, & adj.)."
51. Tarkovsky, *Time Within Time*, 91.
52. For "mastery" in Stalin-era discourse, see Chudinov, "Zametki o ritoricheskom masterstve."
53. Prieto, "Reading Mandelstam on Stalin."
54. For this call, see Chudakova, "Vecher, posviashchennyi 120-letiiu so dnia rozhdeniia O.E. Mandel'shtama."
55. Tarkovsky, *Time Within Time*, 163.
56. Widdis, *Visions of a New Land*, 128.
57. Widdis, *Visions of a New Land*, 122.
58. For aviation technology, propaganda, and pilots under Stalin, see Zubov, *Stalin's Falcons*.
59. See Amad, "From God's-Eye to Camera-Eye."
60. For Chkalov's death, see Bergman, "Valerii Chkalov," 137.
61. A shot of a plane having nose-dived into the ground in *Ivan's Childhood* also conveys Tarkovsky's critique of mechanized air travel.
62. See Werth, "Surrogate for War."
63. Sax, *Aviation Illuminations*, 305.

64. See Braun, *Picturing Time*.
65. Doane, *Emergence of Cinematic Time*, 25.
66. Cartwright, *Screening the Body*, 40.
67. Tarkovsky, *Sculpting in Time*, 94.
68. Bird, *Andrei Tarkovsky*, 210.
69. See Svensson, "On Tarkovsky's *The Sacrifice*," 112–17.
70. Tarkovsky, *Sculpting in Time*, 159, 162.
71. The sight of Writer and Professor at the Zone's threshold recycles an earlier image of the two standing in the tavern's doorway, when Professor warns Writer against reentering to collect his cigarettes. Professor here observes a Russian superstition that one should not return after leaving home for something forgotten. Professor's superstitiousness explains why, despite his ostensible commitment to reason, he aborts his attempt to destroy the Zone with a bomb and does not enter the wish-room, perhaps fearful of its supernatural powers.
72. Dyer, *Zona*, 189.
73. Earlier in the film, Writer accuses Stalker—and then physically attacks him—for lying about the Zone's magical properties: "You hypocritical louse. I can see through you. You don't give a damn about others. You make money from others' misery. Here you get to pretend you're tsar, God." Writer's remarks remind us of Dorothy's rebuke of the Wizard of Oz, who, she learns, is just an ordinary huckster: "You humbug. You're a very bad man." Metacinematically understood, Writer and Dorothy express frustration after having the illusion of cinema dispelled.
74. Dyer, *Zona*, 65.
75. Bellour, "Hitchcock—The Animal, Life and Death," 293–94.
76. See White, "Dark Side of an Auteur." Hitchcock infamously described his actors as "cattle" to be used as he saw fit. See Holliday, "'Actors Are Cattle!' Says Director Alfred Hitchcock."
77. Modleski, "Master's Dollhouse," 632.
78. Tarkovsky's eroticization of levitating women also reminds us of the airborne (and naked) heroine in Bulgakov's *The Master and Margarita*, perhaps the most famous instance of human flight in Soviet culture.
79. Tarkovsky, *Sculpting in Time*, 225, 228.
80. See LaFrance, "How the Bicycle Paved the Way for Women's Rights."
81. For the aesthetic and thematic overlap of bicycle and cinematic technologies, see Bennett, *Cycling and Cinema*, 2–6.
82. Tarkovsky, *Sculpting in Time*, 228.
83. Newson, "Preserving Wilderness," 164.
84. Tarkovsky, *Interviews*, 72.
85. Robinson, *Sacred Cinema of Andrei Tarkovsky*, 307.
86. For the cultural lore of roosters, see Potts, *Chicken*, 64–90.
87. Potts, *Chicken*, 74.

88. Sax, *Aviation Illuminations*, 206.
89. For the gendered symbolism of hens, see Sax, *Aviation Illuminations*, 216–24.
90. Freud, *Three Essays on the Theory of Sexuality*, 23.
91. Potts, *Chicken*, 98.
92. Terekhova, "'Rubit' golovy petukhu?"
93. Surkova, "Khroniki Tarkovskogo. Zerkalo."
94. Tarkovsky, *Sculpting in Time*, 109–10.
95. Terekhova, "'Rubit' golovy petukhu?"
96. Williams, *Hard Core*, 204.
97. Sax, *Aviation Illuminations*, 206–207.
98. Mulvey, *Visual and Other Pleasures*, 22.
99. Mulvey, *Visual and Other Pleasures*, 22.
100. Mulvey, *Visual and Other Pleasures*, 22.
101. Williams, *Hard Core*, 39.
102. Williams, *Hard Core*, 39–41.
103. Williams, *Hard Core*, 41.
104. Williams, *Hard Core*, 325; Burt, *Animals in Film*, 105.
105. Williams, *Hard Core*, 169.
106. Tarkovsky, *Sculpting in Time*, 109.
107. See *Oxford English Dictionary*, "cuck (*n.*)."
108. Gura, *Simvolika zhivotnykh*, 708–10.
109. See Kwok, "When Parenting Goes Cuckoo."
110. See *Oxford English Dictionary*, "cuckoo (*adj.*)."
111. See Tearle, "Meaning and Comedic Origins of Cloud Cuckoo Land."
112. See Goulding, *Five Filmmakers*.
113. Dostoevsky, *Notes from Underground*, 34.
114. Giralt, "Andrei Tarkovsky's Adaptation of Motifs," 77.
115. Tarkovsky, *Interviews*, 177.
116. Tarkovsky, *Interviews*, 182.
117. Soles, "'And No Birds Sing,'" 528; Josephson et al., *An Environmental History of Russia*, 191.
118. Carson, *Silent Spring*, 2.
119. Tarkovsky, *Interviews*, 172.
120. Quoted in Moreman, "On the Relationship Between Birds and Spirits of the Dead," 13.
121. See Jung, *Archetypes and the Collective Unconscious*.
122. Moreman, "On the Relationship Between Birds and Spirits of the Dead," 19.
123. Todd, *Sparrow*, 8.
124. For this photograph, see Chiaramonte and Tarkovsky, *Instant Light*, 128–29.
125. Soëlle, *Mystery of Death*, 5.
126. Soëlle, *Mystery of Death*, 5.

FOUR

COWS

THE MOST NOTORIOUS EPISODE OF animal violence in Andrei Tarkovsky's cinema—the burning of a cow—occurs in *Andrei Rublev*, a biopic about the storied fifteenth-century Russian iconographer. However, because of the film's troubled production history, few viewers saw this appalling image until decades after the film's (very) limited release in 1971.[1] The epigraph to this book—a quote from a 2006 interview with Ukrainian filmmaker Kira Muratova in which she recalls her horror after learning that the "rumors and talk" were true and that Tarkovsky had, indeed, burned a cow alive—confirms the grisly image's delayed reception.[2] What "rumors" was Muratova referring to? And why did it take so long for the cow's image to (re)emerge? Most importantly, why did Tarkovsky set a cow on fire—surely one of the most disturbing events in the history of moving images—at all?

After signing a contract in 1962 to make an epic film about Russia's greatest medieval painter, Tarkovsky and his cowriter, Andrei Konchalovsky, were offered considerable state resources—1.6 million rubles—to pursue their work, a fact that complicates any perception of Tarkovsky as a uniquely persecuted artist.[3] Yet Soviet authorities panned the resultant picture and thwarted its release for years, turning *Andrei Rublev* into one of the most scandalous Soviet films of all time, in no small part thanks to Tarkovsky's image of a burning cow.

The ordeal began in September 1965, several months after Tarkovsky started filming. A climate scientist at the University of Latvia, Professor Natālija Temņikova, published an open letter in *Izvestia*, a leading Soviet newspaper, decrying Tarkovsky's "barbaric footage" of a cow burning alive after being "doused in kerosene."[4] Temņikova's outrage—"Imagine how the animal must have suffered, running around in fire and grunting!"—reflected the heightened concern for animal life in postwar Soviet culture, which, explored in chapter 2, saw animal compassion as a marker of a morally healthy community in contrast to the nation's dark Stalinist past.[5] Temņikova claimed that an acquaintance in Suzdal', one of the small towns where Tarkovsky filmed parts of *Andrei Rublev*, had alerted her to the rank animal cruelty taking place on Tarkovsky's set.

Jolted by the inflammatory accusations, several journalists for *Izvestia* clamored for clarification, prompting the general director of Mosfil'm, the USSR's flagship studio financing *Andrei Rublev*, to issue a missive: "Wishing to truly and powerfully depict the horrors" of medieval Russia, Tarkovsky's "film crew, in one scene, showed . . . a cow running out of a burning barn, engulfed in flames. . . . For this purpose, one cow was used, which was then sent to the slaughterhouse after filming. The film crew has been instructed that such use of animals is strictly prohibited."[6] This directive, while disapproving, nevertheless echoes Tarkovsky's own explanation of why he had to burn a cow alive if he truly wanted to capture the cruelty of life in medieval Russia: "If you study what is said by any historian about those times, you will see that every page of Russian history . . . oozes blood. . . . It suffices to see all this blood on screen."[7] Some of Tarkovsky's contemporary viewers might have encountered the image of the burning cow—in rare color footage, no less—in a short documentary about the making of *Andrei Rublev* that aired on Soviet television in late 1965 to (somewhat ironically) promote the film.[8]

Notwithstanding the gratuitous violence in the first cut of *Andrei Rublev*, which initially bore the more biblical title *The Passion according to Andrei* (*Strast' po Andreiu*), Mos'film submitted it to the state artistic council for approval in August 1966 without demanding major edits.[9] Intermittently screened for select audiences in the intervening months, Tarkovsky's film garnered more and more controversy due to its graphic violence, particularly the image of the burning cow, and state authorities became increasingly circumspect about its prospects.[10]

Things came to a head on December 24, 1966—on the eve of the film's industry premiere—when a little-known critic, I. Soldatov, published an impassioned article in the popular Soviet newspaper *Evening Moscow* (*Vechernaiai Moskva*) titled ". . . And a Cow Burst into Flames" (". . . *I zapylala korova*"), a source of inspiration for *this* book's title.[11] Sharing Professor Temņikova's sense of moral emergency as elicited by Tarkovsky's animal cruelty, Soldatov wrote:

> [The cow's] agonized moans and cries echoed around, scaring not only children but also adults. And those adults who had been standing nearby must have looked on with sorrow in their eyes at the poor animal, which they

themselves had just set on fire.... They poured gasoline on it and lit it ablaze. No, they were neither bandits nor barbarians, nor cold-hearted people.... Each of them likely wanted to rush to the cow to smother the flames and save it. But the imperious hand of the director stopped all their attempts. The cow, a living cow, was consumed by fire—this was a sacrifice offered on the altar of art cinema at the command of the filmmaker.[12]

Motivated by either a concerted and cynical effort to discredit the film—and, therefore, its impetuous director—or genuine concern for animal welfare in step with the Thaw's "petishistic" culture (or perhaps an honest mix of both), Soldatov's article, which also criticized Tarkovsky's excessive use of nudity and gore, magnified the concerns about *Andrei Rublev*, leading even those who supported Tarkovsky's project to back away from it. To appease state censors, Tarkovsky made serious alterations and excised all the images of the burning cow. This editing process, however, only further bogged down the release of *Andrei Rublev*, causing it to fall out of favor entirely and languish in "administrative limbo for five years."[13] *Andrei Rublev* became the most famous film to *not* be released in the USSR.[14] Eventually, in 1971, Soviet officials granted an extremely limited release of a heavily redacted version of the film without, as Tarkovsky noted, "a single poster" or word of praise for it.[15] While Tarkovsky came to prefer this pared-down version of *Andrei Rublev*, he initially claimed that the edits had ruined it, betraying the centrality of graphic animal cruelty to his original vision.[16]

Unknown to all, the uncut version of *Andrei Rublev* was secretly preserved by one of the film's editors, Lyudmila Feiginova (who kept it stowed under her bed); it only reemerged in 1987 amid the liberal atmosphere under Mikhail Gorbachev, two years after Tarkovsky's death and in the twilight days of Soviet power.[17] *Andrei Rublev*'s circuitous release, then, gave Tarkovsky ample cover and plausible deniability about whether he had ever actually immolated a cow, and the scandal faded from view during his lifetime. In his remarks about the incident, Tarkovsky either outright rejected the "monstrous insinuations" that he had incinerated a cow (specifically referencing Soldatov's incendiary article) or conceded that, even if he *had* lit the cow on fire, he had covered it in asbestos beforehand—not in gasoline, as the rumor mill alleged—so that the animal would not unduly suffer.[18]

As if encasing the cow in flame-retardant fabric could somehow justify lighting an animal on fire and insulate Tarkovsky from charges of animal cruelty, Tarkovsky absolved himself of all responsibility. Without available footage, it was difficult to substantiate Tarkovsky's refutations, which conflated the accusations levied against him with a state propaganda campaign to undermine *Andrei Rublev*. If anything, rumors about the cow's burning conferred on Tarkovsky a halo of martyrdom—"the *succès de scandale*"—and enabled him to play the time-honored role of Russian artist hounded by the state, not unlike Rublev.[19] The criticism engulfing *Andrei Rublev* is not only critical for our understanding of the film's vexed backstory; it is also a linchpin detail of what made Tarkovsky "Tarkovsky." Gossip about the burning cow—discussed even by the Central Committee of the Communist Party—lent *Andrei Rublev* a mystique that helped propel Tarkovsky into the pantheon of the cinematic canon.[20] Indeed, Tarkovsky used the cow's burning to spin a story about his own creative freedom and victimization, a textbook case of a strategy behavioral psychologists identify in those racked with a guilty conscience, who use it to diffuse responsibility, manipulate others, and cope with past actions.[21] With *Andrei Rublev*, Tarkovsky deflected the hostility—or, in his words, "the zoological hatred"—against him by obscuring the facts about the true victim of his own gratuitous act of "zoological hatred."[22] The story of *Andrei Rublev*—indeed, that of Tarkovsky's career trajectory—is also, in part, a story about a cow.

A final twist in the biography of Tarkovsky's burning cow came after the Soviet Union's collapse in 1991. Rather unpredictably, the American director Martin Scorsese—a dedicated film preservationist who had just established the nonprofit Film Foundation—procured the original copy of *Andrei Rublev* during his visit to Moscow.[23] The prestigious American home-video distribution company Criterion Collection released it on LaserDisc in 1994 (then on DVD in 1999 and again on Blu-ray in 2018). As expected, the unearthed director's cut contained the infamous cow burning scene, confirming all suspicions that Tarkovsky had lit an animal on fire. Yet this revelation also coincided with the publications of the first English-language books dedicated to Tarkovsky, whose haunting cinema, obliquely critical of Soviet communism, only rose in stature during the USSR's final days and eventual fall (Tarkovsky, for instance, was posthumously awarded the Lenin Prize in 1990).[24] The optimism of the early post-Soviet period cemented Tarkovsky's august reputation, impervious to the "new" footage of the burning cow.

Since the resurfacing of *Andrei Rublev*'s original cut, many in Tarkovsky's professional orbit have come to his defense concerning his treatment of the cow. Tamara Ogorodnikova, the production manager of *Andrei Rublev*, said that the cow, covered in asbestos, "got scared and ran around" after being set on fire but did not die: "You watch the scene and see not only the cow burning—people are burning, too, and you don't think that they're actually on fire. This is normal cinema."[25] Similarly, *Andrei Rublev*'s cameraman, Vadim Iusov, stated that while the cow suffered "some burns," it "walked off set on its own four legs."[26] Yet others involved in the making of *Andrei Rublev* who had less at stake in the film's reception have said that the cow did, in truth, burn to death. Alisa Aksenova, former director of the Vladimir-Suzdal' State Museum who served as a historical consultant for Tarkovsky's film crew, said, "Why mislead? They burned the cow. Alive."[27] Likewise, the Russian poet Stainslav Kuniaev, who dedicated a poem to Tarkovsky's cow, reported that the Soviet diplomat Evgenii Samoteikin, tasked with managing press coverage of *Andrei Rublev*, wrote, "Was the cow burned? Of course it was."[28] As a rule, those nearest to Tarkovsky—those who could be construed as complicit in the controversy—deny that he burned the cow to death, while those more distant say differently. This book, *And the Cow Burned*, allies itself with the latter camp. The "and" of its title introduces an interjection into the debate by affirming what Tarkovsky and his acolytes have long disputed through understatement, evasion, and falsehood.

For us, though, does it (or should it) matter whether Tarkovsky *actually* burned a cow to death? Would the image of a cow smothered in flames in *Andrei Rublev* be any less disturbing if it could be authenticated as a perverse cinematic illusion, not unlike the faux decapitation of a cockerel in *Mirror*? If our concern about the cow's safety could be allayed by taking Tarkovsky at his word—by accepting his halfhearted assurances about asbestos—what would *Andrei Rublev*'s image of a burning cow *still* have to communicate not only about Tarkovsky but also about our readiness to exculpate him? That Tarkovsky continually and indignantly minimized the severity of the cow's burning betrays a certain self-consciousness that his actions went beyond the pale. Tarkovsky's medieval epic, one theme of which centers on the evil lurking in all human beings, culminates in a "medieval" act of brutality against a defenseless animal that exposes the ruthlessness at the core of his filmography. The burning cow raises the stakes of Tarkovsky's desire for artistic control as he takes life and death into his own directorial hands. What Tarkovsky *intends* for us to imagine happening to the cow through the image of its immolation, whatever its true fate, is just as vital to our understanding of its significance, steeped in psychoanalytic, gendered, cinematic, and philosophical implications.

MOTHER COW

Set in the latter half of Russia's two-hundred-year occupation by the Mongols, *Andrei Rublev* depicts the terror and violence of Mongol rule, most notably in a vignette entitled "The Raid," in which the Russian town Vladimir is pillaged. The image of the burning cow appears during this sequence, when the camera

The burning cow, an image Tarkovsky long denied and defended, is central to a full understanding of Tarkovsky's cinema. Still from *Andrei Rublev*, 1966.

enters a barn the Mongols have set on fire. We see what appears to be an amorphous fireball before the sounds of agitated mooing reverberate within the frame. The smoldering heap, we realize, is a *cow*. As the hellish image comes into focus, we see the cow engulfed by flames, attempting to shake off the inferno. The cow appears on screen for six seconds before staggering below the camera's line of sight; it does not reappear within the visual field. This nightmarish footage prompts an obvious—yet rarely posed—question: Why did Tarkovsky set a cow on fire?

The first answer to that question lies in the symbolic significance of cows. In Russia, as in other cultures, cows have long been associated with women and maternal figures because of their milk-producing capacity.[29] Indeed, human beings often anthropomorphize cows with idealized characteristics of their own mothers: unselfishness, tenderness, fertility. These idyllic qualities explain cows' focal presence (often near buxom milkmaids) in landscape paintings, as in the work of the Dutch painter Paulus Potter, whose bovine scenes inspired those of nineteenth-century Russian artist Mikhail Clodt von Jürgensburg.[30] The very word for "cow" in Russian, *korova*, is grammatically feminine, proceeding from the proto-Slavic for "horned beast."[31] An ordinary animal, neither exotic nor exciting, the cow signifies a magnanimous, nonthreatening power; a cow, in effect, "is the Mother of all humans."[32] It is not by chance that cows play a pivotal role in many creation myths, including the cowlike creatures often depicted near the Slavic goddess Mokosh, the only female deity among the ancient gods of Slavic mythology.[33] Cows' tendency to evoke human gratitude for their maternal attributes has informed their portrayals in popular culture. This is evident in Dariush Mehrjui's film *Cow* (*Gav*, 1969), which centers on a farmer's bovine fixation, and a banned story by Soviet writer Andrei Platonov, "The Cow" ('Korova', 1938)—rereleased during the early days of Tarkovsky's career—about a boy who becomes hopelessly attached to his family's cow.[34] These works explore the affection popularly expressed toward cows, particularly by men in want of maternal nourishment.

Tarkovsky, however, appears to symbolically repudiate—literally doom by fire—cows' maternal personification. A basis for Tarkovsky's antipathy toward the cow perhaps lies in his fraught relations with his own mother, Maria Vishnyakova. Despite growing up in Stalin's Russia, Tarkovsky enjoyed a relatively peaceful childhood. His serene adolescence ended when his father, acclaimed poet Arseny Tarkovsky, abandoned his family to pursue another woman in 1937. "I lived with mother, grandmother, and sister," Tarkovsky recalled. "Family without a man. This had considerable impact on my character.... I have always missed my father."[35] The absence of a father haunted Tarkovsky for his whole life, and his mournful cinema is, in part, an attempt to reconcile with the traumatic shock of that singular loss.[36] Indeed, many of Tarkovsky's brooding male heroes seek out—and sometimes become—surrogate father figures.

According to Evgeny Tsymbal, a leading authority on Tarkovsky, the impact of paternal abandonment was equally as devastating for Tarkovsky's mother.[37] At times, Vishnyakova would emotionally withdraw from her children out of an unwillingness to accept the loss of her husband, whose memory, as Tsymbal shows, she preserved through ritualistic acts of devotion. One of the opening shots of *Mirror*, Tarkovsky's autobiographical film in which Vishnyakova cameos, portrays the film's mother-protagonist (Margarita Terekhova) gazing into the distance, hoping against hope for her husband's return. "If he turned from the tree toward our house," the off-screen narrator says in reference to a wandering male figure, "then it was father."[38] Despite her presence in her children's lives, Vishnyakova, whose behavior Tsymbal analyzes through the "dead mother complex" plotted by French psychoanalyst André Green, sometimes retreated from everyday life: a remote, pensive disposition exquisitely captured by Terekhova in *Mirror*.[39]

Though Tarkovsky did express his love for Vishnyakova—he dedicated *Mirror* and *Nostalghia* to her—none of Tarkovsky's biographers doubt the ambivalence and resentment he harbored toward her: "Despite his deep feelings of gratitude towards his mother . . . Tarkovsky, in growing up, also felt oppressed by her will, her nervousness, her principles and her pride."[40] What Tarkovsky perceived as his mother's emotional unavailability redoubled the anguish occasioned by his father's disappearance, so much so that Tarkovsky blamed *her* for his father's neglect. In this light, is it coincidental that Tarkovsky abandoned his first son and wife, Irma Raush—who herself played a dead mother character in *Ivan's Childhood*—for another woman, a production assistant on *Andrei Rublev*, Larisa Kizilova? It is as if Tarkovsky emulated his father's biography by re-creating the act of paternal desertion, sentencing his first son to a similarly estranged childhood with an emotionally evacuated mother.

Psychoanalytically evaluated, the burning cow in *Andrei Rublev* could indicate Tarkovsky's symbolic assault on motherhood. Indeed, the graphic image of a cow on fire cannot help but evoke a highly visceral reaction; its affective charge—and the heated controversy it elicited—eschews any form of emotional detachment. Whereas horses represent Tarkovsky's ideal yet remote vision of masculinity, indicative of his absent father, the burning cow in *Andrei Rublev* may signify what Tarkovsky might have internalized as the failed promise of motherhood. Is Tarkovsky here trying to overcome the memories of what he perceived as his mother's inability to devote herself fully to her son by extracting from a cow the ultimate sacrifice any living being could be forced to make? The burning of the cow in *Andrei Rublev* also resonates with the finale of *The Sacrifice*, discussed below, when the protagonist unexpectedly burns his house down. This act promises a rebirth for the man's son, an escape from the past, "but at the cost of the father's self-inflicted withdrawal."[41] Tarkovsky uses fire to purge boyhood trauma, damning the cow in his Oedipal psychodrama.

Tarkovsky's attack betrays a popular view of cows, at least in the industrialized West, as fundamentally disposable beings: "Without complaint and in a gentle manner, [a cow] provides male calves in the fields, nourishes humans with milk, and provides manure for fuel and fertilizing of crops. . . . She is a precious commodity" that is "just there and always providing."[42] Cows are often taken for granted, whether for their bodies or by-products—just as human beings (particularly men) are liable to become overly accustomed to maternal care. The notion that mothers are preternaturally selfless has deep cultural origins stemming from the Christian cult of the Virgin Mary, which powerfully shaped Tarkovsky's views on women.[43] "What is a woman's driving-force?" Tarkovsky wrote. "Submission, humiliation in the name of love."[44] This vision of female piety is immortalized by Andrei Rublev's icon *The Trinity* (*Troitsa*, 1411), which appears in *Andrei Rublev*, *Solaris*, and *Mirror*. Women, in Tarkovsky's eyes, have little purpose beyond their sons and husbands. As a sacristan says to a young woman in *Nostalghia*, practically lifting lines straight from Tarkovsky's diaries, "A woman is meant to have children and to raise them with patience and self-sacrifice." The ease with which patriarchal idealization of mothers translates into fetish, disregard, and misogyny also parallels the way humanity's affection for cows seamlessly backslides into ethical unconcern. Nearly three hundred million cows are slaughtered each year all over the world, despite (or perhaps because of) their revered maternal connotations.[45] The presumed expendability of cows in human society, exemplified by Tarkovsky's decision to burn one alive, resonates with the misogynistic assumption that human mothers exist solely for their children. However, the immolated cow in *Andrei Rublev* is more than a mere repository for Tarkovsky's "mommy issues"; it functions as a site on which Tarkovsky also discharges his deeper anxieties about sex and gender.

The postwar identity crisis of Russian masculinity, detailed in chapter 1, made complaints against the rise of the Western feminist movement omnipresent in late Soviet culture, which blamed women for the phenomenon of male dislocation.[46] "All of them!" Tarkovsky once exclaimed of feminists, "Horrible!"[47] He said elsewhere that "a solitary woman is an abnormality" because she has achieved independence by deprioritizing motherhood and domesticity.[48] In *The Sacrifice*—a film set in Sweden, the epicenter of second-wave feminism—Tarkovsky's protagonist recounts how his sister, whose blond hair, he says, resembled Lady Godiva's, once cut it short like a boy's "in the style of the day," which brought her father to tears. This anecdote betrays Tarkovsky's essentialist, almost comically reductive ideas of womanhood, measured by appearance alone. Tarkovsky, in other words, understood the promise of feminism as a false idol, a golden calf: "I know you want to be happy," a man says disapprovingly to a stylishly dressed and romantically unattached woman in *Nostalghia*, "but there are more important things in life."

Tarkovsky's antipathy toward feminism explains why, in *Andrei Rublev*, he chastens a temptress character for trying to seduce Rublev during a pagan ceremony. As Rublev approaches her, his cloak catches on fire, symbolizing the energy aroused by a "solitary woman"; Rublev is "singed by the spectacle of naked female flesh," foreshadowing the reactionary gender politics subtending the image of the burning cow.[49] To underscore the temptress's prurience, Tarkovsky filmed her topless in what critics—like Soldatov, mentioned above—lambasted as one of the most erotic scenes in Soviet cinema's otherwise prudish history.[50] The only other major female character in *Andrei Rublev* is the holy fool girl (*durochka*) who rides away with the Mongols after being enchanted by their shiny armor, which she uses as a crude mirror. Carnal, insubordinate, and frivolous, the women of *Andrei Rublev* are punished: the *durochka*, played by Raush (Tarkovsky's first wife), abducted and the temptress arrested.[51] As Robert Bird points out, three different actresses portrayed the temptress during her arrest, suggesting that "the camera sees her through Andrei's carnal gaze, which constructs her as a mutable object of desire instead of as a person."[52]

The demeaning portrayals of women in *Andrei Rublev* anticipate Tarkovsky's merciless treatment of the blond, Botticelli-esque translator Eugenia (Domiziana Giordano) in *Nostalghia*, who epitomizes what he considered the deleterious values of Western feminism. Constantly talking about women's social liberation, Eugenia exposes her breasts, gets spanked, and succumbs to hysterical fits of laughter and rage. The sound of her hair dryer even replicates the noise of a buzz saw, sonically enacting her dangerous sexuality. Her baggy designer clothes de-emphasize her womb; in a country church in Tuscany, she struggles to genuflect while the sound of her high heels reverberates on the church's stone floor, conveying her barrenness in contrast to the images of the pregnant Madonna—Piero della Francesca's *Madonna del Parto* (1457)—seen throughout the film.[53] "You're only interested in Madonnas," Eugenia says dismissively to Andrei Gorchakov (Oleg Iankovskii), Tarkovsky's autobiographical protagonist, who refuses her. For his part, Gorchakov continually dreams of his pregnant (brunette) ex-wife (Patrizia Terreno), who, for him, represents the traditionalist ideals of his Russian homeland. Eugenia's unflattering portrayal channels Tarkovsky's depictions of the naive nurse in *Ivan's Childhood*; the doting alien-ghost of Kelvin's ex-wife in *Solaris*; the grieving mother in *Mirror* (who doubles as the hero's wife); and the overbearing matriarch Adelaide (Susan Fleetwood) in *The Sacrifice*, who, per Tarkovsky, is "barely capable of reflection" as she jockeys with her daughter for a man's affection.[54] Tarkovsky "does not allow women a normal range of thoughts and feelings," which accounts for the "total absence of women as equals and fellow travelers on the inner journeys of his heroes.... In Tarkovsky's world the women are incapable of—or perhaps also do not need—the spiritual transformation which his men undergo. Theirs is a self-contained, at times mysterious, but basically an unchanging physical and emotional universe."[55]

Only Stalker's wife (Alisa Freindlich) aligns with what Tarkovsky hailed as a feminine ideal. At the end of *Stalker*, we see her fill a bowl with milk for her husband's new pet dog. Despite her misgivings about adopting an animal, Stalker's wife immediately assumes the role of maternal caretaker. She nurtures the animal with milk, just as she nurtures Stalker during his nervous breakdown, undressing him, escorting him to bed, and soothing him as she would a child. She says to the camera, as if justifying herself before our gaze: "He's a Stalker. I knew there'd be a lot of sorrow, but I'd rather know bitter happiness than a grey, uneventful life." The character, whose name in Tarkovsky's screenplay is simply "Stalker's wife," defines herself wholly in relation to her husband.[56] She reminds us of Sonia in Dostoevsky's *Crime and Punishment* (*Prestuplenie i Nakazanie*, 1866), the heroine who accompanies Raskolnikov, another misunderstood renegade, to a Siberian prison camp (another kind of Zone).[57] "Women," Tarkovsky said, "don't understand that they only find their dignity in a male-female relationship, in total devotion to the man."[58] The image of a burning cow in *Andrei Rublev* signifies what Tarkovsky saw as humanity's doomed fate, triggered by women who, unlike Stalker's wife, forsake domesticity and decenter their husbands and children.

It stands to reason, then, that Tarkovsky intended the destruction of the cow in *Andrei Rublev* to represent the broader assault on society's social cohesion being waged by women. The cow in Russian culture "gives meaning to transformations *within* the nation's sense of community. It refers to the nation as a metaphorical family.... The symbolic domain of the cow is that of the Russian Motherland, that is, *Rodina*."[59] The burning of a cow in *Andrei Rublev* is Tarkovsky's vision of matricide, a comment on a society that has fallen out of touch with motherhood: "There is no doubt that women are human beings like men, but their function and role in human existence is quite different from the function and role of men. And it's not only wrong to forget this, but it's going against nature to do so. To me, man, in his substance, is essentially a spiritual being and the meaning of his life consists in developing this spirituality. If he fails to do so, society deteriorates."[60] Independent women, per Tarkovsky— that is, women who have stopped aiding men's spiritual development—are to blame for the topsy-turvy state of modern life. Right after the image of the burning cow in *Andrei Rublev*, we see Rublev's apprentice, Foma (Mikhail Kononov), pleading with his attacker, an ethnic Russian: "Brother! What are you doing? We're both Russians!" Foma's call to stop the fraternal violence is a response to what Tarkovsky understood as the social discord that has long bedeviled (mother) Russia.[61] Tarkovsky's attack on the cow signifies the fraying of Russia's fabric, an assault on the national hearth launched by predacious foreigners (i.e., Mongols, feminists, etc.) and their domestic coconspirators (i.e., Russian liberals, modernizers, opportunists etc.). An overlooked detail in the scene with the cow is the presence of a peasant woman, depicted as a prototypical Russian *babushka*, who cries out for her own mother—"Oh, mommy!" (*Oi, mamochka!*)—upon seeing the beleaguered animal before being slain by a Mongol invader's spear herself. Tarkovsky's cow figuratively exemplifies the destruction of the motherland.

The burning of a cow in *Andrei Rublev* thus allies Tarkovsky with the more rearguard voices of late Soviet culture vilifying the modern world's supposed degeneracy.[62] Indeed, its reactionary implications channel the fire-and-brimstone rhetoric of Aleksandr Solzhenitsyn, the ultraconservative Russian novelist deeply admired by Tarkovsky who was exiled from the Soviet Union in 1974 for ideological nonconformity.[63] Despite his misgivings about communism, Solzhenitsyn also deplored what he saw as the "abyss of human decadence" enveloping the West—which, in his infamous 1978 commencement address at Harvard University, he blamed on everything from democracy to pornography to feminism.[64] Soviet communism *and* Western capitalism, per Solzhenitsyn, are equal but opposite cultural systems eroding traditional human values. In his novella *Matryona's House* (*Matrenin dvor*, 1963), Solzhenitsyn uses a cow to symbolize "the idealized values of home and family" that have been lost in modern life.[65] The burning cow in *Andrei Rublev* conveys what Tarkovsky viewed as the loss of these traditionalist values; it betrays Tarkovsky's combustible yearning for a return to gender conventionalism in which women stop insisting "on their similarities with men" and reaffirm "their uniqueness as women"—that is, as self-effaced caretakers always and only devoted to men.[66]

CARNO-PHALLOGOCENTRISM

That Tarkovsky burns a cow alive in *Andrei Rublev* and degrades female characters should be seen as continuous phenomena. This blend of cruelty against animals and women points toward the logic of "carno-phallogocentrism," a characteristically abstruse neologism coined by French philosopher Jacques Derrida.[67] According to Derrida, as touched on in chapter 2, Western thought adheres to a view of humanity that is rational and language based, originating from an oppositional perception of animals as instinctual and nonlinguistic creatures. Yet Derrida argues that this configuration of humanity is troublesome because it is constituted through a network of exclusionary relations that negatively impact humans and animals alike. He employs the term "carno-phallogocentrism" to deconstruct this dominant category of "the human."

The word "carno-phallogocentrism," in reverse order, first underscores the paramount importance of *logos*—the Greek term for "speech"—in the Western tradition. The backend of Derrida's neologism "refers us to the privileges and priorities granted" to "rational, self-aware, self-present, and speaking subjects"—that is, human beings in contrast to nonlinguistic creatures.[68] The middle section of Derrida's coinage, *phallo-*, emphasizes "the quintessentially virile and masculine aspects of Western social institutions and conceptions of subjectivity."[69] Derrida argues that Western culture's patriarchal precedents generate an ambient notion of man as the default subject. Finally, the prefix *carno-* suggests that meat eating is at the heart of what it means to be human: "Who would stand any chance of becoming a *chef d'Etat* (a head of State), and of thereby acceding 'to the head,' by publicly, and therefore exemplarily, declaring him- or herself a vegetarian? The *chef* must be an eater of flesh."[70] Deliciously punning on the French word *chef*, Derrida argues that participating "in the processes and rituals of killing and eating animal flesh is almost a necessary prerequisite of being a subject"; those who adopt vegan or vegetarian diets "resist carnivorous practices and institutions" and are outside dominant forms of social hierarchies, politics, and economic exchange.[71] Acknowledging the inescapability of meat eating in modern life, Writer in Tarkovsky's *Stalker* says, "My conscience wants vegetarianism to win over the world, but my subconscious is yearning for a juicy piece of steak." Though Writer recognizes the benefits of vegetarianism, he cannot avoid carnivorous activity if he wants to fully participate in his society, especially as a man with a gratuitous sexual appetite, hinted at by his insistent references to "chicks" (*baby*) and "groupies" (*poklonnitsy*) throughout the film.[72]

In Derrida's final analysis, to be human—humanism—consists of a mix of "*sacrificial* (carno-), *masculine* (phallo-), and *speaking* (logo-)" that extends beyond the simplistic human-animal binary posited by Cartesian philosophy.[73] These axes determine who counts as a full subject and, consequently, who is accorded moral and legal consideration: "What Derrida is trying to get at with this concept is how the metaphysics of subjectivity works to exclude not just animals from the status of being full subjects but other beings as well, in particular women, children, various minority groups, and other Others who are taken to be lacking in one way or another of the basic traits of subjectivity."[74] While the exploitation of humans and animals "occurs along distinct historical and institutional lines, and the effects of this marginalization have been uneven," Derrida's "joint examination of human and animal subjection can help render undeniably clear the potentially violent nature of the exclusionary logic of the metaphysics of subjectivity."[75] Analyzed side by side—as the slaughter of a rooster for supper by a cowed woman in *Mirror* makes apparent—Tarkovsky's images of women and animals (and, albeit less frequently, his portrayals of ethnic non-Russians) disclose how Derrida's three vectors of carno-phallogocentrism intersect.

Toward the end of *Solaris*, the alien-ghost of Kelvin's ex-wife, Hari (Natalia Bonderchuk), drinks liquid oxygen in a suicide attempt. The sequence begins with a long take of Hari's frostbitten body on the floor, sparsely veiled by a nightgown. Kelvin's hands enter the visual field and begin examining her corpse, lingering on her chest. Kelvin, we see, wears only underwear and a leather jacket, reminding us of the leather-clad James Dean in Nicholas Rey's *Rebel without a Cause* (1955): the quintessential manly man, Hollywood's ultimate sex symbol. Their skimpy attire, Hari's prostration, and Kelvin's roving hands suggest a macabre postcoital moment that channels the scene from Tolstoy's *Anna Karenina* (1878) in which Vronsky, after consummating his romance with Anna, looks at her and "felt what a murderer must feel when he looks at the body he has deprived of life."[76] As the frost generated by the liquid oxygen melts off Hari, her nightdress becomes translucent, revealing her skin, and the camera zooms in on her exposed breasts. Hari's body then judders into action. The alien ghosts generated by the planet Solaris seem incapable of dying, so Kelvin, playing the role of physician, monitors Hari's heartbeat as she convulses and comes back to life. Though Hari is undergoing a painful regeneration, it seems as if she is in the throes of sexual pleasure, quaking on the ground.[77]

Analogously, in *Stalker*, as Stalker's wife protests her husband's departure to the Zone, she collapses to the floor. For a full minute, the camera holds its gaze on her splayed-out body, which resembles Hari's corpse in *Solaris*. Stalker's wife wears a thin nightdress, her breasts visible as the camera magnifies her torso. While her convulsions and moans imply agony, she looks like she is experiencing sexual gratification as she tosses her arms behind her head, submitting. This image of Stalker's wife accords with Tarkovsky's ideal of female "humiliation in the name of love." Her writhing movements are backdropped by the sound of a roaring train and music from the overture of Richard Wagner's *Tannhäuser* (1845)— an opera about the struggle between sacred and profane love—two sonic motifs that are, for Tarkovsky, symbols of the destructive values endemic to modern life: hubris, progress, and industry. This scene, then, reminds us of the connection posited by the fathers of psychoanalysis, Sigmund Freud and Karl Abraham, between the mechanical agitation of train travel and female sexual arousal.[78] The thrill of railway locomotion, they claimed, paralleled early riders' anxieties about the terrifying irrepressibility of erotic desire, which translated into popular fears, a "collective psychosis," about runaway trains and derailment.[79] In *Stalker*,

Tarkovsky links the wild sexuality of Stalker's wife to a fugitive train, implying that modernity has unbridled women's destructive passions. (A train is also heard in the opening scene of *Mirror* as the lone heroine, waiting for her husband, is solicited by a stranger.)[80] These instances fold gender into Tarkovsky's loathing of trains—his siderodromophobia, detailed in chapter 2.

Similarly, in *The Sacrifice*, Aleksandr's wife Adelaide breaks down after the world plunges into nuclear war. Yelling, in English, "Do something!" (further evidence of what Tarkovsky depicts as her bourgeois affectation), Adelaide crumples onto the ground in a fit of screams. Like Hari and Stalker's wife, Adelaide is eroticized as her spread legs become visible. Vulgarizing this scene even more, Tarkovsky has Adelaide cry out "Oh, God!" and "Please!" while—like Hari in *Solaris*—she is cradled by a male physician: her daughter's husband, Victor (Sven Wollter), for whom Adelaide earlier expressed attraction. Tarkovsky described Adelaide's outburst not as a thunderous train but more dramatically as a "nuclear explosion" wrought by the "destructive power" of sexual independence.[81] In all these instances, Tarkovsky simultaneously sexualizes and *industrializes* his images of suffering women, implying that female sexuality is somehow coterminous with the modern technologies menacing humankind: liquid oxygen, railway locomotion, and atomic bombs.

Tarkovsky's images of spasmodic female bodies entertain long-standing tropes about women's pathological degeneracy, no better expressed than by Freud's treatment of Anna von Lieben in his *Studies on Hysteria* (1895).[82] Media historian Lisa Cartwright demonstrates how images of hysterical women have, indeed, been central to cinema since the medium's inception.[83] These portrayals, which Cartwright calls "neurological motion studies," redoubled patriarchal imperatives to medicalize women for their emotional excess, what Tarkovsky euphemistically called women's "surplus of spirit."[84] In *The Sacrifice*, Adelaide is literally sedated by a male physician, who then forcibly administers a sedative to Adelaide's daughter (with whom he has had secret relations). "It's absolutely necessary," the doctor says, despite the girl's protestations, lest she, too, succumb to her mother's hysterical eruption. Resonating with what Cartwright labels the "neurological gaze," Tarkovsky's psychosexual presentations of distraught women betray a fascination with female bodies beset by "involuntary tics, tremors, or seizures" that "strip movement of its functionality."[85] Tarkovsky eroticizes women by indulging in fantasies of their physiological perversion. Across his filmography, women become targets not only of Tarkovsky's eroticizing gaze but also of a *neurological* one that reinforces stereotypes about women's hereditary instability. Tarkovsky's leitmotif of women's "hysteroepileptic fits"—these radioactive, Chernobyl-like meltdowns—substantiates his work's *phallo*-centric essence.[86]

Tarkovsky's portrayals of "hysterical" women, whom he eroticizes and industrializes: Hari's spasmodic body paired with liquid oxygen; Stalker's wife with a train; and Adelaide with nuclear war. Stills from *Solaris*, 1972; *Stalker*, 1979; *The Sacrifice*, 1986.

Additionally, the paroxysms of Hari, Stalker's wife, and Adelaide visually replicate the thrashings of the burning cow in *Andrei Rublev*. Groaning as it runs around the barn in flames, the cow reflexively responds to its predicament. Its erratic behavior parallels the fits to which Tarkovsky's female characters succumb as a consequence of what he implies to be their unstable psycho-emotional constitutions. An image that follows the burning cow in *Andrei Rublev* presents a horse lying on the ground as a peasant slits its throat. The slaughtered animal flails its legs and shudders in response to the pain, again reenacting the spasms of Hari, Stalker's wife, and Adelaide. The animal violence of Tarkovsky's cinema—its carnivorous qualities—unmistakably intermixes with his depictions of hysterical women. "In hysteria," Akira Mizuta Lippit writes, the "animal world erupts onto the surface of human consciousness as a kind of primal scene."[87] In Tarkovsky's films, sexual and species exploitation unfold as separate yet interrelated spectacles.

Having demonstrated how two of the axes of carno-phallogocentrism bisect in Tarkovsky's work, how can we account for the third vector, *logo*centrism? In Western philosophy, it is argued that human beings' capacity for language constitutes our paramount difference from animals. The consensus holds that, while animals do communicate, only humans are capable of conveying their subjectivity through language, and this uniqueness metaphysically ennobles us as a species. "All the philosophers," Derrida writes, "all of them say the same thing: the animal is deprived of language. Or, more precisely, of response, of a response that could be precisely and rigorously distinguished from a reaction; of the right and power to 'respond' and hence of so many other things that would be proper to man."[88] Across his films, Tarkovsky depicts characters coming into language, often re-creating the genesis of human speech, to affirm this extraordinary trait. At the start of *Mirror*, for example, a stuttering teenager recovers his voice with the help of a speech pathologist—"I can speak!" he cries—and the film concludes with a boy yelling at the top of his lungs, discovering the awesome power of his voice. The two speech acts bookending *Mirror*, Tarkovsky's most personal film, imply that he, too, found his voice, his creative freedom, through this most autobiographical of films.

Analogously, toward the end of *Andrei Rublev*, a young bell caster who suffers from a noticeable stutter succeeds against all odds in creating an exquisite bell, the mellifluous and resonant toll of which contrasts with his halting, staccato speech. As the bell ringers prepare the massive object, Tarkovsky's camera dwells on a close-up of the thick rope tied to the "clapper," the bronze shaft used to make a bell toll or, as it were, speak. In Russian, a bell's clapper is called *iazyk*: the word for "tongue," a term designating both the muscle of the human speech organ and, more idiomatically, language itself. Foregrounding the bell's tongue, Tarkovsky suggests that, by making a great work of art, the bell caster has successfully entered language and overcome his stutter. Tarkovsky, then, compares the ringing of the bell to a speech act, which, in turn, inspires Andrei Rublev to break his sixteen-year vow of silence and resume painting. "You'll cast bells, I'll paint icons," Rublev tells the young bell caster, cradling him like a (surrogate) father. Through creative activity, Tarkovsky's characters (re)discover language; the proverbial cat no longer has their tongues. The image of the bell's tongue in *Andrei Rublev*, moreover, reminds us of the shadow of a boom mic dangling in the background during the opening sequence of *Mirror* as the stammering teenager recovers his voice. This tongue-like image redoubles how Tarkovsky reasserts his individuality in *Mirror*—his *kino-iazyk*—by making great art in the repressive world of late Soviet society.[89]

The importance of language for Tarkovsky helps explain why the child in *The Sacrifice*, known as Little Man (Tommy Kjellqvist), has undergone throat surgery, which has deprived him of speech. Early in the film, we see Little Man

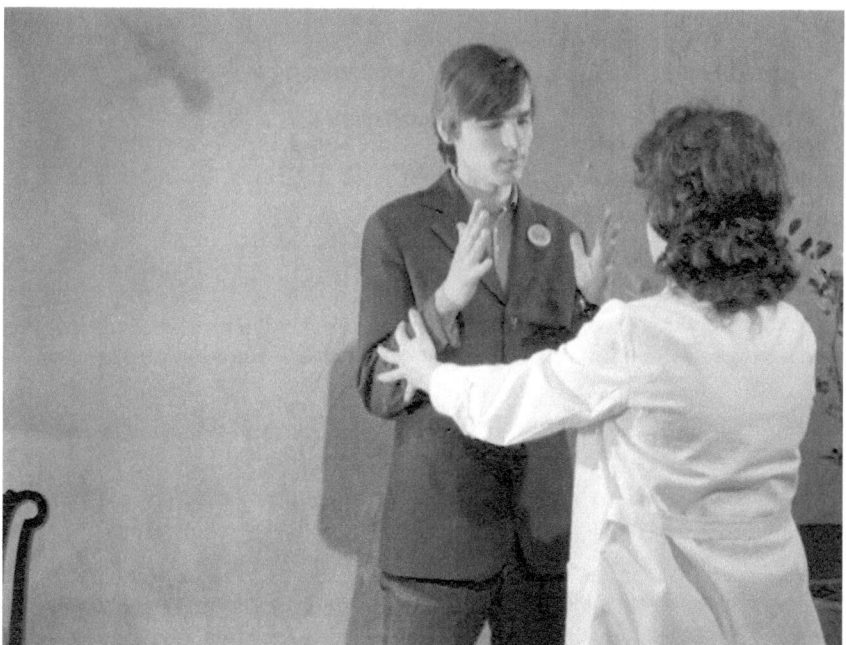

These dangling, tongue-like images—one of a rope used to make a bell toll, *iazyk* in Russian, and the other a shadow of a boom mic—suggest the importance Tarkovsky accords language. Stills from *Andrei Rublev*, 1966, and *Mirror*, 1975.

crawling on grass with weeds in his mouth and growling, not unlike an animal, while his father decries the "savagery" of modern society, in which people have stopped doing anything meaningful and shed their very humanity. However, after Little Man inspires his father to save the world, he heals and matures into a talking (bipedal) subject. Per Derrida's logic of carno-phallogocentrism, Little Man develops into a speaking *big* man (presumably a carnivore). A doctor even exudes upon examining the boy's mended tonsils at the end of the film, "He's got the makings of a real man." Additionally, on the magnificent bell in *Andrei Rublev*, we see emblazoned a horse, the animal Tarkovsky most closely associated with masculinity. In one fell swoop, the young bell caster, like Little Man in *The Sacrifice*, recoups both his voice and his masculinity. Tarkovsky upholds a conviction that language offers humanity—specifically men—a self-possession unavailable to animals. "In the beginning," Little Man says, quoting the book of John, "was the word." In a way, Little Man tells the story of human evolution: man's trajectory from mute quadrupeds to linguistic, upright, enlightened subjects.

Somewhat ironically, though, we remember Tarkovsky's films not for their dialogue but for their silence. Tarkovsky's movies are marked by long stretches of quietude in which the incessant chatter of human life—the propaganda, for instance, spouted by Soviet astronauts at a press conference in *Solaris*—fades. These intervals of quiet and stillness facilitate opportunities for deep thinking. Tarkovsky wrote, "One may talk of the idea of the image, describe its essence in words.... But none of this can be understood in any cerebral sense. The idea of infinity cannot be expressed in words or even described, but it can be apprehended through art," which, through silent contemplation, "makes infinity tangible."[90] Great art, for Tarkovsky, induces silence as a necessary precondition for reflection on life's biggest, most vexing questions. Cinema appealed to Tarkovsky because of its capacity to let audiences "hear" silence once again. Accordingly, Tarkovsky's characters themselves take vows of silence that seemingly remove them from society's logocentric paradigms. As mentioned above, Andrei Rublev adopts a sixteen-year-long vow of silence, and in *Nostalghia*, Domenico (Erland Josephson) silences himself by retreating into a bunker for seven years in anticipation of the apocalypse. Might we consider Tarkovsky's fascination with muteness as a *challenge* to Western philosophy's predominant conception of human subjectivity based on language? Do Tarkovsky's silences perhaps locate the settings and characters of his films closer to the speechless world of animals?

Animals, incapable of generating words, are said to convey their feelings through noise. "The mere making of sounds," Aristotle memorably wrote, "serves to indicate pleasure and pain, and is thus a faculty that belongs to animals in general.... But language serves to declare what is advantageous ... and it is the peculiarity of man, in comparison with other animals, that ... makes a family and a city."[91] A rationally ordered society, a *polis*, rests on linguistic intelligence, which, for Aristotle, is far more important than the sensory experiences governing animal life. The difference between humans and animals, then, is not language per se but the unintelligibility of a being's utterances and one's discretion in exercising those communicative faculties. If animals are speechless, they are hardly silent. "One might say, then, animals can *not* respond to the inquisition or requisition of a stimulus," Derrida writes, "According to this somewhat naïve philosophy of the animal world, one may nevertheless observe that animals are incapable of keeping or even having a secret, because they cannot *represent as such*, as an *object* before consciousness, something that they would then forbid themselves from showing.... An animal can neither choose to keep silent, nor keep a secret."[92] In this light, animals' cries are understood as unmediated, mimetic responses to their behavior and surroundings. What is animal, then, "is the *inability* to refrain from self-exhibition; that language may best be considered to follow from the capacity for silence—restraint—rather than as a function of self-determination and expression."[93] Animals reflexively disclose their presence; their communication is affective, not discursive; animals cannot help *but* speak, albeit nonverbally.

Echoing these ideas, French philosopher Jean-François Lyotard writes that animals are only "mute" insofar as "the root *mu* connotes closed lips which suggest keeping still or talking in a muted voice. From the root connotes *murmurer* (to murmur), *mugir* (to low), *mystère* (mystery) and the vulgar [low] Latin *muttum*, which yielded to *mot* (word) in French."[94] The burning cow in *Andrei Rublev*, groaning as it runs around the barn, speaks in an impossible, mute language of moos. The cow's nonlinguistic essence, per Derrida, creates the conceptual conditions for its relegation to a lower ontological status, which enables human beings to torture and abuse it with impunity; its lack of what we recognize as language invites and permits the cruelty against it. Thus, Tarkovsky's cow, *the* maternal symbol, typifies how gender (*phallo-*), violence (*carno-*), and language (*logo-*) fortify one another in the exercise of human dominion. "The animal dies the moment it is thrust into contact with abstraction, with language. Killed by the word, the animal enters a figurative empire (of signs) in which its death is repeated endlessly... preserved (taxidermically) in the slaughterhouse of being, language."[95] The burning cow's lows—its mute moos—disclose the power denied to it by language.

Rather than dislodging the presumed preeminence that language bestows humanity, Tarkovsky, in fact, *redoubles* his commitment to a self-aware, elevated notion of humanness by way of silence. "Time is necessary to man," Tarkovsky said, "so that, made flesh, he may be able to realise himself as a personality"; that is, human beings require bouts of stillness to contemplate and affirm their difference from purely reactive, flesh-bound animals.[96] Humans can assert their superiority by, counterintuitively, *refusing* language. Andrei Rublev's vow of silence marks his difference from the animals that are awash in incessant, garbled noise—not unlike, in Tarkovsky's view, the clamor of modern human society. Referring both to Soviet propaganda and American commercialism, Tarkovsky wrote that human speech has "become mere chatter, empty of meaning."[97] The protagonists of Tarkovsky's films (and his unnervingly quiet settings) disavow language to *avow* it by way of negative example. The silences of Tarkovsky's cinema are wordless declarations of enlightenment that, in the end, capitulate his belief in the preciousness of language.

Revealingly, during his sixteen-year vow of silence, Andrei Rublev also chooses to abstain from eating meat. Residing at a monastery, Rublev sustains himself on a strict diet of apples and vegetables. When he notices his companion—the holy fool girl he befriended in Vladimir, the *durochka*—eating chunks of meat, he (wordlessly) rebukes her by forcibly squeezing the food out of her mouth. Their diet, he reminds her, consists only of fruits and plants to repent for their sins; they have removed themselves from the wanton carnage of their medieval world, which indiscriminately inflicts violence against humans and animals alike. On its face, Rublev's vegetarianism rejects the "carnivorous practices" of human society, which make all of us, at least to some degree, complicit in slaughter.

Yet Rublev's diet, like his vow of silence, does not ultimately subvert the logic of carno-phallogocentrism. Rublev's abstemiousness, in step with Orthodox customs of fasting and selective vegetarianism, affirms that certain individuals, if they have the requisite willpower, can indeed restrain themselves from indulging their carnal appetites (unlike Writer in *Stalker*, played by the same actor performing Rublev, Anatoly Solonitsyn).[98] The same self-possessed resolve that Rublev exhibits in refraining from language enables him to abstain from meat eating. Rublev's vegetarianism does not, per Derrida, dislodge human exceptionalism on behalf of animals but rather reiterates Rublev's (and, by extension, Tarkovsky's) vision of a noble, stoic human subject capable of overcoming his base animal instincts. Hence, when a band of Mongols arrives at the monastery, Rublev rejects their offerings of horsemeat, which they use to rile up a pack of dogs. Yet the *durochka*, who expresses herself in animal-like cries and groans, is enthralled by the Mongols' fresh meat—and their sexual overtures—so she elects to ride away with them

Rublev forces the *durochka* to spit out meat in order to reaffirm their separation from society's violence vis-à-vis vegetarianism. Still from *Andrei Rublev*, 1966.

and abandon Rublev, leaving him alone at his monastery, in silence with his apples. Tarkovsky contrasts Rublev's self-control not only with the rapacious dogs wrangling over horsemeat but also with the human beings around him (the *durochka*, the Mongols), who cannot, it appears, resist the temptations of animal flesh. Rublev conquers his physical needs and worldly wants; he achieves peak humanity, a Cartesian ideal, and becomes all mind, no body. Rublev's vegetarianism is, in fact, additional evidence of his enlightened humanness.

The horsemeat incident in *Andrei Rublev* further expounds Derrida's intersectional theory of carno-phallogocentrism: just as Tarkovsky parallels his degrading depictions of women and animals, so too does he debase his representations of Russia's ethnic minorities. The Mongols in *Andrei Rublev*, performed by Kyrgyz actors like Bolot Beyshenaliyev, are portrayed as savages who terrorize pious Russians through bounty, torture, and sexual violence. Tarkovsky justified his primitive caricatures of central Asians with the same logic that led him to burn a cow: a desire to depict medieval Russia, which the Mongols ruled brutally, as truthfully as possible. Yet such a pretext allows for a crude representation of racial otherness that Tarkovsky pits against an excessively idealized vision of Russianness, embodied by Rublev. Russian, for

A Mongol invader feeds horsemeat to dogs; Tarkovsky portrays the Mongols as bloodthirsty colonizers against pious Russians. Still from *Andrei Rublev*, 1966.

Tarkovsky, signifies the normative, ambient category of man against which all others—women, animals, non-Russians—should be defined and evaluated. The Mongols in *Andrei Rublev*, as well as the film's female characters and tormented animals, occupy a shared space of exclusion from Tarkovsky's humanist ideals; each group is, therefore, prone to overlapping forms of insult, injury, and abuse. Tarkovsky's exclusivist model of human subjectivity refers us to the cutting-edge work of present-day theorists exploring the ways in which humanity's deep-seated prejudices against animals negatively impact not only animal life but also human beings.[99] These critics argue that humanism rests on a series of reductive dualisms—human versus animal, man versus woman, nature versus culture, white versus nonwhite—that must be disrupted to develop "more complex taxonomies of power," such as Derrida's carno-phallogocentrism, which can better account for how social and cultural othering lead to distinct yet intersecting forms of exclusion.[100]

Tarkovsky's animal cruelty, then, is complicit in *both* his misogynistic treatment of women and his degrading, fetishistic presentations of ethnicity. After all, what kind of people, Tarkovsky insinuates vis-à-vis the Mongols in *Andrei Rublev*, would eat *horses*, the animals he held most dear? While horsemeat has been consumed in central Asia for millennia, it has never appealed to ethnic Russians, particularly during the Soviet era, when horsemeat was used by the state as a low-grade beef substitute to offset food shortages.[101] Tarkovsky portrays the horse-eating Mongols as people closer to animals—as bloodthirsty beasts. In turn, Rublev's mindful refusals of language, sex, and (horse) meat reassert *his* humanity. In its elaboration of ethnic, linguistic, species, cultural, and gender difference, *Andrei Rublev* maps onto the Derridean logic of carno-phallogocentrism, which, as the image of the burning cow makes abundantly clear, is fortified by violence and slaughter.

THE BURNING

Whatever the burning cow's symbolic implications in *Andrei Rublev*, the action of its burning exceeds metaphor. It is an eruption of "the real" into Tarkovsky's fictional world that confronts us with the bracing documentary fact of an animal burning alive. Tarkovsky immolates not an abstract idea but a real, living cow that strains cinema's representational limits.

While filming *Andrei Rublev*, Tarkovsky championed an observational style he called "chronicle-ness" (*khronikal'nost'*) to provide an accurate view of reality.[102] The notion of chronicle-ness is indicative of the documentary turn of postwar avant-garde cinema: the unvarnished films of Italian neorealism; the *cinema vérité* productions of the French New Wave, such as Jean Rouch and Edgar Morin's *Chronicle of a Summer* (*Chronique d'un été*, 1961); and the clear-eyed films of postwar Soviet society that rejected Stalinist propaganda, like *Ordinary Fascism* (*Obykonvennyi fashizm*, 1961) by Mikhail Romm, Tarkovsky's student adviser.[103] These works, committed to "the goal of restoring belief in film images," relied on newsreel footage, amateur actors, handheld cameras, and nonstudio locations to present unembellished views of reality.[104] Analogously, Tarkovsky wanted to film *Andrei Rublev* "as if a hidden camera was placed on the streets of a medieval town ... to avoid the look of stylized historical illusions in favor of achieving the appearance of direct observation."[105]

Tarkovsky's term "chronicle-ness" also references the genre of medieval compilation writing, which documented the happenings of a particular territory or people over time. Tarkovsky most likely had in mind *The Primary Chronicle* (*Povest' vremennyykh let*), one of the most important medieval texts compiled in Kiev around 1113 by Nestor the Chronicler, which presents an unparalleled view into the origins of the Slavic people.[106] Mostly written by monks, chronicles plot history in ostensibly objective terms by according equal weight to all events, suggesting that an occurrence acquires significance through the act of its recording. Describing *Andrei Rublev* as a "chronicle," Tarkovsky imbued it with both documentary merit and deep national significance. The film's episodic structure, marked by titles, seasons, and dates spanning a quarter of a century, mimics the format of *The Primary Chronicle*. Through *Andrei Rublev*, Tarkovsky stylized himself as a modern-day Nestor, a medieval chronicler with a movie camera.

Despite professing to be rooted in fact, medieval chronicles, like all texts, cannot help but disclose the penchants and biases of their creators, who, like all authors, write in pursuit of certain sociocultural ends. As the historian Hayden White notes, chronicles are "products of possible conceptions of historical reality, conceptions that are alternatives to, rather than failed anticipations of, the fully realized historical discourse that the modern history form is supposed to embody."[107] The boundary between historical fact and invention in any chronicle is highly fluid. Tarkovsky's *Andrei Rublev*, then, is a doctored portrayal of medieval life; the "fervent debate" ignited by its rife historical inaccuracies and anachronisms upon its release belied Tarkovsky's apparent commitment to realism—not least of which included the fact that Tarkovsky's medieval monks speak in "neutral-contemporary Russian dialogue" and not Church Slavonic.[108]

Yet Tarkovsky did not want *Andrei Rublev* to be scrutinized from a strictly historiographical perspective: "In my opinion, historical accuracy does not mean historical reconstruction of events; the important thing for what we want to show is that it should possess all attributes of plausibility."[109] In *Andrei Rublev*, Tarkovsky sought to present a believable rendering of medieval times—"the atmosphere of the years past"—not through historically precise dialogue, costumes, or set design.[110] Rather, he pursued his version of realism through cinema's own aesthetic resources—a torpid aestheticization of time, coarse black-and-white film, disorienting camerawork, and graphic images of violence, such as a burning cow. "In order to achieve the truth of direct observation," Tarkovsky wrote, "what one might almost term physiological truth, we had to move away from the truth of archaeology and ethnography."[111] In *Andrei Rublev*, Tarkovsky decouples authenticity from facticity, veracity from validity, to capture what he perceived as the texture of medieval life. *Andrei Rublev*'s documentary aesthetic generates not reality but a *reality effect* to apprehend Rublev's lived experience on a more affective, sensory register. The image of a burning cow, then, is not a fact about Rublev's biography but a cinematic fact about Tarkovsky's pursuit of capturing medieval Russia's physiological reality. The "horrors that Andrei Rublev sees are indispensable to our subject matter. In so far as our narrative is very realistic, we could not limit Rublev's sufferings to the moral level, and only show the spiritual reflection of the trials he underwent: that would have taken us elsewhere, stylistically."[112] Tarkovsky burns a cow to convey the authenticity—the "plausibility," "atmosphere," "physiology," and "texture" (*faktura*)—of Rublev's unforgiving world. Tarkovsky is more interested in what the cow's burning means for film than for the animal itself.

That Tarkovsky relies on an animal to heighten *Andrei Rublev*'s reality effect is not incidental. Throughout film history, images of animals have been interpreted as special markers of the real. The early Hungarian film theorist Béla Balász wrote that the "absolute evidence of reality" is uniquely possible in wildlife films because "animals do not act for the director. And since such glimpsed scenes cannot be imaginary, they possess something metaphysically unsettling" for the spectatorial experience.[113] Animals, for Balász, confound distinctions between the real (i.e., reality) and the reel (i.e., cinema) because of their obliviousness to the fact that they are participating in a film; animals destabilize the illusionism necessary for an immersive cinematic experience, as we are aware that *they* are unaware of the camera's operations. Although an animal "on screen can be burdened with multiple metaphorical significances, giving it an ambiguous status that derives from what might be described as a kind of semantic overload, the animal is also marked as a site where these symbolic associations collapse into each other as our attention is constantly drawn beyond the image and, in that sense, beyond the aesthetic and semiotic framework of the film."[114] Images of animals expand cinema's documentary relation to reality. As the postwar film theorist André Bazin memorably wrote, "Animal films reveal the cinema to us" because animals are examples of authenticity and contingency indifferent to the artifice of film.[115]

Yet animals can be trained in ways that can reinforce cinema's illusionistic qualities, even if said animals remain unaware that they are being recorded. "In fact, if one is to consider what it means for an animal *to act* then one has to take into account not just the mechanics of training, but the whole network of interactions between animal and humans including the general effects sought by the filmmakers and their impact on an audience.... Trainers are often dressed up as extras on set or concealed within it so they can direct the animal's attention via auditory or visual cues."[116] Through training, animals—not unlike human actors performing "a form of agency and something under the direction of somebody else"—can make a film seem more real, even if, on some level, we never lose sight of the fact that, however well trained, they are playacting for the audience.[117] Darkly, then, the authenticity inherent to cinematic images of animals is most palpably registered through images of animal pain, suffering, and, ultimately, death, which introduce an "intractable reality surplus" on screen.[118] Images of animals in pain, in excess of their training, function as the ultimate denotations of the real because animals, unlike humans, are unwilling (or unable) to perform their own anguish. Even if animals can be trained to lie still and play dead, it is difficult for an animal to fake dying: distress, struggle, and expiry. Images of animals in pain are thus *more* real than other kinds of images because they confront us with nonsimulated immediacy.

Describing a 1951 film by Pierre Braunberger titled *Bullfight*, which depicts a matador impaling a bull with "diabolical skill," Bazin writes, "Death is surely one of those rare events that justifies the term . . . *cinematic specificity*," for death attests to cinema's capacity to archive reality's unvarnished, irreplicable details.[119] The image of the slaughtered bull represents "real presence"—an experience of "total cinema"—for it brings viewers as close as (humanly) possible to the most inescapable fact of life: death.[120] In *Mirror*, as if citing Bazin, Tarkovsky splices into his otherwise fictional movie real footage of a matador slaying a bull, proposing "a certain pre-mimetic condition where the artistic realm is approached not by means of imitating nature, but by pointing to something which is already there."[121] Beleaguered animals are *the* ultimate authenticators of the physiological realism, the end of figurative representation, that Tarkovsky tried to capture in *Andrei Rublev*. The burning cow confronts us with a "ferocious reality" because its pain within the frame instantiates its pain outside of it, unlike the peasant woman who playacts her death alongside the animal.[122] She suffers within the film, whereas the cow suffers *for* the film.

For his part, Bazin—a self-professed animal lover—balked at recordings of animal suffering and referred to images of animal death as "an ontological obscenity."[123] By contrast, Tarkovsky embraced images of tortured animals in *Andrei Rublev*, as have many directors throughout cinema's history (discussed more in chapter 5).[124] One of the first canonical films, Thomas Edison's *Electrocuting an Elephant* (1903), "makes visible the often overlooked fact that animal sacrifice constituted something of a founding symbolic and material gesture of early electrical and cinematic culture."[125] The one-minute documentary captures the execution of a circus elephant named Topsy, responsible for the deaths of several trainers on Coney Island, as she receives a fatal shock delivered by a jury-rigged mechanism built by Edison.

The film, which inaugurated the use of the electric chair in the United States as a form of capital punishment, consists of two shots.[126] The first presents several animal trainers leading Topsy to Edison's apparatus, and the second shows Topsy standing in front of the camera as smoke begins to rise. Crucially, we do not witness how Topsy is tethered to Edison's machine. We only see her enter the frame and then be electrocuted. This elision—accomplished, as Mary Ann Doane notes, through one of cinema's first jump cuts—privileges Edison's lethal experiment at the expense of Topsy's life activity.[127] Whatever complications arose in affixing Topsy to Edison's machine, dangerous work to which Topsy would not have passively yielded, are expunged by the editing. *Electrocuting an Elephant* betrays an anthropocentric notion of what constitutes a cinematic event by erasing Topsy's agency (and likely resistance) to Edison's spectacle. Similarly, in *Andrei Rublev*, Tarkovsky does not disclose the cow's activity before its burning (e.g., whether it was covered in asbestos or, worse, kerosene). Its suffering on camera is privileged over its "previous" life. In *Electrocuting an Elephant*, Topsy's charred body emitting smoke grimly portends the fate that awaits Tarkovsky's cow. Though Edison's film, per Bazin, is liable to stir viewers' existential anxiety through its graphic account of animal death, it also substantiates the use of cinema as a violent ocular technology capable of exerting control over living beings.

As Cartwright argues, *Electrocuting an Elephant* corroborates how cinema began as a tool with antecedents in early twentieth-century medicine, a surgical apparatus to control and manipulate subjects under its gaze, "even those as physically and symbolically powerful as the elephant."[128] Film "was a crucial instrument in the emergence of a distinctly modernist mode of representation in Western scientific and public culture—a mode geared to the temporal and spatial decomposition and reconfiguration of bodies as dynamic fields of action in need of regulation and control."[129] Edison commits an elephant's death to celluloid to assert mastery over it: to make death legible, knowable, and superable. Topsy's electrocution is a kind of necropsy—an au(Topsy)—intended to demystifies the enigma of death. *Electrocuting an Elephant* "is evidence of widespread popular interest in the power of technology to regulate and discipline bodies ... a means for lay-audience participation in the 'scientific' pleasure of conducting visual analysis and thereby vicariously exerting control over" life itself.[130]

In this light, Tarkovsky's decision to burn a cow suggests an analogous exercise of control.[131] Just as Edison felled a mighty elephant, Tarkovsky assumed the role of a Zeus-like figure who wields power through fire, a premodern form of electricity befitting *Andrei Rublev*'s medieval diegesis. That both Tarkovsky and Edison recorded their pyrotechnics relays their demiurgic view of the movie camera. The animals under their gaze are *"cinefied,"* a neologism used by film scholars with a prefix, "cine-," that binds "by secret homonym" two terms denoting the residue left by mechanical emissions of light—explosions (cinders) or photographs (cinema).[132] "To *cinefy*: to make move, to make cinema, and to incinerate, to reduce to ashes. Traces and residues of movement, and the movement of ashes. *Cinefaction*."[133] Tarkovsky's burnt cow sears itself into the history of film. It is, like ash, a material trace of the ruthless artistic drive that led Tarkovsky, like Edison, to smite an animal and indulge a fantasy of omnipotence.

NIETZSCHE'S COW

In 1973, several years after finishing *Andrei Rublev*, Tarkovsky visited a doctor, who told him his health was "terribly neglected" and advised "serious treatment."[134] In 1978, Tarkovsky suffered a heart attack. These signs pointed to a more serious condition that eventually took his life. In December 1985, while shooting *The Sacrifice*, Tarkovsky was diagnosed with bronchial cancer.[135] The illness and treatment, which included blood transfusions—"This nausea, despair, not pain, but fear, animal fear, and the lack of hope are indescribable"— hastened the end of Tarkovsky's career, even forcing him to miss *The Sacrifice*'s premier at the 1986 Cannes Film Festival, where it won the Grand Prix.[136] *The Sacrifice*, Tarkovsky's final film, is a meditation on death, specifically his own: a topic for which he long voiced morbid fascination.

"Last night I dreamt that I had died," Tarkovsky wrote in 1974. "But I could see, or rather feel, what was going on around me.... I felt I had no strength or will, I was only capable of witnessing my own death, my own corpse."[137] Over a decade before his illness, Tarkovsky foresaw his own demise, and he used his films as a testing ground to prepare himself for that inevitability. In *The Sacrifice*, for example, Tarkovsky re-creates his cadaverous dream by having Aleksandr envision his own death, the image found on this book's cover. "What is known as the moment of death is also the death of individual time: the life of a human being becomes inaccessible to the feelings of those remaining alive."[138] By extinguishing his characters through murder or suicide, by using his own body to playact a corpse in *Mirror*, and by recording instances of animal slaughter, Tarkovsky strives to make death legible on screen, "accessible" to those "remaining alive." Though Tarkovsky denied death's finality—"Everybody dies, you will say. No: everything changes, and we call these changes death, but nothing disappears"—the frequency with which he reflects on mortality betrays his pitched sense of anxiety about life's finitude.[139] "Throughout his life," Tarkovsky wrote after his diagnosis, "a person knows he is going to die, but he doesn't know when, and to make it easier to live his life, he relegates that moment to some indefinite point in the future. But I do know, and now nothing is going to make it easier for me to live."[140] The unexpected appearance of cows in *The Sacrifice*, the film nearest to Tarkovsky's death, which he finished editing from a hospital bed, reflects both his existential disquietude and hope for everlastingness.

The Sacrifice begins with its protagonist, Aleksandr (Erland Josephson), a retired actor who lectures on philosophy at local universities, musing about the importance of rituals to his son, Little Man. Aleksandr is interrupted by his postman, Otto (Allan Edwall), who veers into the frame on a bicycle. They greet each other, but their conversation quickly turns to a headier topic after Otto brings up a "peculiar" character from Friedrich Nietzsche's philosophical novel *Thus Spoke Zarathustra* (1885), the dwarf who memorably induces Nietzsche's protagonist to faint.[141]

Though Otto confesses that he is no expert on Nietzsche, he gets distracted by "silly things" like Nietzsche's idea of the "eternal recurrence."[142] Otto says, "We live, we have our ups and downs. We hope. We wait for something. We hope; we lose hope; we move closer to death. Finally, we die and are born again. But we remember nothing. And everything begins again." As Otto speaks, Little Man, playing the part of Nietzsche's mischievous dwarf, fastens Otto's bicycle to a shrub so that when Otto tries to ride away, he falls off his bike, collapsing just as Zarathustra does. From its outset, *The Sacrifice* positions itself in direct dialogue with Nietzsche.[143] Members of Tarkovsky's crew also recall him quoting Nietzsche on set, and he raised the idea of "the eternal return" in his diaries.[144]

In *Thus Spoke Zarathustra*, as Zarathustra recounts being felled by a dwarf, he describes the idea of the eternal return, a concept Nietzsche first broached in *The Gay Science* (1882).

> What, if some day or night a demon were to steal after you into your loneliest loneliness and say to you: "This life as you live it now and have lived it, you will have to live once more and innumerable times more; and there will be nothing new in it, but every pain and every joy and every thought and sigh and everything unutterably small or great in your life will have to return to you, all in the same succession or sequence.... The eternal hourglass of existence is turned upside down again and again, and you with it, speck of dust!"[145]

The notion of the eternal return, according to Nietzsche, bears the potential to crush the human spirit because it denies the idealizations of a better world that drive most religious doctrines. There is no afterlife in Nietzsche's cosmology, only a permanent "now-ness." The anxiety stirred by the absence of an afterlife suggests that humans have failed to value their present as they have been too busy disparaging this life on Earth in the hope of otherworldliness. The eternal return asks us to judge whether our lives in the here and now are truly worth living.

In *The Sacrifice*, Aleksandr expresses malaise about the state of the world, echoing Domenico's critique of modern society in *Nostalghia*: "Humanity is on the wrong road.... Man has constantly violated nature. The result is a civilization built on power, fear, dependence." Aleksandr has given up on the present tense; he epitomizes Nietzsche's "world-weary cowards," who deprecate their lives in the present through either wistfulness for the past or fear of the future.[146] Interestingly, during Aleksandr's monologue, we hear a shepherd's high-pitched herding call, known in Swedish culture as *kulning*, beckoning cows from distant pastures.[147] Tarkovsky filmed *The Sacrifice* in a nature preserve on the Swedish island of Gottland in homage to the films of Ingmar Bergman, in which Josephson, the actor playing Aleksandr, often starred.[148] Through *kulning*, Tarkovsky links Aleksandr's world weariness—precisely the sort of ennui castigated by Nietzsche—to cows, who have a key role to play in *Thus Spoke Zarathustra*.

Late in Nietzsche's novel, Zarathustra approaches a herd of cows huddled together on a grassy knoll. He discovers that the cows are accompanied by a mountain sermonizer who has taken up residence with the animals to discover the secrets of "happiness on earth."[149] To be happy, he says, human beings must "become as cows.... For there we ought to learn one thing from them: chewing the cud. And verily, what would it profit a man if he gained the whole world and did not learn this one thing: chewing the cud!"[150] Unlike human beings, cows have no sense of the past or the future; they are fully immersed in the present as they absentmindedly and assiduously graze.

> Consider the cattle, grazing as they pass you by: they do not know what is meant by yesterday or today, they leap about, eat, rest, digest, leap about again, and so from morn till night and from day to day, fettered to the moment and its pleasure or displeasure, and thus neither melancholy nor bored. This is a hard sight for man to see; for, though he thinks himself better than the animals because he is human, he cannot help envying them in their happiness—what they have, a life neither bored nor painful, is precisely what he wants, yet he cannot have because he refused to be like an animal. A human being may well ask an animal: "Why do you not speak to me of your happiness but only stand and gaze at me?" The animal would like to answer, and say, "The reason is I always forget what I was going to say"—but then he forgot this answer, too, and stayed silent.[151]

Cows, for Nietzsche, have language but lack memory; their whole existence is based on the capacity to forget. Yet cows are not to be pitied for their obliviousness, but rather *envied*. "The ones who have excelled the most are these cows: they invented chewing the cud for themselves and lying in the sun. They also refrain from all grave thoughts, which bloat the heart."[152] A cow's existential unconcern is an expression of ontological freedom, exemplifying Nietzsche's theory of the eternal return. "Everything goes, everything comes back; eternally rolls the wheel of being," the animals tell Zarathustra. "In every Now, being begins; round every Here rolls the sphere There, the center is everywhere. Bent is the path of eternity."[153] Unlike human beings, "who believe themselves to occupy unique moments in time, to be bound by singularity," Nietzsche's cows are "inhabited by singular moments: as each moment dies and sinks back into oblivion, the animal passes into another moment, another world, another history.... The animal survives time," which is a patently human construct.[154] What, then, do cows mean for *The Sacrifice*, Tarkovsky's most Nietzschean movie?

Aleksandr eventually learns that the world has plunged into nuclear war, and he greets the news by saying, "I've waited my whole life for this." Up until this point, Aleksandr has lived in a state of suspended animation, regretting the past and dreading the future at the expense of savoring life in the present. The prospect of annihilation, however, inspires Aleksandr to change, so he appeals to a higher power to spare the world with the hope that he might be granted a chance to live differently. If the world is saved, Aleksandr resolves he will "relinquish everything that binds [him]" to life in order to immerse himself in the fullness of existence. The next morning, Aleksandr realizes he has survived, so, fulfilling his promise, he abandons his family, burns his house down, and gives up language. At first glance, Aleksandr's muteness recalls Rublev's sixteen-year-long vow of silence. But whereas Rublev affirmed the sacredness of language—and, in turn, human superiority—by negative example, Aleksandr does the exact opposite, implied by *The Sacrifice*'s recourse to Nietzschean philosophy.

In *Thus Spoke Zarathustra*, the murmuring cows evoke within the protagonist a disquieting solitude, what Nietzsche called "the loneliest loneliness," for they threaten to remove Zarathustra from the human community: "By engaging the animals, Zarathustra . . . plummets from the edifice of world (language and memory) into the immemorial open of a time before world. And this time before world, this prehistory of man, returns humanity to the figure of the animal."[155] The cows unmoor Zarathustra from the coherence of a world premised on language, and he undergoes an existential crisis as a result, not unlike Aleksandr in *The Sacrifice*. For Nietzsche, however, the collapsing edifice that is Zarathustra's subjectivity is not a desperate affair but an ecstatic occasion, a "robust health" that represents the "possibility of a new beginning" for a rejuvenated, fearless human subject: a "superman" (*Übermensch*).[156] The creation of a superman does not, as popularly conceived, signal physical strengthening so much as rejecting—*overcoming*—the dominant view of humanity as a metaphysically lofty or noble category of being. The human, for Nietzsche, is not the apex of evolution but its nadir. "Humans are in no way the crown of creation.

All beings occupy the same level of perfection.... And even this is saying too much: comparatively speaking, humans are the biggest failures, the sickliest animals who have strayed the most dangerously far from their instincts."[157] One becomes an *Übermensch*, then, by unleashing the animal within and entering a zone of proximity, physical and conceptual, with supposedly inferior animals. "I beseech you," Zarathustra says, "*remain faithful to the earth*, and do not believe those who speak to you of otherworldly hopes! Poison-mixers are they, whether they know it or not. Despisers of life, decaying and poisoned themselves."[158] Zarathustra affirms "the importance of thinking in depths rather than heights."[159] (Here is a Nietzschean explanation of the failure of Efim's skyward ambitions in *Andrei Rublev*.)

In *The Sacrifice*, though Aleksandr nearly succumbs to his world weariness by committing suicide, he triumphs over it by embracing the atavistic qualities indicative of animals: irrationality, extemporaneity, and muteness. Aleksandr recognizes that the virtues said to ennoble humanity—reason, history, language, awareness of death—are the very sources of its malaise. Aleksandr becomes *like* a Nietzschean cow, indifferent to all that which makes humans "human." It is fitting, then, that Tarkovsky cast Josephson, the actor who in *Nostalghia* played Domenico, the modern-day Cynic who valorizes canine behavior (detailed in chapter 2), as Aleksandr. If Rublev's silence reaffirms humanism, Aleksandr's is a declaration of *anti*humanism. Whereas Rublev's speechlessness recapitulates the notion of an enlightened human subject—a self-possessed being who consciously removes himself from language to affirm its preciousness—Aleksandr's wordlessness makes him a Nietzschean superman, nearer to animals. Aleksandr goes mute to heed the earthly wisdom of cows, whose lows pervade *The Sacrifice*'s eerily quiet soundscape. It is as if these cows ask Aleksandr whether he, like Zarathustra, is prepared to go under, to slip out of the human condition once and for all. It is not by chance that cows in *The Sacrifice* are first heard (but not seen) during Aleksandr's and Otto's conversation about Nietzsche and the eternal return in the film's opening sequence. At the precise moment Otto utters the phrase "eternal recurrence," a conspicuous moo is heard off-screen, disclosing the final destination of Aleksandr's philosophical-spiritual journey. Thus spoke Zarathustra: "He that has ears to hear, let him hear!"[160]

In addition to relinquishing language, Aleksandr decides to burn down his family home. Far from an act of Christian self-sacrifice, his choice reflects Nietzsche's ideal of "squandering."[161] Whereas sacrifice suggests "selflessness," squandering is "constituted by egoism"; to squander is to experience an "overflowing and explosion of the self."[162] Aleksandr *squanders* that which confines him to the past and tethers him to the future, opting for an unattached present, not unlike a grazing cow. It is as if Aleksandr (silently) asks himself, at the end of this film entitled *The Sacrifice*, the decisive Nietzschean question: "Why sacrifice? I squander what is given to me, I a squanderer with a thousand hands; how could I call that sacrificing?"[163] Nietzsche, moreover, associates squandering with animals, because their activity is almost always self-directed and self-preserving; animals' inability to rationalize time allows for nothing else. An animal, for Nietzsche, revels in the actualities of its present life because that is all it *can* do. The pointlessness of Aleksandr's activity is, thus, a victory over the joyless reason that constitutes the human condition. "Aleksandr breaks irrevocably with the world and with its laws," Tarkovsky wrote at his most Nietzschean, "put[ting] himself outside all accepted norms. . . . He can sense the danger, the destructive force driving the machinery of modern society as it heads toward the abyss. And the mask must be snatched away if humanity is to be saved."[164] Scampering about the sodden grounds of his estate while his home smolders in the background, Aleksandr resembles not only a mischievous child—Zarathustra's dwarf—but also an animal: an impulsive being uninterested in or incapable of explaining himself to others, reveling in the mess he has made.[165] Squandering the customs of human life, Aleksandr recognizes what Zarathustra learned from the cows: "The kingdom of heaven" is not up in the clouds, but here "among the cows"—an infinite present unburdened by the exigencies of death.[166] Unlike most of us, Aleksandr refuses to refuse becoming like an animal.

What Aleksandr consigns to flames, then, is not just his house but *all* Tarkovsky's houses: "all those nests of stored memories and congealed time" throughout his cinema, anchoring "the self to the past and fatally undermining the joy of the present through a yearning for another time."[167] Tarkovsky's cloying attachment to otherworldliness, typified by *Nostalghia*'s final image of a Russian cottage inside an Italian cathedral, goes up in smoke in *The Sacrifice*. Tarkovsky ends his cinema with a self-affirming experience of squandering, communicating his hope, at the end of his life, to remain in the world of the living, in the here and now among the cows.

The scene after Aleksandr's housefire unexpectedly presents a herd of grazing cows. We see Maria, the witch with whom Aleksandr had sexual relations, gazing at the animals. Her black-and-white headscarf rhymes with the polka-dotted cows (reiterating Tarkovsky's association between the female and the bovine). Despite the threat of nuclear war, these cows graze as if nothing ever happened or ever will. They meet the task posed by Zarathustra—the turning of the "eternal hourglass"—completely free of existential dread: "Was *that* life?

By juxtaposing images of fire and cows at the end of his final film, Tarkovsky summons the memory of the burning cow. Stills from *The Sacrifice*, 1986.

Well then! Once more!"¹⁶⁸ Cows return to *The Sacrifice*'s northern grasslands, just as to Tarkovsky's cinema, invoking the memory of the very first cow to have appeared in his work: the burning cow of *Andrei Rublev*. Tarkovsky's filmography folds in on itself like a Möbius strip, ending where it began over twenty years earlier, with images of fire and cows, as if enacting Nietzsche's philosophy of the eternal return on screen.

In *The Sacrifice*, Tarkovsky's lifelong yearning for otherworldliness gives way to a desire for endless now-ness. Staring down his mortality, Tarkovsky recognized all that has passed and all that has yet to be cannot enjoy the Nietzschean gift of presence. Hence, one of the final sights of Tarkovsky's lofty, philosophical cinema is an improbably mundane one of cows "chewing the cud," an image of animals ponderously dwelling in space, indifferent to the ebb and flow of time.

SACRED COW

By alternating between images of fire and cows at the end of *The Sacrifice*, Tarkovsky suggests that, decades later, he was still thinking about—and perhaps haunted by—the immolated cow of *Andrei Rublev*. It is as if revisiting the cow's memory helped Tarkovsky, at the end of his life, prepare for his own death. This compulsion to repeat traumatic events from one's past, as the Freudian critic Peter Brooks writes, manifests in a "death instinct," a psychobiological drive to imagine and, ultimately, surrender to the prospect of nonexistence.¹⁶⁹ "Freud argues that the pleasure principle is a 'tendency operating in the service of a function whose business it is to free the mental apparatus entirely from extinction or to keep the amount of excitation in a constant or to keep it as low as possible.' This function is concerned 'with the most universal endeavor of all living substance—namely to return to the quiescence of the inorganic world.'"¹⁷⁰ As discussed in chapter 3 through images of ascendant birds, Tarkovsky believed that death was a prologue for a new, more peaceful—albeit unknowable—state of being: "What we call death is not death. It's a rebirth. A caterpillar becomes a cocoon. I think there is life after death, and it is that that is unnerving."¹⁷¹

While Tarkovsky's indebtedness to the Western philosophical tradition is inarguable, as apparent through his recourse to Nietzsche, Tarkovsky's work (like Nietzsche's) also draws on Eastern sources to make sense of the world.¹⁷² In *The Sacrifice*, Aleksandr listens to Japanese flute music and wears a kimono-like robe with a yin-yang symbol, an insignia of Taoist thought representing opposite but equal forces. In *Stalker*, Tarkovsky's monk-like protagonist quotes the *Tao Te Ching*, an ancient Taoist text. Stalker's description of the Zone's

mutable topography, which mirrors the flow of its inhabitants' consciousness—
"The Zone is a very complicated system of traps. . . . It may seem capricious, but it is what we've made it with our minds"—echoes what the Buddha said in the *Dhammapada*: "Our life is the creation of the mind."[173] Even in his diaries, Tarkovsky, who studied at the Moscow Institute of Oriental Studies for a year before beginning his career in film, quoted the Zen monk Urabe Kenkō and recorded several translations of Japanese haiku.[174]

Ultimately, though, Tarkovsky betrayed a highly superficial view of Eastern spirituality, indicative of the global fad for New Age beliefs that gripped the stifled cultural atmosphere of late Soviet society in the 1970s and '80s.[175] This eclectic movement, it was popularly believed, could reenchant jaded Westerners living in stagnating industrial societies during the final decades of the Cold War through the arrogation of Eastern philosophies and practices.[176] "The latent Orientalism that propels [Tarkovsky's] romantic invocations of Eastern plenitude, frozen in an arcadian past, is troubling—especially in light of Russia's own vexed history in relation to the Orient. . . . The Universalism he sought was undeniably rooted in a Euro-Russian cultural and epistemological terrain; that is why, Daoist philosophy or Japanese flute music could be invoked as the supplementary Other."[177] Tarkovsky's embrace of the East, however clumsy, served as a balm to what he viewed as the soul-crushing ideologies and platitudes of both Western capitalism and Soviet communism. Confronted with the pressures of exile and illness, Tarkovsky was drawn to mystical theories of everlastingness: "I am convinced that life is only the beginning. I know I can't prove it, but we instinctively know that we are immortal. . . . I just know that a man who ignores death is a bad man."[178] Besides Nietzsche, then, Tarkovsky's musings about eternal return also borrow from one of the most important beliefs shared by many Buddhist, Hindu, Sikh, and Jain communities concerning spiritual passage: reincarnation. "There's no death," Tarkovsky said a year before his own, "There's immortality."[179]

A tenet of reincarnation is the notion of ahimsa, an appeal to do no harm to others because every being's essence begins a new life in a different body after death. This process of spiritual migration is governed by *karma*, the sum total of the moral contributions made by one's actions, which determines the quality of one's next life.[180] This philosophy intrigued Tarkovsky: "Karma is a buddhistic belief. . . . The good or evil of our future lives will equally depend upon our efforts to avoid evil and do good in this world."[181] For many believers of reincarnation, animals are not excluded from those deserving compassion, as both humans and animals, according to the logic of spiritual passage, are linked "through eons of transmigration"; our "spirits have been embodied by every other creature on the planet."[182] Belief in reincarnation envisions a world "in which the quality and quantity of violence is reduced and in which sentient entities might come to live together in a way that reflects the fullness and beauty of their ethical and ontological unity."[183] Throughout his work, however, Tarkovsky neglected to show kindness toward others—humans and animals alike—thus failing one of the basic tests posed by reincarnation. Though Tarkovsky, when asked what animal he would like to be, said, "Perhaps I'd like to be an animal that caused the least harm possible," he often left animals worse for their encounters with him.[184]

Tarkovsky's tendency toward cruelty is epitomized by his decision to burn alive a cow, an animal that, in many corners of Eastern thought, is accorded sacred status.[185] As recounted by the Sri Lankan philosopher Hammalawa Saddhatissa, the Buddha valorized cows as "our great friends, like our mother, father, brother, and other relations," who give "food, strength, beauty, health—knowing these benefits, they [the Brahmins] did not kill cattle."[186] Cows are (maternal) symbols of plenty that beget harmony, and they exemplify the interspecies community fostered by proponents of reincarnation because of their life-giving power of milk production. Even in the godless culture of Soviet society, images of cows acquired pseudoreligious status after World War II, as in Petr Konchalovskii's 1947 painting *At Midday* (*Na Poldni*), symbolizing the "victory of life over death."[187] Cow's milk has, indeed, long been regarded as a "mystical and precious substance" that nurtures infants, restores the weak, and counteracts disease.[188] Milk is the drink of "sages, seers, and saints" because, unlike alcohol, it acts as "an aid to serenity and spirituality"; milk does not "induce worldly desires or distract" from "higher metaphysical truths."[189] We would expect Tarkovsky, given his concerns about humanity's spiritual condition, to depict milk with profound reverence. As Andrei Rublev points out, "It's a sin to waste milk." Yet the milk encountered across Tarkovsky's cinema is not depicted as restorative or nutritious—rather, it is continually spilled, leaked, or wasted.[190] In *Andrei Rublev, Mirror, Stalker, Nostalghia*, and *The Sacrifice*, Tarkovsky draws our attention to milk's unrealized potential, and his insistent focus on spattered milk—viscous, frothy-white liquid that can also be interpreted as misspent semen—captures what he saw as the world's discordant state: nature in conflict with culture, men with women, West with East, superficial materialism with spiritual immanence. Contemporary society, in Tarkovsky's view, is beyond nourishment. Variously spilled and undrunk, milk loses its sacred status in Tarkovsky's cinema; even the milky white walls of a cathedral in *Andrei Rublev* are besmirched by coarse black paint (evoking

Jackson Pollock's paintings, which Tarkovsky saw as modern desecrations of true art). It is especially striking, then, that the cow in *Andrei Rublev*—one of the few cows encountered in Tarkovsky's cinema—is not associated with milk, that "white elixir," but with *fire*, the element most indicative of annihilation and destructive (male) passion.[191] Fire is, in a way, milk's compositionally opposite substance.

The cow's burning in *Andrei Rublev* conveys what Tarkovsky perceived as humanity's penchant for desecrating the sacred, including the gift of life itself. The shot before the image of the burning cow presents a church's facade obscured by flames, conjuring an image of hell and priming viewers for the sulfureous cow. Tarkovsky suggests that people in the modern world have abandoned any moral or religious code.[192] "The scene," Tarkovsky wrote referring to newsreel footage in *Mirror* of Hiroshima—another fiery catastrophe of human history—"was about that suffering which is the price of what is known as historical progress, and of the innumerable victims whom, from time immemorial, it has claimed."[193] (In *Solaris*, Kelvin warns about human destructivity, yelling, "Remember Hiroshima!") Re-creating the savagery of the medieval period vis-à-vis the image of a burning cow, Tarkovsky proffered commentary about his *own* era, the twentieth century, in which all that was precious was under assault.[194] There is, for Tarkovsky, no such thing as historical progress. Humanity since the Middle Ages has been in the business of defiling all that is sacred; Tarkovsky burns a cow to deny any hint of postwar optimism.

Yet Tarkovsky's critique of humanity's disregard for the sacred undercuts itself. Tarkovsky assays humanity's incapacity to cherish precious things by dooming a defenseless cow, indulging the very barbarism he abhorred. He backslides into the most common logical mistake in ethical philosophy, the ultimate fallacy of relevance: whether two wrongs make a right. In his films, Tarkovsky implores us to confront humanity's bottomless capacity for brutality *by way of* brutality, suggesting how his moral compass, too, had been warped by the horrors of the twentieth century. The presence of cows at the end of *The Sacrifice*, especially juxtaposed against images of fire, suggests that Tarkovsky may have been worried about his own karmic condition, about *his* actions that inflicted harm onto others, including animals. "Please, whenever you talk about me," Tarkovsky purportedly said before his death, "remind people I want to be remembered as a sinner, as somebody who committed many sins."[195]

That cows—and not, as one might expect, horses—are the last animals to appear in Tarkovsky's cinema is not incidental. If Tarkovsky expressed a longing for eternal life in *The Sacrifice* by counterposing images of cows and fire to ponder his karmic fate, then the cow burned in *Andrei Rublev* signifies a kind of eternal death. Because the cow's agony is imprinted on celluloid and can be rewound and rewatched, it is denied the terminating, sacred singularity that death typically affords a living being. The cow dies on loop, over and over again on screen. As Bazin writes:

> I cannot repeat a single moment of my life, but cinema can repeat any one of these moments indefinitely before my eyes. If it is true that, for consciousness, no moment is equal to any other, there is one on which this fundamental difference converges, and that is the moment of death. For every creature, death is the unique moment par excellence. The qualitative life is retroactively defined in relation to it.... Thanks to film, nowadays we can desecrate and show at will the only one of our possessions that is temporarily inalienable: dead without a requiem, the eternal dead—again of the cinema![196]

Preserved on film, Tarkovsky's burning cow is condemned to die in perpetuity, enacting another version of Nietzsche's theory of the eternal return. "In every Instant being begins," Zarathustra is told, but for the cow, "being" only means dying. The cow's life, as Tarkovsky presents it, consists of nothing more than fiery suffering. We see the cow's death throes but not the moment of death, a finality deferred. The cow's memory is always and only burning, nearing but never crossing into nonexistence. Tarkovsky's cow, embalmed on celluloid, escapes death only to be granted the gift of life as an ongoing form of death; it is kept alive dying on film forever. As Bazin might say, Tarkovsky's cow "dies every afternoon," as if stuck in hell.[197]

In this light, the pacific cows at the end of *The Sacrifice* may be understood as Tarkovsky's last-ditch gambit to save the burning cow of *Andrei Rublev*, to release from eternal torment what had been his cinema's only image of a cow. It is not by chance that Tarkovsky presents a herd of (living) cows in *The Sacrifice* as opposed to the single (dying) cow in *Andrei Rublev*. To kill an animal, as theorists have grimly pointed out, is one way to "suggest that animal's individuality, disturbing the frequent representation of animals as constituting packs or hordes."[198] Singularity is ascribed to humanity, whereas multiplicity "is said to define animality," so to destroy an animal is to—perversely, paradoxically—recognize its uniqueness and allow it, briefly, "to become human."[199] By burning the cow, Tarkovsky cannot help but acknowledge the individual (ir)reducibility of its existence, a singularity that imbues human lives with poetic and sacred meaning.[200] The cow in *Andrei Rublev* is not an allegory for cows as an abstract category of species but a historically locatable being with a life (and death) of its own.

By contrast, in *The Sacrifice*, Tarkovsky portrays cows as an anonymous horde. Cows once again signify the totalizing idea of "the cow," which generalizes—that is, depersonalizes—these animals. The distant, featureless cows in

The Sacrifice (filmed in a landscape shot, no less) are more animal—remote, indistinguishable, backgrounded—than the individuated, burning cow in *Andrei Rublev*'s foreground. The contrast between Tarkovsky's two depictions of cows troublingly suggests that he accorded some animals individual subjecthood only through torment and death, which single them out from the herd. It is as if in *The Sacrifice*, Tarkovsky compensates for having burned a cow alive—and bestowed it humanlike significance—by offering cows the gift of nondescript, deindividualized *in*significance associated with animal hordes. Tarkovsky inadvertently reveals that human beings burn cows (i.e., kill animals) because animals are not conceived as unique subjects like us. But by killing animals, we singularize them and make them more humanlike, which requires us to reestablish animals' status *as* animals—as faceless, indistinct multiplicities—so we can continue killing them unabatedly and with impunity.

Just like Tarkovsky's image of an immolated cow, real-life animals are stuck in a kind of death loop in which they acquire the very traits that could save them in the eyes of their (human) killers only through slaughter: singularity, recognizability, piteousness. Tarkovsky's parting gift to the herd of cows in *The Sacrifice*—the gift of anonymous animality that saves them from being singled out—is perhaps his attempt at atonement, a penitential tribute, for having set a cow on fire some twenty years earlier, an indirect and all-too-belated confession from his deathbed that yes, the cow did burn.

NOTES

1. For a detailed account of the film's making, see Johnson and Petrie, *Films of Andrei Tarkovsky*, 79–82.

2. Muratova, "Kogda ia uznala."

3. Soviet officials supported Tarkovsky's project as part of a campaign to glorify Russia's medieval history during the Cold War. In 1960, authorities celebrated Rublev's six hundredth anniversary, and Tarkovsky attended a retrospective on Rublev's art in Moscow, where he decided to make the film. See Skakov, *Cinema of Tarkovsky*, 42.

4. For this letter, see "'Andrei Rublev'—Istoriia sozdania fil'ma—Arkhivnye Dokumenty (Chast' 4)."

5. "Andrei Rublev'—Istoriia sozdania fil'ma—Arkhivnye Dokumenty (Chast' 4)."

6. "'Andrei Rublev'—Istoriia sozdania fil'ma—Arkhivnye Dokumenty (Chast' 4)."

7. Tarkovsky, *Interviews*, 27–28.

8. The short film, entitled "Soviet Cinema No. 2" (*Sovetskoe kino No. 2*), was shot by Lev Danilov, a young filmmaker working at Moscow's Central Studio for Documentary Films (CSDF). For this film, see "Goriashchaia korova."

9. Johnson and Petrie, *Films of Andrei Tarkovsky*, 80.

10. See "'Andrei Rublev'—Istoriia sozdania fil'ma—Arkhivnye Dokumenty (Chast' 5)"; see also Kosinova and Fomin, *Kak Sniat' Shedevr*, 338–40.

11. Soldatov, ". . . I zapylala korova," 3.

12. Soldatov, ". . . I zapylala korova," 3.

13. Johnson and Petrie, *Films of Andrei Tarkovsky*, 81.

14. In 1969, the edited version of *Andrei Rublev* "sold to a company representing Columbia for foreign distribution," which led to its premier in an "out-of-competition, unofficial screening" at the Cannes International Film Festival. There, it won the International Critics' Prize "much to the discomfiture of the Soviet authorities, who then made strenuous efforts to prevent its planned opening in Paris and refused to screen it at the 1969 Moscow Film Festival." Johnson and Petrie, *Films of Andrei Tarkovsky*, 81–82.

15. Tarkovsky, *Time Within Time*, 53.

16. Tarkovsky, *Interviews*, 29.

17. Blasco, "Interview with Marina Tarkovskaya and Alexander Gordon."

18. Tarkovsky, "Bespretsedentnost' spiska popravok"; Tarkovsky, "*Passion according to Andrei.*"

19. Johnson and Petrie, *Films of Andrei Tarkovsky*, 82.

20. Johnson and Petrie, *Films of Andrei Tarkovsky*, 81; "'Andrei Rublev'—Istoriia sozdania fil'ma—Arkhivnye Dokumenty (Chast' 4)." Thanks in part to *Andrei Rublev*'s controversial reputation, it regularly appears—more so than any of Tarkovsky's other films—on best-of lists, including *Sight and Sound*'s decennial "Greatest Films of All Time," where it has ranked as high as twelfth place. See "The Greatest Films of All Time . . . in 1982."

21. Kets de Vries, "Are You a Victim of the Victim Syndrome?"

22. Tarkovsky, *Interviews*, 158.

23. For Scorsese's intervention, see Rance, "Mark Rance on *Andrei Rublov*."

24. See, e.g., Le Fanu, *Cinema of Andrei Tarkovsky*; Green, *Andrei Tarkovsky*.

25. Quoted in Turovskaya, *7 s ½ ili Fil'my Andreia Tarkovskogo*, 73.

26. Iusov, "Zhivotnye na s"emkakh 'Andreia Rubleva.'"

27. Aksenova, "Zhertvoprinosheniia."

28. Kuniaev, *Moi pechal'nye pobedy*, 562.

29. Velten, *Cow*, 67–72.

30. Velten, *Cow*, 86–87.

31. See "Proiskhozhdenie slova korova."

32. Velten, *Cow*, 69.

33. Rosenholm, "'There Is No Russia Without the Cow,'" 89–90.

34. For the story's publication, see Platonov, *Soul*, 329.
35. Quoted in Tsymbal, "Tarkovsky's Childhood," 17.
36. On Tarkovsky and mourning, see Sandler, "Absent Father, the Stillness of Film."
37. Tsymbal, "Tarkovsky's Childhood," 18–21.
38. This sequence ends with a recitation of a poem by Tarkovsky's father, "First Meetings" (*Pervyie svidaniia*, 1962).
39. Tsymbal, "Tarkovsky's Childhood," 20.
40. Synessios, *Mirror*, 97.
41. Goscilo, "Fraught Filiation," 267.
42. Velten, *Cow*, 67.
43. See Elkins, *Mary, Mother of Martyrs*.
44. Tarkovsky, *Time Within Time*, 99.
45. Velten, *Cow*, 156–78.
46. For these critiques, see Ruthchild, "Sisterhood and Socialism."
47. Quoted in Menzel, "Tarkovsky in Berlin," 383.
48. Tarkovsky, *Interviews*, 106.
49. Bird, *Andrei Rublev*, 49.
50. See Sadovskii, "Obnazhennoe telo," 92.
51. The holy fool girl, with her expressive face, is distinctly reminiscent of the clown character Gelsomina in a film Tarkovsky admired, Federico Fellini's *La strada* (1954). Gelsomina was, in fact, performed by Fellini's wife, Giulietta Masina, just as Raush, Tarkovsky's first wife, played the *durochka*. Tarkovsky saddles himself to Fellini's legacy through the demeaning portrayal of his wife.
52. Bird, *Andrei Rublev*, 50.
53. For the significance of this painting in *Nostalghia*, see MacGillivray, "Andrei Tarkovsky's *Madonna Del Parto*."
54. Tarkovsky, *Sculpting in Time*, 225.
55. Johnson and Petrie, *Films of Andrei Tarkovsky*, 246.
56. Tarkovsky, *Collected Screenplays*, 373–416.
57. Dostoevsky based Sonia on the trope of the Decembrist wives, who followed their husbands into exile after their failed uprising in 1825. Additionally, Stalker's ramshackle home reminds us of Raskolnikov's "closet-like" dwelling (*kamorka*).
58. Tarkovsky, *Interviews*, 108.
59. Rosenholm, "'There Is No Russia Without the Cow,'" 70.
60. Tarkovsky, *Interviews*, 94.
61. The theme of medieval Russia as an "unhappy family" plagued by political infighting inspired Russian writers and leaders to emphasize "hierarchies of obedience and clan loyalty, beginning with an eleventh-century story in which the machinations of the sons of Grand Prince Vladimir end in fratricide." Kahn et al., *History of Russian Literature*, 82. This theme of clan loyalty continues to inform

modern-day Russia's authoritarian political culture. Additionally, in *Andrei Rublev*, Foma's attacker says, "I'll show you 'Russians,' you Vladimir swine!" (*Ia pokazhu tebe russkie, svoloch' Vladimirskaia!*) in a barnyard aside pigs, conveying how, for Tarkovsky, even brothers can devolve into sectarianism and dehumanization.

62. For reactionary conservatism in late Soviet culture, see Robinson, *Russian Conservativism*.

63. For Tarkovsky on Solzhenitsyn, see Tarkovsky, *Interviews*, 152. For his part, Solzhenitsyn criticized *Andrei Rublev* for not glorifying Russian history more. See Solzhenitsyn, "Fil'm o Rubleve."

64. Solzhenitsyn, "World Split Apart."

65. Rosenholm, "'There Is No Russia without the Cow,'" 81.

66. Tarkovsky, *Interviews*, 110. In this light, Tarkovsky's image of a burning cow inside a barn also inverts the conciliatory portrayal of serene, comforting, and feminized cows that soothe an otherwise distraught Konstantin Levin inside a cowshed in Lev Tolstoy's *Anna Karenina* (1878).

67. Derrida, "Force of Law," 19.

68. Calarco, *Animal Studies*, 41.

69. Calarco, *Animal Studies*, 41.

70. Derrida, "'Eating Well,'" 114.

71. Calarco, *Zoographies*, 132.

72. When Writer is introduced, he is fawning over a woman clad in a fur shawl, which he lustfully strokes, further reflecting Derrida's idea that the killing of animals—for meat and for fur—underpins human constructions of gender, status, and power. Additionally, as Writer flirts with the woman, he refers to the Greek philosopher Pythagoras, describing the mathematically fixed relations between the sides of a triangle. Besides his geometrical theorem, Pythagoras was also one of the earliest proponents of vegetarianism. He believed "in the transmigration of souls from humans to animals," which "meant that he objected" to meat "on the grounds that humans could end up eating human souls." Pythagoras's challenge to prevailing conceptions of eating resonates with Writer's ethical waffling on vegetarianism. Ryan, *Animal Theory*, 9.

73. Calarco, *Zoographies*, 131.

74. Calarco, *Zoographies*, 131.

75. Calarco, *Zoographies*, 132.

76. Tolstoy, *Anna Karenina*, 149.

77. While shooting *Solaris*, Tarkovsky and the actress playing Hari, Natalia Bonderchuk, began a torrid love affair that drove Bonderchuk, like her character in the film, to contemplate suicide. For details about the affair, see "Tarkovskii bez gliantsa. Chast' XI. Natal'ia Bonderchuk." It could be speculated, in an Oedipal key, that Tarkovsky pursued an affair with Bonderchuk to get back at her father, Sergei Bonderchuk, whom Tarkovsky never forgave—"hated everything

he stood for"—for stealing the limelight from *Andrei Rublev* in the late 1960s with his own historical (eight-hour) epic *War and Peace* (*Voina i mir*, 1967), which became one of the few Soviet films to win an Oscar. See Johnson and Petrie, *Films of Andrei Tarkovsky*, 80–81.

78. For this connection, see Schivelbusch, *Railway Journey*, 77–79.
79. Schivelbusch, *Railway Journey*, 83.
80. Later in *Mirror*, the heroine is likened to the mad and licentious Maria Timofeyevna in Dostoevsky's novel *Demons* (*Besy*, 1871–72) while ruthlessly criticized for her "nonsensical emancipation," implying that she has had multiple sexual partners since her husband's sudden departure, to the detriment of her children.
81. Tarkovsky, *Sculpting in Time*, 225.
82. See Reilly, "Story of Freud's Patient."
83. See Cartwright, *Screening the Body*.
84. Cartwright, *Screening the Body*, 48; Tarkovsky, *Interviews*, 134.
85. Cartwright, *Screening the Body*, 47, 53.
86. Cartwright, *Screening the Body*, 66.
87. Lippit, *Electric Animal*, 103–104.
88. Derrida, *Animal That Therefore I Am*, 32.
89. At one point in *Mirror*, Tarkovsky foregrounds an image of a teacup and biscuits, evoking the madeleine episode in Marcel Proust's *In Search of Lost Time* (*À la recherche du temps perdu*, 1913–27) that triggers the protagonist's recollections about his childhood and one of the biggest literary experiments with the written word. In *Mirror*, Tarkovsky undertakes a similarly Proustian project of self-discovery vis-à-vis (cinematic) language.
90. Tarkovsky, *Sculpting in Time*, 38–39.
91. Aristotle, *Politics*, 11.
92. Derrida, "How to Avoid Speaking Denials?," 86–87.
93. Lippit, *Electric Animal*, 30.
94. Quoted in Lippit, *Electric Animal*, 50. See also Lyotard, "Inarticulate, or the Differend Itself."
95. Lippit, *Electric Animal*, 48.
96. Tarkovsky, *Sculpting in Time*, 57.
97. Tarkovsky, *Sculpting in Time*, 229.
98. See "Fasting Rules in the Orthodox Church."
99. See, e.g., Boisseron, *Afro-Dog*; Cordeiro-Rodrigues and Mitchell, *Animals, Race, and Multiculturalism*.
100. Calarco, *Animal Studies*, 116.
101. See "Zapretnoe miaso: Pochemy russkie ne eli koninu"; "Pochemu v magazinakh SSSR ne prodavali koninu?" For additional context, see, too, Forrest, "Troubled History of Horse Meat."
102. Quoted in Mandušić, "Truth of Direct Observation," 86.

103. Mandušić, "Truth of Direct Observation," 91.
104. Mandušić, "Truth of Direct Observation," 89.
105. Mandušić, "Truth of Direct Observation," 92.
106. After signing the contract to make a film about Andrei Rublev in 1962, Tarkovsky and Konchalovsky worked on the script for more than two years and steeped themselves in biblical texts, medieval chronicles, and saints' biographies.
107. White, "Value of Narrativity in the Representation of Reality," 10.
108. Mandušić, "Truth of Direct Observation," 92.
109. Tarkovsky, "Andrei Tarkovsky on *Andrei Rublev*."
110. Tarkovsky, "Andrei Tarkovsky on *Andrei Rublev*."
111. Tarkovsky, *Sculpting in Time*, 78.
112. Tarkovsky, *Interviews*, 28.
113. Balász, *Der Geist des Films*, 84.
114. Burt, *Animals in Film*, 11–12.
115. Bazin, "Les films d'animaux nous révèlent le cinema," 8.
116. Burt, *Animals in Film*, 32, 53.
117. Burt, *Animals in Film*, 32.
118. de Luca, "Natural Views," 221.
119. Bazin, "Death Every Afternoon," 29.
120. Bazin, "Death Every Afternoon," 30–31.
121. Skakov, *Cinema of Tarkovsky*, 125–26. The image of a bull being slain by matadors in *Mirror* also channels Tarkovsky's abiding interest in Hemingway, noted in chapter 1, who immortalized scenes of bullfighting in *The Sun Also Rises* (1926). Translated into Russian in 1935, the novel was recirculated in the post-Stalin period at the onset of Tarkovsky's career. See Parker, "Hemingway's Revival in the Soviet Union," 491.
122. Sobchack, *Carnal Thoughts*, 247.
123. Bazin, "Death Every Afternoon," 31.
124. See Lippit, "Death of an Animal"; O'Brien, "Why Look at Dead Animals?"
125. Shukin, *Animal Capital*, 150–52.
126. Oliver, "See Topsy 'Ride the Lightning.'"
127. Doane, *Emergence of Cinematic Time*, 145.
128. Cartwright, *Screening the Body*, 18. Cartwright also notes that Topsy, an African elephant, can be understood as "a specimen of colonial plunder" whose death entertains "fantasies of colonial authority."
129. Cartwright, *Screening the Body*, xi.
130. Cartwright, *Screening the Body*, 18.
131. Perhaps inspired by Tarkovsky, Ingmar Bergman—another great auteur—made a film a few years after *Andrei Rublev* titled *The Passion of Anna* (*En passion*,

1969), in which, toward the end of the film, a barn bursts into flames and the soundtrack is flooded by the sounds of the cows trapped therein.

132. Lippit, *Atomic Light*, 33.
133. Lippit, *Atomic Light*, 33.
134. Quoted in Bird, "Omens."
135. Tarkovsky was a lifelong smoker, and he wryly portrays cigarettes throughout his films. In *Ivan's Childhood*, Tarkovsky's child protagonist admonishes his mentor for smoking, and, in *Nostalghia*, Domenico says, "I ask for a cigarette when I don't know what to say. But I've never learned to smoke, it's too difficult. Instead of smoking, one should learn to do important things."
136. Quoted in Bird, "Omens."
137. Tarkovsky, *Time Within Time*, 106.
138. Tarkovsky, *Sculpting in Time*, 57.
139. Tarkovsky, *Time Within Time*, 354.
140. Tarkovsky, *Time Within Time*, 389.
141. Nietzsche, *Thus Spoke Zarathustra*, 155–60.
142. "Otto" was the birth name of Anatoly Solonitsyn, an actor who appeared many of Tarkovsky's films. Tarkovsky wanted Solonitsyn to play Aleksandr in *The Sacrifice*, but Solonitsyn's death from cancer in 1982 made this impossible. Naming the postman Otto, Tarkovsky preserves Solonitsyn's memory on screen: "He [Solonitsyn] died of the illness ... which a year later was to afflict me." Tarkovsky, *Sculpting in Time*, 220. Like Tarkovsky, Solonitsyn may have contracted cancer from the radioactive set of *Stalker*.
143. For Nietzsche and *The Sacrifice*, see Moliterno, "Zarathustra's Gift."
144. Alexander-Garrett, "Never Be Neutral," 23; Tarkovsky, *Time Within Time*, 332. Tarkovsky also considered "The Eternal Return" as a title for *The Sacrifice*. See Tarkovsky, *Collected Screenplays*, 590.
145. Nietzsche, *Gay Science*, 273.
146. Nietzsche, *Thus Spoke Zarathustra*, 191.
147. See Rosenberg, "Kulning."
148. Josephson had also played Nietzsche himself in Liliana Cavani's *Beyond Good and Evil* (*Al di là del bene e del male*, 1977).
149. Nietzsche, *Thus Spoke Zarathustra*, 269.
150. Nietzsche, *Thus Spoke Zarathustra*, 269.
151. Nietzsche, *Untimely Meditations*, 60–61.
152. Nietzsche, *Thus Spoke Zarathustra*, 271.
153. Nietzsche, *Thus Spoke Zarathustra*, 217–18.
154. Lippit, *Electric Animal*, 68.
155. Lippit, *Electric Animal*, 71.
156. Lippit, *Electric Animal*, 72.
157. Nietzsche, *Anti-Christ*, 12.
158. Nietzsche, *Thus Spoke Zarathustra*, 13.

159. Ryan, *Animal Theory*, 53.
160. Nietzsche, *Thus Spoke Zarathustra*, 157.
161. Nietzsche, *Thus Spoke Zarathustra*, 238.
162. Lemm, *Nietzsche's Animal Philosophy*, 79–80.
163. Nietzsche, *Thus Spoke Zarathustra*, 238.
164. Tarkovsky, *Sculpting in Time*, 227.
165. Some critics (Cole, "Oeuvre: Tarkovsky: The Sacrifice") note the humor to this scene as Aleksandr, appearing like a character from a Charlie Chaplin or Buster Keaton film, runs away from his family, repeatedly stumbling and pratfalling. One critic refers to these kind of moments in Tarkovsky's cinema as a form of "sublime slapstick" (Kane, "Sublime Slapstick"). The unexpected comedy here, I argue, stems from Aleksandr behaving like an animal. As French philosopher Henri Bergson argues, humans laugh when we recognize a faintly distorted resemblance of ourselves in other beings and things (i.e., children, animals, objects, etc.). "You may laugh at an animal, but only because you have detected in it some human attitude or expression.... Several have defined man as 'an animal which laughs.' They might equally well have defined him as an animal which is laughed at; for it, any other animal, or some lifeless object, produces the same effect, it is always because of some resemblance to man, of the stamp he gives it or the use he puts it." Bergson, "Laughter," 2. At the end of *The Sacrifice*, Aleksandr's behavior evokes laughter because he now only *resembles* a human being; he has, like Zarathustra, slipped out of the human condition and ended up nearer to the cows.
166. Nietzsche, *Thus Spoke Zarathustra*, 270.
167. Moliterno, "Zarathustra's Gift."
168. Nietzsche, *Thus Spoke Zarathustra*, 157.
169. Brooks, "Freud's Masterplot," 291.
170. Brooks, "Freud's Masterplot," 294–95.
171. Tarkovsky, *Interviews*, 175.
172. The name "Zarathustra" refers to the founder of Zoroastrianism, an ancient Iranian religion.
173. *Dhammapada: The Path of Perfection*, 1.
174. Tarkovsky, *Time Within Time*, 78, 164.
175. See Panchenko, "Ancient Wisdom, Stigmatised Knowledge, and Sacred Landscapes."
176. In *Nostalghia*, Tarkovsky satirizes New Age trends vis-à-vis Eugenia's decision to travel to India—with an Italian gangster—and a philistine day tripper's fascination with Chinese music, which, he claims, "beats Verdi." This critique suggests that Tarkovsky believed that there was a wrong way and a right way (e.g., his way) to engage Eastern spiritualism.
177. Sarkar, "Threnody for Modernity," 255.
178. Tarkovsky, *Interviews*, 47.

179. Tarkovsky, *Sculpting in Time*, 13.
180. See Harvey, *Introduction to Buddhism*, 32–49.
181. Tarkovsky, *Time Within Time*, 169.
182. Kemmerer, *Animals and World Religion*, 114.
183. Calarco, *Boundaries of Human Nature*, 48.
184. Tarkovsky, *Interviews*, 87.
185. See Velten, *Cow*, 74–80.
186. Saddhatissa, *Sutta-Nipata*, 33.
187. Rosenholm, "'There Is No Russia without the Cow,'" 79.
188. Velten, *Milk*, 35.
189. Velten, *Milk*, 42–43.
190. Only in *The Steamroller and the Violin* (*Katok i skripka*, 1959), Tarkovsky's student diploma film, do we see a boy drink a bottle of milk with a (surrogate) father figure.
191. Velten, *Milk*, 35.
192. Ironically, one of the early critiques levied against Tarkovsky while he was filming *Andrei Rublev* was his recklessness, especially his crew's use of live fire while filming in and around ancient churches. See "'Andrei Rublev'—Istoriia sozdania fil'ma—Arkhivnye Dokumenty (Chast' 4)."
193. Tarkovsky, *Sculpting in Time*, 130.
194. The image of a cow in a smoldering barn alongside a screaming peasant—and the long take of a burning barn in *Mirror*—surely evoked traumatic memories borne by Tarkovsky's contemporaneous Soviet viewers concerning the Nazi campaign against Soviet partisans (Ivan in *Ivan's Childhood*, for example) that entailed burning whole villages on the Eastern Front during World War II. Inspired by Tarkovsky's cinema, Elem Klimov infamously re-created a barn burning in *Come and See* (*Idi i smotri*, 1985), which also features a graphic sequence of a slain cow, a symbol of the suffering motherland during wartime.
195. Tarkovsky apparently uttered these words to the Polish filmmaker Krzysztof Zanussi, as Zanussi recounts in the documentary *Meeting Andrei Tarkovsky* (2008) by Dmitry Tarkovsky (no relation).
196. Bazin, "Death Every Afternoon," 30–31.
197. Bazin, "Death Every Afternoon," 31.
198. Lippit, "Death of an Animal," 11.
199. Lippit, "Death of an Animal," 11.
200. The American filmmaker John Waters, in a characteristic bout of dark humor, acknowledged the grim relation between animal slaughter and singularity when discussing the chicken killed on the set of *Pink Flamingos* (1972): "We bought [the chicken] at a market that advertised 'freshly killed chickens,' so they were about to cut its neck and hand it over to us. Instead, it got to . . . become famous! You could honestly argue we made the chicken's life better." See Waters, "John Waters on *Pink Flamingos*."

FIVE

HORSES OF ANOTHER COLOR

IN TARKOVSKY'S PENULTIMATE FILM, *NOSTALGHIA*, the Italian madman Domenico (Erland Josephson) climbs atop the *Equestrian Statue of Marcus Aurelius* at the Piazza del Campidoglio in Rome—a replica of the ancient imperial monument—and sets himself on fire in a futile attempt to save humankind. Burning alive, Domenico wobbles on the statue before plummeting to the ground. Besides recalling the burnt cow in *Andrei Rublev*, Domenico's death reminds us of yet another of *Andrei Rublev*'s slaughtered animals: the horse that falls down a flight of stairs, breaks its back, and flails in the dirt before being stabbed. Just as Tarkovsky alludes to the incinerated cow by alternating between images of fire and cattle in *The Sacrifice*, in *Nostalghia* he recycles a semantic web of horses, falling, and death that evokes the ghost of *Andrei Rublev*'s slain horse. The animals killed for Tarkovsky's earlier films haunt his later work.

By having a living being tumble to his ruin off a horse monument in *Nostalghia*, Tarkovsky stages a morbid, perhaps even repentant homage to the felled horse of *Andrei Rublev*. Equine statues, designed to imbue their creators with the mighty and regal qualities anthropomorphized by horses, have proliferated in European cities for centuries, as evidenced by *The Bronze Horseman* (*Mednyi vsadnik*) erected in Saint Petersburg in 1782 under Catherine the Great and immortalized in verse by Aleksandr Pushkin.[1] Tarkovsky's cinema has itself become a kind of monument to horses, animals that confer on his films beauty, verve, and grace. "For me," Tarkovsky once said, "the horse symbolizes life."[2] It is all too fitting, then, that Tarkovsky would spotlight a Roman shrine to horses in *Nostalghia*. Yet Tarkovsky associates this horse statue—like the horse in *Andrei Rublev*—not with life but with death. Paradoxically, Tarkovsky often venerates horses through grim portrayals of them.

After lighting himself on fire, Domenico falls off a horse statue, invoking the ghost of the felled horse. Stills from *Nostalghia*, 1983, and *Andrei Rublev*, 1966.

This funereal form of admiration tracks with what French anthropologist René Girard describes as the ritualistic cycle of sacrificial killing, which rotates between feelings of reverence, contempt, and nostalgia for the sacrificial object.[3] The sacrificial victim is first exalted by those around it, whereafter it is killed with scorn and then resurrected in nostalgic memory, a pernicious cycle of exaltation, degradation, and commemoration. In his films, Tarkovsky similarly glorifies, slays, and poignantly eulogizes horses. This three-pronged process is perfectly encapsulated by Tarkovsky's allusion to the horse's fall in *Andrei Rublev* vis-à-vis Domenico's collapse off the *Equestrian Statue of Marcus Aurelius*, Tarkovsky's guilt-ridden atonement (in a film entitled *Nostalghia*, no less) for having killed a horse for his art. While chapter 1 focused on how Tarkovsky exalts horses and mourns their absence—the first and latter segments of Girard's postulation concerning ritualistic killing—this chapter concentrates on the middle section of Girard's hypothesis: Tarkovsky's vicious treatment of the horses he adored.

This chapter begins by exploring the link between horses and visions of the apocalypse, a cultural association sedimented by the book of Revelation and invoked in the great works of nineteenth-century Russian literature. The brutalized horse of *Andrei Rublev* conveys Tarkovsky's anxieties about what he perceived as civilization's imminent collapse. Beyond foreshadowing the apocalypse, however, Tarkovsky's images of equine suffering also suggest his mournfulness concerning horses' disappearance in modern life lapses into what Sigmund Freud called the pathology of "melancholia," which inspires one to debase—and even destroy—the object of mourning in an attempt to overcome feelings of loss. Tarkovsky had a horse butchered on screen in response to his seemingly moribund psychological condition. The apparent disposability of equine life in *Andrei Rublev* betrays Tarkovsky's understanding of animals as fundamentally meaningless. Such a view echoes the German philosopher Martin Heidegger's theory of animals' metaphysical "poverty," which upholds that because animals cannot conceive of death, their lives are worthless, so their slaughter is ethically permissible.[4] A Freudian-Heideggerian reading of Tarkovsky's felled horse in *Andrei Rublev* circles back to the Cartesian theory of animal soullessness—and, therefore, ontological inferiority—that commenced this book.

In cinematic terms, Tarkovsky's slain horse locates him in a dark subcurrent of avant-garde cinema replete with animal violence. Arthouse filmmakers have long relied on animal cruelty to probe the existential matters of life and death on screen. This chapter argues that Tarkovsky killed a horse to secure his place in an ethically suspect corner of art cinema, ironically uniting his creative practice with the 1920s Soviet avant-garde from which he took pains to distance himself.

If chapter 1, which explored Tarkovsky's living horses, ended with an exploration of John Berger's essay "Why Look at Animals?," then this final chapter concludes with a question posed by more recent scholars, given cinema's bleak history of animal carnage: Why look at *dead* animals?[5] Why does cinema turn, "if not with consistent frequency then with remarkable intensity, to the extinguishment of animal life"?[6] Footage of real animal death disrupts all of cinema's representational codes, yet we can hardly consider these cadaverous images truly transgressive, for what could be more commonplace than "animals dying at human hands"?[7] On-screen animal deaths make spectacles out of ordinary violence. Grisly scenes of animal killing foster an ethically bound mode of spectatorship but never, to be sure, a compensatory one. How, then, should we look—or should we look at all—at the slaying of the horse in *Andrei Rublev*, one of the most gratuitous instances of bloodshed ever committed to celluloid?

APOCALYPSE

Halfway into the film *Ivan's Childhood*, set on the Eastern Front during World War II, Tarkovsky's child protagonist (Nikolai Burlyayev) asks to see an album of prints by the fifteenth-century German artist Albrecht Dürer that his Russian comrades have stolen from the retreating Nazi soldiers. Leafing through the volume, Ivan pauses on one of Dürer's most famous engravings, *The Four Horsemen of the Apocalypse* (1498). It depicts a scene from the book of Revelation, the final book of the New Testament, about the end of the world in which four horsemen (representing pestilence, war, conquest, and death) visit Earth as harbingers of the Last Judgment. Ivan describes Dürer's demonic figures as the "same Fritzes on motorcycles" who razed his village and killed his mother. Ivan's comparison of apocalyptic equestrians and Nazi motorists (besides reiterating Tarkovsky's lifelong amaxophobia) echoes John Berger's thesis of animal vanishing, detailed in chapter 1, which maintains that animals have been replaced by technological facsimiles, with calamitous effect in modern life. Even the first shot of *Ivan's Childhood* consists of Ivan lurking behind a spiderweb, the knotted texture of which rhymes with the images of barbed wire encountered throughout the film. The organic world is devoured and then reconstituted by the lethal technologies of modern warfare.

As Ivan gazes at *The Four Horseman of the Apocalypse*, the camera assumes his point of view and zooms in on Dürer's picture, magnifying the most frightening of the horsemen: an emaciated old man in tatters, whom Ivan describes as "skin and bones," astride a gaunt stallion.[8] This is the fourth rider of the apocalypse—death—and Tarkovsky's attention to it foreshadows Ivan's demise when, at the end of the film, he is hanged in a Nazi prison. Dürer's apocalypse "becomes the Apocalypse of Ivan's life," and it "provide[s] an outlet" for Tarkovsky's anti-German sentiments, "still strong in Soviet war films" of the 1960s.[9] Yet besides its nationalistic symbolism, the spotlighting of Dürer's engraving serves more existential purposes.

Dürer composed *The Four Horsemen of the Apocalypse* in the late fifteenth century in response to prophecies emanating from Italy (the country where Tarkovsky filmed *Nostalghia*) that envisaged the world's end in 1500.[10] Attributed to the Turkish conquest of Constantinople in 1453—and stoked by the doomsday sermons of the Italian monk Girolamo Savonarola (not unlike Domenico in *Nostalghia*)—expectations of the apocalypse swirled in Renaissance Europe and shaped the work of artists like Sandro Botticelli, whose visuals inspired Tarkovsky's painterly aesthetic. "I want to find out about Savonarola. About his relationship with Botticelli," Tarkovsky wrote in his diaries, expressing interest in this turn-of-the-sixteenth-century apocalypticism.[11] Through *The Four Horseman of the Apocalypse* in *Ivan's Childhood*, Tarkovsky interpolates not only anti-German commentary into his debut feature film but also eschatological anxiety.

Tarkovsky's cinema is, indeed, pervaded by a sense of apocalyptic dread, conveyed through his reflections on nuclear catastrophe in *The Sacrifice*, use of footage of the bombing of Hiroshima in *Mirror*, dystopic view of space travel in *Solaris*, aestheticization of pillage and plunder in *Andrei Rublev*, and readings from the book of Revelation in *Stalker*. The end of the world, per Tarkovsky, is an imminent event that could perhaps restore humanity by, counterintuitively, annihilating it. "If mankind gets prepared," Tarkovsky said, "it is possible to head off the Apocalypse, but personally I don't have any belief that mankind wants to get ready. Modern man negates it all. Yes, I am talking about a spiritual crisis: the lack of spirituality in the world needs to be opposed and so the Apocalypse itself is, so to speak, creating a spiritual balance."[12] The apocalypse, Tarkovsky claimed, could have a purgative effect on humankind. In *Nostalghia*, we learn that in anticipation of the apocalypse, Domenico hid his family in a bunker for six years and achieved spiritual peace. By way of destroying us, the world's end will demonstrate the spiritual and metaphysical dimensions of existence that, in Tarkovsky's estimation, we have perilously chosen to ignore. Horses play a significant albeit understudied role in Tarkovsky's cinematic millenarianism.

During the opening credits in *Nostalghia*, we see a black-and-white image of what appears to be the Russian countryside shrouded in mist. A group

An apocalyptic white horse looms in the countryside. Still from *Nostalghia*, 1983.

of people, whom we later learn to be the abandoned family of the film's protagonist, Andrei Gorchakov (Oleg Iankovskii), traverses the landscape. The Russian folk song "Godmothers" (*Kumushki*) backdrops this scene; it is then replaced by Italian composer Giuseppe Verdi's *Requiem* (1874), funereal music that establishes *Nostalghia*'s lachrymose atmosphere.[13] Gorchakov's ambling family—accompanied by a German shepherd—meanders toward a looming white horse blanketed by fog.[14] This horse recalls Dürer's *The Four Horsemen of the Apocalypse* because, as some Christian theologians maintain, Christ himself will be astride a white steed as he leads the horsemen out of heaven's gates to vanquish Earth's sinners in the book of Revelation: "And I looked, and behold, a white horse. He who sat on it had a bow, and a crown was given to him, and he went out conquering and to conquer."[15] Drawing on themes of damnation and salvation, Tarkovsky uses a white horse to signify spiritual reckoning. It is as if the characters in *Nostalghia*'s opening, now at the end of the world, hesitantly approach the horse for divine judgment.

The procession toward the horse, however, unexpectedly stops; Tarkovsky's film abruptly turns into a photograph. The credits begin to roll, and "Nostalghia" appears on screen in white block letters. The sudden introduction of photography into the diegesis redoubles the theme of death expressed by the white horse. Photographs, writes André Bazin in his essay "The Ontology of the Photographic Image," inevitably point viewers toward the dead: "If the plastic arts were put under psychoanalysis, the practice of embalming the dead might turn out to be a fundamental factor in their creation."[16] Unlike visual arts that rely on materials (paint, clay, ink, etc.) to represent their content, "photography captures the rays that reflect directly from the subject's body."[17] Photographs force their subject matter into a different temporal dimension, facilitating our encounter with an uncannily preserved absence. "To preserve, artificially, his bodily appearance is to snatch it from the flow of time, to stow it away neatly ... in the hold of life."[18] Throughout his cinema, Tarkovsky associates photographs with the dead: the Nazi executioner's mug shot of Ivan in *Ivan's Childhood*; the freeze-frame shot of the grassy topsoil before Efim's fatal crash in *Andrei Rublev*; the headshots of Kelvin's late mother and wife in *Solaris*; and the ghostly face of a dead soldier in a snapshot in *The Sacrifice*. "Photography is an elegiac art, a twilight art," wrote the legendary American critic Susan Sontag. "All photographs are *memento mori*. To take a photograph is to participate in another person (or thing's) mortality, vulnerability, mutability. Precisely by slicing out this moment and freezing it, all photographs testify to time's relentless melt."[19] The interpolation of photography in *Nostalghia*'s twilight opening, complemented by Verdi's *Requiem*, reenacts the stillness of death. The photographic immobility of the looming white horse, which alludes to the cosmic death occasioned by Christ's second coming, redoubles the moment's apocalyptic insinuations.

The horse in *Nostalghia* is not the sole apocalyptic white steed in Tarkovsky's work. There is the white horse in the deleted scene from *The Sacrifice* (found on this book's cover) that appears in the protagonist's dream about his death—much like Tarkovsky's own, discussed in the previous chapter—and in *Andrei Rublev*, white horses are ridden by medieval raiders who rain death onto innocent people. We see a power-hungry Russian prince astride a white stallion leading the charge against the town of Vladimir in "The Raid." The prince has united with the Mongols to usurp his brother's throne. Atop his white horse, he converses with and rides alongside his Mongol coconspirator who, dressed in black, rides a jet-black stallion. Their opposite color patterns—an aesthetic signature of horse-laden American Western films like John Ford's *The Man Who Shot Liberty Vance* (1962)—suggest that the Russian prince has allied himself with the powers of evil to advance his political agenda, a Faustian bargain made not in the Wild West but in medieval Russia's Wild East. "[The scene] where the Russian prince gallops across the countryside on a white horse, and

Through the clashing color patterns of horses—one black, one white—
Tarkovsky suggests that the medieval Russian prince has allied
himself with the forces of evil. Still from *Andrei Rublev*, 1966.

the Tatar is on a black horse ... attempts to express the state of a soul and to throw light on the nature of the relationship between two men."[20] Tarkovsky depicts not Christ astride a white stallion in *Andrei Rublev* but an anti-Christ who has appealed to satanic (Mongol) forces. Through images of equestrians barreling onto Vladimir, Tarkovsky shows how the "Fritzes on motorcycles" in *Ivan's Childhood*, evoked by Dürer's *The Four Horsemen of the Apocalypse*, are but the latest iteration of a long series of foreign invaders who have laid waste to Russia. This legacy of incursion, in more recent times, has been used to justify Russia's *own* menacing imperial designs.[21]

By the end of *Andrei Rublev*, the graceful and pacific horses foregrounded throughout the film have been supplanted by demented and brutalized analogs. This contrast evokes a similar shift in equine imagery described by French philosopher Georges Bataille in his essay "The Academic Horse," cited in chapter 1.[22] Analyzing the symmetrical, elegant, regal images of horses in ancient Greece, Bataille finds their compositional opposites in Gallic culture. In response to "the platitudes and arrogance of [Greek] idealists," the Gauls warped images of horses to portray social chaos, as if celebrating the reintroduction of barbarism into human life.[23] The Gauls' aesthetic degradations of horses, Bataille argues, are "not merely the result of some technical lapse" but "illustrations of a disordered life that is unfamiliar with the high ideals of harmony and perfection," a "form of transgression and rebellion against the arrogance of a rationalist culture's idealism."[24] In *Andrei Rublev*, Tarkovsky at times gives us images of horses more befitting of the Gauls than the Greeks, indicative of a society slipping into entropy. This descent into pandemonium is no more apparent than in the image of a horse falling down a flight of stairs, reenacting world culture's fall to the revanchist forces of atavism—from Greece to Gaul.

It is not by chance that the sequence following the horse's collapse depicts Mongol raiders bursting into an Orthodox church. Tarkovsky depicts the sanctum of traditional Russian culture penetrated by anarchic foreigners astride correspondingly manic horses. The wild-eyed horses in "The Raid" mirror how Tarkovsky aestheticizes the Mongols, who, depicted as monstrous, torture and torment their Russian victims, not unlike animals. Tarkovsky blurs the line between human and beast in his depiction of the Mongols and the animals on which they ride, betraying his own ethnic allegiances and prejudices. The dehumanized Mongols destroy—mongrelize—what Tarkovsky understood as the fruits of Russian humanism, typified by Rublev's paintings, which the raiders remorselessly desecrate.

While Tarkovsky's images of wild and brutalized horses resonate with their Gallic antecedents, they are also distinctly *Russian*. The image of the collapsed horse in *Andrei Rublev* cannot help but call to mind the slain carthorse in Fyodor Dostoevsky's *Crime and Punishment* (*Prestuplenie i nakazanie*, 1866), which bears "indisputable *apocalyptic* resonance."[25] Before committing a pair of murders, Raskolnikov, Dostoevsky's neurotic protagonist, has a nightmare in which a female horse, "a bedraggled nag (*kliacha*)"—a far cry from the powerful male steeds (*kon'*) Tarkovsky admired—is beaten to death by a drunken crowd.[26] Dostoevsky's horse not only foreshadows Raskolnikov's heinous act but also symbolizes, on a grander scale, "the silent (non-verbal), long-suffering" condition of (mother) Russia herself, especially the social tumult of the mid-nineteenth century that motivates Raskolnikov's crime.[27] "Living in a later, more skeptical time, and fearing that the 'religion' of rationality that the 'men of the sixties' had imported from the West would lead to universal destruction, Dostoevsky reverses the terms of the chivalric epic—the genre in which a poet like Spenser could still equate England's progress toward a New Jerusalem of ideal governance with a knightly quest on horseback."[28] Through the slaying of a horse, Dostoevsky conveys his pessimism about Russia's future. Similarly, Tarkovsky slaughters a horse in *Andrei Rublev* to project his anxieties about civilizational decline. Indeed, Tarkovsky's horse collapses in a comparable fashion to the one in Raskolnikov's dream, a (night)mare: the "wretched mare staggers, sinks down, tries to pull, but another full swing of the crowbar lands on her back, and she falls to the ground as if all four legs had been cut from under her."[29] Both Tarkovsky and Dostoevsky chop down horses in a premonition of the end times, suggesting that, in their view, human history has reached a kind of terminus. Present-day society, like these horses, has become paralytic; it is incapable of appreciating the qualities embodied by these stunning animals. In *Andrei Rublev*, Tarkovsky extrapolates the chaos of the medieval era to air concerns about the present. The film's exquisite, Hellenic images of horses are gradually replaced by their apocalyptic, Dostoevskian antipodes.

MELANCHOLIA

Tarkovsky's grisly scenes of horse death in *Andrei Rublev* are counterbalanced by his gorgeous equine imagery, the topic of chapter 1. As discussed, a palpably mournful quality pervades Tarkovsky's portrayals of horses. Through the figure of the horse, Tarkovsky laments the loss of beauty, masculinity, nature, and genuine cinematic art in modern life. Horses in Tarkovsky's films anthropomorphize the traits he believed could stave off civilizational collapse and, in turn, help him overcome his own mournful psychological state. As Freud contended, the process, or even "work," of mourning consists in withdrawing oneself from the source of loss and abandoning one's "libidinal position," which clings to the absent object through "hallucinatory wishful psychosis" so as to prolong its existence for the self-gratification of the mourner.[30] Gradually, "respect for reality"—a clear-eyed acceptance "that the loved object no longer exists"—prevails, enabling the ego to "become free and uninhibited again."[31] The leitmotif of lachrymose horses in Tarkovsky's cinema betrays his films' cloying attachment to the object of loss (i.e., horses), leading him to lengthen horses' presence on screen through cinema's unique aesthetic resources: long takes, tracking shots, and slow motion. Freud's theory of mourning implies that, with time, Tarkovsky could surmount his wistfulness about horses' disappearance and begrudgingly accept their absence in modern life, completing the grief cycle.

For Tarkovsky, however, humankind, at least in its current state, could not change in any way that would ameliorate his pitched sense of despondency.

> Modern man is too preoccupied by his material development.... He's like a predatory animal that doesn't know what to go after. Man's interest in a transcendent world has disappeared. Right now man is developing into a kind of earthworm: a tube that swallows up material and leaves little piles of waste behind him. Don't be surprised if one day the earth disappears because man has swallowed it all. What good is it to go out into space if it's only to distance ourselves from the fundamental problem of man: the harmonizing of the spiritual and the material world.[32]

The qualities Tarkovsky believed were necessary for spiritual salvation had, in his eyes, vanishingly little chance of being recovered, suggesting the inescapability of Tarkovsky's hopeless state. If mourning is "a painful dejection" occasioned by loss—whether of a loved one or "of some abstraction" like "one's country, liberty, or ideal," which, for Tarkovsky, meant horses—his mourning stood functionally no chance of resolution.[33] Indeed, Tarkovsky's plaintive depictions of horses merely recapitulate his films' feelings of loss occasioned by horses' ongoing disappearance. There is little evidence that Tarkovsky yielded to this reality over the course of his career. If anything, he became *more* distraught later in life: "I see a very dim future if man does not realize that he's fooling himself.... He can't just perish like a hemophiliac in his sleep, bleeding to death because he scratched himself before he went to sleep."[34]

This inability to disentangle oneself from the lost object, Freud elaborated, generates the conditions for "melancholia," which impoverishes the ego "on a grand scale."[35] A "loved object" existed at one time in a person's life, but the nature of that "object-relationship was shattered" by its disappearance.[36] In particularly intense cases of grief in which the mourner fails to extricate themselves from the object of loss, Freud writes that "the result was not the normal one of a withdrawal of the libido, from this object and displacement of it on to a new one, but something different.... It [the libido] was withdrawn into the ego," thereby establishing "an *identification* of the ego with the abandoned object."[37] The "shadow of the object," in turn, falls "upon the ego" as an "object-loss" eventually "transformed into an ego-loss."[38] In other words, feelings of loss for something external metastasize into feelings of remorse for *ourselves*—"a regression" to "original narcissism," which makes disentangling the ego from the absented object exceedingly difficult, if not impossible.[39] The ego is ineradicably warped by such identification.

Ego-loss, a result of failed mourning that constitutes melancholia, foments violence toward the lost object as punishment for having immiserated the ego: "If love for the object ... takes refuge in narcissistic identification, then hate comes into operation on this substitutive object, abusing it, debasing it, making it suffer and deriving sadistic satisfaction from its suffering ... which have been turned round upon the subject's own self."[40] Aggression against the object of loss functions as a coping mechanism to escape the unendurability of melancholia, unburden the ego, and maybe complete the work of mourning. "Just as mourning impels the ego to give up the object by declaring the object to be dead and offering the ego the inducement of continuing to live, so does each single struggle of ambivalence loosen the fixation of the ego to the object by disparaging it, denigrating it and even, as it were, killing it."[41] Freud's theories of mourning and melancholia clarify how Tarkovsky's cinema accommodates both hauntingly beautiful images of horses and antithetically ghastly scenes of their death; these contradictory modes of equine representation are indivisibly bound—two sides of the same coin.

The scene of horse death in *Andrei Rublev* begins with a horse standing at the top of a flight of wooden stairs. A man is astride the horse, but he jumps to safety as it stumbles—a result of being stabbed, pushed, or, as rumors suggest, shot in the neck.[42] The horse loses control of its forelegs and collapses onto its chest. It struggles to regain composure, and blood streams out from its underbody, whereafter the horse begins spluttering down the stairwell. The horse then topples over the stairway and crashes onto the ground some twenty feet below, breaking its lower back on impact. This is where the episode ends in the edited version of *Andrei Rublev*, as if Tarkovsky (and his Soviet censors) intuited that viewers would tolerate only so much brutality.

In the director's cut, however, Tarkovsky holds the camera's focus on the horse for more than ten seconds as it writhes on the ground. A man in armor enters the visual field and disinterestedly looks at the horse as he marches across the frame, communicating the nonchalance of violence in medieval life. The camera pans away from the horse and shows a group of Mongol men standing over a peasant woman with bared legs, an image that implies serial rape, another example of how animal cruelty and gendered violence go hand in glove in Tarkovsky's cinema.[43] After glimpsing at the rape, the camera pans *back* to the horse, which, having risen, stands with its rear end toward the frame. It wobbles before emitting an anguished cry and pitches backward, almost somersaulting into the camera. The suddenness of the animal's movement is registered by the camera's quick downward swivel, searching for the best angle to capture the horse's final moments. The man who crossed the frame earlier reenters the visual field and plunges a spear into the horse's chest. Its body convulses, and its eyes wrench open before rolling back into its skull. Like *Andrei Rublev*'s earlier image of a beaten dog, which recycles that of twitching rabbits from Jean Renoir's *Rules of the Game* (*La règle du jeu*, 1939), Tarkovsky's horse brings viewers as close as humanly possible to the instant of death.[44]

Regarding documentary recordings of death, media theorist Vivian Sobchack argues that there are six types of gazes used to negotiate the ethical quagmire of filming (human) death: "accidental," "helpless," "endangered," "interventional," "humane," and "professional."[45] These gazes encode the director's subjective position in relation to the filmed instance of death in ways that are variously exculpatory and implicative. Tarkovsky's gaze onto the felled horse in *Andrei Rublev*, however, does not align with any of Sobchak's typologies: it is not coincidental,

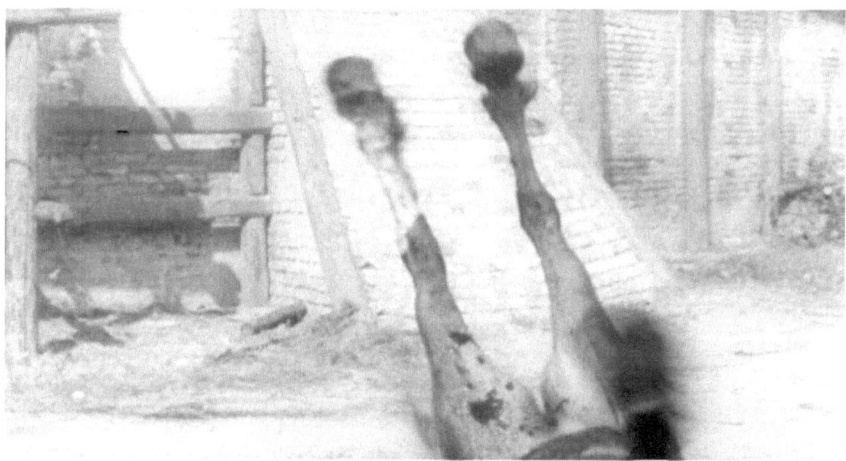
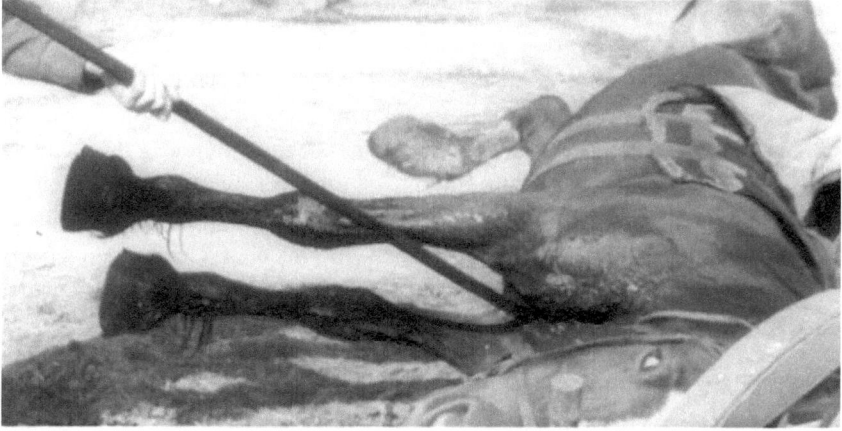

The sequence of the horse's death after its fall, one of the most gruesome instances of animal slaughter ever committed to celluloid. Stills from *Andrei Rublev*, 1966.

impotent, threatened, interruptive, tender, or clinical. Quite contrarily, Tarkovsky tracks the horse's death with macabre fascination as the camera follows its every move. "Avowedly cooperative and even instrumental in the production of" these sordid images, Tarkovsky's gaze onto the horse finds expression "only in spurious cinematic legend—what Sobchack describes as the 'apocryphal' genre of snuff films."[46] Two qualities stand out in Tarkovsky's grotesque, snuff depiction of equine death, and each radiates Freudian implications: the camera's inability to pry itself away from the bloodshed and the way in which the horse's collapse inverts the trajectory of the rolling horse at the film's start.

In his *Studies on Hysteria* (1895), Freud, in collaboration with the Viennese physician Josef Breuer, identified "the communicative powers of animal magnetism" as essential in delineating the nature of human consciousness. Derived from the quack theories of Franz Anton Mesmer in the eighteenth century, animal magnetism posited that incredibly powerful yet invisible forces circulate through all beings and can, if harnessed properly, helpfully affect a person's mental state.[47] Subjecting an individual to these pressures, Freud and Breuer claimed, could shock the body into a convulsive state, enabling desires and drives foreclosed by one's consciousness to (re)surface and be redressed accordingly. Curiously, Mesmer relied on hypnosis, namely verbal repetition and somnambulance, to elicit animal-like passions that activated a patient's unconscious phenomena, "the wildside" of human experience.[48] Though Freud eventually rejected mesmerism—"I have been able to say that psychoanalysis proper began when I dispensed with the help of hypnosis"—his goal of eliciting the irrepressible forces that determine behavior through dream interpretation, talk therapy, and free association nevertheless involved an "appropriation of animal magnetism into the body of psychoanalysis," an attempt "to wrest animal magnetism from its association with magic."[49] Animals' instincts captivated Freud because they teased access into the "supersemiotic field of the unconscious," beyond language, rationality, and memory.[50] In *Mirror*, Tarkovsky betrays his apparent fascination with not only dreams but also hypnosis in determining the nature of human subjectivity: the film begins with a speech pathologist entrancing a teenager—not unlike a quack mesmerist—to recover his speech. How, then, does Tarkovsky's interest in Freudian pseudoscience inform his depiction of horses, the animals that loom largest in his and his characters' imaginations in the form of dreams, memories, and (repressed) desires? Horses, it appears, structure the unconscious of the Tarkovskian cinematic universe.

In *Andrei Rublev*, Tarkovsky's camera falls under the spell of the wild energy—the animal magnetism—bursting forth from the dying horse in Vladimir. As the horse lurches down the flight of stairs, the camera holds focus on its out-of-control body, creating an unnerving visual contrast between the cinematography's steadiness and the horse's erratic gesticulations. When the horse topples off the stairwell, the camera follows its descent and lingers with laser-like precision on the animal as it writhes in the dirt, appearing to take a kind of sadistic pleasure in its pain. Dwelling on the flailing horse for ten seconds, the camera reluctantly pulls its gaze elsewhere in a lateral pan, then circles *back* to the horse. The affective intensity of the horse seems to exert a gravitational pull on the camera's attention, as if drawn by the overpowering force of the psychoanalytic phenomenon of animal magnetism. The hypnotic vitality of animals, which energizes Freud's early writing, is, in *Andrei Rublev*, reframed as hypnotic morbidity elicited not by the hypnotist's eye but by a camera's, which cannot pry itself away from the shuddering sight before its gaze. Far from being repulsed by this violence, Tarkovsky's camera is irresistibly attracted to it, mesmerized by the "narcissistic object-choice" of loss.[51]

The horse's collapse represents the second great fall of the film. The opening scene of *Andrei Rublev*, discussed previously, consists of a medieval balloonist's crash landing. Losing control of his jury-rigged hot-air balloon, the eccentric peasant Efim plummets out of the sky to his death. The image transitions to a gorgeous horse spooling back and forth in the dirt, encapsulating, as argued in chapter 1, the entire aesthetic history of cinema and juxtaposing the folly of human ambitions—exemplified by Efim's voyage—to distance ourselves from the Earth. The horse rolls on the ground before lifting itself up, a reversal of Efim's aerial trajectory that insinuates another critique of humanity's stratospheric aspirations to conquer the heavens. The horse triumphs as it rises and trots out of the frame toward horizons unknown, whereas the human, whose fate has reached its terminus, lies in the mud amid the wreckage of his technological dreams. The horse anthropomorphizes the qualities Tarkovsky hoped humanity would recover to salvage its historical destiny: beauty, grace, power, simplicity.

These traits are not just absent in *Andrei Rublev*'s aestheticization of horse death—they are inverted. If the horse in the film's prologue reverses the course of Efim's flight, "take off—flight—crash—wallow—leaving," then the horse that falls during "The Raid" capsizes *that* horse's trajectory: stand, crash, flounder, stillness.[52] These paradoxical portrayals of horses bear disconcerting resemblance. The nimble rolls undertaken by the horse in the prologue—a volitional activity that communicates a horse's comfort and lively spirit—are grimly transposed by the horse's backward somersault in "The Raid," a reflexive response to its pain. Both these horses reel in the dirt, but for different reasons: the former in pleasure, the latter in agony. To capture each of these instances,

Tarkovsky uses his signature long take—both last upward of ten seconds—so that one horse's rolls and another's death throes can be observed in their unadulterated fullness. Equally but oppositely, then, the two most iconic horses of *Andrei Rublev* epitomize the nature of Tarkovsky's animal representation as it oscillates between elegiac beauty (i.e., mourning) and grisly violence (i.e., melancholia). The breathtaking sight of equine vitality that began *Andrei Rublev* returns as a spectacle of morbidity, suggesting the lapse of Tarkovsky's mourning into melancholic sadism. All Tarkovsky's horse images, in other words, "archive an 'unconscious' death wish" that is "radically, yet productively, at odds with the fetishistic signs of life."[53] The two rolling horses of *Andrei Rublev* are not so different from one another; they are troublingly interdependent, evidence of how Tarkovsky's pathological view of modern life affected his treatment of horses.

METAPHYSICAL POVERTY

Besides its psychoanalytic timbre, the apparent expendability of horses in *Andrei Rublev* resonates with a broader philosophical understanding of animals in the Western intellectual tradition, one grounded in what has been termed their metaphysical "poverty."[54]

Though an extended discussion of animals is absent in Heidegger's magnum opus, *Being and Time* (1927)—a key text of modern philosophy that aspired to provide the study of anthropology with a conceptual bedrock—Heidegger spends much of this work expounding the concept of "world."[55] Heidegger is interested in exploring how humanity's unique relationship to the world separates it not only from animals but also from other forms of life, such as plants and inorganic things, like minerals and rocks. Heidegger rejects the assumption that human beings, simply because they are more sophisticated organisms, are intrinsically superior. This line of reasoning, for Heidegger, elides the specific nature of the relations between beings and their surroundings. Hierarchical evaluations of human primacy mistakenly characterize the differences between human beings and other entities in terms of degree rather than quality. Instead, Heidegger stresses "the abyssal differences" between humans and other forms of existence in order to plot an ontological schema that can better account for humankind's uniqueness.[56]

In a lecture delivered a few years after the release of *Being and Time*, Heidegger claimed that "man is not merely part of the world but is also master and servant of the world in the sense of 'having' world. . . . But then what about the other beings, which like man, are also part of the world: the animals and plants, the material things like stone. . . . Certain distinctions immediately manifest themselves here. We can formulate these distinctions in the following three theses: [1] the stone (material object) is *worldless*; [2] the animal is *poor in the world*; [3] man is *world-forming*."[57] To illuminate this three-pronged hypothesis, Heidegger construed as an example a lizard lying on a rock as it "basks in the sun."[58] The stone, per Heidegger, has "no possible access to anything else around it"—that is, the stone is deprived of world (i.e., worldless) because it has no relational structure to grant it access to other things. The lizard, by contrast, enjoys a degree of accessibility to the world around it. The lizard affectively experiences the heat of the sun, the smoothness of the rock, and the sounds and smells invisibly churning through the air. The lizard, indeed, modulates its behavior in relation to the sun-drenched rock. Still, the lizard does not relate to these phenomena as humans do. The lizard, Heidegger argues, cannot apprehend these things as discrete phenomena unto themselves, as "stone," "heat," "sunlight."

Only human beings, Heidegger continued, engage with things as *such*. "One is tempted to suggest that what we identify as the rock and the sun are just lizard-things for the lizard, so to speak. . . . When we say a lizard is lying on the rock, we ought to cross out the word 'rock' in order to indicate that whatever the lizard is lying on . . . is not known to the lizard *as* a rock."[59] Animals have a world, yet they are circumscribed in their relations to it. They are capable of orienting themselves to—"going along with"—their surroundings, but they cannot know the world in its integral properties the way humans can.[60] Animals are, thus, metaphysically "poor." Heidegger is "unwilling to relinquish the animal entirely from the topoi of being," so he "sets the animal forth into the recesses of worldly poverty."[61] The animal world exists, but as a world apart.

Above all, it is lack of language that impoverishes an animal's experience of world. "Language alone brings what is, as something that is, into the Open for the first time. Where there is no language, as in the being of a stone, plant, and animal, there is also no openness of what is," to other forms of alterity.[62] Language creates the conditions for humans to relate to others, objects, and, ultimately, themselves in their quintessence: things as they are, things *as such*. The realm inhabited by animals, in this light, is a "space of exclusion" in which the ontological categories governing human life dissolve, thereby totally altering an animal's sense of existence, as explored in chapter 4 through Nietzsche's idea of "the eternal return," on which Heidegger draws.[63] "The mortals are human beings. They are called mortals because they can die. To die means to be capable of death as death. Only man dies. The animal perishes. It has death neither ahead of itself nor behind it. Death is the shrine of Nothing, that is, of that which in every respect is never something that merely exists, but which nevertheless presences, even as the mystery of Being itself. As the shrine of Nothing, death harbors within itself the presence of Being."[64] Humanity's awareness of death, based in language, lifts it out of animality: "Where there is no language, there is no openness of being, nonbeing, nor absence of being. And this, in turn, is inseparable from the question of death. For world is also the place of nothing, the space in which nothing takes place. In the case of being, death signifies the presence of nothing in the world."[65] Death, then, is an exclusive feature for beings (i.e., humans) who can reflect on and articulate the nature of their subjectivity.

While ethologists have shown that certain animals—elephants, crows, spiders—do exhibit a certain, albeit peculiar, relation to death, Heidegger suggests that animals never "properly die"; they simply perish, disintegrate, or expire into the void in which they dwell, croaking into nothingness.[66] Without "the capacity to name the disappearance of being from the world—the world itself ceases to appear as the foundation that gives existence its place . . . the animal falls . . . beyond the existential abodes of humanity—the very situation of its worldly being falls into doubt."[67] An animal's death is rendered opaque and insignificant, a "caesura in the flow of that philosophy of being."[68] Heidegger's theory of metaphysical poverty thus recalls Descartes's idea of animal soullessness—and, therefore, meaninglessness—that begins this book. Heidegger "brings to the fore the 'gnawing, ruminant, and silent voracity of such an animal-machine and its implacable logic.' . . . If the animal doesn't die, that is, if one can put it to death without 'killing' it or murdering it, without committing murder, without 'Thou shalt not kill' concerning it or regarding me in the context of it . . . it is because the animal remains foreign to everything that defines sanctity . . . which coordinates the relation between ethics or metaphysics and the command 'Thou shalt not kill' or 'You will not commit murder,' namely responsibility."[69] Caught in a certain light and pushed to its logical extreme, Heidegger's theory of animals' metaphysical poverty removes the ethical guardrails from slaughter. If an awareness of morality is a precondition to the recognition of life's value, then what moral concern should (or could) be extended to beings who cannot die as such? One could easily extrapolate Heidegger's ideas to justify the mass animal killing underway in human society. It is perhaps not by chance, then, that Heidegger bore a worryingly ambivalent relationship to Nazism, the ideological underpinning of the twentieth century's worst instance of mass extermination. "When Heidegger risked" a comparison between "the Nazi Holocaust with the mistreatment of animals" in "his infamous 'mechanized food industry' remark," it was called "scandalously inadequate" because of his "subsequent silence about the Nazi Holocaust, especially in view of his own support of Nazism."[70] Heidegger's frightening disregard for animal life maps along a troubling continuum.

For his part, Tarkovsky echoed Heidegger's view of animals' metaphysical poverty and the cold-blooded ease with which their lives can be dispatched. Discussing the felled horse in *Andrei Rublev*, Tarkovsky said: "And we took the horse from the slaughterhouse. If we didn't kill her that day, she would have been killed the next day in the same way. We did not think up any special torments, so to speak, for the horse."[71] The horse, in Tarkovsky's view, was *already* dead. What difference did it make whether it was slaughtered on a film set or in the dark of an abattoir? Tarkovsky viewed the horse's life as inconsequential—poor—because its death would not amount to what human beings know, per Heidegger, as death. Tarkovsky's horse, as the French philosopher Alexandre Kojève argues, "can only *suffer* its end without ever being able to prepare for it.... Death does not actually exist *for it*, and one cannot say of it: '*it is dying*.'"[72] It is highly telling that Tarkovsky even called attention to the role of language in his justification of the horse's slaying: his film crew did not think of any "special torments" for the horse, "so to speak" (*tak skazat'*). It is precisely humanity's capacity for language—the ability to communicate figuratively and abstractly—that constitutes the chasm between human beings and animals. An animal's wordlessness, according to Heideggerian philosophy, accords it an impoverished worldliness. It occupies a lusher world than a rock but still not one deserving much consideration. The "strained logic of Western metaphysics" confers ethics only to those with richer ontologies.[73]

Yet it is impossible to watch the horse die in *Andrei Rublev* and not be struck by its anguish. Tarkovsky's horse, whatever the nature of its alterity, surely deserved better treatment than *this*. And this sort of affective response to the sight of a suffering animal is precisely what prompted eighteenth-century thinker Jeremy Bentham to identify physical sensation, pleasure and pain—not abstract notions of right and wrong or, in Heidegger's taxonomy, "world-poor" and "world-forming"—as the guiding principles of moral philosophy. Bentham's memorable formulation: "The question is not, Can they *reason*? nor Can they *talk*? But, Can they *suffer*?" shifts attention away from metaphysics and onto experience as the basis of ethics.[74] "'Can they suffer?' asks Bentham simply yet so profoundly.... The form of this question changes everything. It no longer simply concerns the *logos*, having it or not, nor does it concern, more radically, a *dynamis* or *hexis*, this having or manner of being, this having or manner of being, this *habitus* that one calls a faculty or 'capability,' this can-have or the power one possesses (as in the power to reason, to speak, and everything that that implies)."[75]

Rather, Bentham's question refers us to animals' lived actualities, their material conditions and status as they exist alongside us. The horse in *Andrei Rublev* unambiguously suffers, which, per Bentham, morally impugns those exacting its pain, a fact conceded by Tarkovsky through his use of the nonneutral term "torments" (*muchenii*) to describe the horse's treatment. While Tarkovsky's crew did not think up any "special torments" for the horse, they nevertheless committed a morally suspect act that required subtle rhetorical defense. No "*special* torments"—"so to speak"—were directed against the horse, just the sort of commonplace cruelty we have normalized in our dealings with animal life, what Derrida calls humanity's systematic "war against its neighbors."[76]

Writing more than a century before Heidegger, Bentham focused on suffering as a basis for the treatment of animals, introducing a "postanthropocentric logic" into Western thought by uncoupling ethics from metaphysics; that is, Bentham argued that, contra Heidegger, animals deserve some level of moral consideration, whatever the nature of their being.[77] Bentham's oft-cited question about animal suffering emerged out of a treatise on moral behavior in which he contended that the morality of any action can best be determined by measuring the amount of benefit it brings a society against its negative effects. But Bentham, the father of what became known as the doctrine of utilitarianism, implicitly assumed that an animal's well-being is of *less* importance than a human's, meaning that negative actions targeted against an animal, while not ethically neutral, generate less severe moral consequences than violence against a person. Bentham's utilitarianism ascribes to "a hierarchical view about the value of animals' lives, arguing that various cognitive capacities enhance individuals' capacities for enjoyment and suffering in ways that give their lives special moral significance."[78] Animals, indeed, are not the center of Bentham's moral universe; his question "Can they *suffer*?" is tellingly relegated to a footnote in a larger discussion about the rights of enslaved peoples.[79] An animal in pain, for Bentham, is far less adversely impactful for social order than a comparably ill-treated human. There is, in other words, a humanist undertow to Bentham's latently postanthropocentric logic.

Though the horse in *Andrei Rublev* suffers, eliciting ethical concern, Tarkovsky argued that its death bore *utilitarian* value that outweighed the moral cost of its slaying: "I can name films that show much more cruel things, compared to which ours looks quite modest. True, we showed this aspect of life in concentrated fashion, but . . . the time was so cruel in this manner, increasing the tension in individual parts, we were able to preserve the necessary balance between the dark and light aspects of the time, a balance that was required by our fidelity to historical truth."[80] The horse's slaughter purportedly bolsters the historicity of Tarkovsky's medieval epic. The ethical toll of killing a horse—which Tarkovsky understood as already minimal—is offset by what its suffering lends *Andrei Rublev*. "We wanted to show that Andrei Rublev's art was a protest against the order that reigned at that time, against the blood, the betrayal, the oppression. . . . We found it extremely important, both from the historical and the contemporary viewpoints, to express these thoughts."[81] Tarkovsky's actions divulge how Bentham's utilitarian moral calculus can beget asymmetrical outcomes for human beings and animals depending on preexisting value judgments. The fuzzy moral math of Tarkovsky's decision to butcher a horse on camera, therefore, threatens to reveal not just this "isolated fact of coercion or cruelty, but the whole system by which such coercion and cruelty are reproduced" in and for human society more generally.[82] Tarkovsky's felled horse should make us question not only Tarkovsky's moral character but also cinema's own carnal appetite, its complicity in humanity's "war against its neighbors." How might film itself partake in an unequal allotment of violence between humans and animals?

TARKOVSKY VERSUS EISENSTEIN

Andrei Rublev's slain horse is by no means an isolated instance of animal slaughter on film. Indeed, death has been central to animals' history on screen. Film historian Johnathan Burt points out that cinema has its most immediate mechanical antecedents in hunting technologies, evident in Étienne-Jules Marey's chronophotographic gun (*fusil photographique*) used to "track," "shoot," and "capture" birds' flight patterns, as if a celluloid form of taxidermy.[83] While seemingly incomparable, animal slaughter and cinema—"the former weighted with the material gravity of death, the latter with the lively business of moving images—can in unexpected ways be seen as sympathetic and continuous." This continuity is thrown into especially sharp relief when considering the fact that postindustrial cineplexes have "come to occupy old abattoirs in many urban centres."[84] Motionless animals are just as important to the history of film as mobile animals, as demonstrated by two of the medium's founding documents discussed in this book, Eadweard Muybridge's *Animal Locomotion* and Thomas Edison's *Electrocuting an Elephant*. The differences between these two early films—one about animal liveliness, the other about animal extermination—also reflect Tarkovsky's divergent portrayals of horses, which vacillate between photogenic vitality and macabre stillness.

The slaughterhouse itself is an important setting for a small yet impactful corpus of (mostly) documentary films that feature scenes of real animal death:

George Franju's *Blood of the Beasts* (*Le sang des bêtes*, 1949), Frederick Wiseman's *Meat* (1976), Michael Moore's *Roger & Me* (1989), Barbara Koppel's *American Dream* (1990), Nikolaus Geyrhalter's *Our Daily Bread* (*Unser täglich Brot*, 2005), and Richard Linklater's *Fast Food Nation* (2006). These documentaries use the slaughterhouse as a metaphor to reflect on human life in the machine age. Yet in so doing, they jolt viewers away from the world of machines and into proximity with animals, forcing us to confront the horrid conditions animals endure in contemporary society. "Thousands of animals teeming with life are fed into the slaughterhouse to meet their deaths, one death at a time, assembly-line style. In one intimate—but endlessly repeated—encounter, a human kills an animal. This, it turns out, is not an assembly line, but a disassembly line, in which life after life is unpacked into parts. The modern meatpacking industry represents the simultaneous mechanization and de-mechanization of life."[85] Slaughterhouse films make metaphors out of the inhuman(e) logic and logistics of modern life. The abattoir stands in for the Holocaust in Franju's *Blood of the Beasts*; the decimation of organized labor in the American Midwest in Moore's *Roger & Me*; and in Linklater's *Fast Food Nation*, the "villainous industry" of late-stage capitalism that makes us all complicit in the unimaginable exploitation of low-wage workers forced to exploit animals unimaginably.[86]

While slaughterhouse films often redouble anthropocentric tropes by using the abattoir as a metaphor for human society—making plain that human beings are the real subjects of their concern—they also communicate a desire for alternative social arrangements that might make life better for all those trapped in the metaphoric slaughterhouse of modern life, human and animal alike. Indeed, slaughterhouse films expose the hypocrisy of contemporary society that, deeply reliant on animals for meat, deems animal killing too unseemly to look at but not so much so as to abstain from it. As Burt documents, in response to changing moral codes in the nineteenth century (and burgeoning concerns about public sanitation), slaughterhouses in industrial societies were gradually moved out of city centers.[87] Early bourgeois reformers—upper-middle-class do-gooders who founded an array of animal welfare societies—argued that slaughter has no place in the public arena, as it has a coarsening effect on civic morality.[88] "If cruelty was to take place, it was to be behind closed doors and under license.... The emphasis is not just visibility but also on what might be called the appropriate seeing of the animal."[89] The anonymous architecture of slaughterhouses, built along urban peripheries (off screen, as it were), emphasized the increasing invisibility of animals in modern life and, ironically, a commensurate uptick in dead animals thanks in no small part to the efficiency of industrial slaughter.[90] Slaughterhouse documentaries, therefore, refuse modern configurations of animal (in)visibility by undermining the ethical-optical norms and hypocrisies—the out of sight, out of mind ease—that make animals (and, by turn, people) disposable in contemporary society.[91]

Tarkovsky claimed that by killing a horse, he had undertaken a project akin to that of a slaughterhouse documentary: to make viewers aware of the violence surrounding them to which they had become disturbingly desensitized, a form of shock therapy. "The monk, Rublyov . . . preached love, goodness, and non-resistance to evil. And though he found himself witnessing the most brutal and devastating forms of violence, which seemed to hold sway in the world and led him to bitter disillusionment, he came back in the end to . . . the value of human goodness."[92] The slain horse in *Andrei Rublev* is used to convey the severity of the historical circumstances that Rublev—and, by inference, Tarkovsky—conquered to reaffirm the value of life and make art. By violently puncturing his representation of medieval Russia with "the documentary presentation of real animals leaving the world," Tarkovsky used the felled horse (and burnt cow) as a conduit linking the "allegorical figuration of the human to a historical, and material, violent real."[93] Tarkovsky's uncouth images of animal cruelty, per this line of analysis, confront viewers with the revoltingness and promiscuity of violence in modern life that we choose to ignore; Tarkovsky takes us inside the slaughterhouse, as it were.

This would-be exposé function of Tarkovsky's equine cruelty resonates with the stated mission of *the* exemplar scene of animal killing in slaughterhouse cinema: a scene in Sergei Eisenstein's *Strike* (*Stachka*, 1925), a work rediscovered and celebrated in the 1960s and 1970s among countercultural filmmakers.[94] Charting the fall of a labor uprising in prerevolutionary Russia, *Strike* ends with shots of subjugated workers interspliced with documentary footage of bulls being slaughtered in an abattoir. The rapid, ballistic-like shot alterations analogize animal killing with capitalist exploitation: "Eisenstein calculated . . . that the dialectical montage generated by the collision of shots in this image sequence would be synthesized by his spectators into a form of revolutionary consciousness, spurring socialist action against the deadening conditions of capitalist labour."[95] Eisenstein conceived of *Strike*, a "workers film," as a tool in the struggle against capitalist production that treats human laborers like cattle or beasts of burden.[96] It is not by chance that class-conscious filmmakers around the globe perennially re-create *Strike*'s stockyard sequence. In Djibril Diop Mambéty's *Touki Bouki* (1973), Charles Burnett's *Killer of Sheep* (1977), and Ermanno Olmi's *The Tree of Wooden Clogs* (*L'Albero degli zoccoli*, 1978), we see footage of livestock being stunned and stabbed—always with dead animal eyes captured in close-up—that replicates the look of Eisenstein's bull. *Strike*'s undiluted scene of animal

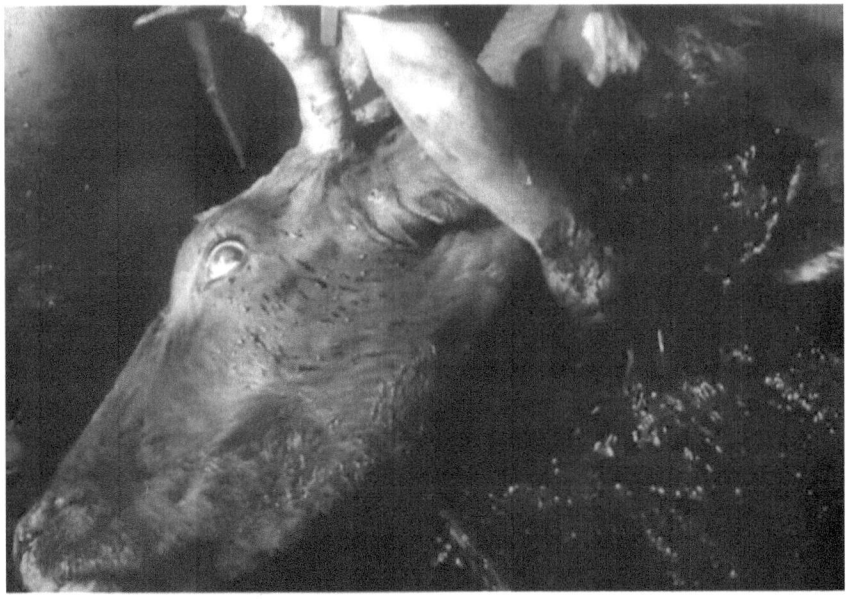

Eisenstein's footage of a bull killed at a stockyard codified a rite of passage in which left-wing directors use slaughter to lay bare the cruelty pervading the industrial economy. Still from *Strike*, 1924.

death codified a rite of passage in which left-wing directors use animal slaughter to lay bare the cruelty pervading the industrial labor economy.

Yet the felled horse in *Andrei Rublev*, despite evoking the memory of Eisenstein's bull, does not pay any sort of political or ideological tribute to it. Tarkovsky harbored a deeply hostile opinion toward Eisenstein, and he vehemently differentiated his creative practice from the renowned Marxist filmmaker. "I am radically opposed to the way Eisenstein used the frame to codify intellectual formulae," Tarkovsky wrote. "My own method of conveying experience to the audience is quite different. . . . Eisenstein makes thought into a despot: it leaves no 'air,' nothing of that unspoken elusiveness which is perhaps the most captivating quality of all art. . . . I want to make films which carry no oratorical, propagandist speech, but are the occasion for a deeply intimate experience."[97] Tarkovsky rejected Eisenstein's didactic filmic practice, which strove to politicize spectatorial consciousness: a view of cinema crystallized by *Strike*'s image of a bull hit over the head with a poleax. "Soviet cinema," Eisenstein wrote, "must cut through to the skull!"[98] The bull in *Strike*, for Tarkovsky, conveys Eisenstein's tendentious understanding of "the spectator as a trainable organism—a bundle of receptors that can, through the science of cinematic affect," be physiologically stimulated."⁹⁹ Eisenstein believed that his audience could be *struck* according to new ideological coordinates vis-à-vis the affective charge of animal slaughter. He "deprives the person watching of that prerogative of film ... the opportunity to live through what is happening on screen as if it were his own life, to take over, as deeply personal and his own, the experience imprinted in time upon the screen, relating his own life to what is shown."¹⁰⁰ Tarkovsky maintained that filmmakers, whatever their political persuasion, should never overpower the viewer with a clear-cut message, hence his own deeply elusive imagery. "If a sense of mystery arises for you," Tarkovsky said of those who encounter his work, "then that for me is an enormous compliment."¹⁰¹

Tarkovsky's critique of Eisenstein should not be taken at face value, however. Like Eisenstein, Tarkovsky in *Andrei Rublev* foregrounds an affectively intense instance of animal slaughter to confront viewers with content that yields "to the form (and force) of the image."¹⁰² In Tarkovsky's own words, "As a director, I always count on the effect shock produces on the spectator: no evasions ... because a short naturalistic scene suffices to put the spectator in a traumatic state, after which he will absolutely believe everything that we show to him."¹⁰³ Could there be a more Eisenstinian proclamation? Both Tarkovsky and Eisenstein slaughter animals on screen to generate an aesthetic in which meaning recedes before affect. Notwithstanding Tarkovsky's self-professed differences with Eisenstein, the felled horse in *Andrei Rublev*, an image expressly designed to traumatize—strike—viewers, establishes Tarkovsky's lineage with the early Soviet avant-garde, from which he took pains to distance himself. Both Eisenstein and Tarkovsky leverage animal killing to jolt spectatorial consciousness, "to cut through to the skull."

Andrei Rublev's felled horse summons the memory not only of the bull in *Strike* but also of another of Eisenstein's dead animals: the white horse of *October* (1927), a film released to commemorate the ten-year anniversary of the October Revolution. In a reenactment of the July Days of 1917, when the urban proletariat took up arms against the Provisional Government on behalf of the Bolsheviks in Saint Petersburg (then Petrograd), Eisenstein depicts a horse collapsing in a melee on the Palace Bridge. As the camera dwells on an image of the fallen horse lying in a pool of its blood, the bridge begins to rise, and the horse's body, which lies at the cross section of the drawbridge, bends and folds as it is lifted into the air. A wide-angle shot observes the horse dangling in the sky before plunging into the Neva River, scores of feet below. Eisenstein's horse anticipates Tarkovsky's, whose collapse down a flight of stairs re-creates both the horse's spectacular free fall in *October* and the goriness of the bull's slaughter in *Strike*.

The similarities between Tarkovsky's aestheticizations of animal slaughter and Eisenstein's suggest that Tarkovsky bore what the literary scholar Harold Bloom calls "the anxiety of influence," the psychoanalytic notion that artists are necessarily encumbered by the ambiguous relationships they harbor with their predecessors.[104] Tarkovsky's and Eisenstein's iconoclastic scenes of animal killing, in comparison, evince what Bloom classifies as a type of anxiety known as "tessera": a desire to "retain the terms" of the "parent-poem" while antithetically resignifying it, thereby refusing and redirecting its ultimate significance.[105] While Eisenstein deploys images of animal killing in *October* and *Strike* to inculcate socialist ideology, Tarkovsky recycles Eisenstein's disturbing visuals to catalyze spectatorial introspection about what he understood as strictly apolitical, *spiritual* content. For Tarkovsky, nonsimulated instances of animal cruelty were to prompt the accursed questions central to nineteenth-century Russian literature: the meaning of suffering, death, truth, and art. In a clear inversion of Eisenstein's collisional shot alterations (i.e., aesthetic strikes), Tarkovsky films the horse's death in a series of tracking shots and long takes. There is a token of recognition of Eisenstinian montage in Tarkovsky's depictions of slaughter, but with the goal of resignifying its purpose and overcoming it, as if a corrective.[106] Indeed, *Andrei Rublev* is itself a corrective to Eisenstein's medical epic *Ivan the Terrible* (*Ivan Grozny*, 1944), rereleased in Soviet society in 1958, just as a young Tarkovsky was beginning his filmmaking career. Tarkovsky's decision to slaughter a horse seems to originate less from a desire to expose the violence permeating modern life than from a more partisan drive to retaliate against Eisenstein. If Tarkovsky burns a cow in *Andrei Rublev*, as detailed in chapter 3, to condemn the failed promise of motherhood, he kills a horse to usurp the throne of artistic renown from the founder—"the father"—of Soviet cinema.[107]

Tellingly, Eisenstein's own claim to cinematic greatness emerged from a similar competitive anxiety played out through animal slaughter. The stockyard scene in *Strike* is a polemical, even Oedipal, response to an episode in his contemporary Dziga Vertov's *Film Eye* (*Kino-Glaz*, 1924) in which Vertov rewinds a bull's slaying to expose the unseen, material processes of the meatpacking industry and the human labor therein. Both Eisenstein and Vertov

> are concerned with the visceral impact of the camera's rendering of real blood and flesh.... Vertov wants the spectator to encounter the slaughter, and the carcass of the bull, *for its own sake*. For Eisenstein, the bull is a means of exerting emotional influence on the spectator. For Vertov, the film eye is an

agent for the discovery of the material presence of the world; for Eisenstein, the physical matter of the bull's carcass creates a visceral shock on the spectatorial eye, but that shock is not an end in itself. Vertov stops at sensation, where Eisenstein proceeds to "consciousness." It was for this that Eisenstein criticized Vertov's use of the slaughterhouse in *Film Eye*: "The abattoir that is merely recorded in *Film Eye*," he claimed, "is gorily effective in *Strike*."[108]

In an Eisensteinian key, Tarkovsky restages the debate about the ideological utility of animal killing in *Andrei Rublev*, a kind of 1960s postscript to what Anne Nesbit describes as "Russian modernism's remaking of the eye" vis-à-vis images of animal slaughter in the 1920s.[109] Whereas Eisenstein sought to outstrip Vertov's observational style by leveraging animal death to alter viewers' political consciousness, Tarkovsky vied to surpass Eisenstein by using animal killing to effect viewers' spirituality, to resensitize us to the barbarism of modern life. In each of these instances, the inheritor of influence destroys their influencer—metaphoric sons killing metaphoric fathers—by way of animal death, which becomes a proxy for cinema's sociopolitical efficacy: a kind of bargaining chip to ratchet up the ante of cinema's capacity to shock. Though Tarkovsky claimed to be above what he viewed as Soviet cinema's crass legacy in propaganda, he nevertheless entered the fray of avant-garde polemics by having a horse butchered on screen.

However, unlike Vertov and Eisenstein, Tarkovsky did *not* use footage from a slaughterhouse for his depictions of animal death; that is, he did not use archival footage (otherwise known as "stock footage") of a real event or site captured outside a film setting and woven into a diegesis. Generally, documentary footage in narrative cinema serves to eschew directors' responsibility over images by creating authorial distance, raising questions about images' origins, authenticity, and eventual appropriation.[110] Filmmakers often use stock footage to depict animal killing to distance their work from the ethical realities of slaughter; doing so relieves them from having to commit an act of killing themselves. (Indeed, Tarkovsky used stock footage of dead human beings and animals in *Ivan's Childhood* and *Mirror* for this very reason.) In the case of slaughterhouse footage, recordings capture institutionalized processes of death and destruction that are already underway in industrial society irrespective of a camera's presence. Scenes from slaughterhouses are not inherently complicit in the violence they depict—they document the institution's intractable presence, posing a series of ethical quandaries about the nature of mechanization, consumption, and, ultimately, the cinematic medium itself.

As media theorist Nicole Shukin has illuminated, celluloid—the very fiber of film—is in part made from boiled-down animal remains: gelatin, which holds the silver nitrate crystals in place on a strip of film.[111] "Extracted from the skin, bones, and connective tissues of cattle, sheep, and pigs," gelatin "is among those seemingly negligible but in fact significant points of entry into the material unconscious of culture," marking a "'vanishing point' where moving images are both inconspicuously and viscerally contingent on mass animal disassembly, in contradiction with cinema's framing semiotic of animation."[112] Film stock is materially dependent on glue extracted from livestock: two terms linked by the word "stock," a surplus of resources—the scraps and waste of industrial slaughter—kept for future use.[113] "In a death-dealing exchange, animal slaughter gives life to film's images."[114] There is an animal ghost in the machine of every celluloid film chamber, haunting the film production, which is "grounded in a project of remorseless amortization of the animal's most striking characteristic, its ability to move."[115] Figuratively glossed, Tarkovsky's slaughtered horse in *Andrei Rublev* portends animals' trajectory from the barnyards of the medieval era to the (dis)assembly lines of industrial modernity, from livestock to film stock.

Yet whereas Eisenstein's *Strike* and Vertov's *Film-Eye* use stock footage, Tarkovsky forgoes any interrogation into the complexities of industrial production (be it labor, meat, or film stock) by using *raw* footage of animal death to prod at the immaterial themes of anguish, truth, and art. Tarkovsky procured a horse from a slaughterhouse to *relive* the spectacle of slaughter. The horse's death, no longer part of the (dis)assembly line of industrial meat production, occurred solely because of a film crew's intervention. In a reversal of what happens at an abattoir—where the leftovers of butchered livestock are converted into the adhesive agent for film stock—Tarkovsky forfeited the only possible utilitarian justification of a slaughterhouse in pursuit of unadulterated cinema. Saved from slaughter only to be slaughtered, but not for meat, Tarkovsky's horse was needlessly extinguished. Whereas the abattoir repurposes the remains of dead animals, Tarkovsky pushed the slaughterhouse's surplus economy of death to its logical extreme by destroying a horse for a raw cinematic effect that could have been achieved otherwise. The horse's excessively graphic demise is an example of *surplus* surplus, a redundant redundancy in excess of the abattoir's culture of violence and waste. Nothing about the horse's fate was inevitable, and its death was all too preventable. Why then, other than to play out his Eisensteinian psychodrama, does Tarkovsky *still* resort to slaughter? The answer leads us straight from the slaughterhouse to the arthouse.

ARTHOUSE AS SLAUGHTERHOUSE

Besides films about slaughterhouses, indexical images of real animal killings abound in movies that have, at least on the surface, very little to do with slaughter. As film scholar Michael Lawrence notes, many nonsimulated scenes of animal killing were produced outside the United States at the height of postwar art cinema in the 1960s–1980s, Tarkovsky's creative milieu.[116] Among the most well-known examples of these productions, including *Andrei Rublev*, are Metin Erksan's *Dry Summer* (*Susuz yaz*, 1964); Jean-Luc Godard's *Weekend* (*Week-end*, 1967); Robert Bresson's *Au Hasard Balthazar* (1966) and *Mouchette* (1967); Federico Fellini's *Satyricon* (1969); Alejandro Jodorowsky's *El Topo* (1970); Werner Herzog's *Even Dwarfs Started Small* (1970); Ted Kotcheff's *Wake in Fright* (1971); Fernando Arrabal's *Viva la Muerte* (1971); Nicolas Roeg's *Walkabout* (1971); John Waters's *Pink Flamingos* (1972); Thierry Zéno's *Wedding Trough* (*Vase de Noces*, 1974); Rainer Werner Fassbinder's *In a Year of Thirteen Moons* (*In einem Jahr mit 13 Monden*, 1978) and *Berlin Alexanderplatz* (1980); Ruggero Deodat's *Cannibal Holocaust* (1980); Michael Haneke's *Benny's Video* (1992); and Béla Tarr's *Sátántangó* (1994). International in scope, each of these narrative films features graphic scenes of *real* animal death, and each filmmaker, like Tarkovsky, had to acquire animals from somewhere beyond the film—from the slaughterhouse, the street, the barn, or the wild—to capture their deaths on camera. None of the animals in these arthouse films needed to die; they were all slaughtered *for* the fictions in which they were conscripted. Animal slaughter is a leitmotif—a macabre *lingua franca*—that unites some of the most storied names of twentieth-century cinematography.

The international film movement in which we encounter images of dead and dying animals with the most disturbing frequency has been called "arthouse," a term that came into use in the late nineteenth century as a noun describing a place where works of art are sold and exhibited. The coinage later entered circulation as an adjective in North America and England (mainland Europeans prefer the term "auteur") to refer to movie theaters and films "specializing in artistic rather than commercial appeal."[117] Arthouse films expressly reject the conventions of mainstream cinema, which, by the late 1940s, had become synonymous with Hollywood. The postwar arthouse established itself vis-à-vis a succession of movements: Italian neorealism, the French *nouvelle vague*, New German Cinema, the Czech Renaissance, and the Brazilian *cinema novo* (along with other "new waves" in Australia, Iran, India, Japan, and Russia).[118] These film movements eschewed everything that made cinema entertaining and, therefore, commercially viable: fast-paced, action-based, forward-moving plotlines populated by identifiable characters (i.e., good guys and bad guys). The arthouse offered viewers a chance to "distinguish themselves from 'ordinary' filmgoers" through "a more intellectual filmgoing experience" that usually entailed offbeat, slow, and foreign-language films.[119] These movies, screened mostly in urban areas at small theaters, festivals, university settings, and galleries, conferred patrons "a sense of prestige and status" in opposition to the mainstream.[120] The arthouse's most important legacy—as Tarkovsky's philosophical films make apparent—is how it revolutionized ideas about what cinema should and could be, elevating the perceived seriousness of film as an art form, as enshrined by the debates on the pages of the postwar French film magazine *Cahiers du cinéma*.[121]

Importantly, film scholar Bert Cardullo draws a useful distinction between "arthouse cinema" and "art cinema," such as Michael Snow's *Wavelength* (1967) and Maya Deren's *The Private Life of a Cat* (1947).[122] Art cinema, while just as committed to challenging Hollywood norms as arthouse cinema, was seen as *too* experimental and commercially unviable for postwar viewers (even the sort of adventurous, educated filmgoers inclined to go see an arthouse flick). The abstract expressionism of postwar art cinema, a descendant of 1920s surrealism and Dada, bears a greater resemblance to moving-image installations or performance art than to cinema proper.[123] Art*house* cinema, then, represents a kind of middle ground between Hollywood and art cinema. Most arthouse films largely "conform with canons of taste established in existing high arts" and are "characterized by the use of self-consciously 'artful' techniques," such as long takes, self-reflexivity, moody atmospherics, philosophical dialogue, opaque characters, and allusions to the other arts, particularly classical music and painting.[124] Unlike art cinema, arthouse films are recognizably, albeit ambivalently, cinematic: they refute and reimagine cinema's dominant codes without rejecting its structuring aesthetic principles wholesale.

The encounter between Tarkovsky—an archetypal figure of the postwar European arthouse—and Stan Brakhage, an American pioneer of experimental art cinema, has become a thing of world-cinema lore; it perfectly illustrates the differences between postwar art and arthouse cinema.[125] Event organizers at the 1983 Telluride Film Festival arranged for Brakhage to present a lifetime achievement award to Tarkovsky, who was invited to attend a private screening of several of Brakhage's films.[126] In Brakhage's retelling, Tarkovsky "hammer[ed] away in incredibly rapid Russian" during the screening and, ever the priggish aesthete, exasperatedly exclaimed (via a translator): "What is this? It does not mean anything, it's just capricious."[127] Ironically, Tarkovsky's reaction toward Brakhage's work matches the response of some present-day viewers to *Tarkovsky's* films.[128] In the end, arthouse cinema is still far more thematically and aesthetically coherent than recondite art cinema, which poses greater interpretive difficulties than Tarkovsky ever could, even at his most enigmatic.[129] Tarkovsky's and Brakhage's meeting represents the clash, the metaphoric car crash, between arthouse and art cinema: each anti-Hollywood but each differently innovative, poetic, and (semi)abstract. As recounted by numerous film critics, Tarkovsky "screamed in a non-stop rage" during Brakhage's films, claiming that they were "hurting his eyes," while Brakhage called Tarkovsky "one of the meanest men" he had ever met.[130]

However revolting Tarkovsky found Brakhage's esotericism, there is nothing remotely as disturbing in all Brakhage's catalog as the episode of horse slaughter in *Andrei Rublev*. Nothing about the history of arthouse or its differences with postwar art cinema could possibly account for the images of dead and dying animals it regularly coughs up. Graphic scenes of slaughter are an aesthetic "innovation" of the arthouse: the supposedly more sophisticated, allusive alternative to vulgar and mainstream Hollywood film. "Whereas Hollywood generally avoids showing violence to animals, it does however frequently show violence done to human bodies"; in arthouse cinema, "the presentation of human violence and animal death is reversed."[131] Arthouse filmmakers frequently rely on images of animal suffering to amplify the existential concerns raised by their "cultured" movies and declare their independence from Hollywood. These all-too-avoidable episodes of animal killing erase the distance between violence and its representation. They constitute metaphors made flesh—antimetaphors, anatropic figures at the end of figuration—that overwhelm a film's thematic content by ushering into the diegesis a lacerating charge of the real too powerful for Hollywood audiences, who have grown accustomed to legal and ethical taboos on images of animal cruelty.[132]

Once cinema became a dominant form of entertainment in the 1920s, an organization in the United States called American Humane (AH), founded in 1877, began petitioning against animal cruelty allegedly emanating out of Hollywood.[133] One of the country's first animal welfare societies, AH reserved particular umbrage for productions in which horses were injured or killed, films like Fred Niblo's *Ben-Hur: A Tale of the Christ* (1925), Michael Curtiz's *The Charge of the Lightning Brigade* (1936), and John Ford's *Stagecoach* (1939). Despite calls to regulate the use of animals in Hollywood, AH failed to secure reform until 1940. The break came with the release of Henry King's *Jesse James* (1939), which features a scene of the eponymous protagonist astride a horse leaping off a cliff into a river seventy feet below. To get the horse to make the plunge, it had to be blindfolded, and a greased platform was rigged to the cliff top so that the horse would lose balance as it approached the edge.[134] Sliding off the cliff and somersaulting through the air before plummeting into the river, the horse broke its back on impact and drowned, not unlike the horses that fell to their death in Tarkovsky's *Andrei Rublev* and Eisenstein's *October*. The scene in *Jesse James* drove AH to protest the film, which impelled the Motion Picture

Producers and Distributors of America (MPPDA), the group representing the major Hollywood studios, to require the presence of animal handlers on set.

This reform was part of the American film industry's self-monitoring standards—the Production (or Hayes) Code—that lasted from 1933 until 1968 and had the stated goal of presenting films as "directly responsible for spiritual or moral progress, for higher types of social life, and for much correct thinking."[135] In this vein, the code proscribed the "branding of" and "apparent cruelty to children or animals" under the subheading "repellant subjects," in addition to the sight of "a woman selling her virtue," which again suggests the conflation of exploited women, children, and animals so pertinent to not only Tarkovsky's cinema but also film history more broadly.[136] However, a series of decisions issued by the United States Supreme Court in the 1960s, which argued that directors are entitled to the freedoms of speech protected by the First Amendment, weakened the code, with positive effects for Hollywood but devastating consequences for animals on screen. "Through the final days of the '60s and then into the '70s, it was bleak," said Karen Rosa, a longtime executive at AH. "We were banned from film sets. There was a push for a gritty realism in those days of filmmaking. And they didn't like to be told they could or could not do something with animals."[137] Though critics blame the code for eroding the quality of postwar American cinema, it had a largely salutary effect for animals, as evidenced by the deregulated scenes of cruelty in postcode films like Sam Peckinpah's *Pat Garrett and Billy the Kid* (1973) and Francis Ford Coppola's *Apocalypse Now* (1979).

The worsening fate of animals on screen culminated in *Heaven's Gate* (1980), a film directed by Michael Cimino and suffused with animal violence: cocks fighting, steers bled from the neck, and a horse blown to smithereens with dynamite. The outcry incited by *Heaven's Gate* galvanized two powerful Hollywood organizations—the Screen Actors Guild (SAG) and the Alliance of Motion Picture & Television Producers (AMPTP)—to contractually obligate film crews to accommodate animal rights groups.[138] The disclaimer "No animals were harmed in the making of this film," which first appeared in Byron Ross Chudnow's *The Doberman Gang* (1972), became a hallmark of Hollywood films after *Heaven's Gate*. This tagline promises viewers that films have had rigorous animal supervision. As Akira Mizuta Lippit writes,

> As a film nears its end and the credit sequence begins, films that have depicted violence against animals disavow—in those final moments of the film, at the threshold of the diegesis—that violence against animals. "No animal was harmed" marks the intervention of a linguistic phrase that attempts to frame the picture and limit the responsibility of the film and its fictions. *It*

states, as it were, for the animal that cannot speak, that cannot defend its rights. A kind of animal right, or writing. The disclaimer and entire credit sequence signal the return of the film to the order of language.[139]

The phrase "No animals were harmed" attempts to separate a film from the world that produced it, one where animal cruelty abounds. Animals are harmed so often off screen that we need assurance that they are not harmed on screen as well; film has come to act as a kind of sanctuary, a virtual animal reserve.

The historical coincidence of anticruelty reform in Hollywood and the rash of images of animal death in the postwar arthouse is, thus, not coincidental. Arthouse filmmakers aestheticize animal violence as an intentionally polemical and countercultural statement. If anything, the lessening of animal violence on screen became associated with Hollywood reformism, which contributed to its proliferation in films attempting to transgress mainstream taboos. The controversy surrounding *Heaven's Gate* only recapitulates how the history of animal welfare on screen is, ultimately, a *Hollywood* affair—a story of mainstream American cinema regulating itself to sustain its appeal for run-of-the-mill audiences.[140] The threat animal cruelty posed to cinema's commercial viability led the market to correct itself by assuring audiences that "no animals were harmed" in the making of a film. The goal of resisting Hollywood's pernicious influence, a task embraced by arty directors like Tarkovsky, entailed, in part, spectacles of animal massacre. Importantly, most arthouse directors operated in foreign studio systems where, unlike in Hollywood, there existed scant regulations (until very recently) on the use and abuse of animals.[141]

Upholding the law of opposites, then, animal slaughter becomes a feature, a *bona fide*, of the anti-Hollywood arthouse. Graphic images of animal death intensify the arthouse's already heady content, which deals with existential, Dostoevskian questions of life, death, art, and suffering in ways that lily-livered Hollywood filmmakers—ever indisposed to offending popular taste—rarely take up. It is as if the butchered animals of arthouse cinema are necessary casualties in the struggle against commercial film, governed by a sacrificial logic that understands animal slaughter as a symbolic destruction of Hollywood. Is it by chance, then, that the felled horse of *Andrei Rublev* re-creates not only Eisenstein's collapsed steed in *October* but also the deposed horse in *Jesse James*, which spurred the onset of anticruelty reform in Hollywood? Tarkovsky's slain horse is a figurative destruction, a metaphor made flesh, of Hollywood conventionalism. For much of the arthouse, animal cruelty is not an injustice but a sort of virtue. The highbrow qualities of the postwar arthouse, which casts itself as a repository of the noblest humanist values of art, culture, and civilization, also entail grim animal violence. That animals *were* harmed in the making of elevated arthouse productions like *Andrei Rublev*—an unwritten disclaimer abridging animal rights—authenticates the productions' perceived philosophical and aesthetic seriousness by reifying arthouse's status as Hollywood's self-appointed antagonist.

The arthouse, then, regards scenes of cruelty as redeemable, even ethically and politically necessary. Per his own admission, Tarkovsky resorts to slaughter in *Andrei Rublev* to make a subversive statement about both Hollywood's inanity and the ways in which viewers avert their gaze from the violence of modern life. "Man's sense of suffering has atrophied," Tarkovsky wrote. "That is dangerous; because it means it is no longer possible now to save humanity by means of blood and suffering. God, what a time to be alive!"[142] Tarkovsky uses a horse to recapitulate life's precarity, the ease by which all beings can fall victim to suffering. Through the horse's death, Tarkovsky evokes what some scholars call a "creaturely gaze," a mode of looking, often triggered by the sight of a dying animal, that confronts us with the material realities of anguish.[143] Scenes of animals in pain, it is argued, disrupt the "defensive inventory of humanness" by reminding us that we are also creatures of the flesh, despite our notions of exceptionalism.[144] Images of dead animals throw into sharp focus life's fragility, the relative defenselessness of all beings, which must be protected against undue harm. The horse's gruesome death in *Andrei Rublev* was intended to make us worry about our *own* skin, our *own* hide.

Somewhat counterintuitively, then, Tarkovsky slaughters a horse—and burns a cow—to jump-start our ethical imagination. Tarkovsky's scenes of animal cruelty accord with what French artist Antonin Artaud memorably terms the "theatre of cruelty" in reference to stage productions that confront spectators with the baseness of human behavior.[145] Artaud reasons that depictions of cruelty function as a "spiritual therapeutic" that can resensitize viewers to the corporeal, emotional, precarious, and exuberant dynamics of being alive.[146] "The Theatre of Cruelty," Artaud writes, "has been created in order to restore to the theatre a passionate and convulsive conception of life, and it is this sense of violent rigour and extreme condensation . . . on which it is based must be understood. This cruelty, which will be bloody when necessary . . . can thus be identified with a kind of severe moral purity which is not afraid to pay life the price it must be paid."[147] Scenes of bracingly violent action can shock us out of our moral complacency toward the suffering of others—an indifference that, if left unchallenged, is liable to fuel ever-worse forms of cruelty. Similarly, Tarkovsky "sought to remove aesthetic distance" by bringing his viewers "into direct contact with the dangers of life" through graphic images of cruelty, turning the screen "into a place where the spectator is exposed rather than protected."¹⁴⁸ This exposure is to elicit feelings of outrage and pity that lay bare life's precariousness and, therefore, its preciousness. Tarkovsky's grisly images—his cinema of cruelty—is to develop in viewers moral and aesthetic antibodies against cruelty. Is this rationale defensible, though?¹⁴⁹ Can arthouse scenes of animal butchery serve a redemptive function? Do they engage us in any meaningful way?

While exposing viewers to graphic images of animal suffering may heighten ethical concern—and, in some cases, spur reform—it is not guaranteed to do so. Spectacles of cruelty can just as easily occasion feelings of revulsion, recoil, or, even worse, desire for *further* retaliation. The intended response to the sight of animal cruelty is ethically agnostic. As Anat Pick astutely writes,

> the threat of violence hangs over the encounter with alterity.... To encounter [an animal] is to come into being via the threat of violence and the possibility of care. Like talk of "inalienable rights," the prohibition of killing would be unnecessary if life were not already exposed to violence (and rights were precisely alienable). And so, ... vulnerability and violence are co-present.... Vulnerability functions as a *provocation* and an *invitation*, and the relation between the two is tautological, for where else would violence turn if not toward the vulnerable?... Vulnerability offers violence the path of least resistance. To imagine the flow of violence in the other direction, toward power, is to imagine politics under the condition of zero gravity.¹⁵⁰

Though vulnerability is a universal fact of life, it is disproportionately endured and unevenly distributed. "If vulnerability connects humans and animals via our shared corporeality, it also sets animals apart from most humans . . . in the scale and reach of the infliction of harm."¹⁵¹ In human society, violence with the fewest obstacles—legal, moral, political, or otherwise—is exercised against animals precisely because they are comparatively defenseless, singled out as outliers at the mercy of human desires and needs. The asymmetrically vulnerable horse in *Andrei Rublev*, then, *provokes* Tarkovsky's cruelty, if for no other reason than the fact that animals are so lopsidedly prone to human might.

Far from buttressing some lofty cause or hard truth, arthouse episodes of animal butchery like the horse death scene in *Andrei Rublev* merely redouble the commonplace violence already directed against the most vulnerable creatures among us. There is vanishingly little transgressive in arthouse cinema's (ab)use of animals, rather something all too conventional. Arthouse filmmakers consistently rebuff opportunities for care in favor of aggression, exploiting animals for their own parochial purposes and locking them in the same death spiral—premised on suspect notions of utilitarianism, Cartesian soullessness, and reductive symbolism—as does mainstream society and Hollywood. The distressingly frequent images of animal death in arthouse cinema not only undercut the humanist values it supposedly exemplifies (beauty, grace, moral education) but also disclose the brutality endemic to the whole philosophical edifice of human exceptionalism, which fortifies itself vis-à-vis capricious violence in service of a rigid species hierarchy: Tarkovsky kills a horse because he *can*, burns a cow because he *can*. The noble humanism Tarkovsky espoused is ever liable to backslide into anthropocentric terror and sadism. The problem of Tarkovsky's animal cruelty is not the result of too little humanism—"a so-called 'humanist deficit'"—and it could not, therefore, be remedied by "more humanity."[152] If, as Tarkovsky hoped, images of animal violence would enflame his viewers against violence, they do so not because of Tarkovsky, but in spite of him. The pointless suffering Tarkovsky inflicts on animals should heighten our desire to safeguard them from *Tarkovsky's* brutal applications of power; his rejection of cruelty vis-à-vis its exhibition generates only more cruelty that necessitates further disavowal. Tarkovsky's cruelty, like the arthouse's more broadly, betrays that lurking beneath humanism's righteous goals lie the propensities for contradiction and moral exclusivism, which always find a way to legitimate violence against animals for humanity's benefit. Tarkovsky's humanism—his aggressive, recalcitrant humanism—succumbs to its own cruelty, to the excessiveness of his own humanist commitments.

If anything, the ethic generated by *Andrei Rublev*, which indulges the very brutality it abhors, is an appeal for *more* violence targeted against the weak. Ruthlessness, Tarkovsky makes apparent, proliferates where there are the fewest obstructions. *Andrei Rublev* reveals that Hollywood has, at least in principle, tendered a safer habitat for animals than the arthouse, which, at times, duplicates on screen the carnage of a slaughterhouse. Whatever Tarkovsky set out to accomplish through the obscene scenes of slaughter in *Andrei Rublev*—to test the limits of cinematic representation, to violate Hollywood taboos, to visualize the mystery of death, to kick-start his viewers' humanist sympathies—there is nothing whatsoever redemptive about his "sacrificial economy of suffering."[153] To read significance into Tarkovsky's scenes of animal cruelty, perhaps some of the most unnecessarily gruesome instances of bloodshed ever committed to celluloid, is to invent useful meaning where none is to be found.

NOTES

1. See Meier, "Why Are Cities Filled with Metal Men on Horseback?"
2. Tarkovsky, *Interviews*, 25.

3. See Girard, *Violence and the Sacred*.
4. See Heidegger, "Letter on Humanism," 268.
5. See Lippit, "Death of an Animal"; O'Brien, "Why Look at Dead Animals?"
6. O'Brien, "Why Look at Dead Animals?," 33.
7. O'Brien, "Why Look at Dead Animals?," 36.
8. Ivan himself is described as "skin and bones," and repeated close-ups of his skeletal ribs allude to wartime famine.
9. Skakov, *Cinema of Tarkovsky*, 30; Johnson and Petrie, *Films of Andrei Tarkovsky*, 253.
10. See Hall, "Before the Apocalypse."
11. Tarkovsky, *Time Within Time*, 60.
12. Tarkovsky, *Interviews*, 160.
13. See Pontara, *Andrei Tarkovsky's Sounding Cinema*, 104–12.
14. This image echoes with the white horse veiled in mist in Yuri Norstein's *Hedgehog in the Fog* (*Ezhik v tumane*, 1975), an existential Soviet cartoon film about belonging, purpose, and desire that resonates with *Nostalghia*'s themes.
15. Quoted in Lenski, *Interpretation of St. John's Revelation*, 223.
16. Bazin, *What Is Cinema?*, 9.
17. Lippit, *Electric Animal*, 171.
18. Bazin, *What Is Cinema?*, 9.
19. Sontag, *Essays of the 1960s & 70s*, 538.
20. Tarkovsky, *Interviews*, 54.
21. See Hill, "Deep-Rooted Russian Fear of the West Has Fueled Putin's Invasion of Ukraine."
22. Bataille, *Undercover Surrealism*, 236–39.
23. Bataille, *Undercover Surrealism*, 238.
24. Timofeeva, *History of Animals*, 19.
25. Bethea, *Shape of the Apocalypse in Modern Russian Fiction*, 57.
26. Bethea, *Shape of the Apocalypse in Modern Russian Fiction*, 70.
27. Bethea, *Shape of the Apocalypse in Modern Russian Fiction*, 70.
28. Bethea, *Shape of the Apocalypse in Modern Russian Fiction*, 58.
29. Dostoevsky, *Crime and Punishment*, 58.
30. Freud, "Mourning and Melancholia," 244.
31. Freud, "Mourning and Melancholia," 244–45.
32. Tarkovsky, *Interviews*, 173.
33. Freud, "Mourning and Melancholia," 243–44.
34. Tarkovsky, *Interviews*, 173–74.
35. Freud, "Mourning and Melancholia," 246.
36. Freud, "Mourning and Melancholia," 249.
37. Freud, "Mourning and Melancholia," 249.
38. Freud, "Mourning and Melancholia," 249.

39. Freud, "Mourning and Melancholia," 249.
40. Freud, "Mourning and Melancholia," 251.
41. Freud, "Mourning and Melancholia," 257.
42. See Billson, "Chicken Decapitation and Battered Cats."
43. As noted in chapter 4 about an image of a topless pagan woman, censors rebuked Tarkovsky for using sexually explicit scenes in *Andrei Rublev*. In the end, these scenes were excised.
44. This close-up of the horse's death also anticipates the footage of a dying giraffe in *Sans Soleil* (1983), an avant-garde documentary by Chris Marker, a devotee of Tarkovsky who, in 2000, made a documentary about Tarkovsky, *One Day in the Life of Andrei Arsenevich* (*Une journée d'Andrei Arsenevitch*).
45. Sobchack, *Carnal Thoughts*, 249.
46. O'Brien, "Why Look at Dead Animals?," 37.
47. See Fara, "An Attractive Therapy."
48. Lippit, *Electric Animal*, 101.
49. Cited in Lippit, *Electric Animal*, 111, 120–21.
50. Lippit, *Electric Animal*, 121.
51. Freud, "Mourning and Melancholia," 250.
52. Skakov, *Cinema of Tarkovsky*, 44.
53. Shukin, *Animal Capital*, 91.
54. Heidegger, "Letter on Humanism," 268.
55. See Heidegger, *Being and Time*.
56. Calarco, *Zoographies*, 22.
57. Heidegger, *Fundamental Concepts of Metaphysics*, 177.
58. Heidegger, *Fundamental Concepts of Metaphysics*, 197.
59. Heidegger, *Fundamental Concepts of Metaphysics*, 198.
60. Calarco, *Zoographies*, 26.
61. Lippit, *Electric Animal*, 62.
62. Heidegger, *Poetry, Language, Thought*, 73.
63. Lippit, *Electric Animal*, 56.
64. Heidegger, *Poetry, Language, Thought*, 178–79.
65. Lippit, *Electric Animal*, 57.
66. Derrida, *Animal That Therefore I Am*, 154; see, also, McCarthy and Moussaieff Masson, *When Elephants Weep*.
67. Lippit, *Electric Animal*, 58.
68. Lippit, "Death of an Animal," 18.
69. Derrida, *Animal That Therefore I Am*, 38, 111.
70. Calarco, *Zoographies*, 110.
71. Tarkovsky, "Passion According to Andrei."
72. Kojève, *Introduction to the Reading of Hegel*, 255.
73. Lippit, "Death of an Animal," 18.

74. Bentham, *Introduction to the Principles of Morals and Legislation*, 308.
75. Derrida, *Animal That Therefore I Am*, 27.
76. Derrida, *Animal That Therefore I Am*, 96.
77. Calarco, *Boundaries of Human Nature*, 81.
78. Varner, "Sentience," 367.
79. Calarco, *Boundaries of Human Nature*, 79–80.
80. Tarkovsky, "Passion According to Andrei."
81. Tarkovsky, "Passion According to Andrei."
82. Burt, *Animals in Film*, 141.
83. Burt, *Animals in Film*, 112.
84. Shukin and O'Brien, "Being Struck," 187.
85. Wood, "Bunnies for Pets or Meat," 35.
86. Wood, "Bunnies for Pets or Meat," 26.
87. Burt, "Illumination of the Animal Kingdom."
88. For nineteenth-century anticruelty societies, see Nelson, "Body of the Beast."
89. Burt, "Illumination of the Animal Kingdom," 208.
90. It is telling, in this light, that animal rights activists often use secret, undercover films of slaughterhouses to shock public opinion on behalf of animal welfare. See, also, Young, "Siting the Slaughterhouse."
91. Slaughterhouse documentaries channel the muckraking spirit of *The Jungle*, Upton Sinclair's 1905 novel about the wretched conditions at the Chicago stockyards that catalyzed legislative reform on behalf of both humans and animals. See Rüdiger, "Truth in the Jungle of Literature, Science, and Politics."
92. Tarkovsky, *Sculpting in Time*, 208.
93. Lawrence, "Haneke's Stable," 79.
94. Bordwell, *Cinema of Eisenstein*, 260.
95. Shukin and O'Brien, "Being Struck," 189.
96. Eisenstein, *Sergei Eisenstein*, 65.
97. Tarkovsky, *Sculpting in Time*, 183.
98. Eisenstein, *Sergei Eisenstein*, 64.
99. Shukin and O'Brien, "Being Struck," 194.
100. Tarkovsky, *Sculpting in Time*, 183.
101. Tarkovsky, *Interviews*, 137.
102. Shukin and O'Brien, "Being Struck," 190.
103. Tarkovsky, *Interviews*, 28.
104. See Bloom, *Anxiety of Influence*.
105. Bloom, *Anxiety of Influence*, 14.
106. In *Solaris*, Tarkovsky foregrounds a close-up of broken eyeglasses, replicating a shot from *Battleship Potemkin* (*Bronenonsets Potemkin*, 1925), further

suggesting that Tarkovsky solicited comparisons to Eisenstein, as if—implied by this shot of broken spectacles—he could see more clearly than his predecessor.

107. See Barratt, "In the Name of the Father."
108. Widdis, *Socialist Senses*, 127.
109. Nesbitt, *Savage Junctures*, 18.
110. See Elsaesser, "Ethics of Appropriation."
111. Shukin, *Animal Capital*, 108–109.
112. Shukin, *Animal Capital*, 91, 104.
113. *Oxford English Dictionary*, "stock (n.)."
114. McMahon, "Screening Pigs," 205.
115. Murphet, "Pitiable or Political Animals?," 102.
116. Lawrence, "Haneke's Stable," 64.
117. *Oxford English Dictionary*, "arthouse (n. & adj.)."
118. The most important factor contributing to the rise of the postwar arthouse was film industries around the world beginning to support home-grown productions, directors, and "independent" studios to counter the dominance of American culture and cinema. See Neale, "Art Cinema as Institution."
119. Wilinsky, *Sure Seaters*, 3. The flourishing population of college students around the world additionally fueled demand for more intelligent, "adult" movies, which went hand in hand with the rise of the 1960s and '70s counterculture movement and growing disillusionment with mainstream consumerism. For the ballooning of postwar higher education, see Hobsbawm, *Age of Extremes*, 295–301.
120. Wilinsky, *Sure Seaters*, 2. The arthouse's appeal was also aided by the lessening of economic discrepancies during the postwar boom, which led consumers to put greater emphasis on taste and culture as a way to differentiate themselves.
121. See Bickerton, *Short History of Cahiers Du Cinéma*; Elsaesser, *European Cinema and Continental Philosophy*.
122. Cardullo, "Art-House Cinema, Avant-Garde Film," 1–2.
123. Art cinema's "truly famous practitioners"—Andy Warhol, for instance—"made their fame and fortune either through other activities" or by moving into the arena of arthouse filmmaking, such as Derek Jarman, Peter Greenaway, and Chantal Akerman. Cardullo, "Art-House Cinema, Avant-Garde Film," 1.
124. Cardullo, "Art-House Cinema, Avant-Garde Film," 1.
125. See Brakhage, "Brakhage Meets Tarkovsky."
126. These works, all silent, included *Window Water Baby Moving* (1959), a detailed recording of the birth of Brakhage's first child; *Dog Star Man, Part IV* (1964), a hallucinogenic depiction of a woodsman on a hike with his dog; *Untitled No. 6* (1975), a kaleidoscopic jumble of burnt autumnal brown and yellow colors (not unlike the hues of Monkey's headscarf in *Stalker*); *Made Manifest* (1980), footage of blue sparks; *Arabic 3* (1980), a rainbow collage of celluloid

frames Brakhage painted over; and *Murder Psalm* (1980), a psychotic re-creation of "Little Red Riding Hood."

127. Brakhage, "Brakhage Meets Tarkovsky," 43–44.

128. Indeed, Tarkovsky's reaction mirrors the hostile reaction of the bureaucrats in *Solaris* after an astronaut, Henri Burton, shows them a recording from outer space: "That's it? You only filmed clouds." Tarkovsky intended this scene to convey Soviet officialdom's bewildered response to *his* work.

129. See, also, White, "Brakhage's Tarkovsky and Tarkovsky's Brakhage."

130. Hoberman, *Vulgar Modernism*, 97; quoted in White, "Brakhage's Tarkovsky and Tarkovsky's Brakhage," 81.

131. Lawrence, "Haneke's Stable," 64.

132. Lippit, "Death of an Animal," 10.

133. Farley, "Horrific True Story Behind the 'No Animals Were Harmed' Disclaimer."

134. Klein, "Protecting Animals in Films."

135. See "Motion Picture Production Code of 1930," 286.

136. "Motion Picture Production Code," 289–90.

137. Quoted in McCarthy, "Hollywood's Long History of Animal Cruelty."

138. McCarthy, "Hollywood's Long History of Animal Cruelty."

139. Lippit, "Death of an Animal," 10.

140. The animal cruelty in *Heaven's Gate* blighted the film's box-office success; the film earned less than one-fifteenth of its ($44 million) budget, a particularly poor return considering that Cimino had struck Hollywood gold with his previous film, *The Deer Hunter* (1978). See "Heaven's Gate."

141. See Novozhilova, "Emergence of Animal Protection in Russia"; Martín, Bermejo-Poza, and De la Fuente Vázquez, "Animal Protection in Filming in the Context of Spain."

142. Tarkovsky, *Time Within Time*, 21.

143. Creed, "Animal Deaths on Screen," 26–27.

144. Pick, *Creaturely Poetics*, 192.

145. Artaud, "Theatre of Cruelty," 55.

146. Gorelick, "Life in Excess," 265.

147. Artaud, "Theatre of Cruelty," 66.

148. Jamieson, *Antonin Artaud*, 23.

149. Renouncing cruelty by spotlighting cruelty, Tarkovsky fell into the same trap as did Enlightenment philosophers, who, in the words of Michel de Montaigne, professed to "cruelly hate cruelty," a term that originated in ancient Rome (*crudelitas*) to refer to the most hideous forms of human brutality: crucifixions, gladiatorial games, and human torches. Cited in Toal, *Entrapments of Form*, 2, 9. While Enlightenment thinkers abhorred cruelty, "it had to be talked about, theorized, and even performed. Indeed, what the Enlightenment could ill afford

to tolerate was a lack of cruelty.... The inhuman was a category produced from within the philosophical discourse, one that had to be posited if humanity was to take shape at all.... Instantiations of moral monstrosity in art and literature helped enact humanity as humaneness." Steintrager, *Cruel Delight*, xiii, xiv.

150. Pick, "Vulnerability," 416.
151. Pick, "Vulnerability," 411.
152. Pick, "Vulnerability," 414.
153. Pick, *Creaturely Poetics*, 125.

CONCLUSION

The Wary Gaze

"If you should ever write about me, be sure you don't make me out to be an impossible director—a tyrant. I've heard enough of that in my lifetime."

—Andrei Tarkovsky, quoted in Layla Alexander-Garrett, "Andrey Tarkovsky—Enigma and Mystery," April 1988

IN 2017, A GROUP OF Tarkovsky's relatives, former colleagues, and fans convened in the Russian town of Suzdal, where much of *Andrei Rublev* (including the scene of the burning cow) had been filmed fifty years earlier. They were there to unveil what Tarkovsky's acolytes hailed as the "world's first monument" dedicated to the filmmaker.[1] The statue, made of bronze by the sculptor Mariia Tikhonova, features a life-size replica of Tarkovsky standing in front of a cathedral-like arch, deferentially flanked by two characters from *Andrei Rublev*: Rublev himself, memorably played by Anatolii Solonitsyn, and the young bell caster Boriska, performed by Nikolai Burlyayev, the famous Russian actor turned politician who financed the monument's construction. (Burlyayev also played the child protagonist in Tarkovsky's debut, *Ivan's Childhood*.) These three figures are situated in a semicircle, reenacting the concave position of the angels in Rublev's icon *The Trinity*, which Tarkovsky spotlights in *Andrei Rublev* and again in *Solaris* and *Mirror*.

As Tikhonova said of her metalwork, "On one hand, it's just a trio of people, on the other hand, it's the trinity of Rublev's icon, so people can approach it and genuflect before it."[2] This statue is not only a commemorative site but also a pseudoreligious shrine designed to evoke awe by likening Tarkovsky to Russia's most fabled icon painter, an analogy Tarkovsky would have eagerly welcomed. The monument aims to generate the same sort of spiritual experience solicited by Tarkovsky's lofty filmography, revealing the extent to which Tarkovsky himself shaped the terms of his legacy. This statue, like much of the scholarly literature about him, deifies Tarkovsky.[3]

Foregrounding the significant and at times disturbing role of animals throughout Tarkovsky's cinema, *And the Cow Burned* has hewed to an alternative critical approach. It has sought to unsettle conventional wisdom about Tarkovsky by focusing on his use of animals as symbols in his existentially searching movies and, more importantly, on animals as living beings affected by—and indifferent to—his larger artistic and philosophical project. In chapter 1, I explored how Tarkovsky's elegiac depictions of horses reflect his malaise about what he perceived as the moribund state of modern civilization, the industrial expanse of which has eroded the presence of horses in human society. Tarkovsky's plaintive depictions of horses are complemented by antithetically grisly scenes of their death, which, explored in chapter 5, suggest that Tarkovsky's mournfulness curdled into a pathological condition of melancholia that fomented violence against the object of loss. In chapter 2, I contended that the elusive dogs accompanying Tarkovsky's renegade protagonists tease at a vision of meaningful cross-species companionship. Yet Tarkovsky neuters the possibility for any interspecies camaraderie that might destabilize his anthropocentrism by emphasizing above all what he viewed as dogs' most treasured traits: loyalty and submission. Chapter 3 maintained that Tarkovsky's lyrical depictions of flight, typified by his recurrent motif of airborne birds, suggest his lifelong yearning for creative (and geopolitical) freedom. However, Tarkovsky's longing for independence is undercut by his obsessive fixation on control and authority, disclosed by his aestheticization of birds, the (dis)appearances, sounds, and movement of which he painstakingly manipulated. Finally, in chapter 4, I turned to the burnt cow of *Andrei Rublev*, the centerpiece of this study. This horrific act of violence betrays not only Tarkovsky's view of animal life as disposable but also his reactionary ideas about women, who, associated with the bovine in traditional Russian culture, Tarkovsky blamed for precipitating society's downfall. Exemplified by this image of an immolated cow, Tarkovsky's mobilization of animals exposes his dark, even ruthless, qualities as a filmmaker.

Tarkovsky's disturbing treatment of animals is thus continuous with his more authoritarian tendencies, his retrograde portrayals of women, and his incipient Russian nationalism. These troubling interconnections not only make Tarkovsky's brand of humanism morally untenable but also expose an ethical nerve in humanist thought more generally. The proponents of humanism always seem to find a way to justify moral exclusionism in service of their tendentious claims of human superiority. The violence of human domination casts a shadow over humanism's aspirational beneficence. If anything, Tarkovsky's cruelty demands a *contraction* of humanity: a retreat from the abstract ideas about what humans and animals "are" that underpin interspecies relations. In spite of his cruelty, and not because of it, Tarkovsky reveals that humanity's treatment of animals should instead begin with "a particular comportment toward the finitude, abundance, and vulnerability" of animal life.[4] The all-too-human logic that animals must be granted moral consideration in accordance with humanlike capacities (language, consciousness, reason)—other "euphemisms of power"—stands to be disrupted by greater attunement with animals' material situatedness in their interactions with human beings.[5] An ethics oriented around questions of vulnerability recognizes the ubiquity of human power while imagining its suspension. As Jacques Derrida beautifully writes, "Mortality resides there, as the most radical means of thinking through the finitude that we share with animals, the mortality that belongs to the very finitude of life, to that experience of compassion, to the possibility to sharing the possibility of this nonpower, the possibility of this impossibility, the anguish of this vulnerability, and the vulnerability of this anguish."[6]

In Tarkovsky's dealings with animals, he does not entertain the power of "nonpower," only power's brutal application; he confronts us with grisly spectacles of animal vulnerability but not with the ethics of vulnerability. At times, Tarkovsky's humanism emerges vis-à-vis enactments of flagrant *in*humanity, a kind of "negative anthropology" that abhors cruelty but must still enact and perform it in order to delineate what supposedly separates human beings from animals.[7] Paradoxically, then, Tarkovsky's scenes of animal cruelty are encounters "in which human dominance exercises its prerogative semiautomatically yet at the same time stands to discover, in the midst of its power, its own contingency and automation, its own afflicted animality."[8] Tarkovsky shows us that "the ability to choose cruelty and ignore pity" is yet another property unique to humanity, a grim twist on the philosophy of human exceptionalism; cruelty is the ultimate exercise in human freedom.[9] By way of cruelty, Tarkovsky fails the litmus test he himself posed about the recoverability of humanist values in the postwar world.

The ethical lacuna in humanist philosophy exposed by Tarkovsky's work—his cinema of cruelty—is all the more pertinent and worrisome today. While critics have tended to associate Tarkovsky with the noble traditions of late Soviet dissidence, his films have recently found a receptive audience among deeply conservative, neotraditionalist thinkers on the political right in Russia and abroad, such as Rod Dreher and Eduard Limonov.[10] These right-wing ideologues, never

Tarkovsky's repurposed footage of Red Army soldiers in Crimea reminds us of Russia's geographic mutilation of present-day Ukraine. Still from *Mirror*, 1975.

straying far from tropes of antisemitism, vilify the West's alleged descent into cultural degeneracy and misandry; even Burlyayev, who played the bell caster in *Andrei Rublev* and commissioned the Tarkovsky monument in Suzdal, has become a bellicose member of Russia's lower house of parliament. Sanctioned by the European Union and the United States, Burlyayev has voiced support for Russia's 2022 invasion of Ukraine, which he mendaciously claims fell prey to the forces of "international satanism."[11] It is, indeed, impossible to watch the footage Tarkovsky incorporated into *Mirror* of Red Army soldiers trudging through the lagoons of the Sivash region, which straddles the coast of Crimea, without being reminded of Russia's ongoing mutilation of present-day Ukraine.[12] One shudders to think what kind of commentary Tarkovsky would hazard about Vladimir Putin's military adventurism, which is being waged with the same sort of messianic zeal that energized Tarkovsky's worldview.[13]

Has Tarkovsky been hijacked by a cultural rear guard, or have the more retrograde elements of his ideology been there all along, hidden in plain view amid his haunting images? How can the orgy of animal violence in *Andrei Rublev* be interpreted in any way that does *not* throw into doubt the ethical and political commitments of the man behind the camera? "Tarkovsky had a reactionary streak," writes Alex Ross in a profile on Tarkovsky for the *New Yorker*, and "his drift toward nationalist mysticism can take on an ominous tinge."[14] Should

Tarkovsky's image of a burning cow—and all that it implies—induce the same sort of dismayed reaction it did from Ukrainian director Kira Muratova, who said, bequeathing this book its epigraph, "Tarkovsky, for me, ceased to exist"?[15] To borrow the trendy albeit somewhat glib phrase, should Tarkovsky be "canceled"? Should his statue, like other monuments exalting problematic figures, be torn down? Tarkovsky begs the question posed by the essayist Claire Dederer in response to one of the most contentious debates of the 2010s and 2020s: "What do we do with the art of monstrous men?"[16]

While it is beyond this study's scope to adjudicate whether a work of art can be separated from its creator, Tarkovsky can teach us something in our struggle to resolve the conundrum of how to approach art made by ethically and ideologically troublesome, if not outright repugnant, individuals. Rather than abandoning Tarkovsky, we can use his cinema to interrogate the cultural incentives and industries that have driven his sacralization. What has enabled Tarkovsky to assume such a feted place in film history? What underpins the default idiom of reverence in our discussions about Tarkovsky, and who stands to benefit from such adulation? As Dederer writes, those who profit the most from keeping biography at bay in our analyses of art are "the winners of history"—the already powerful, protected, and adored.[17] The questions raised by Tarkovsky's enigmatic and often disturbing treatment of animals, and his humanist justifications for said treatment, should cast doubt not only on our assumptions about Tarkovsky's moral character but also on our own willingness to overlook the animals—and animal cruelty—at the heart of his cinema.

And the Cow Burned calls for greater circumspection in our appraisals of Tarkovsky, for a *wary* rather than worshipful gaze, a passionate dispassion that reexamines both Tarkovsky's legacy and its entailed indebtedness to classical humanism. There is an obvious danger to being too much in love with what we study and letting that enthusiasm and enchantment determine the shape of our thinking. For its part, this book leerily regards Tarkovsky's relations with those he exercised power over, particularly the disproportionately vulnerable animals encountered across his work. For a filmmaker who has convinced so many of us that, somewhere in the depths of his chimerical movies, the meaning of life itself can be found, how could anything but skepticism and reticence—wariness—be a suitable response?

NOTES

1. See "V Suzdale otkryli pamiatnik Andreiu Tarkovskomy." Though the Suzdal monument is the first stand-alone edifice dedicated to Tarkovsky, a

monument at Moscow's All-Russia Institute of Cinematography (VGIK) was unveiled in 2009 to commemorate three of its most esteemed alumni: Vasily Shukshin, Gennadii Shpailikov, and, of course, Tarkovsky.

2. Tikhonova, "Avtor pamiatnika Andreiu Tarkovskomy."

3. The monument's inscription encapsulates its pathos: "To the best film of all time, *Andrei Rublev*, and its creator, the great Russian filmmaker Andrei Tarkovsky" (*Luchshemu fil'mu vsekh vremen i narodov "Andrei Rublev" i ego sozdateliu—velikomy russkomu rezhisseru Andreiu Tarkovskomy*).

4. Pick, "Turning to Animals between Love and Law," 79.

5. Pick, "Vulnerability," 413.

6. Derrida, *Animal That Therefore I Am*, 28.

7. Steintrager, *Cruel Delight*, xiv.

8. Pick, "Vulnerability," 420.

9. Steintrager, *Cruel Delight*, xv.

10. See Dreher, "Miracle of Montesiepi"; Dreher, "Andrei Rublev Option"; Dreher, "Tarkovsky, Shaw, and the White Birds"; "Eduard Limonov (fotografii)." Limonov, in fact, studied poetry under Tarkovsky's father in the 1960s.

11. Kireeva, "Deputat Burliaev."

12. For Tarkovsky's use of this footage, see Wright, "Rotten Sea."

13. It is telling that in 2023, Putin had Andrei Rublev's *Trinity* icon transferred from its long-standing home in Moscow's Tretyakov Gallery (where Tarkovsky first encountered it) to the Cathedral of Christ the Savior, which, rebuilt under Putin (after having been razed under Stalin), has become a patriotic symbol of modern-day Russian conservativism. Rublev's legacy, like Tarkovsky's, lends itself to nationalist co-optation. See Luchenko, "Sacrificing Art for War."

14. Ross, "Drenching Richness of Andrei Tarkovsky."

15. Muratova, "Kogda ia uznala."

16. Dederer, "What Do We Do with the Art of Monstrous Men?"

17. Dederer, *Monsters*, 37.

FILMOGRAPHY

Aerograd, directed by Oleksandr Dovzhenko, 1934.
L'Albero degli zoccoli [*The Tree of Wooden Clogs*], directed by Ermanno Olmi, 1978.
Al di là del bene e del male [*Beyond Good and Evil*], directed by Liliana Cavani, 1977.
Alien, directed by Ridley Scott, 1979.
American Dream, directed by Barbara Koppel, 1990.
Andrei Rublev, directed by Andrei Tarkovsky, 1966.
Andrei Tarkovskii. Kino kak molitva [*Andrei Tarkovsky: A Cinema Prayer*], directed by Andrei Tarkovsky, 2019.
Apocalypse Now, directed by Francis Ford Coppola, 1979.
Arabic 3, directed by Stan Brakhage, 1980.
L'Argent [*Money*], directed by Robert Bresson, 1983.
L'Arrivée d'un train en gare de La Ciotat [*The Arrival of a Train*], directed by Auguste and Louis Lumière, 1895.
Au Hasard Balthazar, directed by Robert Bresson, 1966.
The Aviator, directed by Martin Scorsese, 2004.
Bakit Dilaw ang Gitna ng Bahaghari? [*Why Is Yellow the Middle of the Rainbow?*], directed by Kidlat Tahimik, 1994.
Barry Lyndon, directed by Stanley Kubrick, 1975.
Beloe solntse pustyni [*White Sun of the Desert*], directed by Vladimir Motyl, 1970.
Belorusski vokzal [*Belorussian Station*], directed by Andrei Smirnov, 1971.
Belyi Bim, Chernoe ukho [*White Bim, Black Ear*], directed by Stanislav Rostotsky, 1976.
Belyi pudel' [*The White Poodle*], directed by Marianna Roshal and Vladimir Shredel', 1955.
Ben-Hur: A Tale of the Christ, directed by Fred Niblo, 1925.
Berlin Alexanderplatz, directed by Rainer Werner Fassbinder, 1980.
Bestiaire, directed by Denis Côté, 2012.

The Birds, directed by Alfred Hitchcock, 1963.
The Black Stallion, directed by Carroll Ballard, 1979.
Bovines, directed by Emmanuel Gras, 2011.
Brilliantovaia ruka [*The Diamond Arm*], directed by Leonid Gaidai, 1968.
Bronenonsets Potemkin [*Battleship Potemkin*], directed by Sergei Eisenstein, 1925.
Cannibal Holocaust, directed by Ruggero Deodat, 1980.
Cendrillon [*Cinderella*], directed by Georges Méliès, 1899.
C'era una volta il West [*Once upon a Time in the West*], directed by Sergio Leone, 1968.
The Charge of the Lightning Brigade, directed by Michael Curtiz, 1936.
Chelovek c kinoapparatom [*Man with a Movie Camera*], directed by Dziga Vertov, 1929.
Chronique d'un été [*Chronicle of a Summer*], directed by Jean Rouch and Edgar Morin, 1961.
Close Encounters of the Third Kind, directed by Steven Spielberg, 1977.
Cow, directed by Andrea Arnold, 2021.
Dai lapu, drug! [*Give Me Your Paw, Friend!*], directed by Ilia Gurin, 1967.
Dama s sobachkoi [*Lady with a Lapdog*], directed by Iosif Kheifits, 1960.
The Deer Hunter, directed by Michael Cimino, 1978.
Il deserto rosso [*Red Desert*], directed by Michelangelo Antonioni, 1964.
Deviat' dnei odnogo goda [*Nine Days of One Year*], directed by Mikhail Romm, 1962.
The Doberman Gang, directed by Byron Ross Chudnow, 1972.
Dog Star Man, Part IV, directed by Stan Brakhage, 1964.
Dzhul'bars, directed by Vladimir Shneiderov, 1935.
Electrocuting an Elephant, directed by Thomas Edison, 1903.
Empire, directed by Andy Warhol, 1965.
Even Dwarfs Started Small, directed by Werner Herzog, 1970.
Ezhik v tumane [*Hedgehog in the Fog*], directed by Yuri Norstein, 1975.
Fantazii Fariat'eva [*Fariatev's Fantasy*], directed by Il'ia Averbakh, 1979.
Fast Food Nation, directed by Richard Linklater, 2006.
Gav [*Cow*], directed by Dariush Mehrjui, 1969.
Germania anno zero [*Germany, Year Zero*], directed by Robert Rossellini, 1948.
Gorodskoi romans [*City Romance*], directed by Petr Todorovskii, 1970.
Granitsa na zamke [*The Border Is Locked*], directed by Vasilii Zhuravlev, 1937.
Grizzly Man, directed by Werner Herzog, 2005.
Gunda, directed by Viktor Kossakovsky, 2020.
Heaven's Gate, directed by Michael Cimino, 1980.
High Noon, directed by Fred Zinnemann, 1952.
Homeward Bound: The Incredible Journey, directed by Duwayne Dunham, 1993.
The Horse Whisperer, directed by Robert Redford, 1998.
Idi i smotri [*Come and See*], directed by Elem Klimov, 1985.

Iiul'skii dozhd' [*July Rain*], directed by Marlen Khutsiev, 1966.
In einem Jahr mit 13 Monden [*In a Year of Thirteen Moons*], directed by Rainer Werner Fassbinder, 1978.
Invasion of the Body Snatchers, directed by Don Siegel, 1956.
Ivan Grozny [*Ivan the Terrible*], directed by Sergei Eisenstein, 1944.
Ivanovo detstvo [*Ivan's Childhood*], directed by Andrei Tarkovsky, 1962.
Jeanne Dielman, 23 quai du Commerce, 1080 Bruxelles, directed by Chantal Akerman, 1975.
Jesse James, directed by Henry King, 1939.
Une journée d'Andrei Arsenevitch [*One Day in the Life of Andrei Arsenevich*], directed by Chris Marker, 2000.
Kashtanka, directed by Roman Balian, 1975.
Katok i ckripka [*The Steamroller and Violin*], directed by Andrei Tarkovsky, 1961.
Killer of Sheep, directed by Charles Burnett, 1977.
Kino-Glaz [*Film Eye*], directed by Dziga Vertov, 1924.
Ko mne, Mukhtar! [*Here, Mukhtar!*], directed by Semen Tumanov, 1964.
Körkarlen [*The Phantom Carriage*], directed by Victor Sjöström, 1922.
Koshka, kotoaria ruliala sama po sebe [*The Cat That Walked by Himself*], directed by Aleksandra Snezho-Boltskaya, 1968.
Kryl'ia [*Wings*], directed by Larisa Shepit'ko, 1966.
Ladri di biciclette [*Bicycle Thieves*], directed by Vittorio De Sica, 1948.
Lassie Come Home, directed by Fred M. Wilcox, 1943.
The Last Temptation of Christ, directed by Martin Scorsese, 1988.
Letchiki [*Pilots*], directed by Iulii Raizman, 1935.
Letiat zhurvali [*The Cranes Are Flying*], directed by Mikhail Kalatozov, 1957.
Made Manifest, directed by Stan Brakhage, 1980.
The Man Who Shot Liberty Vance, directed by John Ford, 1962.
La marche de l'empereur [*March of the Penguins*], directed by Luc Jacquet, 2005.
Marley and Me, directed by David Frankel, 2008.
The Matrix, directed by the Wachowskis, 1999.
Meat, directed by Frederick Wiseman, 1976.
Meeting Andrei Tarkovsky, directed by Dmitry Tarkovsky, 2008.
Mekhanika golovnogo mozga [*Mechanics of the Brain*], directed by Vsevolod Pudovkin, 1926.
Microcosmos: Le peuple de l'herbe [*Microcosmos*], directed by Claude Nuridsany and Marie Pérennou, 1996.
Mimino, directed by Georgii Daneliia, 1977.
Mne dvadstat' let [*I Am Twenty*], directed by Marlen Khutsiev, 1965.
Mouchette, directed by Robert Bresson, 1967.
Murder Psalm, directed Stan Brakhage, 1980.
Napoléon, directed by Abel Gance, 1927.

National Velvet, directed by Clarence Brown, 1944.
Nénette, directed by Nicholas Philibert, 2010.
Nostalghia, directed by Andrei Tarkovsky, 1983.
Obykonvennyi fashizm [*Ordinary Fascism*], directed by Mikhail Romm, 1961.
Ofret [*The Sacrifice*], directed by Andrei Tarkovsky, 1986.
Oktiabr' [*October*], directed by Sergei Eisenstein, 1927.
Old Yeller, directed by Robert Stevenson, 1957.
One Flew over the Cuckoo's Nest, directed by Miloš Forman, 1975.
Operatsiia "Y" i drugie Prikliucheniia [*Operation Y and Shurik's Other Adventures*], directed by Leonid Gaidai, 1965.
En passion [*The Passion of Anna*], directed by Ingmar Bergman, 1969.
Pat Garrett and Billy the Kid, directed by Sam Peckinpah, 1973.
Persona, directed by Ingmar Bergman, 1966.
Pes Barbos i neobychnyi kross [*Dog Barbos and the Unusual Cross*], directed by Leonid Gaidai, 1961.
Le peuple migrateur [*Winged Migration*], directed by Jacques Perrin, 2001.
Pink Flamingos, directed by John Waters, 1972.
PlayTime, directed by Jacques Tati, 1967.
Pogranichnyi pes [*Border Dog Alyi*], directed by Yuliy Fait, 1980.
Polety vo sne i naiavu [*Flights in Dreams and Reality*], directed by Roman Balian, 1983.
Prikliucheniia Elektronika [*Adventures of an Android*], directed by Konstantin Bromberg, 1980.
The Private Life of a Cat, directed by Maya Deren, 1947.
Proshchanie [*Farewell*], directed by Elem Klimov, 1983.
Psycho, directed by Alfred Hitchcock, 1960.
Rebel without a Cause, directed by Nicholas Rey, 1955.
La règle du jeu [*The Rules of the Game*], directed by Jean Renoir, 1939.
Rescued by Rover, directed by Cecil Hepworth and Lewin Fitzhamon, 1905.
Roger & Me, directed by Michael Moore, 1989.
Le sang des bêtes [*Blood of the Beasts*], directed by George Franju, 1949.
Sans Soleil, directed by Chris Marker, 1983.
Såsom i en spegel [*Through a Glass Darkly*], directed by Ingmar Bergman, 1961.
Sátántangó, directed by Béla Tarr, 1994.
Satyricon, directed by Federico Fellini, 1969.
Seabiscuit, directed by Gary Ross, 2003.
The Searchers, directed by John Ford, 1956.
Shichinin no Samurai [*Seven Samurai*], directed by Akira Kurosawa, 1954.
Siberiada [*Siberiade*], directed by Andrei Konchalovsky, 1978.
Skammen [*Shame*], directed by Ingmar Bergman, 1968.

Sluzhili dva tovarishcha [*Two Comrades Were Serving*], directed by Evgenii Karelov, 1968.
Solenyi pes [*Salty Dog*], directed by Nikolai Koshelev, 1973.
Soliaris [*Solaris*], directed by Andrei Tarkovsky, 1972.
La sortie de l'Usine Lumière à Lyon [*Workers Leaving the Factory*], directed by Louis Lumière, 1895.
Soy Cuba [*I Am Cuba*], directed by Mikhail Kalatozov, 1964.
Stachka [*Strike*], directed by Sergei Eisenstein, 1925.
Stagecoach, directed by John Ford, 1939.
Stalker, directed by Andrei Tarkovsky, 1979.
Star Wars: A New Hope, directed by George Lucas, 1977.
La strada [*The Road*], directed by Federico Fellini, 1954.
Suna no Onna [*Woman in the Dunes*], directed by Hiroshi Teshigahara, 1964.
Susuz yaz [*Dry Summer*], directed by Metin Erksan, 1964.
Svoi sredi chuzhikh, chuzhoi sredi svoikh [*At Home among Strangers, A Stranger among Friends*], directed by Nikita Mikhalkov, 1974.
Sweetgrass, directed by Lucien Castaing-Taylor, 2009.
Tempo di viaggio [*Voyage in Time*], directed by Tonino Guerra and Andrei Tarkovsky, 1983.
The Terminator, directed by James Cameron, 1984.
The Thing, directed by John Carpenter, 1982.
Top Gun, directed by Tony Scott, 1986.
El Topo [*The Mole*], directed by Alejandro Jodorowsky, 1970.
Touch of Evil, directed by Orson Welles, 1958.
Touki Bouki, directed by Djibril Diop Mambéty, 1973.
Tret'ia meshchanskaia [*Bed and Sofa*], directed by Abram Room, 1926.
Troe v lodke (ne schitaia sobaki) [*Three Men in a Boat (To Say Nothing of the Dog)*], directed by Naum Birman, 1979.
2001: A Space Odyssey, directed by Stanley Kubrick, 1968. *Ubiitsy* [*The Killers*], directed by Andrei Tarkovsky, 1956.
Umberto D., directed by Vittorio De Sica, 1955.
Unser täglich Brot [*Our Daily Bread*], directed by Nikolaus Geyrhalter, 2005.
Untitled No. 6, directed by Stan Brakhage, 1975.
Up in the Air, directed by Jason Reitman, 2012.
Valerii Chkalov, directed by Mikhail Kalatozov, 1941.
Vase de Noces [*Wedding Trough*], directed by Thierry Zéno, 1974.
Vertigo, directed by Alfred Hitchcock, 1958.
Viva la Muerte [*Long Live Death*], directed by Fernando Arrabal, 1971.
Voina i mir [*War and Peace*], directed by Sergei Bonderchuk, 1967.
Wake in Fright, directed by Ted Kotcheff, 1971.
Walkabout, directed by Nicolas Roeg, 1971.

War Horse, directed by Steven Spielberg, 2011.
Wavelength, directed by Michael Snow, 1967.
Week-end [*Weekend*], directed by Jean-Luc Godard, 1967.
Where the North Begins, directed by Chester M. Franklin, 1923.
Who Framed Roger Rabbit?, directed by Robert Zemeckis, 1988.
Wilbur Wright und seine Flugmaschine [*Wilbur Wright and His Flying Machine*], directed by Société Générale des Cinématographes Eclipses, 1909.
Window Water Baby Moving, directed by Stan Brakhage, 1959.
The Wizard of Oz, directed by Viktor Fleming, 1939.
Zastava v gorakh [*Frontier Post in the Mountains*], directed by Konstantin Iudin, 1953.
Zerkalo [*Mirror*], directed by Andrei Tarkovsky, 1975.
Znoi [*Heat*], directed by Larisa Shepitko, 1964.
Zvenigora, directed by Oleksandr Dovzhenko, 1929.

BIBLIOGRAPHY

Adorno, Theodor W. *Prisms*. Translated by Shierry Weber Nicholsen and Samuel Weber. MIT Press, 1983.

Aksenova, Alisa. "Zhertvoprinosheniia." *Trud*, May 12, 2005. https://www.trud.ru/article/12-05-2005/87512_zhertvoprinoshenija.html.

Alexander-Garrett, Layla. *Andrei Tarkovsky: The Collector of Dreams*. Glagoslav, 2012.

Alexander-Garrett, Layla. "Never Be Neutral." *Sight and Sound* 7, no. 1 (1997): 23.

Amad, Paula. "From God's-Eye to Camera-Eye: Aerial Photography Post-humanist and Neo-humanist Vision of the World." *History of Photography* 36, no. 1 (2012): 66–86.

Anderson, Nathan. *Shadow Philosophy: Plato's Cave and Cinema*. Routledge, 2014.

"'Andrei Rublev'—Istoriia sozdania fil'ma—Arkhivnye Dokumenty (Chast' 4)." Mosfilm, September 26, 2018. https://www.mosfilm.ru/about/news/sozdanie-filma-andrey-rublev-arkhivnye-dokumenty-chast-4.

"'Andrei Rublev'—Istoriia sozdania fil'ma—Arkhivnye Dokumenty (Chast' 5)." Mosfilm, November 21, 2018. https://www.mosfilm.ru/about/news/sozdanie-filma-andrey-rublev-arkhivnye-dokumenty-chast-5.

"Andrei Tarkovsky Photos." Andrei-Tarkovsky. Accessed December 16, 2024. https://andrei-tarkovsky.com/photos.html.

"Andrei Tarkovsky's American Visit in 1983." YouTube video, July 29, 2017. https://www.youtube.com/watch?v=uHtCIhbWb2Y.

Apostolov, Andrei. "Khronika velikoi nevstrechi: Idiot Andreia Tarkovskogo." *Apparatus: Film, Media, and Digital Cultures in Central and Eastern Europe* 10 (2020). https://www.apparatusjournal.net/index.php/apparatus/article/view/139/502/.

Aristotle. *Politics*. Edited by R. F. Stalley. Translated by Ernest Barker. Oxford University Press, 1995.
Artamonov, A., ed. *Posle Tarkovskogo*. Seans, 2016.
Artaud, Antonin. "The Theatre of Cruelty." In *The Theory of the Modern Stage: An Introduction to Modern Theatre and Drama*, edited by Eric Bentley. Penguin, 1968.
Baker, Steve. *Postmodern Animal*. University of Chicago Press, 2000.
Balász, Béla. *Der Geist des Films*. W. Knapp, 1930.
Banerjee, Anindita. *We Modern People: Science Fiction and the Making of Russian Modernity*. Wesleyan University Press, 2012.
Barceló, Marc. "En la Zona de Oz (Stalker / El mago de Oz)." *Cinetransit*, August 3, 2020. http://cinentransit.com/en-la-zona-de-oz-stalker-el-mago-de-oz/.
Barratt, Andrew. "In the Name of the Father: The Eisenstein Connection in Films by Tarkovsky and Askoldov." In *Eisenstein at 100: A Reconsideration*, edited by Al LaValley. Rutgers University Press, 2001.
Bataille, Georges. *Undercover Surrealism: Georges Bataille and Documents*. Edited by Dawn Ades and Simon Baker. MIT Press, 2006.
Bazin, André. "Death Every Afternoon." Translated by Mark A. Cohen. In *Rites of Realism: Essays on Corporeal Cinema*, edited by Ivone Margulies. Duke University Press, 2003.
Bazin, André. "Les films d'animaux nous révèlent le cinema." *Radio Cinéma Télévision* 285, no. 2–3 (1955): 8.
Bazin, André. *What Is Cinema?* Vol. 1. Translated by Hugh Gray. University of California Press, 2005.
Bellour, Raymond. "Hitchcock—The Animal, Life and Death." In *Animal Life & the Moving Image*, edited by Michael Lawrence and Laura McMahon. British Film Institute, 2015.
Bennett, Bruce. *Cycling and Cinema*. MIT University Press, 2019.
Bennett, Jane. *Vibrant Matter: A Political Ecology of Things*. Duke University Press, 2010.
Bentham, Jeremy. *An Introduction to the Principles of Morals and Legislation*. T. Payne and Son, 1789.
Berdnyk, Luda. "How Sweden Found Out About the Chernobyl Disaster and Alerted the Rest of the World." Swedes in the States, April 25, 2022. https://swedesinthestates.com/how-sweden-found-out-about-chernobyl-and-alerted-the-rest-of-the-world/.
Berger, John. *About Looking*. Vintage, 1980.
Bergman, Jay. "Valerii Chkalov: Soviet Pilot as New Soviet Man." *Journal of Contemporary History* 33, no. 1 (1998): 135–52.
Bergson, Henri. *Laughter: An Essay on the Meaning of the Comic*. Translated by Cloudesley Brereton and Fred Rothwell. Dover Publications, 2005.

Bethea, David M. *The Shape of the Apocalypse in Modern Russian Fiction*. Princeton University Press, 1989.
Bickerton, Emilie. *A Short History of Cahiers Du Cinéma*. Verso, 2009.
Billson, Anne. "Chicken Decapitation and Battered Cats: Hollywood's History of Animal Cruelty." *Guardian*, May 24, 2018. https://www.theguardian.com/film/2018/may/24/chicken-decapitation-battered-cats-hollywood-animal-cruelty.
Bird, Robert. *Andrei Rublev*. British Film Institute, 2004.
Bird, Robert. *Andrei Tarkovsky: Elements of Cinema*. Reaktion, 2008.
Bird, Robert. "The Omens: Tarkovsky, Sacrifice, Cancer." *Apparatus: Film, Media, and Digital Cultures in Central and Eastern Europe* 10 (2020). https://www.apparatusjournal.net/index.php/apparatus/article/view/225/488.
Bird, Robert. "Robert Bird on *Andrei Rublev*." Criterion Channel, 2018. https://www.criterionchannel.com/videos/robert-bird-on-andrei-rublev.
Blasco, Gonzalo. "An Interview with Marina Tarkovskaya and Alexander Gordon." *Nostalghia*, November 10, 2003. http://www.nostalghia.com/TheTopics/Marina_and_Alexandr.html.
Bloom, Harold. *The Anxiety of Influence: A Theory of Poetry*. Oxford University Press, 1997.
Boas, George. "Theriophily." In *Dictionary of the History of Ideas: Studies of Selected Pivotal Ideas*, vol. 4, edited by Philip P. Wiener. Charles Scribner's Sons, 1973.
Bohlinger, Vincent. "'The East Is a Delicate Matter': White Sun of the Desert and the Soviet Western." In *(Re)Locating the Frontier: International Western Films*, edited by Cynthia Miller and A. Bowdoin Van Riper. Scarecrow Press, 2014.
Boisseron, Bénédicte. *Afro-Dog: Blackness and the Animal Question*. Columbia University Press, 2018.
Boldyrev, Nikolai. *Stalker, ili Trudy i dni Andreia Tarkovskogo*. Ural, 2002.
Bordwell, David. *The Cinema of Eisenstein*. Harvard University Press, 1993.
Bordwell, David. *The Way Hollywood Tells It: Story and Style in Modern Movies*. University of California Press, 2006.
Bould, Mark. *Solaris*. British Film Institute, 2014.
Bousé, Derek. *Wildlife Films*. University of Pennsylvania Press, 2000.
Boyadzhieva, Lyudmila. *Andrei Tarkovsky: A Life on the Cross*. Translated by Christopher Culver. Glagoslav, 2014.
Boym, Svetlana. *The Future of Nostalgia*. Basic, 2001.
Brakhage, Stan. "Brakhage Meets Tarkovsky." *Chicago Review* 47, no. 4 (2001): 42–46.
Braun, Marta. *Picturing Time: The Work of Etienne-Jules Marey, 1830–1904*. University of Chicago Press, 1992.
Brooks, Peter. "Freud's Masterplot." *Yale French Studies* 55/56 (1977): 280–300.
Bullock, Marcus. "Watching Eyes, Seeing Dreams, Knowing Lives." In *Representing Animals*, edited by Nigel Rothfels. Indiana University Press, 2002.

Bullock, Philip. "The Musical Imagination of Andrei Platonov." *Slavonica* 10, no. 1 (2004): 41–60.
Burt, Johnathan. *Animals in Film*. Reaktion, 2002.
Burt, Johnathan. "The Illumination of the Animal Kingdom: The Role of Light and Electricity in Animal Representation." *Society and Animals* 9, no. 3 (2001): 203–28.
Burt, Johnathan. "John Berger's 'Why Look at Animals?': A Close Reading." *Worldviews* 9, no. 2 (2005): 203–18.
Calarco, Matthew. *Animal Studies: The Key Concepts*. Routledge, 2021.
Calarco, Matthew. *The Boundaries of Human Nature: The Philosophical Animal from Plato to Haraway*. Columbia University Press, 2022.
Calarco, Matthew. *Zoographies: The Question of the Animal from Heidegger to Derrida*. Columbia University Press, 2008.
Cardullo, Bert. "Art-House Cinema, Avant-Garde Film, and Dramatic Modernism." *Journal of Aesthetic Education* 45, no. 2 (2011): 1–16.
Carson, Rachel. *Silent Spring*. Mariner, 2002.
Cartwright, Lisa. *Screening the Body: Tracing Medicine's Visual Culture*. University of Minnesota Press, 1995.
Celenza, Christopher S. "Humanism and the Classical Tradition." *Annali d'Italianistica* 26 (2008): 25–49.
Chernyshova, Natalya. *Soviet Consumer Culture in the Brezhnev Era*. Routledge, 2013.
Chiaramonte, Giovanni, and Andrey A. Tarkovsky, eds. *Instant Light: Tarkovsky Polaroids*. Thames & Hudson, 2006.
Chris, Cynthia. *Watching Wildlife*. University of Minnesota Press, 2006.
Chudakova, Marietta. "Vecher, posviashchennyi 120-letiiu so dnia rozhdeniia O.E. Mandel'shtama." Muzei Mikhaila Bulgakova. Accessed December 17, 2024. https://bulgakovmuseum.ru/mandelstam/.
Chudinov, A. P. "Zametki o ritoricheskom masterstve I. V. Stalina." In *Khudozhestvennyi tekst: struktura, semantika, pragmatika*, edited by L. G. Babenko and Iu. V. Kazarin. Izd-vo Ural, 1997.
"Codex on the Flight of Birds." Library of Congress. Accessed December 17, 2024. https://www.loc.gov/item/2021668201.
Cole, Jake. "Oeuvre: Tarkovsky: The Sacrifice." *Spectrum Culture*, February 27, 2020. https://spectrumculture.com/2020/02/27/oeuvre-tarkovsky-the-sacrifice/.
Cook, Pam. "For a New French Cinema: The Politique des Auteurs." In *The Cinema Book*, edited by Pam Cook. British Film Institute, 2007.
Cordeiro-Rodrigues, Luís, and Les Mitchell, eds. *Animals, Race, and Multiculturalism*. Palgrave MacMillan, 2018.

Costlow, Jane. *Heart-Pine Russia: Walking and Writing the Nineteenth-Century Forest*. Cornell University Press, 2013.

Costlow, Jane, and Amy Nelson. *Other Animals: Beyond the Human in Russian Culture and History*. University of Pittsburgh Press, 2009.

Creed, Barbara. "Animal Deaths on Screen: Film and Ethics." *Relations* 2, no. 1 (2014): 15–31.

Creed, Barbara. *The Monstrous-Feminine: Film Feminism, Psychoanalysis*. Routledge, 1993.

Dax, Max. "'This Is Not a Coincidence': Max Dax Talks to Andrey A. Tarkovsky." *Electronic Beats*, October 29, 2013. https://www.electronicbeats.net/this-is-not-a-coincidence-max-dax-talks-to-andrey-a-tarkovsky/.

Dederer, Claire. *Monsters: A Fan's Dilemma*. Knopf, 2023.

Dederer, Claire. "What Do We Do with the Art of Monstrous Men?" *Paris Review*, November 20, 2017. https://www.theparisreview.org/blog/2017/11/20/art-monstrous-men/.

Deleuze, Gilles. *Cinema 1: The Movement-Image*. Translated by Hugh Tomlinson and Barbara Habberjam. University of Minnesota Press, 1986.

Deleuze, Gilles. *Cinema 2: The Time Image*. Translated by Hugh Tomlinson and Robert Galeta. Continuum, 2009.

Deleuze, Gilles. "On *The Movement Image*." In *Negotiations, 1972–1990*, translated by Martin Joughin. Columbia University Press, 1995.

Deleuze, Gilles. "On *The Time Image*." In *Negotiations, 1972–1990*, translated by Martin Joughin. Columbia University Press, 1995.

Deleuze, Gilles, and Félix Gauttari. *A Thousand Plateaus: Capitalism and Schizophrenia*. Translated by Brian Massumi. Continuum, 2004.

De Luca, Raymond. "Tarkovsky's Cine-Safari: Animal Bodies in the Cinema of Andrei Tarkovsky." *Slavic and East European Journal* 64, no. 3 (2020): 511–36.

De Luca, Raymond. "Tarkovsky Screens Hemingway: Andrei Tarkovsky's First Student Film, *The Killers* (1956)." *Studies in Russian and Soviet Cinema* 13, no. 2 (2019): 172–81.

De Luca, Tiago. "Natural Views: Animals, Contingency, and Death in Carlos Reygadas's *Japón* and Lisandro Alonso's *Los Muertos*." In *Slow Cinema*, edited by Tiago de Luca and Nuno Barradas Jorge. Edinburgh University Press, 2016.

De Luca, Tiago, and Nuno Barradas Jorge, eds. *Slow Cinema*. Edinburgh University Press, 2015.

Derrida, Jacques. *The Animal That Therefore I Am*. Edited by Marie-Luise Mallet. Translated by David Wills. Fordham University Press, 2008.

Derrida, Jacques. "'Eating Well,' or the Calculation of the Subject: An Interview with Jacques Derrida." In *Who Comes After the Subject?*, edited by Eduardo Cadava, Peter Connor, and Jean-Luc Nancy. Routledge, 1991.

Derrida, Jacques. "Force of Law: The 'Mystical Foundation of Authority.'" In *Deconstruction and the Possibility of Justice*, edited by Drucilla Cornell, Michel Rosenfeld, and David Gray Carlson. Routledge, 1992.
Derrida, Jacques. "How to Avoid Speaking Denials?" In *Derrida and Negative Theology*, edited by Harold Coward and Toby Foshay. State University of New York Press, 1992.
Derrida, Jacques. *Memoires for Paul De Man*. Translated by Cecile Lindsay, Johnathan Culler, Eduardo Cadava, and Peggy Kamuf. Columbia University Press, 1989.
Derrida, Jacques. "Violence Against Animals." Translated by Jeff Fort. In *For What Tomorrow?*, edited by Jacques Derrida and Elisabeth Roudinesco. Stanford University Press, 2004.
Descartes, René. *A Discourse on Method of Correctly Conducting One's Reason and Seeking Truth in the Sciences*. Translated by Ian Mclean. Oxford University Press, 2006.
Doane, Mary Anne. *The Emergence of Cinematic Time: Modernity, Contingency, the Archive*. Harvard University Press, 2002.
Donoho, Emily. "Why Do Horses Roll?" *Horse & Hound*, November 2, 2021. https://www.horseandhound.co.uk/features/why-do-horses-roll-657819.
Dostoevsky, Fyodor. *Crime and Punishment*. Translated by Richard Pevear and Larissa Volokhonsky. Vintage Classics, 1993.
Dostoevsky, Fyodor. *Notes from Underground*. Translated by Richard Pevear and Larissa Volokhonsky. Vintage Classics, 1994.
Dreher, Rod. "The Andrei Rublev Option." *American Conservative*, December 9, 2021. https://www.theamericanconservative.com/the-andrei-rublev-option-michael-anton/.
Dreher, Rod. "The Miracle of Montesiepi." *American Conservative*, September 10, 2021. https://www.theamericanconservative.com/st-galgano-miracle-of-montesiepi-italy-nostalghia/.
Dreher, Rod. "Tarkovsky, Shaw, and the White Birds." *American Conservative*, August 31, 2022. https://www.theamericanconservative.com/tarkovsky-shaw-and-the-white-birds/.
Dumančić, Marko. *Men Out of Focus: The Soviet Masculinity Crisis in the Long Sixties*. Toronto University Press, 2021.
Dunne, Nathan, ed. *Tarkovsky*. Black Dog, 2008.
Dyer, Geoff. *Zona: A Book About a Film About a Journey to a Room*. Vintage, 2012.
Ebert, Roger. "Solaris." *Roger Ebert*, January 19, 2003. https://www.rogerebert.com/reviews/great-movie-solaris-1972.
"Eduard Limonov (fotografii)." *LiveJournal*, October 24, 2010. https://ed-limonov.livejournal.com/415666.html?.
Efrid, Robert. *Andrei Tarkovsky: Ivan's Childhood*. Intellect, 2021.

Efrid, Robert. "Deleuze on Tarkovsky: The Crystal-Image of Time in 'Steamroller and Violin.'" *Slavic and East European Journal* 58, no. 2 (2014): 237–54.

Efrid, Robert. "The Holy Fool in Late Tarkovsky." *Journal of Religion and Film* 18, no. 1 (2014): 86–93.

Eisenstein, Sergei. *Sergei Eisenstein, 1922–1934*. Edited and translated by Richard Taylor. I. B. Tauris, 2010.

Elkins, Kathleen Gallagher. *Mary, Mother of Martyrs: How Motherhood Became Self-Sacrifice in Early Christianity*. Wipf and Stock, 2020.

Elsaesser, Thomas. "The Ethics of Appropriation: Found Footage Between Archive and Internet." *Found Footage Magazine* 1 (2015): 30–37.

Elsaesser, Thomas. *European Cinema and Continental Philosophy: Film as Thought Experiment*. Bloomsbury Academic, 2018.

Elsaesser, Thomas, and Malte Hagener. *Film Theory: An Introduction Through the Senses*. Routledge, 2015.

Epstein, Mikhail. *Priroda, mir, tanik vselennoi*. Vysshaia shkola, 1990.

Evlampiev, Igor. *Khudozhestvennaya filosofia Andreia Tarkovskogo*. Aleteia, 2001.

Fainberg, Dina, and Artemy M. Kalinovsky, eds. *Reconsidering Stagnation in the Brezhnev Era: Ideology and Exchange*. Lexington Books, 2016.

Fara, Patricia. "An Attractive Therapy: Animal Magnetism in Eighteenth-Century England." *History of Science* 33, no. 2 (1995): 127–77.

Farley, Lloyd. "The Horrific True Story Behind the 'No Animals Were Harmed' Disclaimer." *Collider*, May 3, 2023. https://collider.com/no-animals-were-harmed-disclaimer-american-humane-history/.

"The Fasting Rules in the Orthodox Church." *Pravmir*, May 26, 2006. https://www.pravmir.com/the-fasting-rules-in-the-orthodox-church/.

Ferguson, Kevin L. "Aviation Cinema." *Criticism* 57, no. 2 (2015): 309–31.

Fitzgerald, Amy J. "A Social History of the Slaughterhouse: From Inception to Contemporary Implications." *Human Ecology Review* 17, no. 1 (2010): 58–69.

"5 Porod sobak, kotorye byli zhutko populiarny v SSSR." *Life*, December 15, 2022. https://life.ru/p/1544067.

Flaim, Denise. "German Shepherd Dog History: Origins of the Working Breed." American Kennel Club, May 15, 2024. https://www.akc.org/expert-advice/dog-breeds/german-shepherd-dog-history/.

Fomina, Nelli. *Costumes for the Films of Andrei Tarkovsky*. Cygnnet, 2015.

Forrest, Susanna. "The Troubled History of Horse Meat in America." *Atlantic*, June 8, 2017. https://www.theatlantic.com/technology/archive/2017/06/horse-meat/529665/.

Foster, David. "Where Flowers Bloom but Have No Scent: The Cinematic Space of the Zone in Andrei Tarkovsky's *Stalker*." *Studies in Russian and Soviet Cinema* 4, no. 3 (2010): 307–20.

Foucault, Michel. *The Order of Things: An Archaeology of the Human Sciences*. Routledge, 2002.
Francione, Gary L. *Introduction to Animal Rights: Your Child or the Dog?* Temple University Press, 2000.
Freud, Sigmund. "Analysis of a Phobia in a Five-Year-Old Boy." In *The "Wolfman" and Other Cases*, translated by Louise Adey Huish. Penguin, 2003.
Freud, Sigmund. "A Difficulty in the Path of Psycho-analysis." In *The Standard Edition of the Complete Psychological Works of Sigmund Freud*, vol. XVII (1917), edited by Alix Strachey and Alan Tyson. Vintage, 2001.
Freud, Sigmund. "Mourning and Melancholia." In *The Standard Edition of the Complete Psychological Works of Sigmund Freud*, vol. XIV (1914–16), edited by James Strachey. Hogarth Press, 1957.
Freud, Sigmund. *Three Essays on the Theory of Sexuality*. Edited and translated by James Strachey. Basic, 1975.
Freud, Sigmund, and Joseph Breuer. *Studies in Hysteria*. Penguin Classics, 2004.
Friedberg, Anne. "Der vierbeinige Andere und die Projektion im Kino." *Frauen und Film* 47 (1989): 4–13.
Fudge, Erica. *Animal*. Reaktion, 2003.
Fudge, Erica. *Pets*. Acumen, 2008.
Fürholzer, Katharina. "Living Oblivion: Poetic Narratives of Dementia and Fatherhood in Pia Tafdrup's *Tarkovsky's Horses*." In *Ageing Masculinities, Alzheimer's and Dementia Narratives*, edited by Heike Hartung, Rüdiger Kunow, and Matthew Sweney. Bloomsbury Academic, 2022.
Gaita, Raimond. *The Philosopher's Dog: Friendships with Animals*. Random House, 2005.
Garber, Marjorie. *Dog Love*. Simon and Schuster, 1996.
"Gilles Deleuze." *Stanford Encyclopedia of Philosophy*. Accessed December 12, 2024. https://plato.stanford.edu/entries/deleuze/.
Giralt, Gabriel F. "Andrei Tarkovsky's Adaptation of Motifs Embedded in Leonardo da Vinci's 'The Adoration of the Magi.'" *Canadian Journal of Film Studies* 14, no. 2 (2005): 71–83.
Girard, René. *Violence and the Sacred*. Translated by Patrick Gregory. Continuum, 2005.
Golstein, Vladimir. "The Energy of Anxiety." In *Tarkovsky*, edited by Nathan Dunne. Black Dog, 2008.
Gorelick, Nathan. "Life in Excess: Insurrection and Expenditure in Antonin Artaud's Theatre of Cruelty." *Discourses* 33, no. 2 (2011): 263–79.
Gorfinkel, Elena. "Weariness, Waiting: Endurance and Art Cinema's Tired Bodies." *Discourse* 34, no. 2 (2012): 311–47.
"Goriashchaia korova—Tarkovskii snimaet 'Andrei Rublev' (1965)." YouTube video, April 4, 2019. https://www.youtube.com/watch?v=HPSo_Mzdm2E.

Gornykh, Andrei. "*Trava-Travlya-Trata*: Tarkovsky's Psychobiography *à la Lettre*." In *ReFocus: The Films of Andrei Tarkovsky*, edited by Sergey Toymentsev. University of Edinburgh Press, 2021.
Goscilo, Helen. "Fraught Filiation: Andrei Tarkovsky's Transformations of Personal Trauma." In *Cinepaternity: Fathers and Sons in Soviet and Post-Soviet Film*, edited by Goscilo and Yana Hashamova. Indiana University Press, 2010.
Goulding, Daniel J., ed. *Five Filmmakers: Tarkovsky, Forman, Polanski, Szabo, Makavejev*. Indiana University Press, 1994.
"The Greatest Films of All Time . . . in 1982." British Film Institute, June 17, 2021. https://www.bfi.org.uk/sight-and-sound/polls/greatest-films-all-time/1982.
Green, Peter. *Andrei Tarkovsky: The Winding Quest*. Palgrave Macmillan, 1993.
Greene, Ann Norton. *Horses at Work: Harnessing Power in Industrial America*. Harvard University Press, 2008.
Gruen, Lori, ed. *Critical Terms for Animal Studies*. University of Chicago Press, 2018.
Guichet, Jean-Luc. "Animality and Anthropology in Jean-Jacques Rousseau." In *A Cultural History of Animals in the Age of Enlightenment*, edited by Matthew Senior. Berg, 2007.
Gunning, Tom. "An Aesthetic of Astonishment: Early Film and the (In)Credulous Spectator." *Art and Text* 34 (1989): 114–33.
Gura, A. V. *Simvolika zhivotnykh v slavianskoi narodnoi traditsii*. Izd-vo Indrik, 1997.
Hall, Cynthia A. "Before the Apocalypse: German Prints and Illustrated Books, 1450–1500." *Harvard University Art Museums Bulletin* 4, no. 2 (1996): 8–29.
Haraway, Donna. *The Companion Species Manifesto: Dogs, People, and Significant Others*. Prickly Paradigm Press, 2003.
Haraway, Donna. "A Manifesto for Cyborgs: Science, Technology, and Socialist Feminism in the 1980s." In *Simians, Cyborgs, and Women: The Reinvention of Nature*, edited by Donna Jeanne Haraway. Routledge, 1990.
Haraway, Donna. *When Species Meet*. University of Minnesota Press, 2007.
Harte, Tim, and Marina Rojavin, eds. *Soviet Films of the 1970s and Early 1980s: Conformity and Non-conformity amidst Stagnation Decay*. Routledge, 2021.
Harvey, Peter. *An Introduction to Buddhism: Teachings, History, and Practices*. Cambridge University Press, 2013.
"Heaven's Gate." *Numbers*. Accessed December 11, 2024. https://www.the-numbers.com/movie/Heavens-Gate#tab=summary.
Heidegger, Martin. *Being and Time*. Translated by John Macquarrie and Edward Robinson. Harper and Row, 1962.
Heidegger, Martin. *The Fundamental Concepts of Metaphysics: World, Finitude, Solitude*. Translated by William McNeill and Nicholas Walker. Indiana University Press, 1995.
Heidegger, Martin. "Letter on Humanism." Translated by Frank A. Capuzzi. In *Pathmarks*, edited by Will McNeill. Cambridge University Press, 1998.

Heidegger, Martin. *Poetry, Language, Thought*. Translated by Albert Hofstadter. Harper & Row, 1971.
Hill, Alexander. "Deep-Rooted Russian Fear of the West Has Fueled Putin's Invasion of Ukraine." *Conversation*, March 3, 2022. https://theconversation.com/deep-rooted-russian-fear-of-the-west-has-fuelled-putins-invasion-of-ukraine-178351.
Hoberman, J. *Vulgar Modernism: Writings on Movies and Other Media*. Temple University Press, 1991.
Hobsbawm, Eric. *The Age of Capital, 1848–1875*. Vintage, 1996.
Hobsbawm, Eric. *The Age of Extremes: The Short Twentieth Century, 1914–1991*. Abacus, 1994.
Hodgson, Katharine. "The Poetry of Rudyard Kipling in Soviet Russia." *Modern Language Review* 93, no. 4 (1998): 1058–71.
Holliday, Kate. "'Actors Are Cattle!' Says Director Alfred Hitchcock." *Hollywood Magazine* 30, no. 9 (1941): 19, 68.
"'The Horseless Age,' Volume 1, November 1895 to October 1896." The Henry Ford. Accessed December 16, 2024. https://www.thehenryford.org/collections-and-research/digital-collections/artifact/83950/.
Hunt, Kristin. "The End of American Film Censorship." *JSTOR Daily*, February 28, 2018. https://daily.jstor.org/end-american-film-censorship/.
Hunter-Blair, Kitty. *Poetry and Film: Artistic Kinship between Arsenii and Andrei Tarkovsky*. Tate, 2015.
Ionesco, Eugène. *Antidotes*. Gallimard, 1977.
Iusov, Vadim. "Zhivotnye na s'emkakh 'Andreia Rubleva.'" *Bul'var Gordona* 14, no. 362 (2012). https://www.bulvar.com.ua/gazeta/archive/s14_65328/7423.html.
Jaffe, Ira. *Slow Movies: Countering the Cinema of Action*. Wallflower Press, 2014.
Jameson, Frederick. *The Geopolitical Aesthetic: Cinema and Space in the World System*. Indiana University Press, 1992.
Jamieson, Lee. *Antonin Artaud: From Theory to Practice*. Greenwich Exchange, 2007.
Jenks, Andrew. "Conquering Space: The Cult of Yuri Gagarin." In *Soviet and Post-Soviet Identities*, edited by Mark Bassin and Catriona Kelly. Cambridge University Press, 2010.
Johns, Catherine. *Horses: History, Myth, Art*. Harvard University Press, 2006.
Johnson, Vida T., and Graham Petrie. *The Films of Andrei Tarkovsky: A Visual Fugue*. Indiana University Press, 1994.
Jones, Robert Lee. "Stalking the Sublime: Nature and Affect in Andrei Tarkovsky's *Stalker*." In *The Cinematic Sublime*, edited by Nathan Carroll. Intellect, 2020.
Jónsson, Gunnlaugur Á., and Thorkell Á. Óttarsson, eds. *Through the Mirror: Reflections on the Films of Andrei Tarkovsky*. Cambridge Scholars Press, 2006.

Josephson, Paul, Nicolai Dronin, Ruben Mnatsakanian, Aleh Cherp, Dmitry Efremenko, and Vladislav Larin. *An Environmental History of Russia*. Cambridge University Press, 2013.

Jung, Carl. *The Archetypes and The Collective Unconscious* (Collected Works of C.G. Jung), vol. 9, pt. 1. Princeton University Press, 1981.

Jung, Carl. "Concerning Rebirth." Translated by R. F. C. Hull. In *The Collected Works of C. G. Jung*, vol. 9, edited by Herbert Read, Michael Fordham, and Gerhard Adler. Princeton University Press, 1969.

Kahn, Andrew, Mark Lipovetsky, Irina Reyfman, and Stephanie Sandler. *A History of Russian Literature*. Oxford University Press, 2018.

Kalof, Linda. "Introduction: Ancient Animals." In *A Cultural History of Animal in Antiquity*, edited by Linda Kalof. Berg, 2007.

Kamm, Henry. "Soviet Director Asks Refuge, Citing Restraints on Work." *New York Times*, July 11, 1984. https://www.nytimes.com/1984/07/11/arts/soviet-director-asks-refuge-citing-restraints-on-work.html.

Kämpf, Christian. "Beethoven's Music Gone Astray." *Deutsches Historisches Museum*, December 17, 2020. https://www.dhm.de/blog/2020/12/17/beethovens-music-gone-astray/.

Kane, Eubulus. "Sublime Slapstick: The Divine Comedy of Andrei Tarkovsky." *Medium* (March 5, 2024). https://medium.com/@EubulusKane/sublime-slapstick-the-mistakes-of-a-maestro-c66becda1f86.

Kant, Immanuel. *Critique of Judgement*. Edited by Nicholas Walker. Translated by James Creed Meredith. Oxford University Press, 2007.

Kemmerer, Lisa. *Animals and World Religion*. Oxford University Press, 2011.

Kete, Kathleen. *The Beast in the Boudoir: Pet Keeping in Nineteenth-Century Paris*. University of California Press, 1994.

Kets de Vries, Manfred F. R. "Are You a Victim of the Victim Syndrome?" *Organizational Dynamics* 43, no. 2 (2014): 130–37.

"Khrushchev's Secret Speech, 'On the Cult of Personality and Its Consequences,' Delivered at the Twentieth Party Congress of the Communist Party of the Soviet Union." Wilson Center. Accessed December 12, 2024. https://digitalarchive.wilsoncenter.org/document/khrushchevs-secret-speech-cult-personality-and-its-consequences-delivered-twentieth-party.

Kireeva, Vasilisa. "Deputat Burliaev. Prishlo vremia zapreshchat' v Rossii satanizm." *Parlamentskaia gazeta*, June 24, 2024. https://www.pnp.ru/politics/deputat-burlyaev-prishlo-vremya-zapreshhat-v-rossii-satanizm.html.

Klein, Patricia. "Protecting Animals in Films: Humane Group Credited with Drastically Decreasing Cruelty." *Los Angeles Times*, January 11, 1987. https://www.latimes.com/archives/la-xpm-1987-01-11-me-4007-story.html.

Kojève, Alexandre. *Introduction to the Reading of Hegel: Lectures on the Phenomenology of Spirit*. Edited by Alan Bloom. Translated by James H. Nichols Jr. Cornell University Press, 1969.

Komaromi, Ann. "The Material Existence of Soviet Samizdat." *Slavic Review* 63, no. 3 (2004): 597–618.

Kosinova, Marina, and Valerii Fomin. *Kak Sniat' Shedevr: Istoriia sozdaniia fil'mov Andreia Tarkovskogo, Sniatykh v SSSR*. Kanon+, 2021.

Kozin, Alexander. *Andrei Tarkovsky's Mythopoetics*. Paideia, 2020.

Kozlov, Denis, and Elenory Gilburt, eds. *The Thaw: Soviet Society and Culture During the 1950s and 1960s*. University of Toronto Press, 2013.

Kuniaev, Stanislav. *Moi pechal'nye pobedy*. Algoritm, 2007.

Kutik, Ilya, and Reginald Gibbons. "The Poet Who Survived Stalin's Poems." *Literary Hub*, August 21, 2018. https://lithub.com/the-poet-who-survived-stalins-poems/.

Kwok, Roberta. "When Parenting Goes Cuckoo." *ScienceNewsExplores*, April 18, 2019. https://www.snexplores.org/article/bird-fish-insect-parenting-cuckoo-brood-parasite.

LaFrance, Adrienne. "How the Bicycle Paved the Way for Women's Rights." *Atlantic*, January 6, 2014. https://www.theatlantic.com/technology/archive/2014/06/the-technology-craze-of-the-1890s-that-forever-changed-womens-rights/373535/.

Lane, Melissa. "Thoreau and Rousseau: Nature as Utopia." In *A Political Companion to Henry David Thoreau*, edited by Jack Turner. University of Kentucky Press, 2010.

Lawrence, Michael. "Haneke's Stable: The Death of an Animal and the Figuration of the Human." In *On Michael Haneke*, edited by Brian Price, John David Rhodes, Scott Durham, and Christophe Kone. Wayne State University Press, 2010.

Lawrence, Michael. "Muybridgean Motion/Materialist Film: Malcolm Le Grice's *Berlin Horse*." In *Animal Life & The Moving Image*, edited by Michael Lawrence and Linda McMahon. British Film Institute, 2015.

Lawrence, Michael, and Linda McMahon, eds. *Animal Life & the Moving Image*. British Film Institute, 2015.

Lawton, Anna. "Art and Religion in the Films of Andrei Tarkovskii." In *Christianity and the Arts in Russia*, edited by William C. Brumfield and Milos M. Velimirovic. Cambridge University Press, 1991.

Lears, Jackson. "A Matter of Taste: Corporate Cultural Hegemony in a Mass Consumption Society." In *Recast America: Culture and Politics in the Cold War*, edited by Lary May. University of Chicago Press, 1989.

Le Fanu, Mark. *The Cinema of Andrei Tarkovsky*. British Film Institute, 1987.

"Leksicheskoe znachenie clova dakat'." Tolkovye onlain-slovari russkogo iazyka. Accessed December 15, 2024. https://lexicography.online/explanatory/д/дакать.

Lemm, Vanessa. *Nietzsche's Animal Philosophy: Culture, Politics, and the Animality of the Human Being*. Fordham University Press, 2009.

Lenski, Richard C. H. *The Interpretation of St. John's Revelation*. Augsburg Fortress, 2008.
Lévi-Strauss, Claude. "The Disappearance of Man." *New York Review*, July 28, 1966. https://www.nybooks.com/articles/1966/07/28/the-disappearance-of-man/.
Lévi-Strauss, Claude. *The Savage Mind*. University of Chicago Press, 1966.
Levshakova, Ol'ga. "Angely-khraniteli: O posikovo-spasatel'noi sluzhbe." *Drug: Zhurnal dlia liubitelei sobak* 7, no. 8 (2001): 42–45.
Lewis, Philippa. "Peasant Nostalgia in Contemporary Russian Literature." *Soviet Studies* 28, no. 4 (1976): 548–69.
Lim, Song Hwee. *Tsai Ming-liang and a Cinema of Slowness*. University of Hawai'i Press, 2014.
Lippit, Akira Mizuta. *Atomic Light (Shadow Optics)*. University of Minnesota Press, 2005.
Lippit, Akira Mizuta. "The Death of an Animal." *Film Quarterly* 56, no. 1 (2002): 9–22.
Lippit, Akira Mizuta. *Electric Animal: Toward a Rhetoric of Wildlife*. University of Minnesota Press, 2000.
Long, Christopher P. "Who Let the Dogs Out? Tracking the Philosophical Life Among the Wolves and Dogs of the Republic." In *Plato's Animals: Gadflies, Horses, Swans, and Other Philosophical Beasts*, edited by Jeremy Bell and Michael Nass. Indiana University Press, 2015.
Loughlin, Gerard. "Tarkovsky's Trees." In *Tarkovsky*, edited by Nathan Dunne. Black Dog, 2008.
Lovell, Stephen. "Publishing and the Book Trade in the Post-Stalin Era: A Case-Study of the Commodification of Culture." *Europe-Asia Studies* 50, no. 4 (1998): 679–98.
Luchenko, Ksenia. "Sacrificing Art for War: The Handover of Russia's Trinity Icon." *Carnegie Politika*, June 9, 2023. https://carnegieendowment.org/russia-eurasia/politika/2023/05/sacrificing-art-for-war-the-handover-of-russias-trinity-icon?lang=en.
Lyotard, Jean-François. "The Inarticulate, or the Differend Itself." Lecture, Whitney Humanities Center, Yale University, 1992.
Ma, Ling. *Severance*. Farrar, Straus and Young, 2018.
MacGillivray, James. "Andrei Tarkovsky's *Madonna Del Parto*." *Canadian Journal of Film Studies* 11, no. 2 (2002): 82–99.
MacKay, Marina. "World War II, The Welfare State, and Postwar 'Humanism.'" In *The Cambridge Companion to the Twentieth-Century English Novel*, edited by Robert L. Caserio. Cambridge University Press, 2009.
Madson, Ryan. "Zones: Post-industrial Aesthetics and Environments after *Stalker*." *Offscreen* 27, no. 3–5 (2023). https://offscreen.com/view/zones-post-industrial-aesthetics-and-environments-after-stalker.
Malamud, Randy. *An Introduction to Animals and Visual Culture*. Palgrave Macmillan, 2012.

Malik, Kenan. "Humanism, Antihumanism, and the Radical Tradition." *Pandemonium*, 2012. https://kenanmalik.com/2012/11/06/humanism-antihumanism-and-the-radical-tradition/.

Mandušić, Zdenko. "The Truth of Direct Observation: *Andrei Rublev* and the Documentary Style of Soviet Cinema in the 1960s." In *ReFocus: The Films of Andrei Tarkovsky*, edited by Sergey Toymentsev. University of Edinburgh Press, 2021.

Marks, Johnathan. "Who Lost Nature? Rousseau and Rousseauism." *Polity* 34, no. 3 (2002): 479–502.

Marks, Laura U. *Touch: Sensuous Theory and Multisensory Media*. University of Minnesota Press, 2002.

Martín, Pablo De Damborenea, Rubén Bermejo-Poza, and Jesús De la Fuente Vázquez. "Animal Protection in Filming in the Context of Spain." *Animals* 13, no. 7 (2023). https://www.mdpi.com/2076-2615/13/7/1144.

Martin, Sean. *Andrei Tarkovsky*. Oldcastle, 2011.

Martin, Sean. "The Stilyaga from Siberia: Tarkovsky's VGIK Films Reconsidered." In *Tarkovski: Eterno Retorno*, edited by Philipe Ratton, Matheus Pereira, and Bruno Hilario. Fandação Clóvis Salgado, 2017.

Mascaró, Juan, trans. *The Dhammapada: The Path of Perfection*. Penguin, 1973.

Masing-Delic, Irene. *Abolishing Death: A Salvation Myth of Russian Twentieth-Century Literature*. Stanford University Press, 1992.

McCarthy, Susan. "Hollywood's Long History of Animal Cruelty." Salon, April 2, 2012. https://www.salon.com/2012/04/02/hollywoods_long_history_of_animal_cruelty/.

McCarthy, Susan, and Jeffrey Moussaieff Masson. *When Elephants Weep: The Emotional Lives of Animals*. Random House, 1996.

McHugh, Susan. *Dog*. Reaktion, 2004.

McLean, Adrienne L. "Introduction: Wonder Dogs." In *Cinematic Canines*, edited by Adrienne L. McLean. Rutgers University Press, 2014.

McLendon, Michael Locke. *The Psychology of Inequality: Rousseau's 'Amour Propre.'* University of Pennsylvania Press, 2018.

McMahon, Laura. *Animal Worlds: Film, Philosophy, Time*. Edinburgh University Press, 2019.

McMahon, Laura. "Screening Pigs: Visibility, Materiality, and the Production of Species." In *Animal Life & the Moving Image*, edited by Michael Lawrence and Laura McMahon. British Film Institute, 2015.

McSweeney, Terence. *Beyond the Frame: The Films and Film Theory of Andrei Tarkovsky*. Aporetic Press, 2015.

Meier, Allison C. "Why Are Cities Filled with Metal Men on Horseback?" *JSTOR Daily*, September 16, 2016. https://daily.jstor.org/why-are-cities-filled-with-metal-men-on-horseback/.

Melzer, Arthur. *The Natural Goodness of Man: On the System of Rousseau's Thought.* Chicago University Press, 1990.
Menard, David George. "A Deleuzian Analysis of Tarkovsky's Theory of Time-Pressure, Part 1." *Offscreen* 7, no. 8 (2003). https://offscreen.com/view/tarkovsky1.
Menzel, Birgit. "Tarkovsky in Berlin." In *Tarkovsky*, edited by Nathan Dunne. Black Dog, 2008.
Midgley, Mary. "Beasts, Brutes, and Monsters." In *What Is an Animal?*, edited by Tim Ingold. Routledge, 1994.
Mitchum, Petrine Day. *Hollywood Hoofbeats: The Fascinating Story of Horses in Movies and Television.* CompanionHouse, 2014.
Modleski, Tania. "The Master's Dollhouse: *Rear Window.*" In *Film Theory & Criticism*, edited by Leo Braudy and Marshall Cohen. Oxford University Press, 2016.
Moliterno, Gino. "Zarathustra's Gift in Tarkovsky's *The Sacrifice.*" *Screening the Past*, March 1, 2001. http://www.screeningthepast.com/issue-12-first-release/zarathustras-gift-in-tarkovskys%C2%Aothe-sacrifice/.
Mondry, Henrietta. *Political Animals: Representing Dogs in Modern Russian Culture.* Brill, 2015.
Montaigne, Michel de. "Apology for Raymond Sebond." In *The Complete Works*. Translated by Donald M. Frame. Everyman's Library, 2003.
Moreman, Christopher M. "On the Relationship Between Birds and Spirits of the Dead." *Society and Animals* 22 (2014): 481–502.
Morra, Brian J. "The Near Nuclear War of 1983." *Air & Space Force Magazine*, 2022. https://www.airandspaceforces.com/article/the-near-nuclear-war-of-1983/.
Moss, Anne Eakin. "Cinema as Spiritual Exercise: Tarkovsky and Hadot." In *ReFocus: The Films of Andrei Tarkovsky*, edited by Sergey Toymentsev. University of Edinburgh Press, 2021.
"The Motion Picture Production Code of 1930." In *The Dame in the Kimono: Hollywood, Censorship, and the Production Code from the 1920s to the 1960s*, edited by Leonard J. Jeff and Jerold Simmons. Grove Wiedenfeld, 1990.
Mulvey, Laura. *Death 24x a Second: Stillness and the Moving Image.* Reaktion, 2006.
Mulvey, Laura. *Visual and Other Pleasures.* Palgrave Macmillan, 2009.
Muratova, Kira. "Kogda ia uznala." *Bul'var Gordona* 27, no. 63 (2006). https://www.bulvar.com.ua/gazeta/archive/s27_4155/2399.html.
Murphet, Julian. "Pitiable or Political Animals?" *SubStance* 37, no. 3 (2008): 97–116.
Neale, Steve. "Art Cinema as Institution." *Screen* 22, no. 1 (1981): 11–40.
Nelson, Amy. "The Body of the Beast: Animal Protection and Anticruelty Legislation in Imperial Russia." In *Other Animals: Beyond the Human in Russian Culture and History*, edited by Jane Costlow and Amy Nelson. University of Pittsburgh Press, 2010.

Nelson, Amy. "Bringing the Beast Back In: The Rehabilitation of Pet Keeping in Soviet Russia." In *Companion Animals in Everyday Life: Situating Human-Animal Engagement Within Cultures*, edited by Michal Piotr Pregowski. Palgrave Macmillan, 2016.

Nelson, Amy. "Cold War Celebrity and the Courageous Canine Scout: The Life and Times of Soviet Space Dogs." In *Into the Cosmos*, edited by James T. Andrews and Asif A. Sidiqi. Pittsburgh University Press, 2011.

Nelson, Amy. "A Hearth for a Dog: The Paradoxes of Soviet Pet-Keeping." In *Borders of Socialism: Private Spheres of Soviet Russia*, edited by Lewis H. Siegelbaum. Palgrave, 2006.

Nesbitt, Anne. *Savage Junctures: Sergei Eisenstein and the Shape of Thinking*. I. B. Tauris, 2003.

Newson, Scott. "Preserving Wilderness Versus Enabling Economic Change: Iceland and the Kárahnjúkar Hydropower Project." *Geography* 95 (2010): 161–64.

Nicholl, Charles. *Leonardo da Vinci: Flights of the Mind*. Penguin, 2005.

Nietzsche, Friedrich. *The Anti-Christ, Ecce Homo, Twilight of the Idols and Other Writings*. Edited by Aaron Ridley and Judith Norman. Translated by Judith Norman. Cambridge University Press, 2005.

Nietzsche, Friedrich. *The Gay Science*. Translated by Walter Kaufmann. Vintage, 1974.

Nietzsche, Friedrich. *Thus Spoke Zarathustra: A Book for All and None*. Translated by Walter Kaufmann. Penguin, 1978.

Nietzsche, Friedrich. *Untimely Meditations*. Edited by Daniel Breazeale. Translated by R. J. Hollingdale. Cambridge University Press, 1997.

Novozhilova, Irina. "The Emergence of Animal Protection in Russia." In *The Global Guide to Animal Protection*, edited by Andrew Linzey. University of Illinois Press, 2013.

O'Brien, Sarah. "Why Look at Dead Animals?" *Framework: The Journal of Cinema and Media* 57, no. 1 (2016): 32–57.

Oliver, Kelly. "See Topsy 'Ride the Lightning': The Scopic Machinery of Death." *Southern Journal of Philosophy* 50 (2012): 74–94.

O'Rourke, Jennifer. "The Birth of Film—The Beginning of Motion Picture Making." *VideoMaker*, 2012. https://www.videomaker.com/article/f10/15554-the-birth-of-film-the-beginning-of-motion-picture-making/.

Ott, John. "Iron Horses: Leland Stanford, Eadweard Muybridge, and the Industrialised Eye." *Oxford Art Journal* 28, no. 3 (2005): 407–28.

Oukaderova, Lida. *The Cinema of the Soviet Thaw*. Indiana University Press, 2017.

Oxford English Dictionary. "arthouse (*n. & adj.*)." Accessed December 11, 2024. https://www.oed.com/search/dictionary/?scope=Entries&q=arthouse.

Oxford English Dictionary. "bird's-eye-view (*n.*)." Accessed December 17, 2024. https://www.oed.com/search/dictionary/?scope=Entries&q=bird%27s-eye-view.

Oxford English Dictionary. "cuck (*n.*)." Accessed December 17, 2024. https://www.oed.com/search/dictionary/?scope=Entries&q=cuck.

Oxford English Dictionary. "cuckoo (*adj.*)." Accessed December 16, 2024. https://www.oed.com/search/dictionary/?scope=Entries&q=cuckoo.

Oxford English Dictionary. "master (*n, & adj.*)." Accessed December 17, 2024. https://www.oed.com/search/dictionary/?scope=Entries&q=master.

Oxford English Dictionary. "stalker (*n.*)." Accessed December 14, 2024. https://www.oed.com/dictionary/stalker_n?tl=true.

Oxford English Dictionary. "stock (*n.*)." Accessed December 11, 2024. https://www.oed.com/dictionary/stock_n1?tl=true.

Oxford English Dictionary. "zoon (*n.*)." Accessed December 15, 2024. https://www.oed.com/dictionary/zoon_int.

Packer, George. *The Unwinding: An Inner History of the New America.* Farrar, Straus and Giroux, 2013.

Palmer, Scott. *Dictatorship of the Air: Aviation Culture and the Fate of Modern Russia.* Cambridge University Press, 2006.

Panchenko, Alexander. "Ancient Wisdom, Stigmatised Knowledge, and Sacred Landscapes: Ontologies and Epistemologies of New Age Culture in Post-Soviet Russia." *Journal of Ethnology and Folkloristics* 15, no. 2 (2021): 19–24.

Parker, Stephen Jan. "Hemingway's Revival in the Soviet Union, 1955–1962." *American Literature* 35, no. 4 (1964): 485–501.

Pearson, Susan J., and Mary Weismantel. "Does 'the Animal' Exist? Toward a Theory of Social Life with Animals." In *Beastly Natures: Animals, Humans, and the Study of History*, edited by Dorothee Brantz. University of Virginia Press, 2010.

Perepelkin, Mikhail. *Slovo v mire Andreia Tarkovskogo: Poėtika inoskazaniia.* Samarskii universitet, 2010.

Pesmen, Dale. *Russia and Soul: An Exploration.* Cornell University Press, 2000.

Petrushenko, Viktor. *Nostalgia for the Absolute: The Philosophical Context of Andrei Tarkovsky's Filmmaking.* Our Knowledge, 2024.

Philo, Chris, and Chris Wilbert. "Animal Spaces, Beastly Places: An Introduction." In *Animal Spaces, Beastly Places: New Geographies of Human-Animal Relations*, edited by Chris Philo and Chris Wilbert. Routledge, 2000.

Pick, Anat. "Animal Life in the Cinematic *Umwelt.*" In *Animal Life & the Moving Image*, edited by Michael Lawrence and Laura McMahon. British Film Institute, 2015.

Pick, Anat. *Creaturely Poetics: Animality and Vulnerability in Literature and Film.* Columbia University Press, 2011.

Pick, Anat. "Turning to Animals Between Love and Law." *New Formations* 76 (2012): 68–85.

Pick, Anat. "Vulnerability." In *Critical Terms for Animal Studies*, edited by Lori Gruen. University of Chicago Press, 2018.

Pickeral, Tamsin. *The Horse: 30,000 Years of the Horses in Art*. Merrell, 2006.
Plate, S. Brent. *Religion and Film: Cinema and the Re-creation of the World*. 2nd ed. Columbia University Press, 2017.
Plato. *The Republic*. Edited and translated by Desmond Lee. Penguin, 2007.
Platonov, Andrey. *Soul and Other Stories*. Translated by Robert Chandler and Elizabeth Chandler. New York Review Books, 2007.
"Pochemu v magazinakh SSSR ne prodavali koninu?" *Dzen*, November 7, 2023. https://dzen.ru/a/ZUpkofZbiyZZrv2J.
Pontara, Tobias. *Andrei Tarkovsky's Sounding Cinema: Music and Meaning from* Solaris *to* The Sacrifice. Routledge, 2020.
Pontara, Tobias. "Beethoven Overcome: Romantic and Existentialist Utopia in Andrei Tarkovsky's *Stalker*." *19th-Century Music* 34, no. 3 (2011): 302–15.
Potts, Annie. *Chicken*. Reaktion, 2012.
Pourtova, Elena. "Andrei Tarkovsky: Stalker of the Unconscious." *Journal of Analytical Psychology* 62, no. 5 (2017): 778–86.
Prieto, José Manuel. "Reading Mandelstam on Stalin." *New York Review*, June 10, 2010. https://www.nybooks.com/articles/2010/06/10/reading-mandelstam-stalin/.
"Proiskhozhdenie slova korova." Etimologicheskie onlain-slovari russkogo iazyka. Accessed December 13, 2024. https://lexicography.online/etymology/к/корова.
"Proiskhozhdenie slova loshad." Etimologicheskie onlain-slovari russkogo iazyka. Accessed December 16, 2024. https://lexicography.online/etymology/л/лошадь.
"Proiskhozhdenie slova pes." Etimologicheskie onlain-slovari russkogo iazyka. Accessed December 15, 2024. https://lexicography.online/etymology/п/пёс.
Prokhorov, Alexander. "The Adolescent and the Child in the Cinema of the Thaw." *Studies in Russian and Soviet Cinema* 1, no. 2 (2007): 115–29.
Raleigh, Donald J. *Soviet Baby Boomers: An Oral History of Russia's Cold War Generation*. Oxford University Press, 2013.
Rance, Mark. "Mark Rance on *Andrei Rublov*: The Criterion Edition." *Nostalghia*, accessed December 13, 2024. http://www.nostalghia.com/TheTopics/Rance.html.
Redwood, Thomas. *Andrei Tarkovsky's Poetics of Cinema*. Cambridge Scholars, 2010.
Reilly, Hilda. "The Story of Freud's Patient Anna von Lieben—as Told by Anna von Lieben." *Journal of the Royal College of Physicians of Edinburgh* 53, no. 1 (2023): 57–64.
Robinson, Jeremy Mark. *Andrei Tarkovsky: Pocket Guide*. Crescent Moon, 2023.
Robinson, Jeremy Mark. *The Sacred Cinema of Andrei Tarkovsky*. Crescent Moon, 2008.
Robinson, Paul. *Russian Conservativism*. Cornell University Press, 2019.

Roitman, Yaakov. "Dreaming Birth for an Unborn Child: Poetic Memories of Winnicott's 'Mirror Role of Mother and Family' and Tarkovsky's *Mirror*." *Journal of Child Psychotherapy* 47, no. 2 (2021): 255–68.

Rosenberg, Susanne. "Kulning—An Ornamentation of the Surrounding Emptiness: About the Unique Scandinavian Herding Calls." *Voice and Speech Review* 8, no. 1 (2014): 100–105.

Rosenholm, Arja. "Of Men and Horses: Animal Imagery in the Construction of Russian Masculinities." In *Other Animals: Beyond the Human in Russian Culture and History*, edited by Jane Costlow and Amy Nelson. Pittsburgh University Press, 2009.

Rosenholm, Arja. "'There Is No Russia without the Cow': The Russian Mind and Memory: The Cow as Symbol." In *Understanding Russian Nature: Representations, Values, and Concepts*, edited by Rosenholm and Sari Autio-Sarasmo. Aleksanteri Papers, 2005.

Ross, Alex. "The Drenching Richness of Andrei Tarkovsky." *New Yorker*, February 8, 2021. https://www.newyorker.com/magazine/2021/02/15/the-drenching-richness-of-andrei-tarkovsky.

Rothfels, Nigel, ed. *Representing Animals*. Indiana University Press, 2002.

Rothman, Joshua. "Is Heidegger Contaminated by Nazism?" *New Yorker*, April 28, 2014. https://www.newyorker.com/books/page-turner/is-heidegger-contaminated-by-nazism.

Rousseau, Jean-Jacques. *A Discourse on Inequality*. Translated by Maurice Cranston. Penguin, 1984.

Rüdiger, Graf. "Truth in the Jungle of Literature, Science, and Politics: Upton Sinclair's *The Jungle* and Food Control Reforms during the Progressive Era." *Journal of American History* 106, no. 4 (2020): 901–22.

Rushdie, Salman. "Out of Kansas: Revisiting 'The Wizard of Oz.'" *New Yorker*, May 4, 1992. https://www.newyorker.com/magazine/1992/05/11/out-of-kansas.

Russell, Calum. "The One James Cameron Action Film That Andre Tarkovsky Loved." *Far Out*, July 17, 2021. https://faroutmagazine.co.uk/james-cameron-film-andrei-tarkovsky-loved/.

Russell, Calum. "The Stanley Kubrick Film That Andrei Tarkovsky Hated." *Far Out*, June 26, 2021. https://faroutmagazine.co.uk/the-stanley-kubrick-film-that-andrei-tarkovsky-hated/.

Ruthchild, Rochelle. "Sisterhood and Socialism: The Soviet Feminist Movement." *Frontier: A Journal of Women's Studies* 7, no. 2 (1983): 4–12.

Rutten, Ellen. *Sincerity After Communism: A Cultural History*. Yale University Press, 2017.

Ryan, Derek. *Animal Theory: A Critical Introduction*. University of Edinburgh Press, 2015.

Saddhatissa, Hammalawa, trans. *The Sutta-Nipata*. Routledge, 2013.

Sadovskii, Iakub. "Obnazhennoe telo i ego funktsiia v konstruirovanii obrazov sotsial'noi real'nosti v perestoechnom kinematografe." *Zhurnal sotsial'no-gumanutarnykh issledovanii* 6 (2016): 91–99.

Salynskii, Dmitrii. *Kinogermenevtika Tarkovskogo*. Kvadriga, 2009.

Sandler, Stephanie. "The Absent Father, the Stillness of Film: Tarkovsky, Sokurov, and Loss." In *Tarkovsky*, edited by Nathan Dunne. Black Dog, 2008.

Sarkar, Bhaskar. "Threnody for Modernity." In *Tarkovsky*, edited by Nathan Dunne. Black Dog, 2008.

Sartre, Jean-Paul. "Existentialism Is a Humanism." Translated by Philip Mairet. Marxists Internet Archive, February 2005. https://www.marxists.org/reference/archive/sartre/works/exist/sartre.htm.

Sartre, Jean-Paul. "Letter on the Critique of *Ivan's Childhood*." In *Tarkovsky*, edited by Nathan Dunne. Black Dog, 2008.

Sax, Boria. *Aviation Illuminations: A Cultural History of Birds*. Reaktion, 2021.

Scarry, Elaine. *On Beauty and Being Just*. Princeton University Press, 1999.

Scharf, Aaron. "Marey and Chronophotography." *ArtForum* 15, no. 1 (1976). https://www.artforum.com/features/marey-and-chronophotography-214081/.

Schillaci, Filippo. "The Evolution of Form in Andrei Tarkovsky's Films." *Nostalghia*. Accessed December 16, 2024. http://www.nostalghia.com/TheTopics/Tarkovskij-for-cinemetrics.pdf.

Schivelbusch, Wolfgang. *The Railway Journey: The Industrialization and Perception of Time and Space*. University of California Press, 2014.

Schlegel, Hans-Joachin. "Der antiavantgardistiche Avantgardist." In *Andrej Tarkowskij*, edited by Peter Jansen and Wolfram Schütte. Reihe Film, 1987.

Sellier, Geneviève. *Le culte de l'auteur: Les derives du cinéma français*. La fabrique, 2024.

Senior, Matthew. "The Souls of Men and Beasts, 1630–1764." In *A Cultural History of Animals in the Age of Enlightenment*, edited by Matthew Senior. Berg, 2007.

Sexton, Empiricus. *The Outlines of Skepticism*. Edited by Julia Annas and Johnathan Barnes. Cambridge University Press, 2000.

Shneidman, N. N. "Soviet Theory of Literature and the Struggle Around Dostoevsky in Recent Soviet Scholarship." *Slavic Review* 34, no. 3 (1975): 523–38.

Shukin, Nicole. *Animal Capital: Rendering Life in Biopolitical Times*. University of Minnesota Press, 2009.

Shukin, Nicole, and Sarah O'Brien. "Being Struck: On the Force of Slaughter and Cinematic Affect." In *Animal Life & the Moving Image*, edited by Michael Lawrence and Laura McMahon. British Film Institute, 2015.

Sider, Justin. "Tarkovsky's Horse." *Boston Review*, September 20, 2017. https://www.bostonreview.net/articles/justin-sider-tarkovskys-horse/.

Skakov, Nariman. *The Cinema of Tarkovsky: Labyrinths of Space and Time*. I. B. Tauris, 2012.

Sobchack, Vivian. *Carnal Thoughts: Embodiment and Moving Image.* University of California Press, 2004.
Soëlle, Dorothee. *The Mystery of Death.* Translated by Nancy Lukens-Rumscheidt and Martin Lukens-Rumschedit. Fortress Press, 2007.
Soldatov, I. "... I zapylala korova." *Vecherniaia Moskva*, December 24, 1966.
Soles, Carter. "'And No Birds Sing': Discourses of Environmental Apocalypse in 'The Birds' and 'Night of the Living Dead.'" *Interdisciplinary Studies in Literature and Environment* 21, no. 3 (2014): 526–37.
Solzhenitsyn, Aleksandr. "Fil'm o Rubleve." *Lib.ru*. Accessed December 13, 2024. http://www.lib.ru/PROZA/SOLZHENICYN/s_rublew.txt.
Solzhenitsyn, Aleksandr. "A World Split Apart." The Aleksandr Solzhenitsyn Center. Accessed December 13, 2024. https://www.solzhenitsyncenter.org/a-world-split-apart.
Sontag, Susan. *Essays of the 1960s & 70s.* Edited by David Rieff. Library of America, 2013.
Stamp, Jimmy. "The Past, Present, and Future of the Cuckoo Clock." *Smithsonian Magazine*, May 17, 2013. https://www.smithsonianmag.com/arts-culture/the-past-present-and-future-of-the-cuckoo-clock-65073025/.
Steintrager, James A. *Cruel Delight: Enlightenment Culture and the Inhuman.* Indiana University Press, 2004.
Strugatsky, Arkady, and Boris Strugatsky. *Roadside Picnic.* Translated by Olena Bormashenko. Chicago Review Press, 2012.
Surkova, O. "'Gamlet' Andreia Tarkovskogo." *Iskusstvo kino* 3 (1998). http://old.kinoart.ru/archive/1998/03/n3-article25.
Surkova, O. "Khroniki Tarkovskogo. Zerkalo." *Iskusstvo kino* 7 (2002). http://old.kinoart.ru/archive/2002/07/n7-article20.
Svensson, Owe. "On Tarkovsky's *The Sacrifice.*" In *Soundscape: The School of Sound Lectures 1998–2001*, edited by Larry Sider, Diane Freeman, and Jerry Sider. Wallflower Press, 2007.
Synessios, Natasha. *Mirror: The Film Companion.* I. B. Tauris, 2001.
Tafdrup, Pai. *Tarkovsky's Horses & Other Poems.* Translated by David McDuff. Bloodaxe, 2010.
"Tarkovskii bez gliantsa. Chast' XI. Natal'ia Bonderchuk." *Dzen*, August 25, 2020.
Tarkovsky, Andrei. *Andrei Rublev.* Translated by Kitty Hunter-Blair. Faber and Faber, 1992
Tarkovsky, Andrei. "Andrei Tarkovsky on *Andrei Rublev.*" *Nostalghia*. Accessed December 13, 2024. http://www.nostalghia.com/TheTopics/TarkovskyonRublev.html.
Tarkovsky, Andrei. "Andrei Tarkovsky on *The Sacrifice.*" *Nostalghia*. Accessed December 12, 2024. http://www.nostalghia.com/TheTopics/On_Sacrifice.html.

Tarkovsky, Andrei. "Bespretsedentnost' spiska popravok." Seans. Accessed December 12, 2024. https://chapaev.media/articles/8416.

Tarkovsky, Andrei. *Collected Screenplays*. Translated by William Powell and Natasha Synessios. Faber and Faber, 2003.

Tarkovsky, Andrei. "I'm Interested in the Problem of Inner Freedom." Nostalghia. Accessed December 12, 2024. http://nostalghia.com/TheTopics/interview.html.

Tarkovsky, Andrei. *Interviews*. Edited by John Gianvito. University Press of Mississippi, 2006.

Tarkovsky, Andrei. "*The Passion according to Andrei*: An Unpublished Interview with Andrei Tarkovsky." Nostalghia. Accessed December 11, 2024. http://www.nostalghia.com/TheTopics/PassionacctoAndrei.html.

Tarkovsky, Andrei. *Sculpting in Time: Reflections on the Cinema*. Translated by Kitty Hunter-Blair. University of Texas Press, 1987.

Tarkovsky, Andrei. *Time within Time: The Diaries 1970–1986*. Translated by Kitty Hunter-Blair. Seagull, 2019.

"Tarkovsky's Horse 2008—Full Show (SD)." Vimeo video, July 28, 2014. https://vimeo.com/101883543?share=copy.

Tearle, Oliver. "The Meaning and Comedic Origins of Cloud Cuckoo Land." *Interesting Literature*, 2020. https://interestingliterature.com/2020/09/cloud-cuckoo-land-phrase-meaning/.

Terekhova, Margarita. "'Rubit' golovy petukhu? C kakoi stati? Ia zh artistka, a ne etot samyi—kak ego?—zhivoder.'" *Bul'var Gordona*, November 17, 2010. https://bulvar.com.ua/gazeta/archive/s45_64269/6507.html.

Tikhonova, Mariia. "Avtor pamiatnika Andreiu Tarkovskomy i ego fil'mu 'Andrei Rublev.'" *Art-Reliz*, September 29, 2017. https://арт-релиз.рф/2017/09/29/МАРИЯ-ТИХОНОВА-Автор-памятника-АНДРЕ/.

Timofeeva, Oxana. *The History of Animals: A Philosophy*. Bloomsbury Academic, 2018.

Toal, Catherine. *The Entrapments of Form: Cruelty and Modern Literature*. Fordham University Press, 2016.

Todd, Kim. *Sparrow*. Reaktion, 2012.

Tolstoy, Leo. *Anna Karenina*. Translated by Richard Pevear and Larissa Volokhonsky. Penguin, 2000.

Tomizawa, Roy. "The Transformation of Akasaka Mitsuke in 1964." *Olympians*, January 16, 2018. https://theolympians.co/2018/01/16/the-transformation-of-akasaka-mitsuke-in-1964-where-i-work-today/.

Totaro, Donato. "Nature as 'Comfort Zone' in the Films of Andrei Tarkovsky." *Offscreen* 14, no. 12 (2010). https://offscreen.com/view/nature_as_comfort_zone.

Toymentsev, Sergey. "The Crisis of the Soviet Action-Image: Towards a Deleuzian Taxonomy of Thaw Cinema." In *New Europe College Yearbook*, edited by Irina Vainovski-Mihai. Pontica Magna Program, 2017.

Toymentsev, Sergey. "Introduction: Refocus on Tarkovsky." In *ReFocus: The Films of Andrei Tarkovsky*, edited by Sergey Toymentsev. University of Edinburgh Press, 2021.

Toymentsev, Sergey, ed. *ReFocus: The Films of Andrei Tarkovsky*. University of Edinburgh Press, 2021.

Trotsky, Leon. *Literatura i revoliutsiia*. Izd.-vo politicheskoi literatury, 1991.

Truppin, Andrea. "And Then There Was Sound: The Films of Andrei Tarkovsky." In *Sound Theory/Sound Practice*, edited by Rick Altman. Routledge, 1992.

Tsivian, Yuri. *Early Cinema in Russia and Its Cultural Reception*. Translated by Alan Bodger. London: Routledge, 1994.

Tsymbal, Evgeniy. "Tarkovsky's Childhood: Between Trauma and Myth." In *ReFocus: The Films of Andrei Tarkovsky*, edited by Sergey Toymentsev. University of Edinburgh Press, 2022.

Tumanov, Vladimir. "Philosophy of Mind and Body in Andrei Tarkovsky's *Solaris*." *Film-Philosophy* 20, no. 2–3 (2016): 357–75.

Turovskaya, Maya. *7 c ½ ili Fil'my Andreia Tarkovskogo*. Iskusstvo, 1991.

Turovskaya, Maya. *Tarkovsky: Cinema as Poetry*. Translated by Natasha Ward. Faber and Faber, 1990.

Varner, Gary. "Sentience." In *Critical Terms for Animal Studies*, edited by Lori Gruen. University of Chicago Press, 2018.

Velten, Hannah. *Cow*. Reaktion, 2007.

Velten, Hannah. *Milk: A Global History*. Reaktion, 2010.

Vertov, Dziga. *Kino-Eye: The Writings of Dziga Vertov*. Edited by Annette Michelson. Translated by Kevin O'Brien. University of California Press, 1984.

"Virginia Woolf Reflecting on Peace During an Air Raid." *Guardian*, September 6, 2009. https://www.theguardian.com/world/2009/sep/06/virginia-woolf-second-world-war.

"V Suzdale otkryli pamiatnik Andreiu Tarkovskomy." *RIA Novosti*, July 29, 2017. https://ria.ru/20170729/1499405393.html.

Wakamiya, Lisa Ryok. "Zvyagintsev and Tarkovsky: Influence, Depersonalization, and Autonomy." In *ReFocus: The Films of Andrei Tarkovsky*, edited by Sergey Toymentsev. Edinburgh University Press, 2021.

Walker, Elaine. *Horse*. Reaktion, 2008.

Waters, John. "John Waters on *Pink Flamingos*, Divine, and 50 Years of Filth." *Vogue*, June 30, 2022. https://www.vogue.com/article/john-waters-pink-flamingos-50-years-of-filth.

Waxman, Olivia B. "Aerial Photography's Surprising Role in History." *Time*, May 31, 2018. https://time.com/longform/aerial-photography-drones-history/.

Weil, Kari. *Thinking Animals: Why Animal Studies Now?* Columbia University Press, 2012.

Werth, Karsten. "A Surrogate for War—The U.S. Space Program in the 1960s." *American Studies* 49, no. 4 (2004): 563–87.

White, Edward. "The Dark Side of an Auteur: On Alfred Hitchcock's Treatment of Women." *Literary Hub*, April 26, 2021. https://lithub.com/the-dark-side-of-an-auteur-on-alfred-hitchcocks-treatment-of-women/.

White, Hayden. "The Value of Narrativity in the Representation of Reality." *Critical Inquiry* 7, no. 1 (1980): 5–27.

White, Jerry. "Brakhage's Tarkovsky and Tarkovsky's Brakhage: Collectivity, Subjectivity, and the Dream of Cinema." *Canadian Journal of Film Studies* 14, no. 1 (2005): 69–83.

Widdis, Emma. "Border: The Aesthetic of Conquest in Soviet Cinema of the 1930s." *European Studies* 30, no. 120 (2000): 401–11.

Widdis, Emma. *Socialist Senses: Film, Feeling, and the Soviet Subject, 1917–1940*. Indiana University Press, 2017.

Widdis, Emma. *Visions of a New Land: Soviet Film from the Revolution to the Second World War*. Yale University Press, 2003.

Wilinsky, Barbara. *Sure Seaters: The Emergence of Art House Cinema*. University of Minnesota Press, 2001.

Williams, Linda. *Hard Core: Power, Pleasure, and the "Frenzy of the Visible."* University of California Press, 1999.

Wolfe, Cary. *Animal Rites: American Culture, the Discourse of Species, and Posthumanist Theory*. University of Chicago Press, 2003.

Wolfe, Cary. *Before the Law: Humans and Other Animals*. University of Chicago Press, 2012.

Woll, Josephine. *Real Images: Soviet Cinema and the Thaw*. I. B. Tauris, 2000.

Wood, Winifred J. "Bunnies for Pets or Meat: The Slaughterhouse as Cinematic Metaphor." *JAC* 31, no. 1/2 (2011): 11–44.

Wright, Alan. "The Rotten Sea: Andrei Tarkovsky in the Soviet Archive." *KinoKultura* 53 (2016). http://www.kinokultura.com/2016/53-wright-tarkovsky.shtml/.

Young, Ed. *An Immense World: How Animal Senses Reveal the Hidden Realms Around Us*. Random House, 2022.

Young, Paula Lee. "Siting the Slaughterhouse: From Shed to Factory." In *Meat, Modernity, and the Rise of the Slaughterhouse*, edited by Paula Lee Young. University of New Hampshire Press, 2008.

Young, Peter. *Swan*. Reaktion, 2007.

Yurchak, Alexei. *Everything Was Forever, Until It Was No More: The Last Soviet Generation*. Princeton University Press, 2006.

Zagorin, Perez. "On Humanism, Past and Present." *Daedelus* 132, no. 4 (2003): 87–92.

"Zapretnoe miaso: Pochemy russkie ne eli koninu." *Dzen*, June 22, 2023. https://dzen.ru/a/ZJSGdHBGrnqZa55-.

Zdravomyslova, Elena, and Anna Temkina. "Krizis maskulinnosti v pozdnesovetskom diskurse." In *O muzhe(n)stvennosti*, edited by Sergei Ushakin. Novoe literaturnoe obozrenie, 2002.

Žižek, Slavoj. "Andrei Tarkovsky, or the Thing from Inner Space." In *ReFocus: The Films of Andrei Tarkovsky*, edited by Sergey Toymentsev. University of Edinburgh Press, 2021.

Zubov, Dmitry. *Stalin's Falcons: Exposing the Myth of Soviet Aerial Superiority over the Luftwaffe in WW2*. Casemate, 2024.

INDEX

Abraham, Karl, 180
Abramova, Natasha, 100
"Academic Horse, The" (Bataille), 51–52, 224
Adoration of the Magi (Leonardo da Vinci painting, 1481), 132–33, 157–58
Adorno, Theodor, 119n87
Adventures of an Android [*Prikliucheniia Elektronika*] (Bromberg, 1980), 83, 116n41
Aerograd (Dovzhenko, 1934), 140
Afghanistan, Soviet war in, 93
Akasaka-Mitsuke highway (Tokyo), 59, *60*, 61, 63
Akerman, Chantal, 34, 256n123
Akhmatova, Anna, 140
Aksenova, Alisa, 171
Alexander-Garrett, Layla, 259
Alien (Scott, 1979), 58
Alliance of Motion Picture & Television Producers (AMPTP), 248
"Ambler's Race" [*Beg inokhodtsa*] (Vysotsky, 1970), 55
American Dream (Koppel, 1990), 238
American Humane (AH) organization, 247–48
"...And a Cow Burst into Flames" ["*...I zapylala korova*"] (Soldatov, 1966), 168–69
Andrei Rublev (Tarkovsky, 1966), 55, 88, 245, 259; apocalyptic visions in, 221, 223–25, *224*; aviation technology critiqued in, 141, 231; bird's-eye perspectives in, 126–32, *128*; birds in, *146*; canonicity of, 170, 209n20; careening "horse roll" image in, 34, 35, *35*, 39, 46, 50, 53, 70n9; carno-phallogocentrism in, 188–90, *189*; cats in, 90–91; character coming into language, 184, *185*; cinematic spectacle and the miraculous in, 46; color image of horses, 49, *50*, 63; cuckoo bird in, 155; debased representations of Russia's ethnic minorities, 189–90, *190*; disposability of horses in, 25; documentary about making of, 168, 209n8; as documentary "chronicle," 191–92; dogs harmed in making of, 111–12, *112*; fraternal violence and social discord in, 177–78, 211n61; historical inaccuracies and anachronisms in, 192; horsemeat incident, 188–91, *190*; horses bearing witness to human suffering in, 36, *37*; horses in quadrilateral compositions, 44–45, *45*; humans rendered animalistic, 113; Kantian ideas about beauty in, 48–49; levitation leitmotif in, 135; offscreen barking of dogs in, 98; original title, 168; photographs associated with death, 223; preservation and reemergence of uncut version, 169, 170; script and research for, 213n106; slow motion in, 145; Soviet film censors

297

and, 127, 128, 169, 209n14, 228, 254n43; as spiritualized Western, 45; stillness and motion juxtaposed in, 39–40, *41*; Suzdal monument to Tarkovsky and, 259, 264n3; swan's carcass as metaphor, *131*, 162; Tarkovsky's antipathy toward feminism and, 175–76; two versions of, 70n9; vision of female piety in, 175; wasted milk in, 205. *See also* Mongols, in *Andrei Rublev*

Andrei Rublev, cow burning scene in, 1, 3, 171–72, *172*, 260; animals' nonlinguistic essence and, 187; antipathy toward independent women and, 177; condemnation in Soviet press, 167–69; cows of *The Sacrifice* contrasted to, 207–8; defenders of Tarkovsky, 170–71; degrading treatment of female actors and characters in relation to, 24; documentary "chronicle-ness" of, 191; Domenico's death in *Nostalghia* and, 217; *Electrocuting an Elephant* compared to, 194–95; images of "hysterical" women and, 183; karmic fate of Tarkovsky and, 206–7; Nietzschean "eternal return" and, 203; psychoanalytic evaluation of, 174; "rumors" about, 167; as symbolic assault on motherhood, 174; Tarkovsky's motives and explanations for, 168, 169–70, 171, 192–93, 206, 239, 242, 250; Tarkovsky's mystique and, 170

Andrei Rublev, horse death scene in, 229, 230–32, 235, 246, 247, 254n44; conflicting reports about method of killing, 32; dead animals in Eisenstein's films compared with, 240–44, 249; in different versions of the film, 70n3, 228; Domenico's death in *Nostalghia* compared to, 217, *218*; Tarkovsky's motives and explanations for, 236–37, 239, 250; utilitarian value vs. moral cost, 236–37

"Andrey Tarkovsky—Enigma and Mystery" (Alexander-Garrett, 1988), 259

animality, 4, 15, 207, 208

Animal Locomotion (Muybridge), 154, 237

animal rights groups, 248

animals: autonomy and agency of, 22; Cartesian idea of animal soullessness, 11–12, 61, 219, 234, 251; cinema and authenticity in relation to, 193; consciousness of death lacking in, 219, 233–34; domesticated, 19, 108; encounters with cinema, 2; history of animals on screen, 21; human identity and, 62–63, 66; humans before an animal's gaze, 77–78; indexical images of animal death in arthouse cinema, 244–52; lack of spirituality and, 10–11, 113; language and, 183–84, 186–88, 233; marginalization and invisibility of, 33, 238–39; "metaphysical poverty" of, 219, 232–37; in Nietzschean philosophy, 201; nonhuman gaze, 99; reincarnation beliefs and, 204–5; technological ghosts of, 67–68, *68*; violence against animals paired with images of hysterical women, 183; witchcraft and communication with, 148

animal studies, 2, 3, 22

Animal That Therefore I Am, The (Derrida), 77

"animal turn," 2

animal welfare societies, 238, 247

Anna Karenina (Tolstoy, 1878), 53, 101, 180, 211n66

anthropocentrism, 11, 15, 30n101, 70, 113, 260

anthropomorphism, 30n101

antihumanism, 6, 7, 8, 200

Antonioni, Michelangelo, 42, 120n96

apocalypse, visions of, 219, 220–26, *222*, 224

Apocalypse Now (Coppola, 1979), 248

Appearance of Christ to the People, The (Ivanov, 1837–57), 51

Arabic 3 (Brakhage, 1980), 236–37n126

archetypes, Jungian, 160

Argent, L' (Bresson, 1983), 121n127

Aristotle, 88, 186–87

Arnold, Andrea, 17, 19

Arrabal, Fernando, 245

Arrival of a Train, The [*L'Arrivée d'un train en gare de La Ciotat*] (Lumière, 1895), 129

Artaud, Antonin, 250

Artemiev, Eduard, 73n92, 86

arthouse cinema, animal cruelty in, 244–52

aspect ratios, 40, 51

At Home among Strangers [*Svoi sredi chuzhikh, chuzhoi sredi svoikh*] (Mikhalkov, 1974), 45

At Midday [*Na Poldni*] (Konchalovskii painting, 1947), 205
Aubron, Hervé, 21
Au Hasard Balthazar (Bresson, 1966), 245
auteur theory, 22
automobiles: "horsepower" of, 38, 60; horses replaced by, 60, 62; Tarkovsky's antagonism toward, 61
Averbakh, Il'ia, 134
Aviator, The (Scorsese, 2004), 129

Babeș, Liviu Cornel, 105
Bach, Johann Sebastian, 95, 119n87, 133
Balász, Béla, 193
Balian, Roman, 83, 134
Ballard, Carroll, 44
Banionis, Donatas, 54, 83, 135
Barry Lyndon (Kubrick, 1975), 91
Basil of Caesarea, 88
Bataille, Georges, 51–52, 224
Battleship Potemkin [*Bronenonsets Potemkin*] (Eisenstein, 1925), 255–56n106
Bazin, André, 99, 193, 194, 207, 223
beauty, 70; Kantian notions about, 48–49; replication and begetting associated with, 50–51, 52
Bed and Sofa [*Tret'ia meshchanskaia*] (Room, 1926), 80
Beethoven, Ludwig van, 100, 101, 102, 105, 107, 121n125
Being and Time (Heidegger, 1927), 232
Belorussian Station [*Belorusski vokzal*] (Smirnov, 1971), 73n90
Belov, Vasilii, 55
Ben Hur: A Tale of the Christ (Niblo, 1925), 247
Bennett, Jane, 30n101
Benny's Video (Haneke, 1992), 245
Bentham, Jeremy, 235, 236, 237
Berger, John, 33, 64, 66; on reappearance of animals in technological media, 67; theory of animal vanishing, 69, 156, 159, 220; "Why Look at Animals?" (1977), 23, 62–63, 69, 220
Bergman, Ingmar, 25, 42, 121n124, 143, 158, 198, 213–14n131
Bergson, Henri, 215n165
Berlin Alexanderplatz (Fassbinder, 1980), 245

Bestiaire (Côté, 2012), 17
Beyond Good and Evil [*Al di là del bene e del male*] (Cavani, 1977), 214n148
Beyshenaliyev, Bolot, 189
Bicycle Thieves (De Sica, 1948), 35
Bi Gan, 51
Bird, Robert, 117n59, 176
birds, 1, 4, 21, 260; eroticism in depictions of human flight, 146–55, *149*, *150*, *151*; flight and etymology of, 123; freedom associated with, 125; human commonalities with, 123–24; Jung's archetypes and, 160; Leonardo da Vinci's drawings of, 24; pesticide threat to, 159
Birds, The (Aristophanes, 414 BCE), 157
Birds, The (Hitchcock, 1963), 24, 126, 145, 159
Birman, Naum, 82
Birth of Venus, The (Botticelli painting, 1485), 132
Black Shuck (ghost dog in English folklore), 98
Black Stallion, The (Ballard, 1979), 44
Blade Runner (Scott, 1983), 61, 75n130
Blake, William, 99
Blood of the Beasts [*Le sang des bêtes*] (Franju, 1949), 238
Bloom, Harold, 25, 242
Boléro (Ravel, 1928), 100
Bolsheviks, 6, 14, 80, 81, 84–85, 108
Bondarchuk, Natalia, 58, 135, 211–12n77
Bondarchuk, Sergei, 211–12n77
Border Dog Alyi [*Pogranichnyi pes Alyi*] (Fait, 1980), 93
Border Is Locked, The [*Granitsa na zamke*] (Zhuravlev, 1937), 93
Botticelli, Sandro, 132, 221
Bovines (Gras, 2011), 17
Boym, Svetlana, 67, 136
Brakhage, Stan, 236n126, 246–47
Braunberger, Pierre, 194
Bresson, Robert, 36–37, 42, 245
Breuer, Josef, 230
Brezhnev, Leonid, 134
Brodsky, Joseph, 139
Bromberg, Konstantin, 83
Bronze Horseman, The [*Mednyi vsadnik*] (equestrian statue in St. Petersburg, Russia, 1782), 217

"Bronze Horseman, The" [*Mednyi vsadnik*] (Pushkin, 1833), 53, 217
Brooks, Peter, 203
Brown, Clarence, 44
Bruegel the Elder, Pieter, 135, 136
Buddhism, 10, 86, 116n45, 160, 204. *See also* reincarnation
Bulgakov, Mikhail, 115n20, 117n59, 118n68, 140
Bullfight (Braunberger, 1951), 194
Buñuel, Luis, 42
Burlyayev, Nikolai, 65, 155, 220, 259, 262
Burnett, Charles, 239
Burt, Jonathan, 2, 82, 237, 238
Business as Usual [*Privychnoe delo*] (Belov, 1966), 55

Cahiers du cinéma (French film magazine), 246
Calarco, Matthew, 103
Cameron, James, 100
Cannibal Holocaust (Deodat, 1980), 245
capitalism, 43, 62, 80, 108, 178, 204, 238
Cardullo, Bert, 246
carno-phallogocentrism, 24, 178–91
Carpenter, John, 58
Carson, Rachel, 159
Cartesian philosophy, 11–12, 179, 219
Cartwright, Lisa, 181, 195, 213n128
Castaing-Taylor, Lucien, 17
castration complex, Freudian, 152, 153, 154–55
Castro, Fidel, 81
Catherine the Great, 217
cats, 77–78, 80; Skeptics associated with, 90; Tarkovsky's preference for dogs over, 91
"Cat That Walked by Himself, The" (Kipling), 28n64
Cavani, Liliana, 214n148
Cervantes, Miguel de, 155
Charge of the Light Brigade, The (Curtiz, 1936), 247
Chekhov, Anton, 85, 93, 130
Chernobyl disaster, 24, 116n44, 126, 158–59
Chkalov, Valerii, 140, 141
Christian symbolism, 146, 152, 156, 158
Christ the Redeemer [*Khristos Vsederzhitel'*] (Rublev icon, 1410), 49

"chronicle-ness" (*khronikal'nost'*), 191
Chronicle of a Summer [*Chronique d'un été*] (Morin, 1961), 191
chronophotography, 38, 125, 237
Chrysippus, 89
Chudnow, Byron Ross, 248
cigarettes, in Tarkovsky's films, 214n135
Cimino, Michael, 248, 257n140
Cinderella (Méliès, 1899), 72n68
cinema: "180-degree rule," 57; animal remains and material basis of film, 243–44; animal violence in avant-garde cinema, 219; death of, 59; end of, 42–47; as miracle machine, 47; as mourning apparatus, 68–69; return to nature and, 15–21; Soviet avant-garde (1920s), 220; "total cinema," 194. *See also* technology, cinematic
"cinemality," 21
cinema novo, Brazilian, 245
"cinema of attractions," 129
Cinema of Tarkovsky, The: Labyrinths of Space (Skakov), 3
cinema vérité, 191
City Romance [*Gorodskoi romans*] (Todorovskii, 1970), 134
Close Encounters of the Third Kind (Spielberg, 1977), 54
"Codex on the Flight of Birds" (Leonardo da Vinci, 1505), 133
Cold War, 54, 105, 204, 208n3; reluctant Russian exiles, 139; space race, 127, 128, 141
Come and See [*Idi i smotri*] (Klimov, 1985), 216n194
communism, Soviet, 13–14, 43, 74n97, 170, 178; Orientalism and, 204; view of pet ownership, 80. *See also* Bolsheviks; Soviet Union (USSR)
Cooper, James Fenimore, 86
Copernican Revolution, 102
Coppola, Francis Ford, 248
Costa, Pedro, 37
Côté, Denis, 17
Cow (Arnold, 2021), 19
"Cow, The" [*Korova*] (Platonov, 1938), 173
Cow [*Gav*] (Mehrjiu, 1969), 173

cows, 4, 19, 21; cyclical nature of existence and, 24–25; milk of, 205; in Nietzschean philosophy, 198–99, 201; sacred status in Eastern thought, 205; symbolic significance of, 172–73; Tarkovsky's dream about, 63–64. See also *Andrei Rublev*, cow burning scene in
Cranes Are Flying, The [*Letiat zhuravli*] (Kalatozov, 1957), 134
Creation of Adam, The (Michelangelo, 1512), 160
Crime and Punishment [*Prestuplenie i nakazanie*] (Dostoevsky, 1866), 13, 25, 121n127, 177, 210n57, 225
critical theory, 4, 21
cuckoo birds, 125; "cloud cuckoo land," 157, 158, 163; cuckoldry associated with, 154; as harbingers of death in Russian folklore, 24, 155–56; madness associated with, 157
Curtiz, Michael, 247
Cynics/Cynicism, 23, 79, 103–7, 108–9
Czech Renaissance, 245

Daneliia, Georgii, 134
Daoist philosophy, 203–4
Darwin, Charles, 15, 102, 107
"dead mother complex," 173–74
Dead Souls [*Mertvyie dushi*] (Gogol, 1842), 11
Dean, James, 180
death instinct, 203
Dederer, Claire, 263
Deleuze, Gilles, 16, 22, 36, 112; retelling of film history by, 42; on "time-image," 34, 37, 38
Demons [*Besy*] (Dostoevsky, 1871–72), 13, 212n80
Denis, Claire, 17, 51
Deodat, Ruggero, 245
Deren, Maya, 246
Derrida, Jacques, 24, 63, 90, 211n72, 236; on animals and language, 184, 187; on "carno-phallogocentrism," 178–79, 186; cat's gaze on naked philosopher, 77–78; on vulnerability and mortality, 261
Descartes, René, 11–12, 14, 15, 25, 234
Descombes, Vincent, 6
De Sica, Vittorio, 35, 83

Diamond Arm, The [*Brilliantovaia ruka*] (Gaida, 1969), 119n85
Diogenes (Gérôme, 1860), 93
Diogenes of Sinope, 103, 104, 106–7
Discourse on Method (Descartes, 1637), 11
"Discourse on the Arts and Sciences" (Rousseau), 29n76
dissolve shots, 49, 72n68
Doane, Mary Ann, 194
Doberman Gang, The (Chudnow, 1972), 248
Dog Barbos and the Unusual Cross [*Pes Barbos i neobychnyi kross*] (Gaidai, 1961), 82
Dogmatists, 88, 89, 114
dogs, 1, 4, 19, 21, 23–24; birds contrasted with, 124; at boundary of nature and culture, 109, 113; breeds preferred by Soviet owners, 85–86; as companion species, 107–14; Cynicism as canine-inspired philosophy, 99–107; German shepherd breed in Soviet culture, 93–94; history of dogs in cinema, 79; "kino-eye" reimagined as canine-eye, 99; male philosophers in company of, 92–93; as metaphysical envoys, 93–99; mistreated by Descartes and acolytes, 11–12; as moral exemplars, 79–80; offscreen barking and howling of, 98–99; Pavlov's experiments with, 80; as pets in the Soviet Union, 78–79; as "philosopher's pet," 23; in post-Stalinist Thaw-era films, 82–83, 85; Soviet space dogs, 97, 119n89, 121n116; Tarkovsky's pet Dakus, 78, 82, 92, 97–98, 109–11, 114, 116n36
Dog Star Man, Part IV (Brakhage, 1964), 236n126
Dono, Paolo di, 36
Don Quixote (Cervantes, 1605), 155
Dostoevsky, Fyodor, 12–13, 101, 121n127, 157, 177, 212n80. See also *Crime and Punishment* [*Prestuplenie i nakazanie*]
Dovlatov, Sergei, 94
Dovzhenko, Oleksandr, 16, 30n89, 51, 65, 73n76, 140
Dreher, Rod, 261
Dry Summer [*Susuz yaz*] (Erksan, 1964), 245
"Dubrovskii" (Pushkin, 1841), 115n16
Dunham, Duwayne, 79
Dunne, Nathan, 3

Dürer, Albrecht, 92–93, 220, 221, 222, 224
durochka (holy fool girl), 91, 176, 188–89, *189*, 210n51
Dvorzhetsky, Vitalik, 57
Dvorzhetsky, Vladislav, 59
Dzhul'bars (Shneiderov, 1935), 93

Earhart, Amelia, 141
Earth [*Zemlia*] (Dovzhenko, 1930), 16, 65
"Eastern" [*ostern*] (Soviet film genre), 45
Edison, Thomas, 194, 195, 237
Edwall, Allan, 148, 197
Eisenstein, Sergei, 25, 239–44
Electrocuting an Elephant (Edison, 1903), 194–95, 213n128, 237
Empire (Warhol, 1965), 34
Enlightenment, 6, 11, 13, 119n87, 257–58n149
Epicurus, 88
Epstein, Mikhail, 53
Erksan, Metin, 245
eroticism, in depictions of human flight, 146–55, *149*, 165n78
eternal return, Nietzsche's theory of, 197, 199, 207, 233
Even Dwarfs Started Small (Herzog, 1970), 245
Evgeny Onegin (Pushkin, 1833), 116n45
evolution, Darwin's theory of, 15
existentialism, 7
Eyck, Jan van, 43

Fait, Yuliy, 93
Faithful Ruslan: The Story of a Border Dog [*Vernyi Ruslan: Istoriia karayl'noi sobaki*] (Vladimov, 1975), 115n28
Fanon, Frantz, 7
Faratiev's Fantasy [*Fantazii Fariat'eva*] (Averbakh, 1979), 134
Farewell [*Proshchanie*] (Klimov, 1983), 17
fascism, 54, 111
Fassbinder, Rainer Werner, 25, 245
Fast Food Nation (Linklater, 2006), 238
"Fastidious Horses" [*Koni priveredlivye*] (Vysotsky, 1972), 55
Fedoseenko, Pavel, 141
Feiginova, Lyudmila, 169
Fellini, Federico, 42, 210n51, 245

feminism, 9, 24, 58, 59, 153, 175–76, 178
Film Eye [*Kino-Glaz*] (Vertov, 1924), 242, 243, 244
film history, 21
Fitzhamon, Lewin, 79
Fleetwood, Susan, 176
Fleming, Victor, 49
Flights in Dreams and Reality [*Polety vo sne i naiavu*] (Balian, 1983), 134
flight technology, 127–30
Ford, Henry, 38, 60
Ford, John, 45, 223, 247
Forged Coupon, The [*Fal'shivyi kupon*] (Tolstoy, 1911), 121n127
Forman, Miloš, 157
Forster, E. M., 7
Foucault, Michel, 6–7
Four Horsemen of the Apocalypse, The (Dürer engraving, 1498), 220–21, 222, 224
Franju, Georges, 238
Frankel, David, 79
Franklin, Chester M., 79
Franzén, Filippa, 148
freeze-frame shot, 39, 42
Freindlich, Alisa, 93, 177
Freud, Sigmund, 25, 58, 65, 102, 180, 203; on "castration complex," 152; on melancholia, 219; theory of "hysteria" in women, 181; theory of mourning, *68*, 226, 227–28. *See also* psychoanalysis
Friedberg, Anne, 79–80
Friedrich, Caspar David, 56, 57, 74n101
Frontier Post in the Mountains [*Zastava v gorakh*] (Iudin, 1953), 112
Fudge, Erica, 78

Gagarin, Yuri, 55, 127
Gaidai, Leonid, 82, 119n85
Gance, Abel, 130
Garland, Judy, 49, 88
Gay Science, The (Nietzsche, 1882), 197
genre, in cinema, 42
Germany, Year Zero (Rossellini, 1948), 35, 71n14
Gérôme, Jean-Léon, 93
Geyrhalter, Nikolaus, 238
Ghent Altarpiece (Van Eyck painting, 1432), 43

Ginevra de' Benci (Leonardo da Vinci, 1474–78), 132
Giordano, Domiziana, 132, 176
Girard, René, 219
Gísladóttir, Guðrún, 147
Give Me Your Paw, Friend! [*Dai lapu, drug!*] (Gurin, 1967), 83
Godard, Jean-Luc, 25, 245
"Godmothers" [*Kumushki*] (Russian folk song), 222
Gogol, Nikolai, 11, 53
Golstein, Vladimir, 29n68
Gorbachev, Mikhail, 169
Gorfinkel, Elena, 36
Gras, Emmanuel, 17
Green, André, 174
Greenaway, Peter, 256n123
"Grey Gelding" [*Sivyi merin*] (Paustovskii, 1963), 55
Grinko, Nikolai, 86
Grizzly Man (Herzog, 2005), 103
Guattari, Félix, 112
Guerra, Tonino, 120n96
Guevara, Che, 7
Gunda (Kossakovsky, 2000), 17
Gurin, Ilia, 83

Hadot, Pierre, 46
Hamilton, Margaret, 147
Hamlet (Shakespeare), 96–97
Haneke, Michael, 245
Haraway, Donna, 2, 23–24, 107–8, 109, 112–13
Heart of a Dog [*Sobach'e serdtse*] (Bulgakov, 1925), 115n20
Heat [*Znoi*] (Shepit'ko, 1964), 17
Heaven's Gate (Cimino, 1980), 248, 249, 257n140
Hedgehog in the Fog [*Ezhik v tumane*] (Norstein, 1975), 83, 253n14
Heidegger, Martin, 6, 7, 25, 219, 232–36
Hemingway, Ernest, 213n121
Here, Mukhtar! [*Ko mne, Mukhtar!*] (Tumanov, 1964), 82
Hero of Our Time, A [*Geroi nashero vremeni*] (Lermontov, 1840), 53
Herzog, Werner, 103, 245
High Noon (Zinnemann, 1952), 45

Hitchcock, Alfred, 24, 37, 84, 126, 145
Hobbes, Thomas, 13, 14
Hoffman, E.T.A., 74n100
Hoffmanniana (Tarkovsky, abandoned screenplay), 74n100
Hollywood cinema, 33, 93–94, 180, 252; art cinema and arthouse cinema in relation to, 245, 246–47, 249; dominance of, 42; passage of time in, 37; shot length in films, 34, 70n10; watchdogs in, 107
Homeward Bound: The Incredible Journey (Dunham, 1993), 79
Horse in Motion, The (Muybridge), 38, 40, 43–44, 67–68, 142
"horsepower," of automobiles, 38, 60
horses, 4, 19, 21; ancient elites' view of, 52; in apocalyptic visions, 220–26, 222, 224; beautiful and brutalized images of, 33; beautiful images of, 47–53; as "biotechnology," 43; centrality to Tarkovsky's cinema, 23, 32; disappearance from everyday life, 23, 33–34, 59–70, 219; domestication of, 57, 58; equestrian statues, 217, 218, 219; equine death, 25; fantasy dream images of, 63, 64, 65–67; in film history, 44; in Freudian psychoanalytic theory, 58; images of images of, 65, 65; masculinity and virility associated with, 33, 53–59, 186; mournful/melancholic portrayals, 225–28, 229, 230–32; opposite poles of Tarkovsky's visual ecology and, 33; origins of cinematic technology and, 23; Sallie Gardner in Muybridge's motion studies, 37–38; superiority over humans, 52, 53; Tarkovsky's divergent portrayals of, 49, 217, 219, 237, 260. See also *Andrei Rublev*, horse death scene in
Horse Whisperer, The (Redord, 1998), 44
human–animal relations, 1, 69, 77; in Cartesian philosophy, 12, 13, 179; as companionship, 107–14, 260; intelligence versus ingenuity, 15; "material-semiotic" term and, 3; sexual, 154; violence and vulnerability twinned, 26
humanism, 2, 26, 225; animal cruelty and, 252, 261, 263; carno-phallogocentrism and, 179; postwar humanism, 4–9

Hunt, The (Dono painting, 1465–70), 36
Hunters in the Snow, The (Bruegel painting, 1565), 135, 136

I Am Cuba [*Soy Cuba*] (Kalatozov, 1964), 91
I Am Twenty [*Mne dvadstat' let*] (Khutsiev, 1965), 73n90
Iankovskii, Oleg, 55, 83, 136, 150, 176, 222
Idiot, The (Dostoevsky, 1868–69), 13, 101
immortality, craving for, 161
imperialism, 8
In a Year of Thirteen Moons [*In einem Jahr mit 13 Monden*] (Fassbinder, 1980), 245
individuality/singularity, as human trait, 207, 208
In Search of Lost Time [*À la recherche du temps perdu*] (Proust, 1913–27), 212n89
"In the Land of Unafraid Birds" [*V kraiu nepuganykh ptits*] (Prishvin, 1907), 132
Invasion of the Body Snatchers (Siegel, 1956), 58
Ionesco, Eugène, 6
Iudin, Konstantin, 112
Iusov, Vadim, 170–71
Ivanov, Alexander, 51
Ivan's Childhood (1962), 8–9, 28n37, 70n10, 73n83, 103, 216n194, 259; apocalyptic visions in, 220–21; automobiles in, 61; aviation technology critiqued in, 164n61; cuckoo bird's call as omen, 155–56, 158; dead mother character in, 174; dream images of horses in, 65, 66; escapist fantasies of flight in, 135; horses in, 39; madman with pet bird in, 157; photographs associated with death, 223; rooster kept as pet in, 124; stock footage of dead humans and animals, 243
Ivan the Terrible [*Ivan Grozny*] (Eisenstein, 1944), 242

Jacquet, Luc, 19
Jameson, Fredric, 20
Jarman, Derek, 256n123
Jeanne Dielman, 23 quai du Commerice, 1080 Bruxelles (Akerman, 1975), 34
Jesse James (King, 1939), 247–48, 249
Jodorowsky, Alejandro, 245

Josephson, Erland, 55, 83, 133, 147–48, 186, 196; as Domenico in *Nostalghia*, 200, 217; in films of Bergman, 198; as Nietzsche in Cavani film, 214n148
July Rain [*Iiul'skii dozhd'*] (Khutsiev, 1966), 134
Jung, Carl, 126, 160
Jungle, The (Sinclair, 1905), 255n91
Jürgensburg, Mihail Clodt von, 173

Kaidanovsky, Aleksandr, 83, 138
Kalatozov, Mikhail, 91, 134, 140
Kant, Immanuel, 48, 50
Karatsupa, Nikita, 119n81
Karelov, Evgenii, 74n97
Kasatkin, Nikolai, 80
Kashtanka (Balian, 1975), 83
Kelvin, Lord, 59
KGB apartment raids, 64
Kheifits, Iosif, 86
"Kholstomer" (Tolstoy, 1886), 53
Khrushchev, Nikita, 8, 81, 134
Khutsiev, Marlen, 73n90, 134
Killer of Sheep (Burnett, 1977), 239
King, Henry, 247
Kipling, Rudyard, 28–29n64
Kirby, Joshua, 130
Kizilova, Larisa, 174
Kjellqvist, Tommy, 184
Kliachkin, Evgenii, 91
Klimov, Elem, 17, 216n194
"Kogda ia uznala" (Muratova), 1
Kojève, Alexandre, 235
Komonov, Mikhail, 130
Konchalovskii, Petr, 205
Konchalovsky, Andrei, 17, 167, 213n106
Kononov, Mikhail, 177
Koppel, Barbara, 238
Koshelev, Nikolai, 82
Kossakovsky, Viktor, 17
Kotcheff, Ted, 245
Kryakutnoy's balloon flight, myth of, 127
Kubrick, Stanley, 54, 91, 149
Kuniaev, Stanislav, 171
Kurosawa, Akira, 40, 42

"Lady with a Little Dog" [*Dama s sobachkoi*] (Chekhov, 1899), 85

language, 183–84, *185*, 186–88, 191, 233, 235, 261
Lapikov, Ivan, 44, 111
Lassie Come Home (Wilcox, 1943), 79
Last Judgment, The [*Strashnii sud*] (Rublev icon, 1408), 46
Lawrence, Michael, 245
Leastherstocking Tales (Cooper, 1827–41), 86
Leigh, Janet, 145
Lenin, Vladimir, 13, 43
Leonardo da Vinci, 24, 125, 139, 157–58; art in Tarkovsky's filmography, 132; discourse of mastery and, 139–40; interest in birds and aviation technology, 132–34, 138, 142, 159
Leone, Sergio, 45
Lermontov, Mikhail, 53
"Letter on Humanism" [*Über den Humanismus*] (Heidegger, 1946), 6, 7
Lévi-Strauss, Claude, 7–8, 124
Lieben, Anna von, 181
Limonov, Eduard, 261
Linklater, Richard, 238
Lippit, Akira Mizuta, 21, 63, 67–68, 69, 183, 248–49
"Little Hans" (Freudian case), 58
Ljellqvist, Tommy, 133
Locke, John, 13, 14
long takes, 15, 20, 34; in *Andrei Rublev*, 42, 232; capacity to "sculpt time," 35; in *Nostalghia*, 148; in *Stalker*, 92
Lucas, George, 54
Lumière, Auguste, 38, 129
Lumière, Louis, 38, 44, 61, 129
Lyotard, Jean-François, 187

MacKay, Marina, 7
Made Manifest (Brakhage, 1980), 236n126
madness/insanity, 157
Madonna del parto (Piero della Francesca painting, c.1460), 146, 176
Malamud, Randy, 2
Malick, Terrence, 51
Malik, Kenan, 7–8
Malilck, Terrence, 17
Mambéty, Djibril, 239
Mandelstam, Osip, 140
"Manifesto for Cyborgs, A" (Haraway), 108

Man Who Shot Liberty Vance, The (Ford, 1962), 223
Man with a Movie Camera [*Chelovek c kinoapparatom*] (Vertov, 1929), 39, *41*
March of the Penguins [*La Marche de l'empereur*] (Jacquet, 2005), 19
Marey, Étienne-Jules, 24, 38, 125, 142–43, *145*, 237
Marker, Chris, 254n44
Marley and Me (Frankel, 2008), 79
"Marseillaise, La" (Rouget, 1792), 100
masculinity, 70; absent father and, 174; equine, 53–59, 186; idealized and Romantic vision of, 59; postwar crisis of, 23, 33, 54, 58–59, 175; roosters associated with, 150, 152
Masina, Giulietta, 210n51
Master and Margarita, The [*Master i Margarita*] (Bulgakov, 1928–40), 117n59, 118n68, 140, 165n78
mastery, discourse of, 139–45, *142*
Matrix, The (Wachowski and Wachowski, 1999), 100
Matryona's House [*Matrenin dvor*] (Solzhenitsyn, 1963), 178
Meat (Wiseman, 1976), 238
Mechanics of the Brain [*Mekhanika golovnogo mozga*] (Pudovkin, 1926), 80
Mehrjui, Dariush, 173
melancholia, 25, 219, 226–32. See also mourning
Méliès, Georges, 72n68
Mesmer, Franz Anton, 230
Michelangelo, 133, 160
Microcosmos (Nuridsany and Pérennou, 1996), 17
Mikhalkov, Nikita, 45
mimesis, 40
Mimino (Daneliia, 1977), 134
Mirror [*Zerkalo*] (1975), 29n76, 30n103, 74n100, 140, 162, 181, 259; as autobiographical film, 173–74; birds in, 138; characters coming into language, 184, *185*; cuckoo bird in, 155; dogs in, 83, 97; eroticized depictions of women and flight, 149, *151*; footage of matador slaying a bull, 194, 213n121; Hiroshima

bombing footage in, 221; hypnosis in, 230; "hysterical" woman in, 212n80; indoor rain motif in, 144; Leonardo da Vinci's art in, 132; levitation leitmotif in, 135–36, *137*; music soundtrack, 136; offscreen barking of dogs in, 98, 99; Proustian self-discovery through language, 212n89; repurposed footage of Red Army soldiers in Crimea, 262, *262*; rooster slaughtered in, *150*, *151*, 152–53, 171, 180; Rousseauian return to nature and, 16, *20*; stock footage of dead humans and animals, 243; Tarkovsky as dying protagonist releasing sparrow, 160–61, *161*, *162*, 196; vision of female piety in, 175; wasted milk in, 205

Mizoguchi, Kenji, 42
modernity, 70, 136
Mokosh (Slavic goddess), 173
money, in Tarkovsky's films, 43
Mongols, in *Andrei Rublev*, 52, 90, 118n68, 145; burning cow in Raid vignette, 171–72, *172*; dogfight instigated by, 111–12; horsemeat incident, 188, *189*; portrayed as savages and colonizers, 189–91, *190*, 225; as satanic force, 223, *224*, *224*
Montaigne, Michel de, 90, 105, 257n149
Moore, Michael, 238
Morin, Edgar, 191
Mosfil'm, 123, 155, 168
Moss, Anne Eakin, 46
motherhood, patriarchal idealization of, 175
Motion Picture Producers and Distributors of America (MPPDA), 247–48
Motyl, Vladimir, 45
Mouchette (Bresson, 1967), 245
mourning, 21, 25, 34, 69, 232; Freud's theory of, *68*, 219, 227–28; nostalgic, 69. *See also* melancholia
Mulvey, Laura, 39, 153–54
Muratova, Kira, 1, 27n16, 167, 263
Murder Psalm (Brakhage, 1980), 237n126
Muybridge, Eadweard, 33, 39, 42, 49, 67–68, 142; *Animal Locomotion*, 154, 237; horse motion studies on Stanford's ranch, 37–38. *See also Horse in Motion, The*
mysticism, 157–58

Nabokov, Vladimir, 138, 139
Napoléon (Gance, 1927), 130
nationalism, Russian, 12, 136, 260, 262
National Velvet (Brown, 1944), 44
nature, 20, 86, 104, 148; cinematic return to, 15–21; technical mastery over, 24
Nazism, 93, 124, 155, 156; Beethoven's "Ode to Joy" associated with, 101; burning cow image and, 216n194; Heidegger's relationship with, 6, 234–35; visions of apocalypse and, 220–21
Nelson, Amy, 85
Nénette (Philibert, 2010), 17
neorealism, Italian, 34–35, 83, 191, 245
Neo-Romanticism, 55–56
Nesbit, Anne, 243
Nestor the Chronicler, 191, 192
New German Cinema, 245
New Soviet Man (*Novyi sovetskii chelovek*), 6, 8, 80
New Testament, 43
New Wave, French (*nouvelle vague*), 191, 245
Niblo, Fred, 247
Nietzsche, Friedrich, 157, 203, 214n148; *The Gay Science* (1882), 197; theory of "eternal return," 24–25, 197, 199, 204, 207, 233; *Thus Spoke Zarathustra* (1885), 197–201
Nikulin, Yuri, 71n20
Nine Days of One Year [*Deviat' dnei odnogo goda*] (Romm, 1962), 119n89
Norstein, Yuri, 83, 253n14
Nostalghia (Tarkovsky, 1983), 55, 71n14, 109, 120n96, 201; apocalyptic visions in, 221–23, *222*, 253n14; automobiles in, 61; burned book motif, 117n59; critique of modern society in, 197–98; documentary about making of, 132; eroticism in depictions of human flight, 146–48; escapist fantasies of flight in, 136, 138, *139*; feminism criticized in, 176; fiery death of Domenico in, 217, *218*; horse image in, 39; humans rendered animalistic, 113; indoor rain motif in, 144; madness in, 157; money depicted in, 43; music soundtrack, 222; New Age trends satirized in, 215n176; offscreen barking of dogs in, 98, 99; return-to-nature theme in, 104, *105*, 107; ringing telephone motif,

75n121; vision of female piety in, 175; wasted milk in, 205
Nostalghia, dogs in, 83, 84, 85–86; dog companion's resemblance to Dakus, 110–11; dog stirred by sight of human anguish, 105, *106*; German shepherd as connective tissue, 96, 97
nostalgia, 67, 84, 136, 219
Notes from Underground [*Zapiski iz podpol'ia*] (Dostoevsky, 1864), 157
nuclear war, threat of, 158–59, 221
Nuridsany, Claude, 17

October (Eisenstein, 1927), 241–42, 247
"Ode to Joy" (Beethoven, from Ninth Symphony, 1824), 100, 101, 102, 105, 120n110
Ogorodnikova, Tamara, 57, 170
Old Yeller (Stevenson, 1957), 79
Olmi, Ermanno, 239
Once upon a Time in the West (Leone, 1968), 45
One Day in the Life of Andrei Arsenevich [*Une journée d'Andrei Arsenevitch*] (Marker, 2000), 254n44
One Flew Over the Cuckoo's Nest (Forman, 1975), 157
On the Origin of Species (Darwin, 1859), 102
"Ontology of the Photographic Image, The" (Bazin), 223
Operation Y and Shurik's Other Adventures [*Operatsiia "Y" i drugie prikliucheniia*] (Gaida, 1965), 119n85
Order of Things, The [*Les Mots et les Choses*] (Foucault, 1966), 6–7
Ordinary Fascism [*Obyknovennyi fashizm*] (Romm, 1961), 191
Orientalism, 204
Orthodox Christianity, Russian, 10, 126, 188
Our Daily Bread [*Unser täglich Brot*] (Geyrhalter, 2005), 238
Ozu, Yasujiro, 42

Packer, George, 120n103
Palach, Jan, 105
pantheism, 16
Parajanov, Sergei, 27n16

Passion of Anna, The [*En passion*] (Bergman, 1969), 213–14n131
Pasternak, Boris, 140
Pat Garrett and Billy the Kid (Peckinpah, 1973), 248
Paustovskii, Konstantin, 55
Pavlov, Ivan, 80
Peckinpah, Sam, 248
Pérennou, Marie, 17
Pergolesi, Giovanni Battista, 136
Perkins, Anthony, 145
Perrin, Jacques, 17
Persona (Bergman, 1966), 121n124
Phantom Carriage, The (Sjöström, 1922), 44
Philibert, Nicholas, 17
photography, 21, 142, 223
Pick, Anat, 251
Piero della Francesca, 146, 176
Pilots [*Letchiki*] (Raizman, 1935), 140
pineal gland, soul and, 11, 12
Pink Flamingos (Waters, 1972), 216n200, 245
Pinkhasov, Gueorgui, 122n150
"plane film" genre, 129
Planet Earth (BBC TV series, 2006–), 19
Plate, S. Brent, 46–47
Plato, 2, 79, 88, 99; allegory of the cave, 98, 120n95; *The Republic*, 89, 98
Platonov, Andrei, 173
Playtime (Tati, 1967), 74n110
Pollock, Jackson, 206
posthumanism, 2, 79, 113
Potter, Paulus, 173
POV (point-of-view) shots, 130
Prigov, Dmitrii, 116n45
Primary Chronicle [*Povest' vremennyykh let*] (Nestor the Chronicler, c. 1113), 191–92
Prishvin, Mikhail, 132
Private Life of a Cat, The (Deren, 1947), 246
Production Code (Hayes Code), 248
progress, ideology of, 6, 7
Proust, Marcel, 212n89
Psycho (Hitchcock, 1960), 145
psychoanalysis, 3, 21, 58, 74n108, 150, 160, 180; "anxiety of influence," 242; hypnosis and origins of, 230. *See also* Freud, Sigmund
Pudovkin, Vsevolod, 80
Pushkin, Aleksandr, 53, 115n16, 116n45, 217

Putin, Vladimir, 262, 264n13
Pythagoras, 89, 211n72

Raizman, Iulii, 140
Raphael, 133
rationalism, secular, 157–58
Raush, Irma, 91, 155, 174, 176
Ravel, Maurice, 100
Ray, Nicholas, 180
realism, zoomorphic, 19
reality effect, 192
Rebel without a Cause (Ray, 1955), 180
Red Desert [*Il deserto rosso*] (Antonioni, 1964), 120n96
Redford, Robert, 44
reincarnation, 160, 204–5
Reitman, Jason, 129
religion, 10, 43, 47
Rembrandt, 95, 98
Renaissance, 24, 36, 95, 125, 146;
  expectations of apocalypse during, 221;
  humanist philosophy and, 5–6; Leonardo da Vinci and, 132
Renoir, Jean, 111, 228
repetition, in Tarkovsky's films, 51
Republic, The (Plato), 89, 98
Requiem (Verdi, 1874), 222, 223
Rescued by Rover (Fitzhamon, 1905), 79
Return of the Prodigal Son, The (Rembrandt painting, 1661–69), 95
Reygadas, Carlos, 51
Roadside Picnic [*Piknik na obochine*] (Strugatsky and Strugatsky, 1972), 28–29n64, 102
Roeg, Nicolas, 245
Roger & Me (Moore, 1989), 238
Romanticism, 56, 74n100
Romm, Mikhail, 119n89, 191
Room, Abram, 80
Rosa, Karen, 248
Roshal, Marianna, 82
Ross, Alex, 262
Ross, Gary, 44
Rossellini, Roberto, 35
Rostotsky, Stanislav, 83
Rouch, Jean, 191
Rouget, Claude Joseph, 100

Rousseau, Jean-Jacques, 13–15, 29n76
Rublev, Andrei, 46, 48, 49, 72n67, 156, 237, 259; legacy co-opted by nationalism, 264n13; as Romantic hero, 56; as Russian equivalent of Leonardo da Vinci, 133; six hundredth anniversary (1960), 208n3; vegetarianism of, 188, 189, 191; vow of silence by, 186, 188, 199
Ruin at Eldena (Friedrich painting, 1824), 74n101
Rules of the Game [*La règle du jeu*] (Renoir, 1939), 111, 228
Rushdie, Salman, 118n76
Russian literature, 242; horses in, 11, 53, 55, 219; ominous legacy of trains in, 101; "superfluous man" (*lishnii chelovek*) trope, 54
Russian Village Prose (*derevenskaia proza*), 54

Sacrifice, The (Tarkovsky, 1986), 55, 59, 126, 161; apocalyptic visions in, 221; automobiles in, 61; birdcalls in, 143, 152; Chernobyl disaster and, 158–59; cows contrasted to burning cow of *Andrei Rublev*, 207–8; dream images of horses in, 66–67; eroticized depictions of women and flight, 147; "hysterical" woman in, 181, 183; illusion of untamed nature in, 144–45; juxtaposed images of fire and cows in, 201, 202, 203, 206, 217; language in, 184, 186; Leonardo da Vinci's art in, 132–33; levitation leitmotif in, 135; as meditation on death, 196; money depicted in, 43; Nietzschean philosophy and, 197–203, 215n165; offscreen barking of dogs in, 98, 99; photographs associated with death, 223; ringing telephone motif, 75n121; seagulls in funereal role, 157–59; wasted milk in, 205
Saddhatissa, Hammalawa, 205
sadism, 232
Saint Jerome in His Study (Dürer painting, 1514), 93
St. Matthew Passion (Bach, 1727), 132–33
Salty Dog [*Solenyi pes*] (Koshelev, 1973), 82
Samoteikin, Evgenii, 171

Sandler, Stephanie, 51
Sans Soleil (Marker, 1983), 254n44
Sargsyan, Sos, 64
Sartre, Jean-Paul, 7, 8–9, 28n37
Sátántangó (Tarr, 1994), 245
Satyricon (Fellini, 1969), 245
Savonarola, Girolamo, 221
Scarry, Elaine, 48, 50, 52, 70
Schopenhauer, Arthur, 157
science, 6
science fiction genre, 54, 58
Scorsese, Martin, 129, 170
Scott, Ridley, 58, 61
Scott, Tony, 129
Screen Actors Guild (SAG), 248
Sculpting in Time [*Zapechatlennoe vremia*] (Tarkovsky, 1986), 4, 27n15
Seabiscuit (Ross, 2003), 44
Seagull, The [*Chaika*] (Chekhov, 1895), 130
Searchers, The (Ford, 1956), 45
self-mastery, ideology of, 6
Serf Actress in Disgrace, Breast-Feeding Her Master's Puppy (Kasatkin, 1911), 80
Sergeyev, Nikolai, 155
Seven Samurai (Kurosawa, 1954), 40, 71n34
Sextus Empiricus, 88
Shakespeare, William, 96–97
Shalamov, Varlam, 115n28
Shame [*Skammen*] (Bergman, 1968), 158
Shepit'ko, Larisa, 17, 134
Shneiderov, Vladimir, 93
shot length, 35, 70n10
shot-reverse-shot montage, 57
Shpailikov, Gennadi, 264n1
Shredel, Vladimir, 82
Shukin, Nicole, 243–44
Shukshin, Vasily, 264n1
Siberiade [*Siberiada*] (Konchalovsky, 1978), 17
Siegel, Don, 58
silence, in Tarkovsky's films, 186
Silent Spring (Carson, 1962), 159
Sinclair, Upton, 255n91
Sinyavski, Andrei, 139
Sjöström, Victor, 44
Skakov, Nariman, 3, 99, 118n75
Skeptics, 89–90, 104

slaughterhouse documentaries, 237–39, 255nn90–91
Slavic studies, 2
Slavophile movement, 136, 157
"slow animal documentary," 17, 19, 20, 30n101
slow motion, 40, 42, 47, 132, 145
Smirnov, Andrei, 73n90
Snezho-Boltskaya, Aleksandra, 28n64
Snow, Michael, 246
snuff films, 230
Sobchak, Vivian, 228, 230
Société Générale des Cinématographes Eclipses, 129
Socrates, 103
Solaris (Tarkovsky, 1972), 4, 103, 147, 155, 255–56n106, 259; apocalyptic visions in, 221; automobiles in, 62; birds in, 124, 138; blue-tinted horse as oneiric image, 63, 64; "city of the future" scene, 59–60, 60; Cold War space race critiqued in, 141; cuckoo bird in, 155; dog companion in, 83, 85, 95, 96; eroticism in depictions of human flight, 146; horse image in, 39; horses as leitmotif in, 55–59, 56; "hysterical" woman in, 180, 181, 182; images of images of horses, 65, 65; indoor rain motif in, 144; levitation leitmotif in, 135; money depicted in, 43; offscreen barking of dogs in, 98, 99; Russian Village Prose and, 54–55; soundtrack, 95; Tarkovsky's affair with Bondarchuk during filming of, 211–12n77; vision of female piety in, 175
Soldatov, I., 168–69
Solonitsyn, Anatoly, 44, 86, 116n44, 188, 214n142, 259
Solzhenitsyn, Aleksandr, 24, 139, 178
Sontag, Susan, 223
Sophocles, 5
soul, human, 11, 12, 20; perception of good and, 16; "Russian soul," 138
sound, in cinema, 40
sound, offscreen diegetic, 98
Soviet avant-garde (1920s), 241
Soviet cinema: bird's-eye view in, 140; environmental themes in, 17; escapist fantasies of flight in, 134–35; propaganda legacy of, 243

Soviet Union (USSR): "Aesopian language" in, 118n74; All-Union Institute of Cinematography (VGIK), 35, 122n150; Brezhnev "era of Stagnation," 134, 164n37; Buddhist turn in late Soviet culture, 116n45; concern for animal life in post-Stalinist culture, 167–68; crisis of masculinity in, 54, 58–59, 73n90; decline and fall of, 170; Dostoevsky revival in, 13; ecological destruction in, 17; Enlightenment humanist legacy and, 6, 8; film censors, 4; flight technology and, 128; Neo-Romantic movement in, 55–56; New Age beliefs in late Soviet society, 204; nuclear technology and, 158–59; pet keeping in, 78–79, 81, 83, 111. *See also* Thaw (*ottepel'*) era

"speciesism," 11

Spielberg, Steven, 54

spiritualism, Eastern, 86

spirituality, 9–10, 20; animals' supposed lack of, 10–11, 113; music of Bach and, 119n87

Stabat Mater (Pergolesi, 1736), 136

Stagecoach (Ford, 1939), 247

Stalin, Joseph, 5, 8, 13, 44, 155; death of, 80, 81, 83; discourse of mastery and, 140–41; German shepherd breed and, 93–94

Stalinism, 8, 79, 120n110, 140, 168, 191

Stalker (Tarkovsky, 1979), 24, 28–29n64, 109, 120n103; automobiles in, 61; Chelyabinsk nuclear explosion (1957) and, 116n44; cinematic antecedents of German shepherd in, 93–95; classical music in, 100–101; connection with *Wizard of Oz*, 88, 116–17n47, 118n76; contrast with *Star Wars*, 73n92; critique of materialism in, 121n119; cuckoo bird in, 155; diegetic instability in, 87, 88; disorienting switching of colors in, 86, 88, 91; doglike sniffing out of hidden truths in, 92, 118n75; Eastern philosophy referenced in, 203–4; "hysterical" woman in, 181, *182*; indoor rain motif in, 144; Monkey [*martyshka*] ("mutant daughter" of protagonist), 100, 101–3, *103*, 105, 121n119, 147; monks wandering off-screen, 46; offscreen barking of dogs in, 99; references to late Soviet culture in, 94, 118n74; ringing telephone motif, 75n121; Rousseauian return to nature and, 16–17, 20; soundtrack, 73n92, 86, 101–2; Stalker as dogmatist, 89–90, 91; Tarkovsky's feminine ideal in, 177; Tarkovsky's invisible directorial control in, 143–44; tracking shots in, 91, 92; on vegetarianism and meat eating, 179; wasted milk in, 205; *The Wizard of Oz* compared to, 144, 165n73

Stalker, dog companion in, 83, 84, 86, *87*, 88–93; spatial instability embodied in, 95; Stalinist legacy of German shepherds and, 93–94; suggestion of mythological purpose, 97–98

Stalky & Co. (Kipling, 1899), 29n64

Stanford, Leland, 37, 38, 43

Star Wars: A New Hope (Lucas, 1977), 54, 73n92, 117–18n60

Stephanitz, Max Emil Friedrich von, 93

Stevenson, Robert, 79

Stewart, Jimmy, 84

stilyagi youth movement, 78

stock footage, 243

Stoics, 88

storks, 123, 126, 146

Strada, La (Fellini, 1954), 210n51

Strike [*Stachka*] (Eisenstein, 1925), 239–44, *240*

Strugatsky, Boris and Arkady, 29n64, 102

Studies in Hysteria (Freud, 1895), 181, 230

Sun Also Rises (Hemingway, 1926), 213n21

"superfluous man" (*lishnii chelovek*), 54

Supper at Emmaus (Rembrandt, 1648), 98

swans, 130, *131*

Sweetgrass (Castaing-Taylor, 2009), 17

symbolism, Tarkovsky's disavowal of, 91

Tahimik, Kidlat, 72n49

"Tamara the Bitch" ["Suka Tamara"] (Shalamov, 1959), 115n28

Tannhäuser (Wagner, 1845), 100, 180

Taras Bulba [*Taras Bul'ba*] (Gogol, 1835), 53

Tarkovsky (Dunne, ed.), 3

Tarkovsky, Andrei: affection for dogs, 78–79; cameo film roles, 73n90, 160–61, *161*, *162*,

196; childhood and parents of, 5, 173–74; cinematic realism and, 20; on commercial cinema, 15–16, 43; on cows, 63–64; crisis of masculinity and, 53–59, 74n102; as Cynic, 99–107; death as obsession of, 161–62, 196; on "death" of cinematic art, 47; declining health of, 196; demystified approach to, 3–4; Dovzhenko as cinematic muse of, 16, 30n89, 73n76; Eastern philosophical traditions' appeal to, 203–5; Eisenstein compared with, 239–44; family of, 84, 116n39; favorite films of, 71n34; films and filmmakers praised by, 100, 111, 145; on horses, 32; humanism and, 4–5, 8–9, 27n15, 113, 190, 260–61, 263; ideology of mastery and, 143; in Italy, 132, 138–39; limits to affection for dogs, *112*, 113–14; offscreen diegetic sound used by, 98; pessimism and fatalism of, 9, 22, 23, 33, 47; pet sparrow during Tarkovsky's terminal illness, 161, *162*; scholarship on, 3; as the Soviet Rousseau, 13–15; on spirituality and animals, 9–11; Suzdal monument to, 259–60, 262, 263–64n1, 264n3; trip to United States (1983), 45, 72n49

Tarkovsky, animal cruelty of, 3, 19, 25, 26, 190; cow burning in *Andrei Rublev*, 169, 205; death of horse in *Andrei Rublev*, 32; humanism and, 252, 261, 263; vicious treatment of horses, 219

Tarkovsky, Arseny, 173

Tarkovsky, Soviet censors and, 27n16, 81, 127; *Andrei Rublev*, 122n158, 169, 209n14, 228, 254n43; *Mirror*, 140; *Solaris*, 4, 123

Tarr, Béla, 17, 245

Tati, Jacques, 74n110

"techno-horror," 61

technology, cinematic, 21, 67, 125; equine locomotion and, 39; Muybridge's motion studies as origin of, 142; parallel with aviation technology, 128–29, 131, 132; Technicolor in *Wizard of Oz*, 49, 50, 88

telephone technology, 62, 75n121

Telluride Film Festival (1983), 246

Tempņikova, Natālija, 167–68

Terekhova, Margarita, 135, 149, 152–55, 173, 174

Terminator, The (Cameron, 1984), 100

Terreno, Patrizia, 147, 176

Teshigahara, Hiroshi, 143

Thaw (*ottepel'*) era, 8, 12–13, 80, 134; films about bonds with pet dogs, 82–83; moral rehabilitation mission, 84; "petishistic" culture of, 169

"Theatre of Cruelty, The" (Artaud), 250

Theophanes the Greek, 156

"There Is No More Horrible Beast than the Cat" [*Strashnee koshki zveria net*] (Kliachkin song, 1968), 91

Thích Quảng Đức, 105, 121n124

Thing, The (Carpenter, 1982), 58

Third World liberation struggles, 7

Thoreau, Henry David, 29n76, 81, 115n24

Three Men in a Boat (To Say Nothing of the Dog) [*Troe v lodke (ne schitaia sobaki)*] (Birman, 1979), 82

Through a Glass Darkly [*Såsom i en spegel*] (Bergman, 1961), 143

Thus Spoke Zarathustra (Nietzsche, 1885), 197, 199

Tikhonova, Mariia, 259

"time-image," 34–35, 37, 38

time/temporality: aestheticization of, 192; animals' inability to rationalize, 201; cuckoo clock and, 156; de- and re-temporalization of equine locomotion, 40; "dilated temporality" in art cinema, 36–37; dislocation of space and time, 86; language and, 188; Muybridge's motion studies and, 37–38; passage of time in classical Hollywood cinema, 37; photographs as *memento mori* and, 223; spatio-temporal planes connected by dogs, 96, *97*; swans and space-time continuum, 132; "time-image," 34–35, 37

Timofeeva, Oxana, 13–14

Todorovskii, Petr, 134

Tolstoy, Leo, 53, 101, 121n127, 180, 211n66

Top Gun (Scott, 1986), 129

Topo, El (Jodorowsky, 1970), 245

Touch of Evil (Welles, 1958), 91

Touki Bouki (Mambéty, 1973), 239

Tournachon, Gaspar Felix, 128–29

tracking shots, 57, 91, 132

Tree of Wooden Clogs, The [*L'Albero degli zoccoli*] (Olmi, 1978), 239
Trinity, The [*Troitsa*] (Rublev icon, 1411), 175, 259, 264n13
Trotsky, Leon, 6
Trump, Donald J., 120n103
Tsai Ming-Liang, 37
Tsymbal, Evgeny, 173
Tumanov, Semen, 82
Two Comrades Were Serving [*Sluzhili dva tovarishcha*] (Karelov, 1968), 74n97
2001: A Space Odyssey (Kubrick, 1968), 54, 73n92, 75n112

Ukraine, Russian invasion of (2022), 262
Umberto D. (de Sica, 1955), 83
United States, 159
universalism, 7, 204
Untitled No. 6 (Brakhage, 1975), 236n126
Up in the Air (Reitman, 2012), 129
Urabe Kenkō, 204
utilitarianism, of Bentham, 236, 251

Valerii Chkalov (Kaltozov, 1941), 140
Varda, Agnes, 37
vegetarianism, 179, 188, 189, 211n72
Verdi, Giuseppe, 222
Vertigo (Hitchcock, 1958), 84
Vertov, Dziga, 39, 40, 242–43, 244
Virgin Mary, cult of, 175
Vishnyakova, Maria, 173–74
"Visual Pleasure and Narrative Cinema" (Mulvey, 1975), 153
Viva la Muerte (Arrabal, 1971), 245
vivisection, 12
Vladimov, Georgii, 115n28
von Trier, Lars, 51
Voyage in Time [*Tempo di Viaggio*] (documentary, 1983), 132
voyeurism, 153
Vysotsky, Vladimir, 55–56, 57, 74n97

Wachowski, Lana and Lilly, 100
Wagner, Richard, 100, 180
Wake in Fright (Kotcheff, 1971), 245
Walden (Thoreau, 1854), 81, 115n24
Walkabout (Roeg, 1971), 245

Wanderer above the Sea of Fog (Friedrich painting, 1818), 56
War and Peace [*Voina i mir*] (Bondarchuk, 1967), 212n77
war epics, 45
Warhol, Andy, 34, 256n123
War Horse (Spielberg, 2011), 45
Waters, John, 216n200, 245
Watt, James, 60
Wavelength (Snow, 1967), 246
Wedding Trough [*Vase de Noces*] (Zéno, 1974), 245
Weekend [*Week-end*] (Godard, 1967), 245
Weerasethakul, Apichatpong, 17
Welles, Orson, 91
Western film genre, 42, 45
Westernization, 59
Where the North Begins (Franklin, 1923), 79
White, Hayden, 192
White Bim, Black Ear [*Belyi Bim, Chernoe ukho*] (Rostotsky, 1976), 83
White Poodle [*Belyi pudel'*] (Roshal and Shredel, 1955), 82
White Sun of the Desert [*Beloe solntse pustyni*] (Motyl, 1970), 45
Who Framed Roger Rabbit? (Zemecki, 1988), 154
Why Is Yellow the Middle of the Rainbow? (Tahimik, 1994), 72n49
"Why Look at Animals?" (Berger, 1977), 23, 62–63, 69, 220
Wilbur Wright and His Flying Machine (film, 1909), 129
wildlife films, 19
Williams, Linda, 153–54
Window Water Baby Moving (Brakhage, 1959), 236n126
Winged Migration (Perrin, 2001), 17
Wings [*Kryl'ia*] (Shepit'ko, 1966), 134
Wiseman, Frederick, 238
witches, 147–48, 149
Wizard of Oz, The (Fleming, 1939), 49, 63, 88, 116–17n47, 118n76, 145; "man behind the curtain" in, 144; Toto compared with Lumière's dog, 93–94; Wicked Witch of the West, 147, 149
Wolfe, Cary, 22
Wollter, Sven, 181

Woman in the Dunes [*Suna no Onna*] (Teshigahara, 1964), 143
women, Tarkovsky's views of, 54, 260; animal cruelty paired with gendered violence, 228; ideal of female humiliation in love, 180–81, *183*; portrayals of birds/flight and, 126, 146–55, *149*, *150*, *151*, 165n78; rooster sacrifice scene in *Mirror* and, 152–53, *154*; Tarkovsky's relationship with his mother and, 173–74; Virgin Mary cult and, 175
Woolf, Virginia, 7
Worker and Kolkhoz Woman [*Rabochii i kolokhoznitsa*] (Stalin-era scultpure), 155
Workers Leaving the Factory [*La Sortie de l'Usine Lumière à Lyon*] (Lumière, 1895), 44, 61, 94–95
World War II, 6, 8, 33, 37; disorientation of perception and, 35; ecological destruction and, 17; in *Ivan's Childhood*, 155, 156, 216n194, 220; near suicide of Europe in, 7; spirituality and, 9; Tarkovsky's father in Red Army during, 5
Wright, Wilbur, 129, 130

Zagorin, Perez, 5
Zemecki, Robert, 154
Zéno, Thierry, 245
Zhuravlev, Vasilii, 93
Zinnemann, Fred, 45
Žižek, Slavoj, 65, 95
Zone, The: A Prison Camp Guard's Story [*Zona: zapiski nadziratelia*] (Dovlatov, 1982), 94
zoopraxiscope, 38
Zvenigora (Dovzhenko, 1929), 51

RAYMOND SCOTT DE LUCA is Assistant Professor of Russian Studies in the Department of Russian and East Asian Languages and Cultures (REALC) at Emory University.

For Indiana University Press

Sabrina Black, Editorial Assistant

Anna Garnai, Production Coordinator

Sophia Hebert, Assistant Acquisitions Editor

Samantha Heffner, Marketing Production Manager

Katie Huggins, Production Manager

Alyssa Lucas, Marketing and Publicity Manager

David Miller, Lead Project Manager/Editor

Bethany Mowry, Acquisitions Editor

Jennifer Wilder, Senior Artist and Book Designer

www.ingramcontent.com/pod-product-compliance
Lightning Source LLC
Chambersburg PA
CBHW021819300426
44114CB00009BA/234